SPEAK·TRUTH·TO·POWER

COMMANDER
STEVEN HAINES
ROYAL NAVY

INTERNATIONAL LAW AND
THE PROTECTION OF PEOPLE AT SEA

International Law and the Protection of People at Sea

IRINI PAPANICOLOPULU

OXFORD

UNIVERSITY PRESS

OXFORD

UNIVERSITY PRESS

Great Clarendon Street, Oxford, OX2 6DP,
United Kingdom

Oxford University Press is a department of the University of Oxford.
It furthers the University's objective of excellence in research, scholarship,
and education by publishing worldwide. Oxford is a registered trade mark of
Oxford University Press in the UK and in certain other countries

© I. Papanicolopulu 2018

The moral rights of the author have been asserted

First Edition published in 2018

Impression: 1

Crown copyright material is reproduced under Class Licence
Number C01P0000148 with the permission of OPSI
and the Queen's Printer for Scotland

Published in the United States of America by Oxford University Press
198 Madison Avenue, New York, NY 10016, United States of America

British Library Cataloguing in Publication Data
Data available

Library of Congress Control Number: 2017957341

ISBN 978-0-19-878939-0

Printed and bound by
CPI Group (UK) Ltd, Croydon, CR0 4YY

To my father Eleftherios
and in memory of my mother Giuseppina

Acknowledgements

The sea has always fascinated me, and its law has provided an endless source of intellectual discovery. It was therefore only natural that sooner or later I would have wondered about the law of the sea's lack of engagement with humans. People at sea were a reality, I soon found out, and yet most relevant treaties were silent; even scholars passed them over. The resolve to find some protection led me to international law and its multiple regimes. A research on people at sea thus developed into an inquiry into the potential of international law, as a system, to provide solutions to emerging issues.

This book would not have been possible without the generous funding of the European Union under the FP7 Marie Curie Actions. Further funding was provided by the University of Oxford and the University of Milano-Bicocca. I gratefully acknowledge their contribution.

Thanks to the Marie Curie Fellowship, I was able to spend two years focusing on my research in the congenial environment provided by the University of Oxford. I am truly grateful to colleagues, doctoral candidates, and students at the Faculty of Law and at St. Peter's College, for helping me broaden my perspective and at the same time concretise my research. I wish to express particular thanks to Vaughan Lowe, Dapo Akande, Stefan Talmon, Timothy Endicott, Guy Goodwin-Gill, Cathryn Costello, and Martins Paparinskis.

The actual writing of this book mostly took place in Scotland and Italy, supported by the friendship and encouragement of many colleagues. In Glasgow, my special thanks go to Rosa Greaves, Christian Tams, James Sloan, Claire La Hovary, Akbar Rasulov, Marco Goldoni, and Kyela Leakey. In Milan, I am particularly grateful to Tullio Scovazzi and Tullio Treves, as well as to Maurizio Arcari, Matteo Fornari, and Marco Cottone. Thank you also to Chiara Ragni, Angelica Bonfanti, and all the occupants of the 'stanza d'angolo' for much hospitality.

My work on people at sea and their protection has spanned more than ten years. During this time, I have benefitted from the encouragement, support, and help of many colleagues around the world, who have generously shared their views, provided relevant information, challenged my ideas, and, at later stages, read parts of this book. I would like to express my gratitude to all, and in particular to David Attard, Silvia Borelli, Gianmatteo Breda, Neil Brown, Alessandro Bufalini, Martina Buscemi, Luigi Crema, Malgosia Fitzmaurice, Mary Footer, Erik Franckx, Philippe Gautier, Maria Gavouneli, Martti Koskenniemi, Enrico Milano, Marko Milanovic, Simon Olleson, Bernard Oxman, Efthymios Papastavridis, Anne Peters, Cesare Pitea, Catherine Redgwell, Ashley Roach, Clive Schofield, Antonios Tzanakopoulos and Roberto Virzo. I am most grateful to Joanna Dingwall, Ben MacFarlane, Francesca Mussi, Alice Ollino, Armando Rocha, and Eirianna Sklavounaki, who have provided valuable assistance at various stages of the research and writing of this book, as well as to Ben Stanford, who has revised the text. Finally, I would like to thank Merel Alstein, John Louth, and all the staff at OUP for all their help in transforming a research into a book.

During my solitary roving of the seas and the international law system, I had the comfort of the constant encouragement and love of family and friends. Thank you to all and in particular to my father Eleftherios and my brothers Kostas and Stefanos, and to little Vittoria Giuseppina, who came to brighten up the last stages of writing with her smiles and good humour. And, of course, to Massimo, who makes my circle just.

Table of Contents

Table of Cases

Table of Cases

DOMESTIC COURTS

Table of Treaties

List of Abbreviations

ACHPR	African Charter on Human and People's Rights
ACHR	American Convention on Human Rights
ACommHPR	African Commission on Human and People's Rights
AJIL	American Journal of International Law
CAT	Committee Against Torture
CEDAW	Convention on the Elimination of All Forms of Discrimination against Women
CERD	Convention on the Elimination of All Forms of Racial Discrimination
CESCR	Committee on Economic, Social and Cultural Rights
CJEU	Court of Justice of the European Union
CoC	Code of Conduct for Responsible Fisheries
DOALOS	Division for Ocean Affairs and the Law of the Sea
ECHR	European Convention on Human Rights
ECtHR	European Court of Human Rights
EJIL	European Journal of International Law
EU	European Union
FAO	Food and Agriculture Organization
FSA	United Nations Agreement for the Implementation of the Provisions of the United Nations Convention on the Law of the Sea of 10 December 1982 relating to the Conservation and Management of Straddling Fish Stocks and Highly Migratory Fish Stocks
GC	Grand Chamber
HRC	Human Rights Committee
HSC	Convention on the High Seas
IACHR	Inter-American Court of Human Rights
IACmHR	Inter-American Commission on Human Rights
ICCPR	International Covenant on Civil and Political Rights
ICESCR	International Covenant on Economic, Social and Cultural Rights
ICJ	International Court of Justice
ICLQ	International & Comparative Law Quarterly
ICSID	International Centre for Settlement of Investment Disputes
IJMCL	The International Journal of Marine and Coastal Law
ILC	International Law Commission
ILO	International Labour Organization
IMO	International Maritime Organization
ITLOS	International Tribunal for the Law of the Sea
IUU	illegal, unreported and unregulated
MARPOL	International Convention for the Prevention of Pollution from Ships
MLC	Maritime Labour Convention
MODU	mobile offshore drilling unit
MOU	memorandum of understanding
NGO	non-governmental organization
PCIJ	Permanent Court of International Justice

PSCA	Agreement on Port State Measures to Prevent, Deter and Eliminate Illegal, Unreported and Unregulated Fishing
Recueil des Cours	Collected Courses of The Hague Academy of International Law
Refugee Convention	Convention Relating to the Status of Refugees
RIAA	Reports of International Arbitral Awards
SAR Convention	International Convention on Maritime Search and Rescue
SFV	Convention for the Safety of Fishing Vessels
Smuggling Protocol	Protocol against the Smuggling of Migrants by Land, Sea and Air Supplementing the United Nations Convention against Transnational Organized Crime
SOLAS	International Convention for the Safety of Life at Sea
STCW	International Convention on Standards of Training, Certification and Watchkeeping for Seafarers
STCW-F	International Convention on Standards of Training, Certification and Watchkeeping for Fishing Vessel Personnel
SUA Convention	Convention for the Suppression of Unlawful Acts Against the Safety of Maritime Navigation
TOC Convention	United Nations Convention against Transnational Organized Crime
UDHR	Universal Declaration of Human Rights
UN	United Nations
UNCLOS	United Nations Convention on the Law of the Sea
UNEP	United Nations Environment Programme
UNGA	United Nations General Assembly
UNHCR	United Nations High Commissioner for Refugees
UNSC	United Nations Security Council
UNTS	United Nations Treaty Series
VCLT	Vienna Convention on the Law of Treaties
WGT	world gross tonnage
WTO	World Trade Organization

Introduction

1. A New Field for Research

This is a book about international law and how it can be used to protect people at sea. Its fundamental premise is that international law provides numerous norms that can be used towards this end. These rules take the form either of dedicated regulation, specifically addressing the topic under consideration, or that of rules adopted for other purposes which can nonetheless be applied to 'people at sea'. These particular rules derive primarily from international human rights law and the law of the sea, as well as from other fields of international law, including maritime law, labour law, and refugee law. This book argues that all of these rules can be conceptualized as a *sui generis* special regime of international law, the overarching principle of which is the duty of States to protect people at sea and to adopt all necessary acts with a view towards ensuring enjoyment of their rights.

Interest in people at sea and in the interaction between the two main fields of international law that address this issue—international human rights law and the law of the sea—is gaining momentum in legal discourse. The reasons for this are manifold, but two factors have been particularly significant. The first is that some stories involving persons at sea have attracted widespread attention due to their media coverage. The second is the increase of litigation before international courts, concerning situations in which the conduct of a State with respect to persons at sea is assessed.

Stories about pirates and migrants at sea have featured pre-eminently in media coverage in recent years. Accounts of piratical attacks off the coast of Somalia have rekindled the interest of the public at large into piracy, its root causes, and its effects. The need to address piracy and to ensure the safety of navigation and the regular flow of global trade has stimulated discussion among the international community, where we have seen the participation of most international institutions, from the United Nations (UN) and its agencies to regional organizations.[1] Within the legal community, the arrest, trial, and conviction of pirates has triggered debate among international law scholars—and we have witnessed an unprecedented flourishing of legal literature on the topic.[2]

---

[1] Information on piracy and the efforts by United Nations (UN) bodies and other organizations to combat this threat to maritime navigation may be found on the dedicated webpage of the Division for Ocean Affairs and the Law of the Sea, Office of Legal Affairs, United Nations (DOALOS) at <http://www.un.org/depts/los/piracy/piracy.htm> accessed 18 October 2017.

[2] Among the many scholarly works, see Tullio Treves, 'Piracy, Law of the Sea, and Use of Force: Developments off the Coast of Somalia' (2009) 20 EJIL 399; Bibi van Ginkel and Frans-Paul

International Law and the Protection of People at Sea. Irini Papanicolopulu. © Irini Papanicolopulu, 2018. Published 2018 by Oxford University Press.

Similarly, media revelations concerning the treatment of migrants and asylum seekers trying to reach coastal States' shores has also triggered interest in the issue. The 2011 'left-to-die boat' tragedy in the Mediterranean Sea was instrumental in informing the public at large about the plight of sea migrants, and fuelled discussions on human rights standards to be applied to interception operations at the international level.[3] Some years before, in 2001, on the other side of the world, accounts of the *Tampa* case had a similar effect.[4]

There are however other stories that involve people at sea which have fascinated the public. In 2012, the sinking of the *Costa Concordia* off the Italian island of Giglio was broadcast internationally and has brought issues of maritime safety to the forefront which seemed consigned to the previous century. A hundred years after the sinking of the *Titanic*, we were again reminded that safety of navigation is still an issue, not only for substandard vessels in developing countries, but also for luxury cruise ships sailing in Western Europe. On the other side of the ocean, the stories featured in the 2015 prize-winning series 'The Outlaw Oceans' published by the *New York Times* have exposed a number of human rights violations that happen on a daily basis at sea and brought people at sea a little closer to everyday life.[5]

In addition to all the information now available on people at sea, the issue has attracted the interest of lawyers also due to the fact that an unprecedented number of cases involving these people have been addressed by international judges over the past twenty years. The very first case decided by the International Tribunal for the Law of the Sea (ITLOS), the 1999 *Saiga* case,[6] involved among many other issues, concerns relating to the standard of treatment of people on board vessels during enforcement action. The 2008 *Medvedyev* case decided by the European Court of Human Rights (ECtHR)[7] attracted the attention of human rights lawyers and law of

van der Putten (eds), *The International Response to Somali Piracy* (Martinus Nijhoff 2010); Robin Geiss and Anna Petrig, *Piracy and Armed Robbery at Sea: The Legal Framework for Counter-Piracy Operations in Somalia and the Gulf of Aden* (OUP 2011); Douglas Guilfoyle (ed), *Modern Piracy* (Edward Elgar 2013); Panos Koutrakos and Achilles Skordas (eds), *The Law and Practice of Piracy at Sea: European and International Perspectives* (Hart Publishing 2014); Anna Petrig, *Human Rights and Law Enforcement at Sea. Arrest, Detention and Transfer of Piracy Suspects* (Brill Nijhoff 2014).

[3] *Lives Lost in the Mediterranean Sea: Who Is Responsible?*, Report presented to the Parliamentary Assembly of the Council of Europe (PACE), 23 March 2012 <http://assembly.coe.int/CommitteeDocs/2012/20120329_mig_RPT.EN.pdf> accessed 18 October 2017. See also, among many others, Tullio Scovazzi, 'La tutela della vita umana in mare, con particolare riferimento agli immigrati clandestini diretti verso l'Italia' (2005) 88 Rivista di Diritto Internazionale 106; Efthymios Papastavridis, 'Enforcement Jurisdiction in the Mediterranean Sea: Illicit Activities and the Rule of Law on the High Seas' (2010) 25 IJMCL 569; Seline Trevisanut, 'Search and Rescue Operations in the Mediterranean: Factor of Cooperation or Conflict?' (2010) 25 IJMCL 523.

[4] See discussion and references in Chapter 4, Section 4.2.

[5] Ian Urbina, 'The Outlaw Ocean' *New York Times* (25 July 2015) <https://www.nytimes.com/interactive/2015/07/24/world/the-outlaw-ocean.html> accessed 18 October 2017.

[6] *The M/V 'Saiga' (No 2) (Saint Vincent and the Grenadines v Guinea)* (Judgment of 1 July 1999) ITLOS Reports 1999, 10. The *Saiga* case was numbered '2' in the ITLOS's list. Case no 1 is the *The M/V "Saiga" Case (Saint Vincent and the Grenadines v Guinea), Prompt Release* (Judgment of 4 December 1997) ITLOS Reports 1997, 16. However, since the same factual circumstances were at the basis of the two cases, it can be considered that the 1999 *Saiga* judgment was part of the first case to be decided by the Tribunal.

[7] *Medvedyev and Others v France* App no 3394/03 (Judgment of 10 July 2008). The case was subsequently examined by the Grand Chamber of the ECtHR, see *Medvedyev and Others v France* App no

the sea experts alike, due to the arrest of individuals on the high seas. The 2012 *Hirsi* judgment in the ECtHR[8] consolidated the growing attention towards migrants at sea, as seen in earlier cases reviewed by the Inter-American Commission on Human Rights (IACHR)[9] and the Committee Against Torture (CAT).[10] The 2015 arbitral award in the *Arctic Sunrise* case[11] discussed violations of human rights by Russia during an enforcement action against Greenpeace activists. The *Enrica Lexie* case, which is still pending before an arbitral tribunal,[12] has seen human rights arguments advanced by the two parties, India and Italy. Following a pattern that has informed many recent international judicial proceedings, in all these cases international courts and tribunals were faced with the recurrent problems deriving from cases at the inter-section between two different fields of law—human rights law and the law of the sea.

The availability of practical information and judicial decisions that concern people at sea and the law that applies to them have resulted in a resurgent interest into the legal regulation of this issue. A number of questions, in fact, need to be addressed. Do pirates have human rights? Can migrants at sea be turned back to the State from which they have sailed? How can the crew of vessels be protected against inhuman and degrading working and living conditions? Can States be held liable under international human rights treaties for arresting drug traffickers on the high seas? These

---

3394/03 (Judgment (GC) of 29 March 2010). On this case see Gianmatteo Breda and Jean Paul Perini, 'Legal Issues Surrounding Maritime Counterdrug Operations and the Related Question of Detention as Highlighted in the *Medvedyev and Others v. France* Decision of the European Court of Human Rights' (2008) 47 Military Law and the Law of War Review 167; 'Case Comment *Medvedyev v France* (3394/03)' (2010) 4 European Human Rights Law Review 442; Efthymios Papastavridis, 'European Court of Human Rights *Medvedyev et al v France* (Grand Chamber, Application No 3394/03) Judgment of 29 March 2010' (2010) 59 ICLQ 867.

[8] *Hirsi Jamaa and Others v Italy* App no 27765/09 (Judgment (GC) of 23 February 2012). On this case see Giovanni Cellamare, 'Brevi note sulla sentenza della Corte europea dei diritti dell'uomo nell'affare *Hirsi Jamaa e altri c. Italia*' (2012) 7 Studi sull'integrazione europea 491; Alessia Di Pascale, 'La sentenza *Hirsi e altri c. Italia*: una condanna senza appello della politica dei respingimenti' (2012) Diritto, Immigrazione e Cittadinanza 85; Mariagiulia Giuffré, 'Watered-Down Rights on the High Seas: *Hirsi Jamaa and Others v Italy* (2012)' (2012) 61 ICLQ 728; Federico Lenzerini, 'Il principo del "non-refoulement" dopo la sentenza "Hirsi" della Corte europea dei diritti dell'uomo' (2012) 95 Rivista di diritto internazionale 721; Anna Liguori, 'La Corte europea dei diritti dell'uomo condanna l'Italia per i respingimenti verso la Libia del 2009: il caso Hirsi' (2012) 95 Rivista di diritto internazionale 415; Violeta Moreno-Lax, 'Hirsi Jamaa and Others v Italy or the Strasbourg Court versus Extraterritorial Migration Control?' (2012) 12 Human Rights Law Review 574; Matteo Tondini, 'The Legality of Intercepting Boat People under Search and Rescue and Border Control Operations: With Reference to Recent Italian Interventions in the Mediterranean Sea and the ECtHR Decision in the Hirsi Case' (2012) 18 The Journal of International Maritime Law 59; Maarten den Heijer, 'Reflections on "Refoulement" and Collective Expulsion in the "Hirsi" Case' (2013) 25 International Journal of Refugee Law 265; Irini Papanicolopulu, 'Hirsi Jamaa v. Italy' (2013) 107 AJIL 417.

[9] *The Haitian Centre for Human Rights* et al *v United States* Case 10.675 (Report no 51/96 of 13 March 1997).

[10] *JHA v Spain*, Communication no 323/2007 (Decision of 21 November 2008).

[11] *Arctic Sunrise (The Kingdom of the Netherlands v The Russian Federation)* PCA Case no 2014-02 (Award (merits) of 14 August 2015). For a comment of the case, including its human rights aspects, see Alex G Oude Elferink, 'The "Arctic Sunrise" Incident: A Multi-faceted Law of the Sea Case with a Human Rights Dimension' (2014) 29 IJMCL 244.

[12] *The 'Enrica Lexie' Incident (Italy v India)* PCA Case no 2015-28, still pending; information on the case is available on the website of the Permanent Court of Arbitration (PCA) <https://pca-cpa.org/en/cases/117> accessed 18 October 2017.

questions in turn give rise to more general concerns about how international law can be used to protect the people who are at sea. General concerns can also be framed as research questions: What rules of international law apply to persons who are at sea? What powers can States exercise over them and what limitations are they subject to? Do people at sea have rights? Do States have duties towards people at sea? What actions, if any, are States required to take to protect and safeguard these rights and to enforce these duties?

2. Why 'People at Sea'

One may question the necessity of dealing with 'people at sea' collectively. Why not continue distinguishing between pirates and seafarers? Between fishers and migrants? Between passengers and traffickers?

To some extent, this is a valid point. 'People at sea' is a category that is too wide and, at the same time, too narrow. On the one hand, every individual who is at sea is unique and may be subject to specific rules, as a number of simple examples easily demonstrate. A Somali pirate is committing a criminal offence while a Philippine seafarer working on a Panamanian flagged vessel is exercising a lawful activity. A British engineer employed on board an oil platform in the middle of the North Sea may have different safety needs and may face different issues than a small-scale fisher in Thailand, or a person engaged in food processing on board a factory vessel fishing for krill in the Antarctic Ocean. An American tourist enjoying a cruise in the Mediterranean Sea may have different objectives to a Syrian refugee crossing that same sea to seek asylum on its northern shores. It is therefore impossible to find two individuals who are exactly the same and ultimately, the law will have to be established with regard to the specific person concerned. Even two people participating in the same act of piracy may be subject to different rules, if for example, one is an adult and the other a teenager.

On the other hand, all these people are human beings. As such they share, apart from their human nature, the fact that they are considered, to a growing extent, as the addressees of rights and duties of international law.[13] In this respect, there should be no difference between 'people at sea' and 'people on land', since the capacity to enjoy fundamental human rights does not depend on the place where a person happens to be.[14] To use the celebrated words of the Universal Declaration of Human Rights (UDHR) 'all human beings are born free and equal in dignity and rights' and all are 'entitled to all the rights and freedoms set forth in this Declaration, without distinction'.[15] Why then distinguish, among all individuals who make up humanity, those who are at sea during a specific moment in their lives?

---

[13] Anne Peters, *Beyond Human Rights. The Legal Status of the Individual in International Law* (CUP 2016).

[14] Chapter 4, Section 6.

[15] Universal Declaration of Human Rights, UNGA Res 217 A (III) (10 December 1948), Art 1 and Art 2, respectively.

It is indeed a fundamental assumption of this work that all people are equal and that egalitarian and non-discriminatory treatment should be the basis for legal regulation directed towards persons. Special rules that derogate from well-established legal norms and provide for specific rights and duties, however numerous, should always be the exception and should be justified on the basis of the specific circumstances of each case. Being engaged in a specific activity may in fact provide an appropriate justification for discriminating. For example, pirates may be subject to limitations upon their right to personal liberty because they are engaged in a criminal activity, while navy officers will not suffer such limitations, not because they are humanely different but because they are undertaking a lawful activity. In this case, however, a person should be treated differently only because of and to the extent justified by the activity in which she or he is engaged. The arrest of a ship by enforcement officers in conformity with international law should be treated differently from the seizure of a ship by people engaged in piracy to demand a ransom. This should not be interpreted to mean that a pirate can be treated differently only because he or she is a pirate.

In conclusion, any classification is, to a certain extent, arbitrary and reposes on the contingent necessities of legal analysis and the development and application of the law. The fundamental issue to consider is how to identify and define a category that is meaningful for legal analysis. It is submitted that the category of 'people at sea' serves this purpose. When the research that has eventually formed the basis of this book began more than ten years ago, this classification was chosen because it included a group of people that did not form the object of any dedicated legal study. 'People at sea' was a working hypothesis for an innovative analysis of two fields of international law which were seldom discussed together: the law of the sea and international human rights law.

The findings of this book demonstrate that, in terms of legal protection, 'people at sea' share some common characteristics, which also differentiate them from people on land. On the one hand, they are all human beings and as such these people can be distinguished from other objects of protection such as marine resources and the marine environment. Considering all people at sea as a single group, notwithstanding their specificities and the particular activity in which they may be engaged at a specific moment in time, allows for an equal treatment of all individuals, which takes into account the equality of individuals and the need to respect every human being. On the other hand, people at sea share the fact that they find themselves at sea, an environment that is physically and juridically different from land. This category of people therefore allows us to take into account the natural and legal specificities of the marine space in the assessment of rules that need to be not only non-discriminatory but also effective.

3. The Need for a New Approach

Given the presence of people at sea, the obvious question for an international lawyer is: What does the international community do for the protection of people at sea? And what role may international law play? Many of the situations discussed above are currently on the agendas of States and international organizations. The focus, so far, has mostly been on the need to integrate the human element into specific law of the sea rules. Recent attempts by international organizations to integrate the two branches have provided evidence of the potential benefits of institutional co-operation. For example, the International Labour Organization (ILO) and International Maritime Organization (IMO) have pressed for uniform maritime labour standards which eventually resulted in the 2006 Maritime Labour Convention (MLC),[16] and the IMO and United Nations High Commissioner for Refugees (UNHCR) are working together on the difficult issues associated with migration by sea.[17]

The need to integrate human rights considerations into activities occurring at sea and involving persons does not stem from any formal incompatibility between the international law of the sea and international human rights law. It is, rather, the consequence of a separate treatment of rules deriving from these two branches of international law, which have always been conceived as independent one from the other. This separate treatment, which is also to be found in a great deal of scholarly writing, is particularly evident in relevant treaties. In fact, legal instruments attached to one field are usually silent with respect to situations governed by the other. Thus, the International Covenant on Civil and Political Rights (ICCPR)[18] and the International Covenant on Economic, Social and Cultural Rights (ICESCR)[19] do not mention the maritime space. The same is true for the other major international human rights treaties, including regional instruments such as the European Convention on Human Rights (ECHR)[20] and the American Convention on Human Rights (ACHR).[21] On the other hand, the United Nations Convention on the Law of the Sea (UNCLOS),[22] the treaty that regulates most maritime activities and has been defined as a 'Constitution for the Oceans'[23]

---

[16] Maritime Labour Convention (adopted 23 February 2006, entered into force 20 August 2013) (MLC). Instruments for cooperation between the ILO and the IMO are discussed in James Harrison, *Making the Law of the Sea* (CUP 2011) 258–68.

[17] The IMO and UNHCR, together with the International Chamber of Shipping, have adopted a guidance for seafarers encountering migrants and refugees at sea: 'Rescue at Sea: A Guide to Principles and Practice as Applied to Refugees and Migrants' (January 2015) <http://www.imo.org/en/OurWork/Facilitation/personsrescued/Documents/RescueatSeaGuideENGLISH.pdf> accessed 18 October 2017.

[18] International Covenant on Civil and Political Rights (adopted 16 December 1966, entered into force 23 May 1976) 999 UNTS 171.

[19] International Covenant on Economic, Social and Cultural Rights (adopted 16 December 1966, entered into force 3 January 1976) 993 UNTS 3.

[20] Convention for the Protection of Human Rights and Fundamental Freedoms (adopted 4 November 1950, entered into force 3 September 1953) 213 UNTS 222.

[21] American Convention on Human Rights (adopted 22 November 1969, entered into force 18 July 1978) 1144 UNTS 123.

[22] United Nations Convention on the Law of the Sea (adopted 10 December 1982, entered into force 16 November 1994) 1833 UNTS 397 (UNCLOS).

[23] Remarks by Tommy TB Koh, President of the Third United Nations Conference on the Law of the Sea, <http://www.un.org/depts/los/convention_agreements/texts/koh_english.pdf> accessed 18 October 2017.

does not mention human rights and 'is not ordinarily considered a human rights instrument'.[24]

Most of the institutional and normative responses given by the international community were motivated by the urgent need to respond to specific situations. If measured against the conditions existing on the ground when regulation was promoted, the results are undoubtedly remarkable. Legal regulation, most usually in the form of binding treaties, has been adopted within relatively little time. However, a scholar who approaches this amount of regulation in an attempt to conceptualize its content may not feel entirely satisfied. In fact, regulation has developed quickly but erratically, pursuing the cogent interest of the moment at the expense of a coherent framework.

The time is therefore ripe to address the topic of 'people at sea' in a coherent and comprehensive manner, in order to ascertain what law applies to them. Applying Higgins' suggestion, this book will try to locate 'the corpus of law at the heart of a difficult issue'.[25] This effort can only partially take stock of and benefit from previous scholarly work. As mentioned above, some issues involving some categories of people at sea have received much attention from those writing on international law. For example, several monographs and edited collections, not to mention journal articles, have addressed aspects of piracy,[26] migration by sea,[27] maritime labour,[28] interdiction of vessels at sea,[29] and maritime security.[30] While these texts provide useful information and perspectives, they do not focus on general issues, except occasionally. This often leads to a sectorial or fragmented analysis that is too closely linked to the specificities of the topic under review and, at the same time, may not sufficiently take into account lessons learned from other fields and may not be easily transposable to other contexts. In addition few works address the general legal framework that applies to people at sea. These works have focused on one aspect of the problem: the relationship between the law of the sea and international human rights law.[31] These writings are, however, in the form of articles and while they

---

[24] Bernard H Oxman, 'Human Rights and the United Nations Convention on the Law of the Sea' (1998) 36 Columbia Journal of Transnational Law 399, 401.

[25] Rosalyn Higgins, 'A Babel of Judicial Voices? Ruminations from the Bench' (2006) 55 ICLQ 791, 792.

[26] Above n 2.

[27] Patricia Mallia, *Migrant Smuggling by Sea. Combating a Current Threat to Maritime Security through the Creation of a Cooperative Framework* (Martinus Nijhoff 2010); Thomas Gammeltoft-Hansen, *Access to Asylum. International Refugee Law and the Globalisation of Migration Control* (CUP 2011); Amedeo Antonucci, Irini Papanicolopulu, and Tullio Scovazzi (eds), *L'immigrazione Irregolare via Mare nella Giurisprudenza Italiana e nell'Esperienza Europea* (Giappichelli 2016); Itamar Mann, *Humanity at Sea. Maritime Migration and the Foundations of International Law* (CUP 2016); Violeta Moreno Lax and Efthymios Papastavridis (eds), *'Boat Refugees' and Migrants at Sea: A Comprehensive Approach. Iintegrating Maritime Security with Human Rights* (Martinus Nijhoff 2017).

[28] Deirdre Fitzpatrick and Michael Anderson (eds), *Seafarers' Rights* (OUP 2005).

[29] Douglas Guilfoyle, *Shipping Interdiction and the Law of the Sea* (CUP 2009); Efthymios Papastavridis, *The Interception of Vessels on the High Seas* (Hart 2014).

[30] Natalie Klein, *Maritime Security and the Law of the Sea* (OUP 2011).

[31] Louis B Sohn, 'International Law of the Sea and Human Rights Issues' in Thomas A Clingan Jr (ed), *The Law of the Sea: What Lies Ahead?* (The Law of the Sea Institute 1988) 51; Bernard H Oxman, 'Human Rights and the United Nations Convention on the Law of the Sea' in Jonathan I Charney and Donald K Anton (eds), *Politics, Values and Functions: International Law in the 21st Century. Essays in*

provide valuable insights into the relationship of these two fields of international law, they do not have the necessary form that would allow the development of a complete conceptual argument.

As a matter of fact, the notional category of 'people at sea' defies any existing legal taxonomy. Although both general international law and many of its specialized regimes contain provisions that consider or have an impact on persons at sea, none of the established regimes adequately regulate this subject matter. On the one hand, we have the law of the sea as codified in the UNCLOS, which contains many detailed substantial rules that address a variety of topics and issues, including navigation, the conservation of living and non-living resources, the protection of the environment, and even illegal activities, but the treaty says very little about people and their rights. On the other hand, international human rights law (and lawyers) seem to generally forget about the existence of the sea. Their legal analysis and research concentrates on situations on land and examples used to illustrate issues and explain rules usually take place on land. While this allows for the elaboration of general principles that apply to most individuals, it does not take into account either the specific dangers and threats faced by people at sea or the complex legal framework within which they find themselves. There are all sorts of rules of law—procedural and substantive— which combine to provide for the safeguarding of human rights. Nevertheless, given the fact that the structure of legal competences and the scope of the rights and duties of States are different at sea, and that the physical circumstances at sea put people into situations that do not always sit comfortably within the paradigms that the drafters of human rights treaties had in mind, the law may apply incompletely or inefficiently or even incorrectly at sea.

The difficulty in addressing and contextualizing, in legal thinking and discourse, the regime applicable to people at sea is evident from the struggle of textbook authors in dedicating some room to the topic. Since many of the issues discussed in this book have gained momentum only recently, earlier textbooks do not discuss aspects of the law that apply to people at sea.[32] The inclusion of some of these issues in recent textbooks has highlighted the need to conceptualize problems relating to persons at sea and to devise a taxonomy of problems and rules. If one uses the 'old' law of the sea framework, the alternative is between trying to fit human issues into other 'well-established' categories, such as navigation or environmental protection,[33] or

---

Honor of Professor Louis Henkin (Martinus Nijhoff 1997) 377, reprinted as Oxman (n 24); Budislav Vukas, 'Droit de la mer et droits de l'homme' in Giuseppe Cataldi (ed), *La Méditerranée et le droit de la mer à l'aube du 21e siècle* (Bruylant 2002) 85; Sophie Cacciaguidi-Fahy, 'The Law of the Sea and Human Rights' (2007) 19 Sri Lanka Journal of International Law 85; Tullio Treves, 'Human Rights and the Law of the Sea' (2010) 28 Berkeley Journal of International Law 1.

[32] For example, Robin R Churchill and Alan Vaughan Lowe, *The Law of the Sea* (3rd edn, Manchester University Press 1999), which is still considered a basic textbook, does not address human rights of persons at sea, nor does it discuss the allocation among States of powers and duties with respect to persons.

[33] Donald R Rothwell and Tim Stephens, *The International Law of the Sea* (Hart 2010) 361, eg, address issues relating to seafarers' rights, including the 2006 Maritime Labour Convention, in the part of the text devoted to the protection of the marine environment from vessels-source pollution.

dividing them in different parts of the analysis.[34] The same difficulties emerge from an examination of the textbooks on human rights, most of which ignore the particularities of the marine context, concentrating their analysis on the application of human rights on land.[35] Even more specific works dealing with particular aspects of international human rights law often do not consider the possibility of applying human rights treaties during activities carried out at sea,[36] or do so only in a cursory manner.[37] Similarly, while the debate on fragmentation is indeed not new to international law, issues relating to the potential conflict between different rules applicable to persons at sea have apparently never been dealt with jointly during this debate, nor has the potential relationship between the two regimes of the law of the sea and international human rights law been considered.[38]

Acknowledging this fragmented picture, this book argues that the different situations that people at sea find themselves in should be seen not as isolated cases, but as parts of a wider picture that needs to be described and assessed in a consistent way, both in its empirical description and in its normative analysis. It therefore advances the proposal that a new paradigm should be applied to the conceptualization of 'people at sea'. This paradigm reposes on two fundamental arguments. The first is that all people at sea should be considered together, for the reasons expounded in the previous section. Any differentiated treatment should be construed as an exception, and not as the general rule. The second is that the development of international law in this field can be construed as leading to the emergence of a special regime. If one examines international law through the lens of 'people at sea' one realizes that the law of the sea and international human rights law, as well as other international law

---

[34] Yoshifumi Tanaka, *The International Law of the Sea* (2nd edn, CUP 2015), eg, mentions considerations of humanity when discussing the material sources of the law of the sea (ibid 15) and the MLC when discussing flag State duties (ibid 159), and port State control (ibid 298).

[35] Henry J Steiner, Philip Alston, and Ryan Goodman, *International Human Rights in Context* (3rd edn, OUP 2007), eg do not refer to the many problems arising from the application of human rights at sea and the same is true of other textbooks on human rights law, eg Sarah Joseph and Adam McBeth, *Research Handbook on International Human Rights Law* (Edward Elgar 2010). A notable exception to this trend is provided by Guy Goodwin-Gill and Jane McAdam, *The Refugee In International Law* (3rd edn, OUP 2007) 267; due to the scope of their book their discussion is limited, however, to protection afforded to asylum seekers travelling by sea.

[36] The fact that a 2010 collection of essays on the right to life (Christian Tomuschat, Evelyne Lagrange, and Stefan Oeter (eds), *The Right to Life* (Martinus Nijhoff Publishers 2010)) does not address the protection of life at sea or the positive obligations of States at all in this context is indicative of this trend.

[37] For example, recent publications on the extraterritorial application of human rights treaties, including Fons Coomans and Menno T Kamminga (eds), *Extraterritorial Application of Human Rights Treaties* (Intersentia 2004) and more recently Marko Milanovic, *Extraterritorial Application of Human Rights Treaties. Law, Principles, and Policy* (OUP 2011), while providing interesting constructions of extraterritorial jurisdiction, do not discuss in depth the application of international human rights treaties at sea and the complexities created by the existence of areas within and beyond national jurisdiction, as well as by the exercise of functional jurisdiction according to law of the sea provisions.

[38] For example, ILC, 'Fragmentation of International Law: Difficulties Arising from the Diversification and Expansion of International Law. Report of the Study Group of the International Law Commission Finalized by Martti Koskenniemi' (13 April 2006) UN Doc A/CN.4/L.682 (Koskenniemi Report), does not discuss possible interactions between the law of the sea and international human rights law and the same is true for Margaret Young (ed), *Regime Interaction in International Law. Facing Fragmentation* (CUP 2012).

regimes, such as maritime law and international labour law contain rules that are addressed at people, or apply to people, or can be used by people to further their interests. All these rules share a common object, which is to ensure a better protection of people at sea. Furthermore, there is a common general principle that underlies the interpretation and application of all these rules. This principle requires States to protect people at sea and to ensure that these people enjoy their human rights while at sea. The general principle and the rules, grouped together, form the special regime of the 'law that applies to people at sea'.

4. A Note on 'Regimes'

A significant part of this book is dedicated to the discussion of regimes. It will describe and assess those regimes of international law that most closely concern people at sea and it will argue in favour of the emergence of a new regime on the protection of people at sea. The term 'regime' is widely used, albeit with different meanings, in both international relations scholarship, and international law scholarship.[39] Although this book engages with the concept and substance of legal regimes, a detailed inquiry into the nature and content of 'regimes' is beyond its scope.[40] At the same time, the attribution of different meanings to this term and the vague triad of 'regime-system-field' may cause confusion and make it appropriate to provide the understanding of the term that will be used in this book.

Following decades of discussion about the nature of international law and the term that should be employed to designate the group of its rules,[41] in 2006 the International Law Commission (ILC) concluded that 'international law is a

---

[39] For a notion of 'regime' in international relations see the classical definition in Stephen Krasner, 'Structural Causes and Regime Consequences: Regimes as Intervening Variables' in Stephen Krasner (ed), *International Regimes* (Cornell University Press 1983) 2 ('Regimes can be defined as sets of implicit or explicit principles, norms, rules, and decision-making procedures around which actors' expectations converge in a given area of international relations'). As this book deals with positive international law, the debate as it is approached in international relations will not be investigated further.

[40] There is much discussion among legal scholars of the meaning and content of 'regimes', in particular in works addressing the fragmentation of international law; for accounts of this discussion see Lorenzo Gradoni, Regime failure *nel diritto internazionale* (CEDAM 2009); Ole Kristian Fauchald and André Nollkaemper (eds), *The Practice of International and National Courts and the (De-) Fragmentation of International Law* (Hart 2012); Gunther Teubner, *Constitutional Fragments. Societal Constitutionalism and Globalization* (OUP 2012); Mario Prost, Unitas multiplex: *Unité et fragmentation en droit international* (Bruylant 2013); Young (n 38); Philippa Webb, *International Judicial Integration and Fragmentation* (OUP 2013); Dirk Pulkowski, *The Law and Politics of International Regime Conflict* (OUP 2014); Mads Andenas and Eirik Bjorge (eds), *A Farewell to Fragmentation: Reassertion and Convergence in International Law* (CUP 2015); Andrzej Jakubowski and Karolina Wierczyńska (eds), *Fragmentation vs the Constitutionalisation of International Law. A Practical Enquiry* (Routledge 2016); Anne-Charlotte Martineau, *Le debat sur la fragmentation du droit international: une analyse critique* (Bruylant 2016).

[41] The triad system-order-regime was a characteristic feature of the international legal discourse at the turn of the century and is still very much in use today. While sometimes the three terms are used interchangeably, it is often the case that one is preferred to the other or that they are used to designate different cognitive objects.

system'.[42] This 'system' can be further divided into 'regimes', which include subgroups of rules that have a certain internal consistency. The ILC identified three types of 'special regimes': (a) 'a particular group of (primary) rules ... accompanied by a special set of (secondary) rules concerning breach and reactions to breach'; (b) 'a set of special rules, including rights and obligations, relating to a special subject matter [which] may concern a geographical area ... or some substantive matter'; and (c) 'all the rules and principles that regulate a certain problem area are collected together so as to express a "special regime".'[43] In the past, these regimes were sometimes referred to as a 'self-contained regime';[44] however, this term is not used anymore, as it has become clear that no regime of international law is entirely self-contained.[45] The general acceptance of the fact that the 'system' of international law is divided into separate 'regimes', of course, does not entail that there is complete agreement on how many regimes there are in international law and what exactly these regimes include. Thus, for example, while the law of the sea is usually classified as one of the 'regimes' of international law, this assumption has not gone unchallenged.[46]

My understanding of legal regimes is very similar to the third category identified by the ILC above which, according to Koskenniemi, means that 'fields of functional specialization, of diplomatic and academic expertise, are described as self-contained (whether or not that word is used) in the sense that special rules and techniques of interpretation and administration are thought to apply'.[47] Each such regime is dominated by its separate 'guild'.[48] A 'regime' therefore will include all those rules of international law, as interpreted and applied at the international and domestic level, that regulate a certain subject matter and that are interpreted and applied as part

[42] ILC, 'Conclusions of the work of the Study Group on the Fragmentation of International Law: Difficulties arising from the Diversification and Expansion of International Law' (18 July 2006) UN Doc A/CN.4/L.702 (ILC Conclusions 2006), para 1: 'International law is a legal system. Its rules and principles (i.e. its norms) act in relation to and should be interpreted against the background of other rules and principles. As a legal system, international law is not a random collection of such norms. There are meaningful relationships between them. Norms may thus exist at higher and lower hierarchical levels, their formulation may involve greater or lesser generality and specificity and their validity may date back to earlier or later moments in time.'
[43] ILC Conclusions 2006 (n 42) para 12.
[44] Bruno Simma, 'Self-Contained Regimes' (1985) 16 Netherlands Yearbook of International Law 112; Koskenniemi Report (n 38) 65.
[45] According to Koskenniemi Report (n 38) 82, 'the notion of a "self-contained regime" is simply misleading. Although the degree to which a regime or responsibility, a set of rules on a problem or a branch of international law needs to be supplemented by general law varies, there is no support for the view that anywhere general law would be fully excluded.' Bruno Simma and Dirk Pulkowski, 'Of Planets and the Universe: Self-contained Regimes in International Law' 17 EJIL 483, 529, consider that 'general international law provides a systemic fabric from which no special legal regime is completely decoupled'.
[46] 'General international law and its various component areas (airspace, outer space, the oceans) cannot usefully be described as a regime, anymore than tort, contract and unjust enrichment can be described as "regimes" of domestic law. . . . It would be better if the word regime is used in a more discriminating way, and in particular was not used to describe branches of general international law' (James Crawford and Penelope Nevill, 'Relations between International Courts and Tribunals: The "Regime Problem"' in Young (n 38) 235, 259).
[47] Koskenniemi Report (n 38) para 129.
[48] Oxman (n 24) 399–400.

of a special subset of rules of international law, guided by its own principles.[49] As such, legal regimes include only a portion of all the rules that make up international law, which is considered as the overarching system within which all the regimes are located.

5. Structure of the Book

Starting from the assumption that few people are familiar with the topic of people at sea, Chapter 1 sets out to describe the factual and legal background which is crucial to digest before turning attention to the protection of these people. Firstly, it provides some background discussion concerning the presence of people at sea and the risks these people face. Secondly, it briefly presents the legal rules that have been adopted specifically to protect some of the categories of people who are at sea. It continues by evaluating whether these rules address all the identified risks before concluding that existing treaties specifically targeting people at sea provide only a partial and uneven protection. Current efforts to address the specific challenges faced by people at sea are not effective, since legal analysis is based upon the identification of a discrete field, often in conjunction with a specific forum, within which the particular problem is addressed. This approach results in piecemeal solutions that do not devote sufficient attention to the human nature of all people who are at sea, resulting in different levels of protection and, sometimes, an unjustified difference in treatment. It is therefore suggested that there is a need to conceptualize the law that applies to people at sea going beyond specific treaties and categories of persons.

Following the first chapter, Chapter 2 rejects the current approach and elaborates upon the proposed new conceptual approach. Drawing upon the systemic nature of international law, this chapter advocates that rules relevant to the protection of people at sea may be found in any field of international law and that it is only through the integration of different rules that better protection of people at sea can be ensured. In order to achieve this objective, the chapter first proceeds to isolate regimes that provide a substantial contribution—the law of the sea, international human rights law, and technical regimes (including international labour law and maritime law)—identifying the core characteristics of each and the elements that may contribute towards its integration with the others. It then singles out the devices that are currently available in order to integrate legal rules and instruments deriving from the discrete regimes of international law.

Having argued in favour of an integrated reading of all international law rules that apply to people at sea, Chapter 3 applies this comprehensive approach in order to identify the scope of States' duties owed to people at sea. Scope is linked with the notion of jurisdiction, which permits the identification of the State or States

---

[49] Koskenniemi Report (n 38) 68: 'One often speaks of "principles of international environmental law", or "principles of international human rights law" with the assumption that in some way those principles differ from what the general law provides for analogous situations.'

that must comply with its legal obligations to protect people at sea. The chapter thus reconstructs the complex web of norms that regulate jurisdiction of States over persons at sea. These rules, it is argued, play a crucial role in determining the State that must protect the rights of people at sea. In particular, in the context of human rights law, it is argued that jurisdiction is relevant both in its *de jure* component, which is to be mostly found in dedicated law of the sea provisions, and in its *de facto* component, which derives from an interpretation of this notion which is specific to international human rights law.

Turning from scope to content, Chapter 4 discusses the content of the legal obligations owed by States to people at sea. It is not the aim of this book to provide a detailed illustration of all duties of States, nor to assess the exact extent to which each human or labour right applies at sea. Rather, this chapter sets out to provide a conceptual framework within which to carry out further codification work and which may serve as a basis for the development of new rules. The chapter first argues in favour of the emergence of a new general principle of international law, according to which States have the duty to protect people at sea and to undertake action to ensure that people enjoy their human rights at sea. The chapter then explores the nature of these duties and the extent to which an extensive range of positive obligations accompany negative ones. This is followed by a discussion of the tension between comprehensiveness and severability, and some measure of scrutiny over the usefulness of the different approaches for the protection of people at sea. Eventually, the chapter discusses the structural change in the content of norms relating to the powers that States exercise at sea. In this respect, the book argues that the widespread acceptance of human rights and the development of detailed regulation providing for the exercise of mandatory legislative and enforcement jurisdiction, when it comes to people at sea, is actually transforming the rights attributed to States under the traditional law of the sea rules into duties.

Summing up the discussion of the content of international law for the protection of people at sea, Chapter 5 conducts a close examination of this law in order to evaluate whether it merely represents an arbitrary collection of rules that actually belong to different fields, or whether it can better be construed as a coherent set of norms that constitute a sub-regime of international law. Two conceptual tools are used in this assessment: 'regime emergence' and a 'human-centered' approach to international law. The book argues that the conceptualization of any group of rules that apply to a certain issue requires a systemic understanding of international law, according to which all rules (deriving from general international law and its specialized regimes) belong to the same system, and therefore have the potential to be functionally combined and to create an unlimited number of functional legal regimes, each focusing on a specific substantive matter. The chapter concludes by sketching the main elements of the new regime of the international protection of people at sea and in discussing its advantages vis-à-vis a fragmented reading of the rules collected in the book. It is thus submitted that the collection of rules pertaining to 'people at sea' is logically meaningful and practically useful, as it allows us to address the real gaps and inconsistencies in the existing law, promoting a coherent development of international law.

The need to challenge the current regime-based approaches and to develop a comprehensive legal framework addressing treatment of people at sea is becoming ever more critical. The recent tragic events in the Mediterranean Sea and the partial and unsatisfactory response by the European Union and its member States provide but one additional instance of the enduring risks for people at sea—not only from the natural elements, but also from unclear and underdeveloped legal frameworks. By setting out to clarify the legal framework, I hope the book will eventually contribute towards a better protection of people at sea.

1

People, the Sea, and International Law

1. Introduction

Since its beginning, humankind has been unable to resist the allure of the sea. And while the perils of the sea were not second to the fate awaiting the victims of the sirens, they have not kept men (and a few women) back. For thousands of years the sea has been exploited as the safest route for the transport of goods and people, as well as being a source of food, a preferred course for migration, at times the theatre of war, and the means for expansion of countries and the creation of new empires.[1]

The technological developments of the last decades have enhanced most of these uses and have introduced new ways of exploitation. In addition to its continued use as a transport route and an economic resource—mining for oil and minerals, farming fish, and producing wind energy have been added to the traditional list of economic activities—the sea is now seen as a major area for recreation and might soon attract uses that do not fall into our intuitive notion of the 'maritime', such as data storage or office space. The sea, broadly construed, is on its way to being turned into a new sort of land, whereupon all kinds of activities may take place.[2]

All uses of the sea presuppose the presence of people and their increase may only result in a corresponding increase in the number of people at sea. Furthermore, the diversification of these uses has induced an enlargement of the types of people that populate the sea. Once the domain of sailors, fishers, merchants, and pirates, marine waters now see holiday goers, refugees, engineers, scientists, entertainers, and people working in food processing, to mention but some. This enlargement is due to the continuous technological and social adaptation of humankind to life in the water, which at the same time pays testament to a changing perception of the sea and maritime enterprise that turns towards the pursuit of pleasure, rather than the threats, of life in the salty waters.[3]

---

[1] Lincoln Paine, *The Sea and Civilization. A Maritime History of the World* (Atlantic Books 2013) provides a captivating account of the maritime history of the world.

[2] Thus already in 1980 René Rodière and Martine Rèmond-Gouilloud, *La mer: droits des hommes ou proie desétats?* (Pedone 1980) 139 concluded that 'le navire n'est plus que l'une des catégories des bâtiments de mer' and asked whether '[l]a vie en mer est-elle aujourd'hui à ce point différent de la vie terrienne pour justifier un statut particulier?'.

[3] 'Today we see pleasure where our forebears saw peril, and we can savor the fruits of maritime commerce without being remotely aware of its existence, even when we live in cities that originally grew rich from sea trade.' Paine (n 1) 10.

International Law and the Protection of People at Sea. Irini Papanicolopulu. © Irini Papanicolopulu, 2018. Published 2018 by Oxford University Press.

The increasing population of the sea by humans should not be taken as proof of the acquired safety of the maritime environment. The sirens' call may be lost in the mythical ages but the perils of the sea are always there, both natural and manmade, to threaten the survival and well-being of people who take to the sea. Harsh weather, a dangerous environment, distance from the coast, and the difficulties in patrolling and controlling the oceans result in a space where dangers cannot be entirely controlled and abuse may take place unchecked. As a result, death and personal injury, inhuman working and living conditions, slavery and forced labour, and disregard for basic guarantees against the arbitrary use of force by the State or the stronger party still characterize many maritime activities.[4]

It logically follows that people at sea need protection against all these threats. They need effective measures to guarantee their safety and security and adequate training to ensure that they know how to face risks and to not constitute a potential threat to each other. Whilst the further development of technological solutions, training, and the promotion of a culture that takes due account of the human element at sea are undoubtedly long-term strategies to ensure the safety and security of people at sea, legal regulation is a necessary component of any solution. It is only the existence of legally binding principles and rules, the attribution and effective use of the power to enforce these rules, the enhanced control of all involved actors, and the possibility to bring forward claims and have them settled according to the rule of law that will ensure the effective protection of people at sea. As the sea is the archetypal area beyond State sovereignty, it is evident that it is not possible to regulate activities therein based on the laws of one State only. It is therefore natural to turn to international law in search of such rules.[5]

Before turning to the rules of international law that purport to protect people at sea, the reader may ask: who are these persons and why should they be protected? The analysis of legal rules cannot begin without briefly addressing the factual background against which these rules should be understood and assessed. Whilst it is not the principal aim of this book to bring to the attention of the public the plight of persons who spend a part of their life at sea, it is important to keep in mind the practical realities that call for better regulation. As a matter of fact, law does not exist in a vacuum but is always related to reality and purports to regulate human conduct. The same should hold true for legal scholarship. Even the most abstract analysis cannot entirely ignore the fact that it is shaped by, and may have an impact on, the practical realities on the ground. The corollary of this is that any meaningful legal analysis must first state the practical realities which shape subsequent legal developments.

---

[4] For accounts of actual violations see Ian Urbina, 'The Outlaw Ocean' *New York Times* (25 July 2015) <https://www.nytimes.com/interactive/2015/07/24/world/the-outlaw-ocean.html>. See also the information provided in Section 3 below.

[5] The comments by Louis B Sohn, 'International Law of the Sea and Human Rights Issues' in Thomas A Clingan Jr (ed), *The Law of the Sea: What Lies Ahead?* (The Law of the Sea Institute 1988) 51, illustrate the usefulness of having international protection for human rights at sea: 'The United States ... has ratified very few [human rights] instruments, perhaps because of the mistaken belief that human rights are adequately protected by our Constitution. Even if this is true on land, it is not true at sea, as some federal courts refuse to apply to persons arrested at sea the safeguards provided for by international law and the United States Constitution.'

This is what this chapter aims to achieve. Beginning with the presumption that most readers are not familiar with the topic, it provides a snapshot of the practical and juridical issues raised by the presence of people at sea. It presents some background information concerning the presence of individuals at sea and its consequences, in particular the issues affecting people at sea. It will also illustrate current normative developments and the efforts of the international community to address old and new problems.

As such an undertaking demonstrates, existing regulation is not only scarce but it is also fragmented, addressing issues in a piecemeal fashion, rather than in the holistic way advocated by the United Nations Convention on the Law of the Sea (UNCLOS).[6] These shortcomings also partly describe current efforts at the lawmaking stage. The conclusion is that there is an urgent need for a holistic approach to the legal regulation of the subject matter of 'people at sea'.

2. The People: A Brief Empirical Account

Who are the 'people at sea', who are the central concern with this book? This generic expression is used throughout the book to identify any person who is, for a certain period of time, physically at sea. A handful of persons may be in the waters of the sea literally, being shipwrecked, having been thrown overboard, or having jumped into the sea deliberately, whatever their purpose may be. However, persons at sea are usually to be found on board vessels and, to a lesser but still significant extent, on board platforms or other man-made structures. In all these cases, the criterion used in order to determine whether a person can be considered as being at sea will be whether the ship or structure is in marine waters.[7]

People take to the sea for three main reasons: work, travel, and crime. They may work on board vessels and platforms, they may use the sea to go from one place to another, or they may engage in unlawful lucrative activities, be that trafficking or depredation, favoured by the vastness of the sea and the lack of control by a source of authority. In addition, people increasingly go to the sea for recreation, sailing in yachts, engaged in recreational fishing, taking cruises or other tours.

One strong reason to deal with persons at sea is their sheer numbers: the already noticeable presence of human beings at sea is constantly increasing and the activities in which they are involved are diversifying. The traditional categories of fishers,[8]

---

[6] Para 3, Preamble, United Nations Convention on the Law of the Sea (adopted 10 December 1982, entered into force 16 November 1994) 1833 UNTS 397 (UNCLOS).

[7] Although artificial islands are also man-made structures, they are treated as land for the purpose of identifying the law that applies to them. Thus, persons on artificial islands will be excluded to the extent that the law that applies to them is that of land, and not the law of the sea.

[8] The gender-neutral term 'fishers' is preferred to the traditional term 'fishermen' since it allows us to take into account the thousands of women engaged in sea fisheries. International organizations have used different terms, as observed in ILO, *Conditions of Work in the Fishing Sector. A Comprehensive Standard (a Convention supplemented by a Recommendation) on Work in the Fishing Sector* (International Labour Office 2003) 3.

sailors, passengers, and pirates are nowadays joined by people working on oil rigs, migrants, drug traffickers, arms traffickers, scientists, and many others. However, one must also consider other workers and entrepreneurs who use the sea in the same way as land was used—as a working space from which to conduct their business in fields entirely unrelated to the maritime environment, such as information technology or data storage.[9]

The following sections will look at these categories more closely.

2.1 Seafarers

Sailors form one of the oldest categories of people working at sea. Traditionally, a sailor was a person 'professionally occupied with navigation' who was often 'a member of a ship's company below the rank of officer'.[10] Sailors, therefore, were people that were necessary for navigating a vessel, from the master to the officers, the engineers, and the mates. Data from the International Chamber of Shipping estimate that over 50,000 merchant ships trading internationally employ 774,000 officers and 873,500 ratings.[11] These people work on vessels that fly different flags, representing all seafaring nations.[12] The constant increase in the number and tonnage of ships has generated an increase in the number of sailors and this trend is likely to continue since projections show a continuous expansion of the world merchant fleet.[13]

---

[9] Plans for the use of vessels as 'land beyond States' jurisdiction' wherein to carry out activities that would not be subject to the legislation of the coastal State, are cyclically elaborated. The use of ships as gambling venues is well documented (Robert D Faiss and Anthony N Cabot, 'Gaming on the High Seas' (1986) 8 New York Law School Journal of International and Comparative Law 105). During the prohibition period some companies organized drinking cruises beyond the US territorial waters. In the 1960s and 1970s, vessels and dismissed oil platforms were used to undertake non-licensed broadcasting (JC Woodliffe, 'Some Legal Aspects of Pirate Broadcasting in the North Sea' (1965) 12 Netherlands International Law Review 365; Horace Robertson, 'The Suppression of Pirate Radio Broadcasting: A Test Case of the International System for Control of Activities Outside National Territory' (1982) 45 Law and Contemporary Problems 71) and for the operation of incinerators (Daniel Suman, 'Regulation of Ocean Dumping by the European Economic Community' (1991) 18 Ecology Law Quarterly 559). In recent years, projects have been developed to operate vessels that would provide working space for IT start-ups or that would store data (Matthew Conroy, 'Sealand: The Next Haven?' (2003) 27 Suffolk Transnational Law Review 127; Stephen Swanson, 'Google Sets Sail: Ocean-Based Server Farms and International Law' (2011) 43 Connecticut Law Review 709; Shane O Balloun, 'The True Obstacle to the Autonomy of Seasteads: American Law Enforcement Jurisdiction over Homesteads on the High Seas' (2011) 24 University of San Francisco Maritime Law Journal 409).

[10] Oxford English Dictionary <http://www.oed.com/view/Entry/169826?redirectedFrom=sailor#eid>.

[11] International Chamber of Shipping, 'Global Supply and Demand for Seafarers' <http://www.ics-shipping.org/shipping-facts/shipping-and-world-trade/global-supply-and-demand-for-seafarers>.

[12] International Chamber of Shipping, 'The World's Major Shipping Flags' <http://www.ics-shipping.org/shipping-facts/shipping-and-world-trade/the-world's-major-shipping-flags>.

[13] International Chamber of Shipping, 'Predicted Increases in World Seaborne Trade, GDP and Population' <http://www.ics-shipping.org/shipping-facts/shipping-and-world-trade/predicted-increases-in-world-seaborne-trade-gdp-and-population>. Transport by sea is still the main means for the transport of goods and around 90 per cent of world trade is carried by the international shipping industry: International Chamber of Shipping, 'Key Facts' <http://www.ics-shipping.org/shipping-facts/key-facts>.

Modern shipping, however, includes not only trading ships, but also many other types of vessels: cruise ships, mobile offshore drilling units (MODUs), research vessels, passenger ships, and navy vessels to mention but some examples.[14] In many cases, not all personnel employed on the vessel are occupied with navigation. One can think of cooks and waiters, scientists and cleaners, entertainers and technicians. Cruise ships provide a good example of instances in which people coming from different parts of the world, with different qualifications and different drives, meet.[15] Finally, when vessels are used to provide office space, people on board may be employed in virtually any job. While most people are employed on board a vessel for at least one voyage, individuals may also work on a navigating vessel on an occasional and temporary basis, as is the case of riding gangs members.

Although they may be engaged in different duties, maritime or not, all persons working on a ship share the same working space and face a range of similar threats to safety and security independent of their actual occupation. This consideration has led to the widespread use of the term 'seafarer', rather than 'mariner' or 'sailor', to designate any person who works on a vessel.[16]

2.2 Navy and coastguard personnel

While usually included within the notion of seafarer, navy personnel, coastguards, and other State organs working at sea and mostly trusted with law enforcement duties are generally excluded from the applicable regulations and might therefore be considered as a group on its own.

Usually a small group, they are worth singling out since their role, and their consequent legal status, is complex. On the one hand, they are individuals and therefore they can be seen as potential victims, as they may also be affected by all the circumstances that impact on other people at sea. On the other hand, they are also State organs and are therefore the means through which States may protect or violate the rights of other individuals.

2.3 Fishers

A cursory glance at international instruments shows that the only group of people who are formally singled out whilst working on a ship are fishers, on the basis of the

---

[14] International Chamber of Shipping, 'Different Types of Ship in the World Merchant Fleet' <http://www.ics-shipping.org/shipping-facts/shipping-and-world-trade/different-types-of-ship-in-the-world-merchant-fleet>.

[15] 'A cruise ship represents nearly the full range of differentiation in the global labour market: low paid staff from developing countries below deck, up to quite highly paid officers on the bridge, which is not only a broad scope of professions and skill levels, but represents a widespread multicultural arena. This is the situation with, for example, 600 members of staff in the relatively small area of 250 x 30 meters or less' (Wolfgang Lukas, 'Leadership: Short-term, Intercultural and Performance-oriented' in Alexis Papathanassis (ed), *Cruise Sector Growth Managing Emerging Markets, Human Resources, Processes and Systems* (Gabler 2009) 65, 66).

[16] For example in Art II(1)(f) Maritime Labour Convention (adopted 23 February 2006, entered into force 20 August 2013) (MLC).

activity in which they engage. Their separate treatment can probably be attributed to their numbers and to the wide differences existing between all people designated by this definition. The type of persons encompassed by this term ranges from artisanal fishers who fish close to coasts, often by themselves or with one or two other people at most on non-decked boats less than ten metres long, to persons employed on large commercial distant fishing vessels, and everything in between.[17] While little less than 90 per cent of all fishers work in Asia, they are often employed in small-scale fishing and subsistence fishing.[18] The contribution of fishers to the 'world's well-being and prosperity' is well-documented. In 2010, capture fisheries and aquaculture supplied about 148 million tonnes of fish, and world trade in fish and fishery products in the same year reached about US$109 billion, with an increase of 13 per cent in value terms compared with 2009.[19] This significant contribution to world trade is matched by a substantial contribution to economic development, since employment in fisheries and ancillary activities supports the livelihoods of about 10–12 per cent of the world's population.[20]

The vast majority of fishing activity occurs through the utilization of vessels. There are however also instances of fishing from offshore platforms, and the use and operation of man-made floating devices is often central to aquaculture. Fishers therefore include both people working on board vessels and those working from platforms.

2.4 People working on extraction platforms

The field in which most people working on platforms are to be found, however, is the offshore mining sector. Technological advances have permitted the exploitation of offshore mineral resources, including oil, gas, and solid minerals, mostly from offshore platforms. These activities require a range of people with technical skills that spend long periods at sea and who are often transported to the platform and back from land by other means of transport. It is not easy to find estimates of persons employed on offshore platforms, but the average oil drilling platform requires 50–100 people. In 2014 more than 64,113 people travelled offshore to oil and gas installations on the British continental shelf. The number of core workers (those working over 100 nights a year offshore) rose to 28,990 in 2014 from 27,749 in 2013.[21]

---

[17] FAO, *The State of World Fisheries and Aquaculture* (FAO 2012) (SOFIA 2012) 47–50.
[18] With an average of 2.1 tonnes per person per year in 2010, compared with 25.7 tonnes in Europe, 18.0 tonnes in North America, and 6.9 tonnes in Latin America and the Caribbean (SOFIA 2012, 46).
[19] SOFIA 2012.
[20] 'Apart from the primary production sector, fisheries and aquaculture provide numerous jobs in ancillary activities such as processing, packaging, marketing and distribution, manufacturing of fish-processing equipment, net and gear making, ice production and supply, boat construction and maintenance, research and administration. All of this employment, together with dependants, is estimated to support the livelihoods of 660–820 million people, or about 10–12 percent of the world's population'. ibid 10.
[21] OIL&GAS UK, 'UK Continental Shelf Offshore Workforce Demographics Report 2015' (2015) 6 <http://oilandgasuk.co.uk/wp-content/uploads/2015/08/EM014.pdf> accessed 25 August 2017.

2.5 Passengers

Turning to people who use the sea to travel, one must consider passengers, migrants by sea, and stowaways. Passengers include all people who embark on a vessel to travel from one place to another. While transoceanic, long-distance travel is now undertaken almost exclusively by airplane, ferries are still very much used for local and regional transportation.[22] In 2004, more than 1.3 billion passengers were carried on 5.9 million crossings globally.[23] Passengers travel by ferry in both developed and developing regions,[24] although the conditions of travel may vary, going from modern, safe ferries to old unsafe ones.

Passengers of cruise vessels are another significant group, and one that is constantly increasing. In 2008, 13 million passengers worldwide travelled on cruise ships while today there are more than 20 million annual passengers.[25] Cruise itineraries cover all continents, including areas that are not easily accessible by other means of travel. If one considers that cruise voyages can last from several hours to several months and that a typical cruise ship now carries up to 3000 passengers and 1000 crew,[26] it is easy to conclude that cruise passengers find themselves for a certain period within a constrained and crowded vessel, which carries many more people than average commercial vessels.

2.6 Migrants, refugees, and asylum seekers

The sea has always served as a road for people to migrate. However, in recent years migration by sea has become central to political debate, as the numbers of migrants by sea are dramatically increasing. Migrant flows often include persons fleeing

---

[22] According to Interferry, 'A ferry is a vessel used to transport passengers and/or vehicles across a body of water on a regular, frequent basis. Ferries can range from small boats carrying passengers across a harbour or river in an urban setting, to large sea-going ships carrying passengers, cars, trucks and other heavy cargo across longer distances where overnight sleeping accommodations are required' (Interferry, 'Ferry Industry Facts' <http://www.interferry.com/communications/ferry-industry-facts>; unless otherwise indicated, all websites in this chapter were accessed on 21 November 2017).

[23] The total number of ferries worldwide as of 1 January 2006 (excluding ferries less than 1,000 gross tonnage) was 1,162, with a combined capacity of 1.15 million passengers. Combined gross tonnage was 12.8 million and the average age of the fleet was twenty-one years. Information available at IMO, 'Safety of Ro-Ro Ferries' <http://www.imo.org/OurWork/Safety/Regulations/Pages/RO-ROFerries. aspx>. According to Interferry, '[t]he global ferry industry transports approximately 2.1 billion passengers per year plus 250 million vehicles and 32 million trailers' (Interferry, 'Ferry Industry Facts' <http:// www.interferry.com/communications/ferry-industry-facts>).

[24] EU data shows that in 2012 more than 370 million people embarked and disembarked in EU ports (Eurostat, 'Country Level—Passengers Embarked and Disembarked in All Ports' <http://appsso. eurostat.ec.europa.eu/nui/show.do?dataset=mar_mp_aa_cph&lang=en>). In 2009, 212.4 million passengers embarked or disembarked in an EU Mediterranean port, accounting for more than half (53.0 per cent) of EU passenger seaborne traffic. In this sea area the main ports where passengers embark and disembark are in Greece (42.0 per cent) and in Italy (43.0 per cent) (Eurostat, 'Mediterranean and Black Sea Coastal Region Statistics' < http://ec.europa.eu/eurostat/statistics-explained/index.php/ Archive:Mediterranean_and_Black_Sea_coastal_region_statistics>).

[25] 'Cruise Ship Industry Statistics' <http://www.statisticbrain.com/cruise-ship-industry-statistics>.

[26] World Health Organization, 'Travel by Sea' <http://www.who.int/ith/mode_of_travel/sea_ travel/en/> accessed 12 August 2017.

violence in their home or host countries who seek asylum elsewhere. By way of example, at the height of the Libyan conflict from January to September 2011, more than 55,000 migrants and asylum seekers fleeing violence in Tunisia and Libya reached the Italian island of Lampedusa.[27] More recently, Syrian refugees fleeing conflict in their country have added to their numbers, bringing the total number of refugees and migrants reaching European shores to more than one million in 2015.[28] These people, who often flee violence and war in their home countries, are particularly vulnerable, both because of their personal circumstances, which leave them at the mercy of people smugglers, and because of the means used to travel, often consisting of old, unsafe, and overloaded boats.[29]

Flows of people are often mixed, that is they may include both refugees and migrants. However, the two categories are legally separate. Refugees and asylum seekers enjoy the protections guaranteed under the 1951 Refugee Convention, first and foremost the right to *non-refoulement*. Migrants, on the other hand, do not have similar specific rights, although they obviously benefit from the protection of applicable international human rights treaties.

2.7 Stowaways

Stowaways are persons, usually migrants or refugees, who hide in a ship in order to travel from one place to another, unnoticed by the crew and customs officers.[30] By hiding in spaces such as empty containers, engine rooms, false panels, or tanks, stowaways risk their lives and often meet an untimely end. While far fewer than that of migrants at sea, their number remains constant, notwithstanding regulatory and

---

[27] Parliamentary Assembly of the Council of Europe, Committee on Migration, Refugees and Population Ad Hoc Sub-Committee on the large-scale arrival of irregular migrants, asylum-seekers and refugees on Europe's southern shores, 'Report on the Visit to Lampedusa (Italy)' (30 September 2011) AS/MIG/AHLARG (2011) 03 REV 2, 2. 'UNHCR reported that 488 vessels have arrived at Italy's borders from January to mid-July 2011. This comprised some 410 vessels arriving from Tunisia, carrying an average number of 60 passengers, and some 78 vessels arriving from the Libyan Arab Jamahiriya, with an average of 300 passengers' (United Nations High Commissioner for Human Rights, 'The Situation of Migrants and Asylum-seekers Fleeing Recent Events in North Africa' UN Doc A/HRC/18/54).

[28] United Nations High Commissioner for Refugees (UNHCR), 'Refugees/Migrants Emergency Response—Mediterranean' <http://data.unhcr.org/mediterranean/regional.php> accessed 12 May 2016.

[29] An account of the means may be found in Amedeo Antonucci, Pasquale Caiazza, and Marco Fantinato, 'L'evoluzione delle norme di diritto internazionale in tema di interventi di polizia in alto mare, con particolare riguardo alle operazioni aeronavali della Guardia di Finanza nel contrasto ai trafficanti di migranti nel Mediterraneo' in Amedeo Antonucci, Irini Papanicolopulu, and Tullio Scovazzi (eds), *L'immigrazione irregolare via mare nella giurisprudenza italiana e nell'esperienza europea* (Giappichelli Editore 2016) 109.

[30] According to the definition in Section 1.A Convention on Facilitation of International Maritime Traffic (adopted 9 April 1965, entered into force 5 March 1967) 591 UNTS 266, as amended (FAL), a stowaway is 'A person who is secreted on a ship, or in cargo which is subsequently loaded on the ship, without the consent of the shipowner or the master or any other responsible person and who is detected on board the ship after it has departed from a port, or in the cargo while unloading it in the port of arrival, and is reported as a stowaway by the master to the appropriate authorities'.

enforcement action promoted by the shipping industry.[31] Particular issues are raised by stowaway asylum seekers.[32]

2.8 Pirates and armed robbers

People engaging in irregular migration, such as stowaways and migrants at sea, should not be confused with people who engage in criminal activities at sea, such as different types of trafficking, terrorism, piracy, and armed robbery.

Pirates, the 'hostis humani generis',[33] are undoubtedly the most well-known criminals at sea. Modern law of the sea distinguishes between 'pirates' and people engaged in armed robbery. On the one hand, 'pirates' engage in acts of depredation against another vessel in areas beyond the territorial waters.[34] Armed robbers, on the other hand, include all those robbers who do not fall within the legal definition of 'pirates', and who operate mostly within the territorial sea and internal waters.[35] The aim however remains the same: the depredation of another vessel, either for the purpose of getting hold of its cargo, as in the case of pirates operating in West Africa and the Strait of Malacca, or to take hostages and then demand a ransom, as in the case of pirates operating off the coast of Somalia.

2.9 Traffickers

Another category of criminals who operate at sea includes traffickers, who engage in the unlawful transport of goods such as arms, drugs, or people. Low transportation costs and a lack of control, often due to the 'protection' of flags of convenience,[36] are among the reasons why the seas are often used by traffickers, who generally

---

[31] 'The presence of stowaways on board ships may bring serious consequences for ships and, by extension, to the shipping industry as a whole; the ship could be delayed in port; the repatriation of stowaways can be a very complex and costly procedure involving masters, shipowners, port authorities and agents; and the life of stowaways could be endangered as they may spent several days hidden, with the risk of suffocation and without any water / provisions' International Maritime Organization, 'Stowaways' <http://www.imo.org/OurWork/Facilitation/Stowaways/Pages/Default.aspx>.

[32] UNHCR, 'Note on Stowaway Asylum-Seekers' UN Doc EC/SCP/51.

[33] On the development of this notion see Daniel Heller-Roazen, *The Enemy of All. Piracy and the Law of Nations* (Zone Books 2009).

[34] Art 101 UNCLOS.

[35] The term 'armed robbery' is defined in Code of Practice for the Investigation of the Crimes of Piracy and Armed Robbery Against Ships, IMO Resolution A.1025(26), para 2.2.

[36] 'Flags of convenience' is the term used to designate cases in which a vessel is registered in a State other than that of the owner, often in order to avoid the more stringent tax, fiscal, or labour regime applicable in the State of ownership. The Oxford English Dictionary in fact defines a 'flag of convenience' as a 'foreign flag under which a ship is registered in order to avoid certain duties, charges'. According to the United Nations Office on Drugs and Crime (UNODC), *Transnational Organized Crime In The Fishing Industry* (United Nations 2011) 19: 'Some registries are targeted due to the inability or unwillingness of the flag State to exercise its criminal law enforcement jurisdiction in terms of international law or because they allow front companies to register as fishing vessels owners which makes the true beneficial owner difficult, if not impossible, to identify. The lack of law enforcement facilitates criminal activities. These flag States are therefore referred to as "flags of convenience" (FOC) or "flags of non-compliance" (FONC)'.

operate within the framework of transnational criminal groups.[37] While it is not easy to find figures about the number of people involved in these activities, it is well-established, for example, that cocaine is usually shipped from South and Central America to North America and Europe, whilst opium and its derivatives are transported by ship towards the US and Canadian markets.[38] In many cases, traffickers show great ingenuity in the means of transportation, as the use of submersible and semi-submersible vessels shows.[39]

What brings together all these people, independent of the object of trafficking, is the fact that they undertake unlawful activities at sea, while the fact that the activity does not directly impact on other people at sea distinguishes them from pirates and armed robbers, and, to a certain extent, from illegal fishers.

3. The Hazards and Dangers of Being at Sea

The second reason justifying this book's engagement with persons as sea consists in the multiple dangers and threats these people face. The marine environment, not being the natural environment in which humans live, is inherently dangerous. In addition, one natural result of the restricted space available on board ships and the long periods many ships spend at sea is that people at sea will encounter some discomfort. However, in addition to the inherent danger of physically being in a hostile environment during their permanence at sea, individuals often risk violations of their fundamental rights from the wilful conduct of other humans, be they acting as State organs or in a private capacity.[40] Furthermore, it should be remembered that the seas are not safe from common crime, in particular murders, thefts, and rapes.

The hazards and threats faced by people at sea may vary according to their personal circumstances, the conditions of their ship or platform, and the geographical area in which they find themselves. It is evident that a migrant sailing on an overcrowded boat faces health and safety threats much more severe than those faced by the passenger of a state-of-the-art cruise ship. Equally, a person slicing and packing tuna on an old and rusty vessel fishing off the coasts of Somalia risks personal injury and kidnapping much more than if the same person were working as a sailor in a vessel sailing the Mediterranean Sea. However, these differences generally relate to the measure of the risk, rather than to its existence. Being at sea, it is worth repeating, is dangerous in and of itself, as persons find themselves in a hostile environment, not intended to accommodate humans, and in areas that are often far off from land and the possibility to apply for protection.

[37] See UNODC, *The Globalization of Crime. A Transnational Organized Crime Threat Assessment* (UNODC 2010) 29–30.

[38] UNODC, 'Drug Trafficking' <http://www.unodc.org/unodc/en/drug-trafficking/index.html>.

[39] UNODC, *Combating Transnational Organized Crime Committed at Sea* (United Nations 2013) 27.

[40] For a historical perspective on the difficulties encountered by seafarers, see Alistair D Couper, 'Historical Perspectives on Seafarers and the Law' in Deirdre Fitzpatrick and Michael Anderson (eds), *Seafarers' Rights* (OUP 2005) 3.

It is therefore more appropriate to address the hazards and threats of being at sea as general categories, without distinguishing, at least at the general level, between different categories of people. A distinction may be useful in assessing the likeliness of the threat. It should however be borne in mind that most dangers are common to all categories of people at sea.

3.1 Death and personal injury

The marine environment is inherently dangerous for human beings and maritime incidents still cause the loss of many lives despite the reduction in the number of ship losses.[41] What is more, deaths and injuries concern all people at sea, be they seafarers, passengers, migrants, or others.

Fishing and shipping remain the two most dangerous occupations worldwide and fatal incidents are commonplace even in developed countries. For example, during 1996 to 2005 the fatal accident rate in the UK fishing industry was 115 times higher than that in the general workforce of Great Britain, twenty-four times higher than in the construction industry and eighty times higher than in manufacturing.[42] In the USA, the fatal work injury rate for fishers and related fishing workers is 152.00, as opposed to the all-worker fatal injury rate of 3.60.[43] Fishers in the UK have a one in twenty chance of being killed on the job during the course of their working lives.[44] Seafarers fare only slightly better, as the fatal accident rate in UK merchant shipping was twelve times higher than in the general workforce of Great Britain, two and a half times higher than in the construction industry, and eight and a half times higher than in manufacturing.[45] Furthermore, the eleven fatalities in the Deepwater

[41] International Chamber of Shipping, 'Reduction in the Number of Ship Losses' <http://www.ics-shipping.org/shipping-facts/safety-and-regulation/reduction-in-the-number-of-ship-losses>. See also <http://www.ics-shipping.org/shipping-facts/safety-and-regulation/lives-lost-at-sea> and IMO, Casualty Statistics and Investigations (16 January 2012) Doc FSI 20/INF.17.

[42] SE Roberts and JC Williams, 'Update of Mortality for Workers in the UK Merchant Shipping and Fishing Sectors, Report for the Maritime and Coastguard Agency and the Department for Transport' (2007). For data on other European States see Commission, 'Commission Staff Working Document. Impact Assessment on the Agreement concluded between the General Confederation of Agricultural Cooperatives in the European Union (COGECA), the European Transport Workers' Federation (ETF) and the Association of National Organisations of Fishing Enterprises (EUROPÊCHE) of 21 May 2012 as amended on 8 May 2013 concerning the implementation of the Work in Fishing Convention, 2007 of the International Labour Organisation' SWD (2016) 144 final.

[43] Bureau of Labor Statistics, 'Census of Fatal Occupational Injuries (CFOI)' <http://www.bls.gov/iif/oshwc/cfoi/cfch0009.pdf> accessed 14 January 2013. See also information provided by National Institute for Occupational Safety and Health (NIOSH) <http://www.cdc.gov/niosh/topics/fishing/#ref1> accessed 14 January 2013.

[44] BBC, 'Fishing: The Most Dangerous Job in the UK' <http://www.bbc.co.uk/news/uk-10923190> accessed 14 January 2013. According to Roberts and Williams (n 42) 'The fatal accident rate in the UK fishing industry during 1996 to 2005, 102 per 100,000 fishermen-years, was 115 times higher than that in the general workforce of Great Britain. The fatal accident rate in fishing was also 24 times higher than in the construction industry and 81 times higher than in manufacturing'.

[45] ibid.

Horizon explosion in 2010 are just some indication of the deaths that can occur in offshore oil and gas operations.[46]

Deaths of migrants and refugees are unfortunately a widespread phenomenon, due to the overcrowding and often unsafe condition of boats and vessels used for travel. In 2011, four States reported 189 incidents involving 14,985 migrants to the International Maritime Organization (IMO)[47] and in 2015, in the Mediterranean Sea alone, 3,771 persons were reported dead or missing.[48] In one incident that attracted much attention, a vessel that had left Libya at the end of March 2011 drifted for two weeks in the Mediterranean Sea, before eventually returning to the Libyan coast, after most of the seventy-two people on board had died.[49] However, deaths are increasing as tragedies, in the worst cases, result in the loss of hundreds of lives at a time.[50]

Passengers of ferries or cruise ships may also face threats to life when travelling on board vessels. Although the sinking of *RMS Titanic* has remained particularly infamous, one does not need to go beyond recent years to realize that deaths at sea are still an issue for passengers. Ferries still experience fatal incidents, causing the deaths of hundreds of people every year. In 1987, the sinking of the Philippine ferry *Dona Paz*, after colliding with an oil tanker, resulted in more than 4000 deaths, mostly of passengers on board the *Dona Paz*.[51] In 1994, the sinking of the *MV Estonia* during a storm caused 852 deaths in the Baltic Sea. In 2008, the sinking of the Philippine ferry *Princess of the Stars* caused hundreds of deaths.[52] In 2014, the sinking of the Korean ferry *Sewol* after colliding with a barge killed 304 people, mostly teenagers on a school trip. These are just some examples that illustrate how much human life is still at danger at sea, mostly because of unsafe, overloaded passenger vessels. However, the dangers of the sea and unsafe navigational practices should never be underestimated. In 2012, the sinking of the cruise ship *Costa Concordia* off the Italian island of Giglio,[53] which led to thirty-two fatalities, has shown that even modern pleasure vessels with strict safety regulations are not immune from fatal incidents.

---

[46] Data for the United States indicate that in the period 2003–10, 'the U.S. oil and gas extraction industry (onshore and offshore, combined) had a collective fatality rate seven times higher than for all U.S. workers (27.1 versus 3.8 deaths per 100,000 workers)', 'Fatal Injuries in Offshore Oil and Gas Operations—United States, 2003–2010' (2013) 62 Morbidity and Mortality Weekly Report 301.

[47] IMO, Unsafe Practices Associated with the Trafficking or Transport of Migrants by Sea (5 January 2012) Doc MSC.3/Circ.21.

[48] UNHCR, 'Refugees/Migrants Emergency Response—Mediterranean' <http://data.unhcr.org/mediterranean/regional.php> accessed 12 May 2016.

[49] Jack Shenker, 'Aircraft Carrier Left Us to die, Say Migrants' *The Guardian* (8 May 2011) <http://www.guardian.co.uk/world/2011/may/08/nato-ship-libyan-migrants> accessed 12 August 2017.

[50] Tania Karas, 'Horrified Shipwreck Survivors Watched as Hundreds Drowned' *UNCHR* (2 May 2016) <http://www.unhcr.org/572753416.html> accessed 12 August 2017.

[51] 'MV Doña Paz' (*Wrecksite*) <http://www.wrecksite.eu/wreck.aspx?59165> accessed 12 August 2017.

[52] BBC, 'Hundreds Missing in Ferry Tragedy' (23 June 2008) <http://news.bbc.co.uk/1/hi/world/asia-pacific/7468493.stm> accessed 12 August 2017.

[53] BBC, 'Costa Concordia: What Happened' (10 February 2015) <http://www.bbc.co.uk/news/world-europe-16563562> accessed 12 August 2017.

Death and personal injury may not always be attributable to the force of natural elements, nor are they merely the result of human error. Death and injury may also stem from wilful conduct. Another cause of death on board ships derives from knowingly throwing people overboard. Stowaways, in particular, are known to have been killed by crew members, as a consequence of violent attacks against them, by being thrown overboard, or by being abandoned in unseaworthy crafts far away from the nearest land.[54]

In addition, death may be the result of a defiantly conspicuous disregard for safety standards and procedures favoured by the globalization of shipping, the current economic environment, and the slackening of control over vessels.[55] The reduction of the crew in most commercial vessels results in long working hours and mounting fatigue, while the multicultural composition of a crew may result in misunderstandings, and may contribute to mounting tension; fatigue and tension, alone or combined, favour human error. Furthermore, the unconcern for the people and a mentality which seeks to ensure profit at all costs have resulted in numerous unseaworthy vessels still navigating the sea, which constitute a threat for those on board and any other ship they may happen to encounter.

3.2 Inhuman working and living conditions

For all people at sea, a vessel or a platform is not only their means of transport or their workplace; it is also their home for as long as they remain in the waters. Poor health and safety conditions on board, therefore, affect not only workers but any other person present.

Working and living conditions on board ships and platforms vary considerably. Modern cruise ships provide a variety of entertainment facilities and even modern commercial vessels or offshore platforms may have levels of comfort unthought of in past decades. However, in contrast to these privileged circumstances, there are many vessels that present degrading and inhuman working and living conditions. The remoteness of vessels, in conjunction with the limited enforcement capabilities of States, have often led to such conditions on board fishing and commercial vessels.[56] While most workers are able to leave their workplace by simply walking out of it, this is not an option for people who work at sea. Despite the absence of any other impediments, people on ships cannot walk away from the ship but have to either wait until the ship docks in a port or to arrange for other means of transportation

---

[54] For accounts of violent death met by stowaways see Fanny Payre, 'Les passagers clandestins' (1996) 14 Annuaire de Droit Maritime et Oceanique 265; Elissa Steglich, 'Hiding in the Hulls: Attacking the Practice of High Seas Murder of Stowaways through Expanded Criminal Jurisdiction' (2000) 78 Texas Law Review 1323.

[55] Alistair D Couper, *Voyages of Abuse: Seafarers, Human Rights and International Shipping* (Pluto 1999) 9–12. For the fishing sector see FAO SOFIA 2010, 46.

[56] Couper, *Voyages of Abuse* (n 55); International Transport Workers' Federation, *Out of Sight, out of Mind. Seafarers, Fishers & Human Rights* (International Transport Workers' Federation 2006); EJF, *All at Sea—The Abuse of Human Rights aboard Illegal Fishing Vessels* (Environmental Justice Foundation 2010).

to reach land. This has a significant impact in emergencies, such as shipwrecks or sickness.

Even when it does not lead to loss of human life directly, recklessness by shipowners and operators may allow for a lack of training, unsafe or abusive practices, defective equipment, unhealthy spaces, which may result in the violation of a number of fundamental human rights. Rusty and overcrowded cabins, dirty galleys, poor hygienic condition of sanitary facilities, a lack of heating, cold showers, insufficient quantities of fresh provisions and the use of expired provisions, heavy floor dirtiness, and a lack of proper food and garbage segregation are just some examples of conditions witnessed on board substandard vessels.[57] These issues affect not only workers, but any person on board. It is therefore wrong to relegate such abuses to 'labour issues', since in many instances they can amount to grave violations of fundamental human rights.

Other treatment can also amount to torture and inhuman and degrading treatment, as well lead to the violation of a number of other human rights, including labour rights. The most serious instances include verbal and physical abuse and sexual harassment. Statements by some of the victims of such behaviour are telling:

One worker, beaten with an iron rod, sustained serious head injuries and, bleeding profusely, was locked up in the bow for three days without food or water. His offence was to ask for leave from the boat. Another fisher, thought to have been chatting with a colleague, was grabbed by the hair and repeatedly punched in the face. After the first assault by the chief engineer, the man was beaten with a thick wooden rod 3ft long on his thigh, stomach and back.[58]

They were expected to sleep 12 to a cabin, with no blankets and for washing were told to stand on deck and 'shower' in the waves.[59]

A lack of training and an absence of safety equipment unfortunately characterizes a number of ships. Moreover, a lack of written employment agreements, a refusal to pay wages, or other practices that result in lack of payment are also often practised. The refusal of medical treatment, victimization, unfair dismissal, refusal of repatriation, and abandonment have been documented. Abandonment in particular is becoming a relevant issue in the shipping industry. As the word suggests, it consists in the practice of abandoning a vessel and the people on board, or a single seafarer, at a port, usually with a backlog of wages owed, without providing repatriation for the seafarers or at least the financial means to return home.[60] Abandonment is seen by reckless shipowners as a cheap way to get rid of a vessel that no longer guarantees a profit.[61]

---

[57] For some instances of inhuman living quarters see the reports published by the Paris MOU under the series 'Caught in the Net' <https://www.parismou.org/publications-category/caught-net> accessed 12 August 2017.

[58] International Transport Workers' Federation (n 56) 20.   [59] ibid 23.

[60] According to Standard A2.5.2(2) Maritime Labour Convention (MLC), 'a seafarer shall be deemed to have been abandoned where, in violation of the requirements of this Convention or the terms of the seafarers' employment agreement, the shipowner: (a) fails to cover the cost of the seafarer's repatriation; or (b) has left the seafarer without the necessary maintenance and support; or (c) has otherwise unilaterally severed their ties with the seafarer including failure to pay contractual wages for a period of at least two months'.

[61] Couper, *Voyages of Abuse* (n 55) 43.

Illegal fishing operations in particular are often characterized by the lowest stand-ards of working conditions and extensive reports of abuse.[62] A lack of safety equip-ment and training, long working hours, a refusal to pay for work, verbal and physical abuse, and the abandonment of crew members have been documented in many cases.[63] However, even fishing vessels that do not employ flags of convenience and those that are regularly licensed for fishing in the maritime zones of a State may engage in unacceptable practices.[64]

A significant challenge faced by States in their efforts to combat these practices is to acquire knowledge and evidence of facts. Most controls over vessels are still conducted when the ships are in ports and most complaints are made by people who leave the vessel and speak with local authorities. Consequently, confined space and distance from land result in the practical impossibility for States to regularly check compliance with safety, security, labour, and human rights standards.

3.3 Human trafficking and forced labour

Sea routes are sometimes used for the trafficking of human beings. However, most of the time, trafficking is the result of irregular migration (also by sea) and takes place once the person arrives at the intended destination. For instance, people trafficked to provide forced labour on board illegal, unreported, and unregulated (IUU) fish-ing vessels or platforms in more than one case started the voyage towards the ship or platform of their own free will, lured by misrepresentations of the situation and without knowing what awaited them.[65]

The impossibility to escape from the ship is probably one of the main reasons why forced labour is becoming more commonplace in the maritime industries.[66] Another significant reason is the development of techniques and practices that allow vessels to spend long periods at sea, such as transhipment, onboard processing, and bunkering. Child labour and the use of trafficked persons are major issues in fisher-ies, even more so with the use of large factory vessels which can stay at sea for long

---

[62] UNODC, *Transnational Organized Crime in Fishing* (n 36); Matthew Gianni and Walt Simpson, 'The Changing Nature of High Seas Fishing' (2005) <http://d2ouvy59p0dg6k.cloudfront.net/down-loads/iiumr.pdf>. The lack of human rights guarantees may also negatively impact on the conservation of marine resources, as discussed in Edward H Allison, Blake D Ratner, Björn Åsgård, Rolf Willmann, Robert Pomeroy, and John Kurien, 'Rights-based Fisheries Governance: From Fishing Rights to Human Rights' (2012) 13 Fish and Fisheries 14.

[63] Recent reports have focused on such instances, see International Labour Office, 'Conditions of Work in the Fishing Sector. A Comprehensive Standard (a Convention supplemented by a Recommendation) on Work in the Fishing Sector' (International Labour Office, 2003); EJF (n 56); International Transport Workers' Federation (n 56).

[64] Christina Stringer, Glenn Simmons, and Daren Coulston 'Not in New Zealand's Waters Surely? Labour and Human Rights Abuses Aboard Foreign Fishing Vessels' (2011) New Zealand Asia Institute Working Paper Series 11-01 <http://docs.business.auckland.ac.nz/Doc/11-01-Not-in-New-Zealand-waters-surely-NZAI-Working-Paper-Sept-2011.pdf> accessed 21 August 2017.

[65] Glenn Simmons and Christina Stringer, 'New Zealand's Fisheries Management System: Forced Labour an Ignored or Overlooked Dimension?' (2014) 50 Marine Policy 74, 75–76; International Organization for Migration, 'Trafficked at Sea. The Exploitation of Ukrainian Seafarers and Fishers 2012' (International Organization for Migration 2013) 64.

[66] International Organization for Migration (n 65).

periods which frustrates the impact of port State control and creates a place of virtual impunity. As one trafficked individual testified:

When the boat went, we were told by those who were on board that they were working 24 hours a day, almost without sleep, no money paid and also that it was impossible to leave since the ship never entered port.[67]

It is worth emphasizing that slavery practices in the fishing and maritime industry should not be seen as isolated phenomena or occasional practices. On the one hand, human trafficking in the fishing sector is part of the wider context of fisheries and is often intertwined with legal activities.[68] On the other hand, trafficking in persons is often just one issue amongst the manifold illegal activities pursued by transnational organized crime.[69]

3.4 Piracy and other security threats

Piracy, a traditional security threat for seagoing people, remains a major concern. Following its peak in the early modern period, piracy was thought of as something relegated to books and films until its recent upsurge, first in South East Asia, then in the Gulf of Aden and parts of the Indian Ocean, and more recently in the Gulf of Guinea.[70] At the peak of Somali piracy in 2011, there were 439 attacks worldwide, resulting in forty-five highjacks,[71] while in 2015, 246 incidents were reported, most of which took place in South East Asia.[72] Piracy happens anywhere, from the high seas to ports and anchorages.

Piracy comes with a high human cost.[73] During piratical attacks members of a crew may be injured or killed and further suffering may result if the ship is high-jacked and crew members are held captive for a ransom. In 2011, 802 persons were held captive, mostly by Somali pirates. While numbers have diminished with the fight against Somali piracy, they have not abated, as in 2015, 271 persons were taken

---

[67] ibid 70.

[68] Traceability gaps often allow the products of forced labour to enter the lawful market, through unmonitored transhipment or their commercialization as raw or semi-processed materials: Kate Hodal, Chris Kelly, and Felicity Lawrence 'Revealed: Asian Slave Labour Producing Prawns for Supermarkets in US, UK' *The Guardian* (10 June 2014) <http://www.theguardian.com/global-development/2014/jun/10/supermarket-prawns-thailand-produced-slave-labour> accessed 12 August 2017.

[69] UNODC, *Transnational Organized Crime in Fishing* (n 36).

[70] James Bridger, 'Piracy in the Gulf of Guinea: Oil Soaked Pirates' *USNI News* (10 March 2014) <http://news.usni.org/2014/03/10/piracy-gulf-guinea-oil-soaked-pirates> accessed 12 August 2017.

[71] Figures provided by the International Maritime Bureau Piracy Reporting Centre <http://www.icc-ccs.org/piracy-reporting-centre/piracynewsafigures>.

[72] An updated map of piracy and armed robbery incidents in South-East Asia may be found on the website of the Regional Cooperation Agreement on Combating Piracy and Armed Robbery against Ships in Asia (ReCAAP) Information Sharing Centre, at <https://portal.recaap.org/OpenMap>.

[73] ICC and Oceans Beyond Piracy, 'The Human Cost of Somali Piracy 2011' (22 June 2012) <http://oceansbeyondpiracy.org/sites/default/files/hcop_2011.pdf> accessed 12 August 2017; Ben Farmer, 'The Human Cost of Piracy: Broken Victims of Violence' *The Telegraph* (10 February 2014) <http://www.telegraph.co.uk/sponsored/culture/captain-phillips-film/10388296/somali-piracy-victims.html> accessed 12 August 2017.

hostage.[74] Hostages may face inhuman treatment and their captivity may last for long periods of time. For example, the crew of the Mongolian flagged, Vietnamese owned bulk carrier, the *MV Hoang-Son-Sun*, composed of 24 Vietnamese, were held captive for more than 240 days, from 20 January to 19 September 2011.[75] During this time, hostages suffer physical and psychological harm[76] and may also have to face other issues, such as loss of wages and lack of repatriation,[77] as well as difficulty in getting reparation.[78]

From a legal point of view, piracy is different from armed robbery. Piracy may take place only beyond the territorial waters and requires the presence of two ships, one of which assaults the other.[79] All other instances of assault against vessels, as well as assaults against platforms, are now defined as armed robbery.[80] While in practice acts of piracy and acts of armed robbery often coincide, the different legal definitions point to separate regimes, the main difference being the right of all States to exercise their jurisdiction against pirates, but not armed robbers. The latter can be apprehended only by the coastal State when they operate in the territorial waters or internal waters, or by the flag State when they are on the high seas. The distinction between piracy and armed robbery has been criticized for drawing a distinction between activities that are very similar. Indeed, the fundamental characteristic that brings pirates and armed robbers together is the activity of depredation, using force, operated against a vessel or platform at sea.

Piracy and armed robbery are not the only security threats that exists at sea. Crimes at sea, terrorist acts, intentional and unlawful damage to the marine environment, and depletion of natural resources have all been identified as security

---

[74] Figure provided by the International Maritime Bureau Piracy Reporting Centre, <http://www.icc-ccs.org/piracy-reporting-centre/piracynewsafigures>.

[75] 'MV HOANG SON SUN Pirated in the Indian Ocean' *EUNAVFOR Somalia* (20 January 2011) <http://eunavfor.eu/mv-hoang-son-sun-pirated-in-the-indian-ocean> accessed 12 August 2017 and 'Motor Vessel HOANG SON SUN Released from Pirate Control' *EUNAVFOR Somalia* (19 September 2011) <http://eunavfor.eu/motor-vessel-hoang-son-sun-released-from-pirate-control> accessed 12 August 2017.

[76] Michael Stuart Garfinkle, Craig L Catz, and Janaka Saratchandra, *The Psychological Impact of Piracy on Seafarers* (The Seamen's Church Institute 2012).

[77] Graham Caldwell, 'Seafarers and Modern Piracy' in Jennifer Lavelle (ed), *Maritime Labour Law Convention 2006. International Labour Law Redefined* (Informa Law 2014) 137.

[78] Séraphine Nga Essomba, 'La protection de la personne physique, victime d'actes de piraterie maritime' (2015) 20 Annuaire du Droit de la Mer 209.

[79] Art 101 UNCLOS provides that 'Piracy consists of any of the following acts: (a) any illegal acts of violence or detention, or any act of depredation, committed for private ends by the crew or the passengers of a private ship or a private aircraft, and directed: (i) on the high seas, against another ship or aircraft, or against persons or property on board such ship or aircraft; (ii) against a ship, aircraft, persons or property in a place outside the jurisdiction of any State; (b) any act of voluntary participation in the operation of a ship or of an aircraft with knowledge of facts making it a pirate ship or aircraft; (c) any act of inciting or of intentionally facilitating an act described in subparagraph (a) or (b)'.

[80] According to IMO, Code of Practice for the Investigation of the Crimes of Piracy and Armed Robbery Against Ships, Resolution A.1025(26), Annex, para 2.2, armed robbery against ships consists of any of the following acts: '(a) any illegal act of violence or detention or any act of depredation, or threat thereof, other than an act of piracy, committed for private ends and directed against a ship or against persons or property on board such a ship, within a State's internal waters, archipelagic waters and territorial sea; (b) any act of inciting or of intentionally facilitating an act described above.'.

threats.[81] Furthermore, they are often linked with other perils. For example, sub-standard ships, which are more likely to pollute the marine environment, are often found to be missing safety equipment and basic accommodation needs, while IUU fishing practices reveal widespread violations of human rights and the employment of forced labour. Security issues may also arise out of lawful activities, as the fishing 'wars' between regularly licensed fishing vessels show.[82]

3.5 Excessive law enforcement activities

The enforcement of existing legislation is key to the protection of people at sea and the safeguarding of their rights, so much so that the lack of effective enforcement is often referred to as one of the reasons for the widespread violation of human rights at sea. However, if carried out without due regard for the people involved and the applicable normative framework, enforcement action undertaken by State officials against vessels may unnecessarily endanger human life, violate the conditions imposed by human rights law for limitation of personal liberty, and may end up in unfair trial and detention.[83]

The threat or use of excessive force against fishing vessels has led to legal disputes before the International Tribunal for the Law of the Sea (ITLOS). In the *Saiga* case, Guinean officers 'fired at the ship itself with live ammunition from a fast-moving patrol boat without issuing any of the signals and warnings required by international law and practice'[84] and, once on board, 'fired indiscriminately while on the deck and used gunfire to stop the engine of the ship'.[85] The lawfulness itself of the interdiction

---

[81]   UNGA 'Oceans and the Law of the sea. Report of the Secretary-General' (10 March 2008) UN Doc A/63/63, para 39.

[82]   Clive R Symmons, 'Use of the Law of Piracy to Deal with Violent Inter-Vessel Incidents at Sea beyond the 12-Mile Limit: The Irish Experience' in Clive R Symmons (ed), *Selected Contemporary Issues in the Law of the Sea* (Martinus Nijhoff 2011) 169, thus describes incidents taking place in the coasts of Ireland: 'The forms of intimidation typically took the form of deliberate ramming of Irish fishing vessels, destruction of nets (including snagging of nets and towing of Irish fishing vessels backwards) and other interferences of a less serious nature such as "close quartering" such Irish vessels'.

[83]   Brian Wilson, 'Human Rights and Maritime Law Enforcement' (2016) 52 Stanford Journal of International Law 243, discusses a number of cases in which national and international courts addressed the lawfulness of law enforcement activities; see also J Ashley Roach and Robert W Smith, *Excessive Maritime Claims* (3rd edn, Martinus Nijhoff 2012) 623 and for a discussion of counter-piracy operations Sofia Galani, 'Somali Piracy and the Human Rights of Seafarers' (2016) 34 Netherlands Quarterly of Human Rights 71. The fairness of trial has been questioned in particular in the case of seafarers charged with pollution of the marine environment. The issue reached the ECtHR and the Court of Justice of the European Union, which however both upheld the lawfulness of applicable rules; see *Mangouras v Spain* App no 12050/04 (Judgment (GC) of 28 September 2010) and Case C-308/06 *Intertanko and Others v Secretary of State for Transport* [2008] ECLI:EU:C:2008:312; Gwendoline Gonsaeles, 'Of Mice and Men: Some Observations on the EU Approach towards Seafarers' Liability for Marine Pollution' in Kris Bernauw, Ralph De Wit, Wouter Den Haerynck, Benoît Goemans, Frank Stevens, and Erik Van Hooydonk (eds), *Free on Board. Liber Amicorum Marc A. Huybrechts* (Intersentia 2011) 317.

[84]   *The M/V 'Saiga' (No 2) (Saint Vincent and the Grenadines v Guinea)* (Judgment of 1 July 1999) ITLOS Reports 1999, 10, para 157.

[85]   *Saiga* (n 84) para 158.

of vessels has been challenged in cases involving drug traffickers,[86] refugees,[87] and members of non-governmental organizations (NGOs) during protest campaigns.[88]

4. Dedicated Legal Instruments and Norms

Having described the various natural and manmade perils that people face at sea, it is now appropriate to turn to the available legal means for protection and redress. This section will present the legal response developed so far by States, as it emerges from existing international legal instruments. This presentation will constitute the basis for the assessment of this regulation in the following section.

A preliminary assessment of international law shows that a small yet significant number of legal instruments and legal norms have been adopted to protect people at sea and to address threats faced by them. These can be divided into three groups. The first includes treaties adopted expressly for the protection of a specific category of people, such as the Maritime Labour Convention (MLC). The second group includes provisions that aim to protect people at sea, found in treaties having a broader scope, such as the UNCLOS. The third category includes treaties that protect people indirectly, by ensuring the safety of navigation and the operation of vessels and structures taking to the sea; the Safety of Life at Sea Convention (SOLAS)[89] is the best known among these instruments.

4.1 Treaties dedicated to the protection of a category of people at sea

It should be clear from the outset that there is no dedicated bill of rights for people at sea. In other words, there is no general treaty, nor any other international legal instrument, that purports to protect all people at sea against the threats identified above. The UNCLOS, the main law of the sea treaty, does not include any part dedicated to the protection of people at sea.[90] Conversely, none of the global and regional human rights treaties has a part specifically devoted to the rights of people at sea.

In a few cases, however, States have adopted treaties dedicated to the protection of a specific category of people at sea. There are two main instruments: the

---

[86] *Rigopoulos v Spain* App no 37388/97 (Decision of 12 January 1999); *Medvedyev and Others v France* App no 3394/03 (Judgment (GC) of 29 March 2010); *Vassis and Others v France* App no 62736/09 (Judgment of 27 June 2013).

[87] *Hirsi Jamaa and Others v Italy* App no 27765/09 (Judgment [GC] of 23 February 2012).

[88] *Women on Waves and Others v Portugal* App no 31276/05 (Judgment of 3 February 2009); *Drieman and Others v Norway* App no 33678/96 (Decision of 4 May 2000); *Arctic Sunrise (The Kingdom of the Netherlands v The Russian Federation)* PCA Case no 2014-02 (Award (merits) of 14 August 2015).

[89] International Convention for the Safety of Life at Sea (adopted 1 November 1974, entered into force 25 May 1980) 1184 UNTS 278, as amended (SOLAS). The SOLAS has been amended many times to reflect technical developments and new issues, in particular concerning security of ships in ports and at sea.

[90] The point is made in Irini Papanicolopulu, 'The Law of the Sea Convention: No Place for Persons?' (2012) 27 IJMCL 867.

MLC and the Work in Fishing Convention, both adopted by the International Labour Organization (ILO). Both of these treaties focus on the rights of the people addressed in the treaty and the duties of the State to protect and promote respect for these rights.[91]

4.1.1 Maritime Labour Convention

Among the many people at sea, seafarers are those that benefit from the most developed legal regime. Seafarers are specifically protected under numerous ILO treaties.[92] All of these instruments are now combined in and superseded by the 2006 MLC,[93] an innovative instrument that was jointly prepared by the IMO and ILO and was adopted by the latter organization.

Whereas the practical starting point for the MLC was the need to protect seafarers, the legal background was one of a fragmented set of rules. Fragmentation derived from the existence of many conventions having a limited scope, uneven ratification, and great differences as to their enforcement procedures and mechanisms. The MLC has brought all of these substantial and procedural rules together in one single instrument, thus also visually embodying the unitary nature of the regime. Furthermore, the MLC has clarified some issues that had given rise to confusion in the past, and it has addressed other issues that had escaped legal regulation, such as non-maritime work carried out on seagoing vessels. Finally, the widespread ratification of the MLC, not only in terms of numbers of States but also of world gross tonnage (WGT), will have a significant impact upon the applicable standards for non-parties, through the 'generally applicable standard' reference in the UNCLOS.[94]

Structurally, the MLC is a composite treaty, made up of the Convention itself, the Regulations, and the Code. The Convention contains a list of fundamental rights and a list of seafarers' rights, some provisions as to their implementation, and the final provisions, which include the amendment procedure. The Regulations and the Code set out a seafarer's rights and State's duties in more detail. In particular, the Code contains provisions for the implementation of these rights, divided into binding Standards and non-binding Guidelines.[95] Unlike previous ILO treaties on the protection of seafarers, the MLC enables States that cannot implement the Regulations as provided for in the Standards to adopt substantially equivalent

---

[91] On the relationship between the rights of individuals and the duties of States *infra*, Chapter 2.

[92] M Anderson, A McDowall, et al, 'International Standards' in Deirdre Fitzpatrick and Michael Anderson (eds), *Seafarers' Rights* (OUP 2005) 39. See also K X Li and Jim Mi Ng, 'International Maritime Conventions: Seaferers' Safety and Human Rights' (2002) 33 Journal of Maritime Law & Commerce 381.

[93] The negotiation process is described in Moira L McConnell, Dominick Devlin, and Cleopatra Doumbia-Henry (eds), *The Maritime Labour Convention, 2006. A Legal Primer to an Emerging International Regime* (Martinus Nijhoff 2011).

[94] Art 94(3)(b) UNCLOS. See Chapter 2, Section 8.2.2, and Chapter 4, Section 3.3.

[95] Visually, the Regulations and Code are combined into a single text, wherein each Regulation is followed by the appropriate Standards and Guidelines.

measures, as long as they fully achieve the general object and purpose of the Standards and give effect to them.[96]

According to Article 3 MLC, the fundamental rights of seafarers include: freedom of association and collective bargain; elimination of forced labour; abolition of child labour; and elimination of discrimination. In addition, Article 4 MLC sets out a seafarer's employment and social rights, which include: the right to a safe and secure workplace; the right to fair terms of employment; the right to decent working and living conditions on board vessels; the right to health protection and social security. The Code expands on these rights in the first four chapters, relating respectively to minimum requirements for working (Title 1); conditions of employment (Title 2); accommodation, recreational facilities, food and catering (Title 3); health protection, medical care, welfare and social security protection (Title 4).

Looking more closely at the MLC requirements, the minimum requirements for working on board a vessel concern age, health, training, and qualifications. Only persons aged sixteen and above may work on vessels[97] and they must have a medical certificate proving that they are medically fit to perform their duties.[98] They must be trained according to the requirements of the relevant IMO conventions, in particular the International Convention on Standards of Training, Certification and Watchkeeping for Seafarers (STCW).[99] In addition, and to prevent the widespread abuses deriving from an uncontrolled recruitment procedure, the MLC provides that seafarers must have access 'to an efficient, adequate and accountable system for finding employment on board ship without charge to the seafarer',[100] and contains detailed Standards and Guidelines concerning recruitment and placement.

Conditions of employment are key to ensuring respect for seafarers' rights. The MLC provides for a written employment agreement, that must be accessible for control by port States,[101] and for the regular payment of work.[102] Other Regulations concern hours of work and rest[103] and paid leave,[104] with exceptions for the safety of persons and cargo on board the vessel, as well as for the safety of life at sea more generally. Due to the contemporary relevance of the issue and the frequent instances of abandonment of seafarers in ports and at sea,[105] the MLC contains detailed regulation of repatriation. Repatriation must be effected without cost to the seafarers and shipowners must provide financial security to this end.[106] The flag State, the port State, and the State of nationality of seafarers may also initiate the repatriation and then claim the cost from the shipowner. Protection is now further strengthened with the adoption of amendments to the MLC in 2014 which set out in more detail the forms of financial security.[107] Other Regulations concern compensation for the loss of the ship[108] and manning of the ship,[109] which are to be given effect in

[96] Art VI(3) and (4) MLC.
[97] Reg 1.1 MLC. Special rules concerning night shifts and exceptions are included in Standard A1.1.
[98] Reg 1.2 MLC.   [99] Reg 1.3 MLC.   [100] Reg 1.4 MLC.
[101] Reg 2.1 MLC.   [102] Reg 2.2 MLC.   [103] Reg 2.3 MLC.
[104] Reg 2.4 MLC.
[105] See ILO, 'Database on Reported Incidents of Abandonment of Seafarers' <http://www.ilo.org/dyn/seafarers/seafarersbrowse.home> accessed 12 August 2017.
[106] Reg 2.5 MLC.   [107] Relating to Standard 2.5.   [108] Reg 2.6 MLC.
[109] Reg 2.7 MLC.

accordance with the relevant IMO conventions, including SOLAS, and career and skills development.[110]

Conditions of life on board are regulated in Title 3, which contains detailed Standards and Guidelines on decent accommodation and recreational facilities on board,[111] as well as food and catering.[112] These rules should be read in conjunction with the similar requirements of treaties on the construction and equipment of vessels, in particular the SOLAS.

Finally, the MLC provides for the protection of health and access to medical care on board the vessel and ashore, which should in principle be provided at no cost for the seafarer.[113] The liability of a shipowner is provided for to protect the seafarer from the financial consequences of sickness, injury, or death occurring in connection with their employment.[114] The MLC requires that seafarers are provided with 'occupational health protection', that they 'live, work and train on board ship in a safe and hygienic environment', and that adequate measures are adopted for accident prevention, in light of analogous requirements in the IMO conventions, in particular the SOLAS.[115] Finally, and in accordance with the ILO tradition, the MLC provides for access to social security protection.[116]

The aforementioned protective measures are all the more important since they apply to almost all people working on board seagoing vessels.[117] The only exceptions concern people working on board warships, ships of traditional build such as dhows and junks, fishing vessels,[118] ships in inland waters,[119] and, if a State so declares, ships of less than 200 GT not engaged in international voyages.[120] Apart from these exceptions, every other ship falls within the scope of the MLC, including cruise ships, MODUs, and research vessels.

The strength of the MLC results not only in the detailed and comprehensive substantial provisions for the protection of seafarers, but also in the well-developed enforcement mechanisms created by it. They combine elements from the IMO treaties (the responsibilities of the flag and port State) and from ILO treaties (the special tripartite committee composed of representatives of governments, shipowners, and seafarers).[121]

According to Article V(1) MLC

Each Member shall implement and enforce laws or regulations or other measures that it has adopted to fulfil its commitments under this Convention with respect to ships and seafarers under its jurisdiction.

---

[110] Reg 2.8 MLC.   [111] Reg 3.1 MLC.   [112] Reg 3.2 MLC.
[113] Reg 4.1 MLC. Access to shore-based welfare facilities is further considered in Reg 4.4 MLC.
[114] Reg 4.2 MLC.   [115] Reg 4.3 MLC.   [116] Reg 4.5 MLC.
[117] Arts II(2) and II(3) MLC provide that: '2. Except as expressly provided otherwise, this Convention applies to all seafarers. 3. In the event of doubt as to whether any categories of persons are to be regarded as seafarers for the purpose of this Convention, the question shall be determined by the competent authority in each Member after consultation with the shipowners' and seafarers' organizations concerned with this question.'
[118] Art II(4) MLC.   [119] Art II(1)(i) MLC.   [120] Art II(6) MLC.
[121] Art XIII MLC.

This broad provision is formulated so as to include any State which, for any reason, may have jurisdiction over the ship or the seafarer.[122] The principal States that bear this responsibility are the flag State[123] and the port State,[124] as well as the State where recruitment and placement services are located with regard to these services.[125] The duties of these States, mentioned in Article V MLC, are further detailed in Title 5 of the Code, relating to 'Compliance and enforcement'.

The responsibilities of the flag State include the duty to establish an effective system for inspection and certification of maritime labour conditions,[126] also through duly authorized public institutions or other organizations.[127] The flag State issues two documents according to the model provided in the MLC, the maritime labour certificate and the declaration of maritime labour compliance,[128] which constitute prima facie evidence that the ship complies with maritime labour standards.[129] Certificates have a five-year validity and in cases specifically provided may be provisional, for at most six months. A detailed inspection and enforcement system has to be in place to verify substantial adherence to the MLC standards.[130] Finally, the flag State must make provisions for an on-board complaints procedure 'for the fair, effective and expeditious handling of seafarer complaints alleging breaches' of the MLC requirements[131] and 'shall prohibit and penalize any kind of victimization of a seafarer for filing a complaint'.[132]

Port State control takes a form similar to that provided in other maritime law conventions, such as the SOLAS and the International Convention for the Prevention of Pollution from Ships (MARPOL). The port State has the right—but not the duty—to inspect vessels in its ports. The maritime labour certificate and the declaration of maritime labour compliance constitute prima facie evidence of compliance with the MLC.[133] However, if the documents are not produced, or are invalid, or if there are clear grounds for believing that the working and living conditions do not conform with the MLC, or that the ship has reflagged for the purpose of avoiding inspections or if there is a complaint, a physical inspection of the ship may take place.[134] Measures that the port State may take include notifying the master of the vessel and requiring the redress of deficiencies by a certain deadline and, where there are clearly hazardous conditions or serious or repeated breaches of the Convention, detention of the ship.[135] In addition, the port State must provide for an on-shore complaint procedure for seafarers entering its ports.[136]

In concluding this brief overview of the MLC, it is worth noting some aspects relevant for present purposes. In the first place, the MLC is a comprehensive instrument that sets out to include all rights of seafarers and duties of States within a single text, thus making the identification of legal norms far easier and avoiding the need for coordination of a number of different legal instruments. Secondly, the MLC

---

[122] See Chapter 3.   [123] Art V(2) and (3) MLC.   [124] Art V(4) MLC.
[125] Art V(5) MLC and Reg 5.3 MLC.   [126] Reg 5.1.1 MLC.
[127] Reg 5.1.2 MLC.   [128] Reg 5.1.3 MLC.   [129] Reg 5.1.1(4) MLC.
[130] Reg 5.1.4 MLC.   [131] Reg 5.1.5(1) MLC.   [132] Reg 5.1.5(2) MLC.
[133] Reg 5.2.1 MLC.   [134] Standard A5.2.1 MLC.   [135] ibid.
[136] Reg 5.2.2 MLC.

provides not only for labour rights, but also for other human rights. Thirdly, the MLC provides obligations not only for flag States, but also makes use and indeed develops the concept of port State control, attributing extensive duties to the port State. In this respect, it is probably the first treaty to expressly introduce port State control as a means for addressing violations of human rights. Fourthly, the special amendments procedure of the Code, which does not require express acceptance by all States for modifications to enter into force, paves the way for a quicker update of States' specific duties of implementation and enforcement. Finally, it has already been ratified by many States, representing more than two-thirds of the WGT.[137] Wide ratification can significantly broaden the scope of the Convention, as it arguably testifies to the MLC's status as part of the 'generally accepted international regulations' that all States, and not only MLC parties, must comply with under Article 94 UNCLOS.[138]

There are however some open issues with this monumental treaty. Its very nature may indeed in some cases not be met with adequate action. In particular, the MLC imposes heavy duties upon port States that want to inspect vessels which may prevent or delay inspections and, consequently, the redress of deficiencies. This threat is partly counter-balanced by the existence of memoranda of understanding on port State control which render mandatory inspection of vessels and which include the MLC within the applicable standards, such as the Paris Memorandum of Understanding on Port State Control (Paris MOU).[139] Furthermore, some of the procedures provided for in the MLC may be of difficult application due to the conditions on board seagoing vessels. In particular, the on-board complaints procedure might not be easily applied on board vessels, where a seafarer is 'at the mercy' of the master, officers, and other seafarers while the vessel is navigating in the seas. This danger was evidently foreseen by the drafters of the Convention, who inserted the provision to avoid victimization of the complainant.[140] It remains to be seen however if this provision will be enough to ensure the protection of those who file complaints, given that the persons in charge of its application are the same persons against whom complaints could be made. Finally, and more generally, it is a pity that a vast portion of maritime workers, which includes fishers but also those working on board platforms when these cannot be considered as vessels, are left outside the scope of protection.

4.1.2 Work in Fishing Convention

As fishers are clearly considered workers, the ILO has engaged in a number of efforts to ensure decent working conditions for them since its inception.[141] While some of the

---

[137] As of 20 August 2017, States parties represented 91 per cent WGT.

[138] Irini Papanicolopulu, 'Seafarers as an Agent of Change of the Jurisdictional Balance' in Henrik Ringbom (ed), *Jurisdiction over Ships. Post-UNCLOS Developments in the Law of the Sea* (Martinus Nijhoff 2015) 301.

[139] Paris Memorandum of Understanding on Port State Control (adopted 26 January 1982 entered into force 1 July 1982) 21 ILM 1, as amended (Paris MOU).

[140] Reg 5.1.5(2) MLC.

[141] In addition to the general conventions that apply to all workers, including fishers, dedicated instruments date back to the ILO Recommendation R007: Hours of Work (Fishing) Recommendation

conventions relevant for this sector are dated, a renewed effort for the elaboration of a modern treaty concerning work in the fishing sector resulted in the adoption of the Work in Fishing Convention[142] in 2007. This treaty applies to all fishers—meaning every person employed or engaged in any capacity or carrying out an occupation on board any fishing vessel.[143] Parties may however exclude the application of some provisions in specific cases.[144] These exclusions aim to reflect the diverse levels of economic and scientific development of States and the peculiarities of certain types of fisheries, for example inland fisheries. Exclusions cannot operate for vessels which are twenty-four metres in length and over, or remain at sea for more than seven days, or normally navigate at a distance exceeding 200 nautical miles from the coast.[145] These provisions effectively exclude a significant number of fishing vessels from the scope of the Work in Fishing Convention, since more than 85 per cent of motorized fishing vessels in the world are less than twelve metres in length, whilst only 2 per cent of all motorized fishing vessels correspond to industrialized fishing vessels of twenty-four metres and above.[146]

Under the Work in Fishing Convention, a State is required to implement and enforce laws, regulations, and other measures to fulfil its commitments 'with respect to fishers and fishing vessels under its jurisdiction'.[147] This broad wording allows the Convention to apply not only with respect to the flag State, but also with respect to the coastal State when the latter exercises jurisdiction over vessels. Responsibility is placed on the vessel owner to ensure that the skipper,[148] who has the responsibility for the safety of the fishers on board and the safe operation of the vessel, is provided with the necessary resources and facilities to comply with the obligations of this Convention.[149] Enforcement rests with the flag State,[150] the port State,[151] and the State where recruitment and placement take place, with respect to these activities.[152] Substantial standards indicated by the

---

(Recommendation concerning the Limitation of Hours of Work in the Fishing Industry) (2nd ILC session Genoa 30 June 1920) and include the Medical Examination (Fishermen) Convention (No 113) (adopted 19 June 1959, entered into force 7 November 1961), the Fishermen's Articles of Agreement Convention (No 114) (adopted 19 June 1959, entered into force 7 November 1961), the Fishermen's Competency Certificates Convention (No 125) (adopted 21 June 1966, entered into force 15 July 1969), and the Accommodation of Crews (Fishermen) Convention (No 126) (adopted 21 June 1966, entered into force 6 November 1968).

[142] Work in Fishing Convention (No 188) (adopted 14 June 2007, entered into force 16 November 2017) (Work in Fishing Convention).

[143] Art 1(e) Work in Fishing Convention, which excludes from its scope 'pilots, naval personnel, other persons in the permanent service of a government, shore-based persons carrying out work aboard a fishing vessel and fisheries observers'. According to Art 1(g) Work in Fishing Convention, 'fishing vessel or vessel means any ship or boat, of any nature whatsoever, irrespective of the form of ownership, used or intended to be used for the purpose of commercial fishing'.

[144] Art 3(1) and Art 4(1) Work in Fishing Convention.

[145] Art 4(2) Work in Fishing Convention.

[146] SOFIA 2012 11.

[147] Art 6(1) Work in Fishing Convention.   [148] The person in charge of a fishing vessel.

[149] Art 8 Work in Fishing Convention.

[150] Arts 40 and 43(1) Work in Fishing Convention.

[151] Art 43(2) Work in Fishing Convention.

[152] Art 22(3) Work in Fishing Convention.

Work in Fishing Convention concern minimum age, medical examination and certification, conditions of service, the obligation to maintain a crew list, fisher's work agreements, repatriation, recruitment and placement, payment, accommodation and food, medical care, health protection, and social security.

The adoption of the Work in Fishing Convention was accompanied by the adoption of a Recommendation having the same object. Like all ILO recommendations, this is not a binding instrument. It is however indicative of those areas that are considered as most necessitating regulation: protection of young persons, medical examination, training, conditions of service, payment, accommodation, medical care, health protection, and social security.

The Work in Fishing Convention is undoubtedly a significant step forward in the protection of fishers' rights, as it provides the principles that should guide States in the implementation of their duties towards fishers. While it is due to enter into force on 6 November 2017, the low number of ratifications[153] does not allow it, for the time being, to have a significant impact globally. In the meantime, fishers are not able to benefit from the MLC, which expressly excludes fishing vessels from its scope.[154] To contrast this rather disappointing situation, it is useful to remember that ILO instruments may influence the development of national legislation even when they are not in force. This has happened, for example, in the European Union. Following the adoption of the Work in Fishing Convention, an Agreement was concluded between the social partners,[155] which calls upon States to ratify the Convention and endorses its content. The Agreement has paved the way for the elaboration of a directive to effectively implement the content of the Work in Fishing Convention.[156]

4.1.3 Migrant workers and stateless seamen

Sailors and people working on board platforms who are migrants, as well as stateless seamen have been the object of dedicated provisions in international treaties dealing, respectively, with migrant workers and with stateless persons.

Migrant workers at sea are among the individuals considered by the International Convention on the Protection of the Rights of All Migrant Workers and Members of their Families (Migrant Workers Convention).[157] The Convention applies to

---

[153] As of 21 July 2017, it has been ratified by ten States.   [154] Art II(4) MLC.

[155] Agreement Between the Social Partners in the European Union's Sea-Fisheries Sector Concerning the Implementation of the Work In Fishing Convention, 2007 of the International Labour Organization (adopted 21 May 2012).

[156] Council Directive (EU) 2017/159 of 19 December 2016 implementing the Agreement concerning the implementation of the Work in Fishing Convention, 2007 of the International Labour Organisation, concluded on 21 May 2012 between the General Confederation of Agricultural Cooperatives in the European Union (Cogeca), the European Transport Workers' Federation (ETF) and the Association of National Organisations of Fishing Enterprises in the European Union (Europêche) [2016] OJ L25/12.

[157] International Convention on the Protection of the Rights of All Migrant Workers and Members of their Families (adopted 18 December 1990, entered into force 1 July 2003) 2220 UNTS 3 (Migrant Workers Convention).

any migrant worker, that is 'a person who is to be engaged, is engaged or has been engaged in a remunerated activity in a State of which he or she is not a national' including seafarers[158] and workers on offshore installations.[159] However, '[s]eafarers and workers on an offshore installation who have not been admitted to take up residence and engage in a remunerated activity in the State of employment' are excluded from the scope of the treaty.[160]

The Migrant Workers Convention provides for the non-discrimination of migrant workers and sets out lists of rights for, respectively, all migrant workers[161] and those who are in a regular situation,[162] as opposed to migrant workers who are in an irregular situation.[163] The Migrant Workers Convention is also notable for providing some protection for people working on offshore installations, a category that is otherwise not the object of legal regulation. However, the scope of protection for migrant workers employed on vessels or platforms is limited by the exception mentioned above.

The Convention relating to the Status of Stateless Persons[164] also contains a provision on 'stateless persons regularly serving as crew members on board a ship flying the flag of a Contracting State'.[165] According to this provision, a State party 'shall give sympathetic consideration to their establishment on its territory and the issue of travel documents to them or their temporary admission to its territory particularly with a view to facilitating their establishment in another country'.[166]

4.1.4 Agreement Relating to Refugee Seamen

A treaty dedicated to a specific category of people at sea, refugee seamen, is the 1957 Agreement Relating to Refugee Seamen.[167] The Agreement was adopted in

---

[158] According to Art 2(2)(c) Migrant Workers Convention, 'the term "seafarer", which includes a fisherman, refers to a migrant worker employed on board a vessel registered in a State of which he or she is not a national'.

[159] According to Art 2(2)(d) Migrant Workers Convention, 'the term "worker on an offshore installation" refers to a migrant worker employed on an offshore installation that is under the jurisdiction of a State of which he or she is not a national'.

[160] Art 3(f) Migrant Workers Convention.

[161] Arts 8–35 Migrant Workers Convention.

[162] Arts 36–56 Migrant Workers Convention. According to Art 5(a) Migrant Workers Convention, migrant workers '[a]re considered as documented or in a regular situation if they are authorized to enter, to stay and to engage in a remunerated activity in the State of employment pursuant to the law of that State and to international agreements to which that State is a party'.

[163] According to Art 5(b) Migrant Workers Convention, migrant workers '[a]re considered as non-documented or in an irregular situation if they do not comply with the conditions provided for in subparagraph (a) of the present article'.

[164] Convention relating to the Status of Stateless Persons (adopted 28 September 1954, entered into force 6 June 1960) 360 UNTS 118.

[165] Art 11 Convention relating to the Status of Stateless Persons.   [166] ibid.

[167] Agreement Relating to Refugee Seamen (adopted 23 November 1957, entered into force 27 December 1961) 506 UNTS 126. The Agreement was amended by the Protocol Relating to Refugee Seamen (adopted 12 June 1973, entered into force 30 March 1975) 965 UNTS 446, to reflect the new definition of 'refugee' incorporated in Art 1(A) Convention Relating to the Status of Refugees (adopted 28 July 1951, entered into force 22 April 1954) 189 UNTS 137 (Refugee Convention), as modified by Art 1 Protocol relating to the Status of Refugees (adopted 31 January 1967, entered into force 4

furtherance of the Refugee Convention, which contains a special provision for refugee seamen. Article 11 of the Refugee Convention requires a State to give sympathetic consideration to the establishment of refugees regularly serving as crew members on board a ship flying its flag and the issue of travel documents to them or their temporary admission to its territory particularly with a view to facilitating their establishment in another country.

This provision has been further developed in the Agreement Relating to Refugee Seamen, that is 'any person who, being a refugee according to the definition in Article 1 of the [Refugee Convention] is serving as a seafarer in any capacity on a mercantile ship, or habitually earns his living as a seafarer on such a ship'.[168] There is no definition of 'seaman' either in the Agreement or in the Refugee Convention. It is therefore doubtful whether this term should be interpreted in accordance with the ILO instruments, which distinguish between people working on fishing vessels and those working on other commercial vessels, or whether it should be interpreted in the same way as the term 'seafarer' in the Migrant Workers Convention. In the absence of any definition and any explicit reduction of its scope, it seems most in conformity with the object and scope of the treaty, that is, the protection of refugees serving on board ships, to include fishers within the term 'seaman'.

The Agreement regulates entry and stay of refugee seamen in the territories of State parties with a view towards identifying a State where the refugee seaman can lawfully stay.[169] It also provides for the right to disembark while the ship on which he or she is serving is in port[170] and the right not to stay on board a vessel for medical reasons.[171] An interesting provision is contained in Article 10, according to which a refugee seaman shall not 'be forced, as far as it is in the power of the Contracting Parties, to stay on board a ship which is bound for a port, or is due to sail through waters, where he has wellfounded fear of persecution'. Unlike other provisions, which apply mostly at the point when the refugee seaman is setting foot onshore, this provision applies also at sea, prohibiting States from obliging seafarers to sail through waters where there is a well-founded fear of persecution.

4.2 Specific provisions for the protection of people at sea

In addition to the treaties presented in the previous sections, there are other treaties which, while having different objects and scope, also contain specific provisions which aim to protect persons at sea. These may be either general treaties, such as the UNCLOS, treaties dealing with maritime security issues, treaties dealing with the

---

October 1967) 606 UNTS 267. P Weis, 'The Hague Agreement Relating to Refugee Seamen' (1958) 7 ICLQ 334.

[168] Art 1(b) Agreement Relating to Refugee Seamen.
[169] Arts 2 and 3 Agreement Relating to Refugee Seamen.
[170] Art 6 Agreement Relating to Refugee Seamen.
[171] Art 9 Agreement Relating to Refugee Seamen: 'No refugee seaman shall be forced, as far as it is in the power of the Contracting Parties, to stay on board a ship if his physical or mental health would thereby be seriously endangered'.

regulation of fishing, or treaties with a non-maritime object, such as the Refugee Convention.

The UNCLOS is the basic treaty for the law of the sea and the starting point for any investigation into the existence of rules concerning any issue at sea. It contains the fundamental principles and rules that regulate activities at sea and includes procedural norms as well as substantial standards. However, the protection of individuals who are at sea does not seem to form an object of the Convention, nor does this treaty contain any general principle establishing the duty to protect people at sea.[172] The UNCLOS, while not attributing any rights directly to individuals, does in a few instances pose the duty upon States to protect and respect specific rights of people.[173]

First, the duty to protect life at sea under Articles 98 and 146 UNCLOS is an expression of the more general positive obligation of States to protect the right to life of individuals.[174] Second, penalties for illegal fishing in the exclusive economic zone 'may not include imprisonment, in the absence of agreements to the contrary by the States concerned, or any other form of corporal punishment', so as to safeguard personal integrity.[175] Third, trials for pollution of the marine environment must be conducted so as to respect the recognized rights of the accused and, except in the case of a wilful and serious act of pollution in the territorial sea, penalties must be monetary only.[176] Fourth, individuals who are operating in the International Seabed Area under a licence are given specific rights to safeguard their interests, including procedural rights.[177]

Apart from these provisions, it is indeed possible to consider that many activities regulated under the UNCLOS are of some benefit to individuals or groups, as Oxman has perceptively argued.[178] It is, however, difficult to extrapolate subjective rights for individuals from generic provisions concerning, for example, the common heritage of mankind, the duty not to pollute the marine environment, or the freedom of all States to fish on the high seas.

Following the example of the UNCLOS, treaties and other instruments dealing with fisheries contain very little detail directly concerning individuals. The 1995 Agreement relating to the Conservation and Management of Straddling Fish Stocks and Highly Migratory Fish Stocks (FSA)[179] briefly mentions that, when a fishing vessel that has been apprehended is brought into port, the 'inspecting State and the flag State and, as appropriate, the port State shall take all necessary steps to ensure

---

[172] The point is discussed in Papanicolopulu, 'The Law of the Sea Convention' (n 90).

[173] Bernard H Oxman, 'Human Rights and the United Nations Convention on the Law of the Sea' (1998) 36 Columbia Journal of Transnational Law 399, 401–02; Sophie Cacciaguidi-Fahy, 'The Law of the Sea and Human Rights' (2007) 19 Sri Lanka Journal of International Law 85, 86; Tullio Treves, 'Human Rights and the Law of the Sea' (2010) 28 Berkeley Journal of International Law 1, 3.

[174] See Chapter 4.   [175] Art 73(3) UNCLOS.   [176] Art 230 UNCLOS.

[177] Arts 153(2)(b), 168(3), 183(c), 187(e), and 190 UNCLOS.

[178] Oxman (n 173) 401.

[179] United Nations Agreement for the Implementation of the Provisions of the United Nations Convention on the Law of the Sea of 10 December 1982 relating to the Conservation and Management of Straddling Fish Stocks and Highly Migratory Fish Stocks (adopted 4 December 1995, entered into force 11 December 2001) 2167 UNTS 3 (FSA).

the well-being of the crew regardless of their nationality'[180] and contains some essential safeguards concerning the use of force during enforcement activities.[181] Similarly, the Code of Conduct for Responsible Fisheries (CoC)[182] contains only one provision concerned with the protection of fishers, requesting States to ensure that 'fishing is conducted with due regard to the safety of human life' and the IMO regulations on marine traffic.[183]

In the same way, the 2009 Port State Control Agreement (PSCA)[184] provides that a vessel shall not be denied the use of port services (one of the measures that the State can adopt against ships engaged in IUU fishing) if their use is 'essential to the safety or health of the crew or the safety of the vessel, provided these needs are duly proven'.[185] The PSCA does not concern, at least apparently, the control of living and working conditions on board the vessel, since it focuses only on the conservation of marine living resources and the elimination of IUU fishing.[186]

Most treaties dealing with maritime security issues contain provisions relevant to the protection of people at sea. In the first place, they provide for the jurisdiction of parties with respect to individuals on vessels flying their flag and, often, individuals who come under their control through other means. While these provisions do not, by themselves, grant any protection to the individuals envisaged, they allow for the application of other standards, as will be discussed in Chapter 3.

Furthermore, recent treaties that regulate enforcement action by States against vessels usually contain a safeguard provision, aimed at protecting human life and the dignity of the persons on board the intercepted vessel. Thus the 1995 FSA provides that the 'inspecting State shall require its inspectors to observe generally accepted international regulations, procedures and practices relating to the safety

---

[180] Art 21(8) FSA.

[181] Art 22(1)(f) FSA. Excessive use of force against fishing vessels and fishers on board is an issue that has come to the forefront in numerous cases. The International Tribunal for the Law of the Sea (ITLOS) addressed this issue in *Saiga* (n 84).

[182] The FAO Code of Conduct for Responsible Fisheries (adopted 31 October 1995) (CoC) is a voluntary instrument that 'provides principles and standards applicable to the conservation, management and development of all fisheries [and] covers the capture, processing and trade of fish and fishery products, fishing operations, aquaculture, fisheries research and the integration of fisheries into coastal area management' (para 1.3 CoC). It is addressed to 'members and non-members of FAO, fishing entities, subregional, regional and global organizations, whether governmental or non-governmental, and all persons concerned with the conservation of fishery resources and management and development of fisheries' (para 1.2 CoC). Although non-binding in itself, the CoC incorporates requirements under binding treaties, such as the UNCLOS and FSA, and has had an impact in the development of national legislations and policies; see Gilles Hosch, Gianluca Ferraro, and Pierre Failler, 'The 1995 FAO Code of Conduct for Responsible Fisheries: Adopting, Implementing or Scoring Results?' (2011) 35 Marine Policy 189.

[183] Para 8.4.1 CoC.

[184] Agreement on Port State Measures to Prevent, Deter and Eliminate Illegal, Unreported and Unregulated Fishing (adopted 22 November 2009, entered into force 5 June 2016) (PSCA).

[185] Art 11(2)(a) PSCA. See also Art 18 (2) PSCA.

[186] While it is to be regretted that this occasion was not properly exploited to also impose a duty to undertake controls concerning humans, this omission should not be overstated. On one hand, the PSCA does not exclude other forms of control that the port State can undertake. On the other, the detailed controls mandated for inspectors under Annex B PSCA cannot but expose some of the practices that amount to a violation of the basic rights of fishers.

of the vessel and the crew'.[187] Similar wording is included in treaties concerning the fight against drug trafficking, people smuggling, and security of navigation.

The United Nations Convention against Illicit Traffic in Narcotic Drugs and Psychotropic Substances (Convention against Illicit Traffic in Drugs) requires parties to cooperate towards the suppression of the illicit traffic of narcotics by sea and provides a jurisdictional framework for doing so. During these actions, 'the Parties concerned shall take due account of the need not to endanger the safety of life at sea, the security of the vessel and the cargo'.[188]

Similar provisions can be found in regional or bilateral agreements, including those providing for 'shipriders'. The Council of Europe Agreement on Illicit Traffic by Sea,[189] for example, provides that when undertaking enforcement action the parties 'shall take due account of the need not to endanger the safety of life at sea',[190] but also that any enforcement action must be 'without prejudice to any right existing under the law of the intervening State of suspected persons not to incriminate themselves'.[191] The Agreement on Trafficking in Narcotic Drugs in the Caribbean Area[192] contains safeguards with respect to the safety of life at sea,[193] as well as a detailed provision on the use of force during enforcement action.[194]

The Protocol against the Smuggling of Migrants by Land, Sea and Air Supplementing the United Nations Convention against Transnational Organized Crime (Smuggling Protocol) establishes a cooperative framework for dealing with people smuggling, which allows for the boarding and inspection of vessels and for further measures against smugglers.[195] At the same time, the Smuggling Protocol requires States to 'ensure the safety and humane treatment of the persons on board'

---

[187] Art 21(10) FSA. See also Art 22(1) FSA.

[188] Art 17(5) United Nations Convention against Illicit Traffic in Narcotic Drugs and Psychotropic Substances (adopted 20 December 1988, entered into force 11 November 1990) 1582 UNTS 165 (Convention against Illicit Traffic in Drugs). Art XV (2) of the Supplementary Arrangement between the Government of the United States of America and the Government of the Republic of Panama for Support and Assistance from the United States Coast Guard for the National Maritime Service of the Ministry of Government and Justice (adopted 5 February 2002) text in AV Lowe and Stefan Talmon, *The Legal Order of the Oceans: Basic Documents on the Law of the Sea* (Hart 2009) 45, provides also that the parties 'shall observe the norms of courtesy, respect and consideration for the persons on board the suspected vessel'.

[189] Agreement on Illicit Traffic by Sea, Implementing Article 17 of the United Nations Convention against Illicit Traffic in Narcotic Drugs and Psychotropic Substances (adopted 31 January 1995, entered into force 1 May 2000) 2136 UNTS 81 (Agreement on Illicit Traffic by Sea).

[190] Art 12(1) Agreement on Illicit Traffic by Sea.

[191] Art 9(2) Agreement on Illicit Traffic by Sea.

[192] Agreement Concerning Co-operation in Suppressing Illicit Maritime and Air Trafficking in Narcotic Drugs and Psychotropic Substances in the Caribbean Area (adopted 10 April 2003, entered into force 18 September 2008) text in Lowe and Talmon (n 188) 789 (Agreement on Trafficking in Narcotic Drugs in the Caribbean Area).

[193] Art 20(4) Agreement on Trafficking in Narcotic Drugs in the Caribbean Area.

[194] Art 22 Agreement on Trafficking in Narcotic Drugs in the Caribbean Area.

[195] Patricia Mallia, *Migrant Smuggling by Sea. Combating a Current Threat to Maritime Security through the Creation of a Cooperative Framework* (Martinus Nijhoff 2010).

and to 'take due account of the need not to endanger the security of the vessel, or its cargo'.[196] It also contains a broad safeguard clause, according to which:

1. Nothing in this Protocol shall affect the other rights, obligations and responsibilities of States and individuals under international law, including international humanitarian law and international human rights law and, in particular, where applicable, the 1951 Convention and the 1967 Protocol relating to the Status of Refugees and the principle of non-refoulement as contained therein.

2. The measures set forth in this Protocol shall be interpreted and applied in a way that is not discriminatory to persons on the ground that they are the object of conduct set forth in article 6 of this Protocol. The interpretation and application of those measures shall be consistent with internationally recognized principles of non-discrimination.[197]

The 2005 Convention for the Suppression of Unlawful Acts Against the Safety of Maritime Navigation (SUA Convention)[198] is also particularly detailed in its human rights guarantees.[199] Apart from the provisions aimed at ensuring contact with national authorities,[200] the safety of life at sea,[201] and the protection of human dignity,[202] it also obliges States to provide for effective remedies against unlawful action by State authorities,[203] fair treatment of persons taken into custody,[204] and prior informed consent for the transfer of a person detained or serving a sentence from one State to another for the purposes of providing evidence.[205] Furthermore, the SUA Convention is one of few law of the sea treaties to contain a non-prejudice clause concerning human rights in general. According to Article 2*bis* (1) of the SUA Convention:

Nothing in this Convention shall affect other rights, obligations and responsibilities of States and individuals under international law, in particular the purposes and principles of the Charter of the United Nations and international human rights, refugee and humanitarian law.

A special feature that distinguishes law of the sea treaties is the fact that they usually contain a specific obligation for a State taking action against a vessel to allow the master, crew, or other persons on board to contact the flag State or, in some cases,

---

[196] Art 9(1)(a) Protocol against the Smuggling of Migrants by Land, Sea and Air Supplementing the United Nations Convention against Transnational Organized Crime (adopted 15 November 2000, entered into force 28 January 2004) 2241 UNTS 480 (Smuggling Protocol).

[197] Art 19 Smuggling Protocol.

[198] Convention for the Suppression of Unlawful Acts Against the Safety of Maritime Navigation (adopted 10 March 1988), as amended by the 2005 Protocol (adopted 14 October 2005, entered into force 28 July 2010) 1678 UNTS 222 (SUA Convention).

[199] While the original 1988 Convention for the Suppression of Unlawful Acts Against the Safety of Maritime Navigation did not refer to human rights, the 2005 version has been amended to take human rights, refugee law, and international humanitarian law into account, also as a result of the UN debates concerning the relationship between measures to combat terrorism and the respect for fundamental human rights. See 2005 Protocol, Preamble para 12.

[200] Art 7 (3) SUA Convention.   [201] Art 8*bis* (10)(a)(i) SUA Convention.

[202] Art 8*bis* (10)(a)(ii) SUA Convention.   [203] Art 8*bis* (10)(b) SUA Convention.

[204] Art 10(2) SUA Convention.   [205] Art 12*bis* (1)(a) SUA Convention.

the State of nationality. Thus, the UNCLOS provides that 'the coastal State shall, if the master so requests, notify a diplomatic agent or consular officer of the flag State before taking any steps [to exercise criminal jurisdiction against a ship in its territorial waters], and shall facilitate contact between such agent or officer and the ship's crew'.[206] The Agreement on Illicit Traffic by Sea furthermore provides for the duty of the State engaged in enforcement action to report as soon as possible to the flag State '[t]he death, or injury of any person aboard the vessel'.[207]

These provisions mirror the definition of consular functions contained in the Vienna Convention on Consular Relations,[208] according to which these functions include:

exercising rights of supervision and inspection provided for in the laws and regulations of the sending State in respect of vessels having the nationality of the sending State, . . . and in respect of their crews, [and] extending assistance to vessels and aircraft mentioned in subparagraph (k) of this article and to their crews, taking statements regarding the voyage of a vessel, examining and stamping the ship's papers, and, without prejudice to the power of the authorities of the receiving State, conducting investigations into any incidents which occurred during the voyage, and settling disputes of any kind between the master, the officers and the seamen, insofar as this may be authorised by the laws and regulations of the sending State.[209]

These provisions can be considered as specific applications of the general right to consular information, notification, and assistance, which all foreign individuals enjoy under Article 36(1) of the Vienna Convention on Consular Relations.[210] Significantly, and as recognized in the International Law Commission (ILC) Draft Articles on Diplomatic Protection, diplomatic protection with respect to a ship's crew is exercised not only by the State of nationality of the individuals, but also by the State of nationality of the vessel on which they sail.[211]

Finally, as mentioned above in relation to the Agreement relating to refugee seamen, the Refugee Convention contains a special provision for refugee seamen, which requires States to give sympathetic consideration to the establishment of refugees regularly serving as crew members on board a ship flying their flag and the issue of travel documents to them or their temporary admission to its territory, particularly with a view to facilitating their establishment in another country.[212]

---

[206] Art 27(3) UNCLOS.   [207] Art 12(3) Agreement on Illicit Traffic by Sea.

[208] Vienna Convention on Consular Relations (adopted 24 April 1963, entered into force 19 March 1967) 596 UNTS 262.

[209] Arts 5(k) and (l) Vienna Convention on Consular Relations. See also Art 37(c) Vienna Convention on Consular Relations providing for the duty of the receiving State to inform the consular post of the sending State 'if a vessel, having the nationality of the sending State, is wrecked or runs aground in the territorial sea or internal waters of the receiving State'.

[210] *LaGrand (Germany v United States of America)* [2001] ICJ Rep 466, para 77.

[211] Art 18 ILC, Draft Articles on Diplomatic Protection <http://legal.un.org/ilc/texts/instruments/english/draft_articles/9_8_2006.pdf> accessed 13 August 2017.

[212] Art 11 Refugee Convention.

4.3 Treaties to ensure safety and security

A further category of treaties that warrants some consideration includes all those instruments which, while not providing for specific rights of individuals, have been adopted with the aim to protect them while at sea. These treaties are useful in determining how international law protects people at sea because they may pose duties on States to take specific measures to protect people at sea.

There are three categories of instruments that are particularly relevant: those relating to the safety of vessels and platforms, which contain measures to ensure that ships and platforms are constructed and equipped so as to ensure the safety of those on board and that maritime incidents are dealt with promptly, so that life at sea may be saved; those relating to the training of crews, which are instrumental to ensure a safe trip for them and for the other people on board; and finally, those targeting threats to maritime security, which aim to combat crime at sea, which may affect the people therein. The latter treaties have been mentioned in the previous section. This section will briefly assess treaties on maritime safety and training.

4.3.1 Safety of vessels and platforms

A safe ship and a safe platform are fundamental for the protection of the right to life of all those on board. At the same time, as ships and platforms are complex structures, safety regulations must necessarily reflect the relevant technical details, lest they prove ambitious but not effective. It is for this reason that the safety of vessels has mostly been pursued in technical bodies of the IMO. In this respect, it should be noted from the outset that, while the safety of commercial vessels is well developed, that of fishing vessels and, in particular, platforms, is lagging behind and is so far unsatisfactory.

Beginning with ships, the SOLAS is probably the best known and most important treaty concerning safety of navigation. Its widespread acceptance, which comes close to a universal application, demonstrates its relevance.[213] Adopted in the aftermath of the Titanic disaster and readopted four times successively, the SOLAS provides minimum standards for the construction, equipment, and operation of ships, in order to ensure their safety and security. The present version was adopted in 1974 and it has been amended several times to reflect technical developments and the ever-changing perception of safety and security threats.

Structurally, the SOLAS is composed of the Convention text, which poses the duty on States to comply with its requirements and contains the final provisions, and the Annex, divided into Chapters, which contains the substantial regulations. The Annex contains regulations on construction; life-saving appliances and arrangements; radio communications; safety services which should be provided by States; carriage of cargoes; carriage of dangerous goods; nuclear ships; the International Safety Management (ISM) Code; high-speed craft; special measures to enhance

---

[213] As of 14 January 2012, there are 162 parties, the combined merchant fleets of which constitute approximately 99.20 per cent of the gross tonnage of the world's merchant fleet.

maritime safety; special measures to enhance maritime security; bulk carriers; verification of compliance; and safety measures for ships operating in polar waters. The SOLAS applies to all ships engaged in international voyages,[214] with the exception of ships of war and troopships; cargo ships of less than 500 tons gross tonnage; ships not propelled by mechanical means; wooden ships of primitive build; pleasure yachts not engaged in trade; and fishing vessels.[215]

As has been pointed out when discussing the threats faced by people at sea, lack of safety of vessels is a primary concern. It is therefore evident how the SOLAS contributes to the protection of people at sea. Guidance as to the design and construction of vessels, furthermore, contributes to ensuring that people on board have sufficient space for living and working, as well as the necessary facilities for dealing with life on board. Hence the cross-reference to the SOLAS standards in the MLC. Finally, the SOLAS is crucial in ensuring the safety of life at sea, not only for those on board but also for people rescued.[216]

In this respect, the SOLAS contains provisions on rescue at sea, which oblige both the master of a vessel and the States to go to the rescue of those in danger of perishing at sea. These duties, similar to those incorporated in Article 98 UNCLOS, require in the first place the master to proceed with all speed to the assistance of persons in distress at sea if in a position to be able to provide assistance.[217] In the second place, a coastal State has the duty to 'ensure that necessary arrangements are made ... for the rescue of people in distress at sea around its coasts'.[218] Furthermore, the SOLAS requires all ships engaged in international voyages to have plans and procedures for the recovery of persons from the water.[219]

A significant innovation introduced by the SOLAS concerns the system adopted to control compliance with its requirements. This system is based on three elements: certificates, flag State inspections, and port State control. The flag State must regularly inspect its vessels to ensure that they comply with the SOLAS requirements. Upon successful completion of the inspection, a certificate is released, which provides prima facie evidence of compliance. Subsequently, when the ship enters into the ports of another State, the latter will inspect the certificates and may proceed to physical inspection only where there are no certificates, or they are expired, or whether there are material grounds for believing that the ship does not comply with the SOLAS requirements. Port State control is particularly noteworthy as it allows for the verification of compliance by a State other than the flag State, traditionally identified as the one with power to control compliance with safety requirements. This has been incorporated in most IMO instruments afterwards.

In conclusion, the SOLAS is a monumental treaty devoted to the safety and security of vessels. While it does not attribute rights to individuals—on the contrary, it contains duties for the master and crew of a ship—it does provide for the duty of States to adopt measures for the safety and security of those on board, and it is therefore

---

[214] Reg 1 SOLAS.   [215] Reg 3 SOLAS.   [216] See Chapter 4, Section 4.2.
[217] Reg 33(1) SOLAS.   [218] Reg 7 SOLAS.
[219] Reg 17(1) SOLAS. See also IMO, 'Guide to Recovery Techniques' (21 November 2014) Doc MSC.1/Circ.1182/Rev.1.

instrumental to the protection of people at sea. Furthermore, it contains significant provisions for rescue at sea and introduces port State control as a means for ensuring compliance with its requirements. Its widespread acceptance makes it a worldwide reference standard. Indeed, its major drawback is the fact that some vessels, principally fishing vessels, are excluded from its scope and that it does not apply to platforms and installations unless they are self-propelled and are travelling as vessels. While in some cases the IMO has encouraged States to apply the SOLAS provisions beyond the scope of the Convention,[220] this does not constitute a duty for States.

Notwithstanding its exclusion from the scope of the SOLAS, the safety of fishing vessels has always been a major issue of concern, since safety greatly impacts the working and living conditions on board, as well as the hazardous nature of fishing. Fishing vessels are generally beyond the scope of IMO maritime safety conventions, either because of their activity or because of their dimensions, which do not reach the minimum required for the application of these treaties. As a consequence, it has been necessary to adopt dedicated treaties.

Since most of the SOLAS provisions do not apply to fishing vessels,[221] in the 1970s the IMO developed the Convention for the Safety of Fishing Vessels (SFV). Following almost two decades of unsuccessful attempts to bring this Convention into force, in 1993 a Protocol was produced with the purpose to facilitate ratification.[222] While this allowed a certain number of States to ratify this instrument, it became evident that the requirements for entry into force needed to be further lowered and a new Protocol was adopted in 2012, which is expected to eventually bring the instrument into force.[223] The SFV, in its present form, will apply to new fishing vessels—that is, vessels used commercially for catching fish, whales, seals, walrus, or other living resources of the sea[224]—of twenty-four metres in length and over. It also applies to fishing vessels processing their catch,[225] but excludes from its scope vessels used *exclusively* for processing fish, for sport or recreation, for research and training, or as fish carriers.[226] National administrations may exempt further categories of vessels from the application of the SFV, provided these vessels conform to requirements adequate to ensure their safety.[227] The SFV also provides rules with respect to certification, flag State responsibilities, port State control, and simplified amendment procedures, in line with the usual content of other IMO treaties.

As to the substantive standards, the SFV contains detailed regulations on construction and equipment, including provisions on fire protection, life-saving appliances and arrangements, emergency procedures, satellite communication systems, and other components of the global maritime distress and safety system. The SFV

[220] See, eg, IMO Resolution MSC.346(91) (adopted 30 November 2012).
[221] Reg I/3(a)(vi) SOLAS. Fishing vessels are however bound by the provisions on safety of navigation in Chapter V. See Reg V/1 SOLAS.
[222] Torremolinos Protocol of 1993 relating to the Torremolinos International Convention for the Safety of Fishing Vessels (adopted 2 April 1993) (SFV Convention).
[223] Cape Town Agreement of 2012 on the Implementation of the Provisions of the Torremolinos Protocol of 1993 Relating to the Torremolinos International Convention for the Safety of Fishing Vessels (adopted 11 October 2012).
[224] Art 2(b) SFV Convention.   [225] Art 3(1) SFV Convention.
[226] Art 3(2) SFV Convention.   [227] Reg I/3 SFV Convention.

contains rules in respect of noise levels,[228] the avoidance of slipping,[229] protection against accidental closing of hinged covers, manholes and other openings,[230] bulwarks, rails, and guards for protection against accidentally falling.[231]

As already mentioned, the SFV has not yet entered into force. While the 2012 modifications are expected to bring this treaty into force, this has not yet happened and it will certainly be some time before it acquires the widespread ratification of the SOLAS, which regulates the same matters with respect to commercial vessels.

If fishing vessels are less protected than other commercial vessels, then platforms are even less protected. There is in fact no international agreement addressing the safety of oil rigs and other platforms used to perform economic and scientific activities at sea. Some protection is provided for at the regional level, in particular within the European Union, which has adopted a Directive on the safety of offshore oil and gas operations.[232] In particular, the Directive contains measures for the safety of installations.[233] Furthermore, detailed but non-binding standards are included in the code developed by the IMO for MODUs.[234]

Finally, safety of life at sea is the main aim of the International Convention on Maritime Search and Rescue (SAR Convention), which provides detailed guidance on the application of the duty set out in Article 98 UNCLOS.[235] Provisions on the safety of life at sea are also contained in the International Convention on Salvage.[236]

4.3.2 Training and certification

Safety of navigation depends not only on the seaworthiness of vessels, but also on the competence and preparedness of the crew, who will be called upon to address any emergency. It is for this purpose that the IMO has worked on instruments to ensure that members of the crew are properly trained.

The International Convention on Standards of Training, Certification and Watchkeeping for Seafarers (STCW)[237] has been adopted to 'promote safety of life and property at sea and the protection of the marine environment by establishing

---

[228] Reg IV/12 SFV Convention.   [229] Reg VI/1(4) SFV Convention.
[230] Reg VI/2 SFV Convention.   [231] Reg VI/3 SFV Convention.
[232] Directive 2013/30/EU of the European Parliament and of the Council of 12 June 2013 on safety of offshore oil and gas operations and amending Directive 2004/35/EC [2013] OJ L 178/66 (Offshore Directive).
[233] The Directive provides that 'installation' means 'a stationary, fixed or mobile facility, or a combination of facilities permanently inter-connected by bridges or other structures, used for offshore oil and gas operations or in connection with such operations. Installations include mobile offshore drilling units only when they are stationed in offshore waters for drilling, production or other activities associated with offshore oil and gas operations'; Art 2(19) Offshore Directive.
[234] IMO Resolution A.1023(26): Code for the Construction and Equipment of Mobile Offshore Drilling Units Code for the construction and equipment of mobile offshore drilling units (adopted 2 December 2009).
[235] International Convention on Maritime Search and Rescue (adopted 27 April 1979, entered into force 22 June 1985) 1405 UNTS 97 (SAR Convention).
[236] International Convention on Salvage (adopted 28 April 1989, entered into force 14 July 1996) 1953 UNTS 165.
[237] International Convention on Standards of Training, Certification and Watchkeeping for Seafarers (adopted 7 July 1978, entered into force 28 April 1984) 1361 UNTS 2 (STCW).

in common agreement international standards of training, certification and watch-keeping for seafarers',[238] so as to ensure that 'seafarers on board ships are qualified and fit for their duties'.[239] Its structure includes the Convention text, the Annex which constitutes an integral part of the Convention,[240] and the Code, which is divided into a mandatory Part A[241] and Part B which includes non-mandatory guidelines. The STCW requirements apply to all ships with the exception of war-ships, fishing vessels, pleasure yachts, and wooden ships of primitive build.[242]

The STCW Annex and Code regulate the training[243] and certification[244] of seafarers in particular, depending on their role on board the vessel. They also address minimum requirements for serving in different roles,[245] and medical examinations to assess the fitness of seafarers.[246] As with other IMO treaties, the primary responsibility for the implementation of the STCW provisions rests with the flag State, which has the duty to train and provide certificates to the people working on board its vessels. A significant role is also given to control by port States.[247] In fact, certificates issued by the flag State constitute prima facie evidence of compliance with the STCW standards and the port State may proceed to further assessment of the ability of seafarers to maintain watch-keeping and security standards only if 'there are clear grounds for believing that such standards are not being maintained'.[248]

Complementing the STCW, the International Convention on Standards of Training, Certification and Watchkeeping for Fishing Vessel Personnel (STCW-F)[249] is instrumental to the safety of fishers. It provides for mandatory minimum requirements for certification and sets out requirements to ensure the continued proficiency of skippers and officers, of chief engineers and second engineer officers, and of radio operators. While there are no requirements for the certification of other persons working on board a fishing vessel, the STCW-F requires that *all* fishing vessel personnel receive basic safety training before being assigned to any shipboard duties.[250] It furthermore sets out basic principles to be observed in watchkeeping. The STCW-F applies to 'personnel serving on board seagoing fishing vessels [mean-ing 'any vessel used commercially for catching fish or other living resources of the sea']'[251] entitled to fly the flag of a Party'.[252] However, a State party, 'without [a] derogation from the principles of safety in the Convention', may limit the certifi-cation requirements in the case of 'fishing vessels of less than 45 metres in length operating exclusively from its ports and fishing within its limited waters'.[253] Finally, the STCW-F provides for enforcement of its provisions by the flag State,[254] the State that has certified the fishing personnel,[255] and by the port State.[256]

---

[238] Preamble, para 1, STCW.   [239] Art 1(2) STCW.   [240] Art 1(1) STCW.
[241] Reg I/1(2) STCW.   [242] Art 3 STCW.   [243] Reg I/6 STCW
[244] Reg I/2 STCW.
[245] Chapters II (master and deck department), III (engine department), IV (radiocommunications and radio operators), and V (special training for certain types of ships) STCW.
[246] Reg I/9 STCW.   [247] Art 10 and Reg I/4 STCW.   [248] Reg I/4(1)(3) STCW.
[249] International Convention on Standards of Training, Certification and Watchkeeping for Fishing Vessel Personnel (adopted 7 July 1995, entered into force 29 September 2012) (STCW-F).
[250] Reg III/1 STCW-F.   [251] Art 2(7) STCW-F   [252] Art 3 STCW-F.
[253] Reg I/2 STCW-F.   [254] Art 7(2) STCW-F.   [255] ibid.
[256] Art 8 STCW-F.

In light of their provisions and notwithstanding their limited subject matter and the fact that the STCW and STCW-F do not attribute rights to fishers (but rather impose duties on them concerning training and certification), these treaties could be considered as a step forward in ensuring the safety and adequate working and living conditions on board a vessel. The main issue with these treaties is that, while the STCW is widely ratified and applies to almost all seagoing vessels, the STCW-F still suffers from a lack of ratification, and consequently leaves most fishing vessels and the people on board unprotected.[257]

5. A Fragmented and Deficient Legal Framework?

Having looked at the people at sea, the threats they face, and the normative response provided so far by States, it is now time to assess whether these rules address all the risks identified and whether they do so in a satisfactory manner. The review of relevant legal norms in the previous sections suggests that the development of international rules on the protection of people at sea has taken one of two forms: dedicated legal instruments or safeguard clauses in broader treaties.

In the first case, a specific legal instrument is adopted to protect a discrete group of people during the time they are present at sea, or to address a specific threat to people, for example lack of vessel safety. The dedicated legal instrument, usually a treaty, provides a list of rights (of individuals) and correspondent duties (of States or other actors), as well as, at times, mechanisms for their implementation. The best example of this model is the MLC. In the second case, the protection of people at sea is achieved through the introduction of safeguard clauses into treaties dealing with other matters, usually the suppression of unlawful activities at sea.

Scholarly treatment of people at sea generally follows the same model, either briefly referring to the people and their rights in the treatment of different subject matters, for example piracy,[258] migration by

---

[257] As of 26 May 2016, the STCW has been ratified by 160 States, representing 98.55 per cent of the gross tonnage of the world's merchant fleet, while the STCW-F has been ratified by nineteen States, representing 4.16 per cent of the gross tonnage of the world's merchant fleet.

[258] Tullio Treves, 'Piracy, Law of the Sea, and Use of Force: Developments off the Coast of Somalia' (2009) 20 EJIL 399; Bibi van Ginkel and Frans-Paul van der Putten (eds), *The International Response to Somali Piracy* (Martinus Nijhoff 2010); Robin Geiss and Anna Petrig, *Piracy and Armed Robbery at Sea: The Legal Framework for Counter-Piracy Operations in Somalia and the Gulf of Aden* (OUP 2011); Douglas Guilfoyle (ed), *Modern Piracy* (Edward Elgar 2013). Interestingly, a significant number of studies has been devoted to the human rights of pirates, see Caroline Laly-Chevalier, 'Lutte contre la piraterie maritime et droits de l'homme' (2009) 42 Revue Belge de Droit International 5; Douglas Guilfoyle, 'Counter-Piracy Law Enforcement and Human Rights' (2010) 59 ICLQ 141; Anna Petrig, *Human Rights and Law Enforcement at Sea. Arrest, Detention and Transfer of Piracy Suspects* (Brill Nijhoff 2014); Cesare Pitea, 'Azioni di Contrasto alla Pirateria e Convenzione Europea del Diritti Umani: Questioni di Attribuzione e di Applicazione Extraterritoriale' (2015) 9 Diritti Umani e Diritto Internazionale 489; Mihaela Ailincai, 'Piraterie et droits de l'homme au sein du Conseil de l'Europe' in Constance Chevallier-Govers and Catherine Schneider (eds), *L'Europe et la lutte contre la piraterie maritime*

sea,[259] maritime interdiction,[260] and maritime security,[261] or, more rarely, focusing upon specific categories of people and their rights.[262]

The adoption of the rules illustrated in the previous sections undoubtedly marks a step forward towards the protection of people at sea, introducing the rule of law into a space that was often considered, at least as far as the people were concerned, beyond the reach of the law. This positive evaluation is further strengthened by the fact that most normative activity has taken place in recent years, and that further developments are underway at the global and regional level. The current picture is therefore rapidly developing and is likely to be further altered in a positive way in the near future.

Nonetheless, it is far from easy to conclude that dedicated legal instruments provide sufficient protection to people at sea. Rather, the opposite is true: the legal framework applicable to people at sea is still, to a great extent, insufficient to fully safeguard these people against the threats and dangers they face during their time at sea. This is due, it is here submitted, to the approach taken so far, which tends to be reactive and fragmented, rather than proactive and comprehensive. As a consequence, the ensuing legal framework is both fragmented and deficient.[263] This fragmentation and these deficiencies relate to the subject matter, the addressees of norms, the scope, and the content of treaties.

Beginning with the issues pertaining to fragmentation, the first problem is that there is no single, comprehensive treaty that sets out how people at sea should be treated. As shown, the UNCLOS is far from able to provide the guiding principles in this field, as it does for almost every other field of activity at sea. All other treaties focus on a single category of people, be they seafarers, fishers, or pirates, or a single issue, such as the safety of vessels or adequate training of people working on board. This fragmentation in respect of the subject matter leads to a deficiency in protection for those categories of people who are not included within the scope of existing treaties, for example people working on oil rigs or those working on aquaculture structures. It also entails uneven protection, as will be discussed below.

Second, the multiplicity of treaties results in a multiplicity of addressees of the norms, both because treaties are ratified unevenly, and because they adopt different legislative techniques. The fact that regulations are contained in treaties, which have

(Pedone 2015) 227; Tullio Treves and Cesare Pitea, 'Piracy, International Law and Human Rights' in Nehal Bhuta (ed), *The Frontiers of Human Rights. Extraterritoriality and Its Challenges* (OUP 2016).

[259] Patricia Mallia, *Migrant Smuggling by Sea. Combating a Current Threat to Maritime Security through the Creation of a Cooperative Framework* (Martinus Nijhoff 2010); Thomas Gammeltoft-Hansen, *Access to Asylum. International Refugee Law and the Globalisation of Migration Control* (CUP 2011).
[260] Douglas Guilfoyle, *Shipping Interdiction and the Law of the Sea* (CUP 2009); Efthymios Papastavridis, *The Interception of Vessels on the High Seas* (Hart 2014).
[261] Natalie Klein, *Maritime Security and the Law of the Sea* (OUP 2011).
[262] Deirdre Fitzpatrick and Michael Anderson (eds), *Seafarers' Rights* (OUP 2005).
[263] The same can be said of much scholarly works dealing with people at sea. While these books provide useful information and points of view, they only examine general issues occasionally. This often leads to a sectoral or fragmented analysis that is often too linked to the specificities of the topic under review and, at the same time, may not sufficiently take into account lessons learned from other fields and/or may not be transposed to other contexts.

to be ratified by States to become binding on them, makes rules applicable only for some States, and therefore only some people. If this uneven ratification is combined with the existence of different flags and the possibility for ships to reflag to avoid stricter measures, it becomes evident that the apparent lack of customary rules or generally accepted standards exacerbates the uneven protection of people at sea. Applicable standards mostly rest on the regulatory framework and the willingness of the single flag State to apply it and, to a limited extent, on the geographical area where the vessel operates. The same person, for example a passenger of a ferry or a rating on a commercial vessel, may be afforded different levels of protection while engaged in exactly the same activity, just because he or she happens to travel under one flag rather than another.

There is an additional way in which legislative techniques affect the addressees of relevant treaties, creating mismatches and, sometimes, confusion. While in most cases relevant instruments set out duties for States, it is not always clear who owns the equivalent right—if there is such an equivalent right. Is it other States? Is it the vessel and its owner? Or is it the people benefiting from the treatment prescribed by the treaty? Rights and duties are not always well coordinated, resulting in issues about standing and options for redress. In the case of the MLC, for example, it is questionable whether the protection granted by it, and even the rights expressly mentioned in it, can be claimed directly by the seafarers. The latter's only option is to use the enforcement mechanisms provided by the MLC itself, for example the on-board complaint procedure. What, however, if there is no on-board complaint procedure, or if the seafarer who lodges a complaint is not treated fairly as a result of their complaint? The same is true for safeguard clauses contained in law enforcement treaties. For example, while it is clear that Article 2*bis* of the SUA Convention reiterates the duties of States under human rights law, refugee law, and humanitarian law, it is open to argument whether this provision attributes rights *directly* to individuals, and whether these rights can be actioned domestically or internationally.

Third, in order to define their particular scope, treaties often make use of a variety of terms. This multiplicity causes a lack of uniformity and generates various issues: the absence of definitions for terms used to describe categories of people who share some common characteristics; multiple and possibly conflicting definitions of the same term; and different terms employed to identify the same category of persons.

In some cases, the people affected may be identified by terms that are not always defined in the treaty itself, as in the case of the term 'migrant', which is often used but never defined. The Migrant Workers Convention thus defines who a migrant worker and a (migrant) seafarer are, but the definition clearly does not include other migrants. The Migrant Smuggling Protocol defines what the smuggling of migrants is, thereby providing a definition that might be used to define who a migrant or an irregular migrant is. The Refugee Convention and Protocol define refugees, thus possibly contributing to the limitations of the term migrant, if the latter is to be interpreted as excluding refugees and asylum seekers. There is no rule however that indicates how these definitions relate to each other and there is no common or uniform definition of the term 'migrant' itself.

In other cases, the same word may be defined in different ways in different treaties, as in the case of the partly different meanings given to the word 'seafarer' by the MLC and the Migrant Workers Convention. According to the MLC, a seafarer is a person working on board a vessel, but not a fisher. According to the Migrant Workers Convention, a seafarer is a person working on a vessel that has a different nationality to that of the vessel, including fishers. Thus the MLC definition is, at the same time, both broader and narrower than the one contained within the Migrant Workers Convention. What does this tell us about the use of the term in other instruments, such as the Agreement on Refugee Seamen, where it is not defined? Are fishers to be included in the definition of seafarer, unless expressly excluded? Is the condition of being a migrant relevant beyond the Migrant Workers Convention?

In yet other cases, different treaties may designate the same category (or similar categories) of people with different words. The case of people working on board vessels exemplifies this problem.[264] Treaties usually refer to the 'crew' and, when appropriate, to the rank of the person. The UNCLOS generally refers to the 'master and crew' of vessels.[265] The SOLAS refers to 'the master and the members of the crew or other persons employed or engaged in any capacity on board a ship on the business of that ship'.[266] The Convention on Facilitation of International Maritime Traffic defines a crew member as '[a]ny person actually employed for duties on board during a voyage in the working or service of a ship and included in the crew list'.[267] However, recent treaties sometimes refer to 'seafarers' without defining this term, as in the case of the STCW.[268] The Paris MOU refers both to 'crew' and 'seafarers',[269] without defining either term. While early labour treaties referred to 'seamen', later instruments changed to the gender-neutral term 'seafarer'.[270] However, the use of a common term has not always been consistent, as definitions of these terms do not always coincide.[271]

It is hard to determine what the relationship between all these terms is. Are they synonyms, or does the more general term incorporate the more specific ones? It could be argued that the term 'seafarers' as defined in the MLC includes all other

---

[264] McConnell, Devlin, and Doumbia-Henry (n 93) 178.

[265] For example Art 94 UNCLOS.

[266] Reg 2(e)(i) SOLAS.

[267] Section 1, A FAL.

[268] The Convention however provides a series of definitions of categories of seafarers, such as 'master', 'officer', and 'rating'. See Reg I/1 STCW.

[269] Compare, eg, Section 3.6 and Section 1 of Annex 1 Paris MOU.

[270] For examples of the first see early ILO treaties, such as the Convention for Establishing Facilities for Finding Employment for Seamen, of 10 July 1920, now superseded by the MLC. 'Seamen' was used also by other contemporary treaties, eg the International Convention for the Safety of Life at Sea (20 January 1914). For a more recent use of the term see the Agreement Relating to Refugee Seamen.

[271] ILO, Sub-Group of the High-Level Tripartite Working Group on Maritime Labour Standards (first meeting), 'Duplicative or Contradictory Text in the Existing Maritime Instruments' Doc no STWGMLS/2002/4, 2.

terms. It has already been mentioned that people working on board a vessel may be engaged not only in navigating that particular vessel, but in many other activities. According to Article II(1)(f) of the MLC *'seafarer* means any person who is employed or engaged or works in any capacity on board a ship' to which the Convention applies. This drafting has provided inclusivity by using a very broad definition, independently from the contractual arrangement (eg self-employed) or the type of duties (eg non-maritime). The result is that no group of workers can be automatically excluded from the scope of the MLC,[272] although the MLC, which differentiates between the definition of a seafarer and the scope of the treaty,[273] contains some exceptions, notably fishers.

Fourth, treaties do not always contain the same rules, or provide the same protection. When comparing, for example, the protection granted to seafarers by the MLC and that granted to fishers by the Work in Fishing Convention, it is evident that the former is more comprehensive, more detailed and, overall, better. Similarly, the different formulations of safeguard clauses inserted in treaties concerning law enforcement against unlawful activities at sea may make it easier or more difficult to assert any violation of those standards. While the SUA Convention expressly safeguards the rights of individuals under 'international human rights, refugee and humanitarian law'[274] the FSA does not contain any reference to human rights or refugee law. Can this be construed to mean that when a State arrests a person under the FSA, then that State may return the person to a State where the person could be persecuted?

Turning now to the deficiencies of the legal framework, these also emerge from the description in the preceding sections. First and foremost, not all categories of people are protected by dedicated legal instruments. For example, people working on platforms which cannot be considered as 'vessels' according to the MLC currently enjoy no protection at all at the international level.[275] The same is true for migrants who travel by sea as they do not form the object of protection of any dedicated treaty unless they are migrant workers. This gap is the more problematic as these people may be negatively affected by measures taken under treaties for the suppression of migrant smuggling. Passengers and stowaways also lack dedicated protection. These gaps in the system emerge more clearly if compared with other categories of people who enjoy (at least some) protection, such as seafarers. The result is not only morally and socially unsatisfactory, but also contrary to basic legal principles, such as the equality of individuals.[276]

---

[272] McConnell, Devlin, and Doumbia-Henry (n 93) 180–82.   [273] ibid 176.

[274] Art 2*bis*(1) SUA Convention.

[275] Apparently, the only (non-binding) instrument that applies to offshore workers is a 1981 ILO code of practice, ILO, *Safety and Health in the Construction of Fixed Offshore Installations in the Petroleum Industry* (International Labour Office 1981).

[276] See Universal Declaration of Human Rights, Preamble, para 1: 'recognition of the inherent dignity and of the equal and inalienable rights of all members of the human family is the foundation of freedom, justice and peace in the world'.

Additionally, there is some incoherence due to the absence of rules and principles concerning the interrelation between different legal instruments and rules. How are rules coming from different legal instruments to be addressed and coordinated? Where is this answer to be found? Should legal characterization provide the answer? For example, there are people belonging to more than one category, such as a seafarer who works on a vessel engaged in drug smuggling: which instruments apply to him or her? How are the rights and duties under those instruments to be coordinated?

The conclusions reached here may appear disheartening. Any effort to determine what international law provides for people at sea, which takes into account only existing treaties specifically targeting these people, leads to an unsatisfactory result since the outcome is only a partial and uneven protection. Consequently, current efforts to address the specific challenges faced by people at sea are not entirely effective, since legal analysis is based upon the identification of a discreet field, often in conjunction with a discreet forum, within which the specific problem is addressed. This approach results in piecemeal solutions that do not devote sufficient attention to the human nature of all people who are at sea and provide different levels of protection, often producing unjustified disparity in treatment.

In this context, it is proposed that we should look at people at sea in a different way. This different outlook rests on two premises. Firstly, people at sea should, in principle, be viewed and treated as a single group, and any special rules for a distinct category, be it seafarers, fishers, or pirates, should be carved out as exceptions to the general rule, rather than as self-standing rules themselves. Secondly, we should explore the entirety of international law, and not solely the law that was designed specifically with a view to protect people at sea.[277] This new outlook does not propose to replace the existing one, but rather to operate alongside and to complement it. In fact, the existing normative development is not in itself wrong, but it is insufficient to effectively protect people and it should be supported by a general normative framework within which more specific normative responses can be contextualized. This is the only way to address in a consistent and comprehensive way the questions concerning the relationship between different legal instruments or lack thereof.

It is therefore suggested that there is a need to conceptualize the law that applies to people at sea, going beyond specific treaties and categories of persons. This can be achieved by adopting a functional, human-centered perspective, which would allow us to detach legal rules from their instruments of origin and categorize them according to the objective to be pursued, in this case the protection of people at sea. This approach consists in identifying a distinct group of legal rules, including both the specific rules detailed in this chapter *and* any other rule and instrument deriving from multiple legal fields which, while not necessarily adopted with people at sea in mind, can nonetheless apply to this conceptual category due to its scope *ratione materiae, loci,* or other linking factor.

---

[277] Reference to other fields of international law, such as human rights and refugee law, in law of the sea instruments serves indeed this purpose, as will be discussed in Chapter 2.

In some respects, this is not only an issue for persons at sea, but for persons everywhere. International law is undergoing developments that could lead to qualitative changes which may affect the place of the individual within the system.[278] The legal analysis that will be carried out in this book, therefore, aims to establish a dialectic relationship with the more general debate, drawing from it but also contributing to its deployment and development by providing examples illustrating the changing place of the individual at sea.

---

[278] Kate Parlett, *The Individual in the International Legal System. Continuity and Change in International Law* (CUP 2010); Anne Peters, *Beyond Human Rights. The Legal Status of the Individual in International Law* (CUP 2016).

2

Protection by the System and Its Regimes

1. Introduction

The previous chapter has provided cogent evidence that people at sea may be negatively affected by many situations. It has been suggested that these situations need to be addressed by legal rules, so as to clarify States' duties and ensure adequate protection of these people. It has also been shown that so far, legal rules drafted for this purpose fall under two broad categories: specialized treaty regimes addressing specific categories of people, such as those relating to seafarers and fishers, and dedicated groups of norms, such as generic safeguard clauses concerning human rights. Finally, it has been argued that these treaties and rules provide only a highly fragmented system of regulation and one which may yield incongruous results. Therefore, they do not provide a satisfactory response to the need to protect people at sea.

These initial findings do not however terminate the study of how international law protects people at sea. This book promotes a different approach, expounding the relevance of systemic thinking in the reconstruction of the law that applies to new issues. Pursuant to this approach, attention will now turn to the system of which treaties are just one element to consider, in order to establish whether international law and its regimes contain other principles and rules that—while not drafted having people at sea in mind—may serve the purpose of protecting them.

This chapter provides the conceptual grounding for the reconstruction of the law that applies to persons at sea. The chapter first presents the analytical framework within which to examine the relationships between different rules that apply to people at sea, analysing the conceptual potential of thinking in terms of regimes and in terms of the system. The selection of these rules and their joint consideration rests upon some basic understandings concerning the nature of international law, the relationship between the system and its components, and the practical difficulties posed by the mental habit of 'regime thinking'. This framework is then applied to the specific topic under consideration (the regulation of the subject matter 'people at sea'). The chapter thus turns to the distinct regimes of international law that contribute rules and analyses their individual contribution. Eventually, the chapter considers the contribution of the various regimes collectively, within a systemic understanding of international law.

International Law and the Protection of People at Sea. Irini Papanicolopulu. © Irini Papanicolopulu, 2018. Published 2018 by Oxford University Press.

2. International Law as a Complete Legal System

The fragmentation debate that dominated international legal discourse at the turn of the twentieth century and divided scholars and practitioners alike, eventually led to upholding the systemic nature of international law against Hartian submissions to the contrary.[1] And while arguments concerning self-contained regimes were still being opposed by those advocating the unity of international law,[2] the debate started moving from opposition to interaction and from conflict to the composition of the conflict. The categorical statement of the International Law Commission (ILC) that 'international law is a legal system', by authoritatively settling the main issue, allowed the discussion to move on and to focus on the consequences of the systemic nature of international law.[3]

Attention was thus polarized by the specific components of the international legal system, drifting from the universe to the planets, in the evocative language of Simma and Pulkowski.[4] Although being one single legal system, international law was recognized as comprising many sub-systems (which eventually might comprise sub-sub-systems, and so on), the existence of which had prompted the debate on fragmentation in the first place.[5] Human rights law, United Nations (UN) law,

---

[1] Compare Hart's comment that 'the rules that are in fact operative constitute not a system but a set of rules' (HLA Hart, *The Concept of Law* (2nd edn, OUP 1997) 236) with Higgins' forceful assertion that '[i]nternational law is not rules. It is a normative system' (Rosalyn Higgins, 'International Law and the Avoidance, Containment and Resolution of Disputes: General Course on Public International Law' (1991) 230 Recueil des cours de l'Académie de Droit International 9, 23).

[2] See amongst many others, Georges Abi-Saab, 'Cours Général de Droit International Public' (1987) 207 Recueil des Cours 9; Pierre-Marie Dupuy, 'L'unité de l'Ordre Juridique International: Cours Général de Droit International Public' (2000) 297 Recueil des Cours 9; Christian Tomuschat, 'International Law as a Coherent System: Unity or Fragmentation?' in Mahnoush Arsanjani (ed), *Looking to the Future: Essays on International Law in Honor of W. Michael Reisman* (Martinus Nijhoff 2011) 323, 334.

[3] ILC, 'Conclusions of the Work of the Study Group on the Fragmentation of International Law: Difficulties Arising from the Diversification and Expansion of International Law' <http://legal.un.org/docs/?path=../ilc/texts/instruments/english/draft_articles/1_9_2006.pdf&lang=EF> accessed 16 August 2017 (ILC Conclusions) para 1. The statement that international law is a system should not however be taken to mean more than it says. Among other issues, it does not clarify whether the system is horizontal or vertical and which actors participate in its making. Furthermore, it certainly does not pre-empt any discussion concerning its formal coherence, as Koskenniemi and Leino have warned us (Martti Koskenniemi and Paivi Leino, 'Fragmentation of International Law? Postmodern Anxieties' 15 Leiden Journal of International Law 553, 558–59).

[4] Bruno Simma and Dirk Pulkowski, 'Of Planets and the Universe: Self-contained Regimes in International Law' (2006) 17 EJIL 483.

[5] Fears concerning the fragmentation of international law were initially prompted by the entry into force of legal instruments that contained well-developed sets of legal rules regulating a certain area and that created institutional mechanisms and judicial or quasi-judicial bodies backing the application of these rules, such as the Statute of the International Criminal Tribunal for the former Yugoslavia (ICTY). The entry into force of the UNCLOS towards the end of 1994 led to the setting up of the ITLOS and the other institutions of the law of the sea. The Uruguay round of negotiations led to the adoption of the Marrakesh agreements in the same year and to the almost immediate operation of the WTO dispute settlement mechanism. Eventually, the adoption of the Rome Statute in 1998 paved the way for the first permanent international criminal tribunal, the International Criminal Court. On the dangers for the unity of international law that the creation of all these regimes and tribunals would produce, see Address of Judge Gilbert Guillaume, President of the International Court of Justice, to the United Nations General Assembly (26 October 2000) <http://www.icj-cij.org/files/press-releases/

international economic law, and the law of the sea are just some examples. While each of these sub-systems may contain its own principles and procedures, all eventually partake of and can be subsumed within the general system of international law.[6]

In the current stage of development of international law, sub-systems comprise the majority of international legal rules but they do not exhaust the content of international law. There still remain a number of overarching rules concerning subjects, sources, and responsibility. Although the applicability of these rules can be modified between certain parties, they are nonetheless generally applicable (unless they are disposed with) and form the rules to which sub-systems can fall back when they are not able to regulate specific issues from within.[7] In order to distinguish the two, I will refer to this set of rules as 'general international law'[8] and will use the term 'regime' to designate the substantial sub-systems among which all other rules are divided.[9]

What went mostly unnoticed is that international law is not only a system, but it is a 'complete' system.[10] In Lowe's words, '[w]hen the elements of a legal system can be combined to build up a normative structure adequate for the needs of the society to which it applies, we may think of the legal system as being complete'.[11] Completeness does not exclude further development but has a significant bearing on

---

9/2999.pdf> accessed 16 August 2017. For a doctrinal perspective see Andreas Fischer-Lescano and Gunther Teubner, 'Regime-Collisions: The Vain Search for Legal Unity in the Fragmentation of Global Law' (2004) 25 Michigan Journal of International Law 999, 1014. Contra Yuval Shany, *The Competing Jurisdictions of International Courts and Tribunals* (OUP 2003).

[6] Entirely self-contained regimes do not exist in international law; ILC, 'Fragmentation of International Law: Difficulties Arising from the Diversification and Expansion of International Law. Report of the Study Group of the International Law Commission Finalized by Martti Koskenniemi' (13 April 2006) UN Doc A/CN.4/L.682 (Koskenniemi Report) para 192; Georges Abi-Saab, 'Fragmentation or Unification: Some Concluding Remarks' (1999) 31 New York University Journal of International Law and Politics 919. See also, in relation to more specific contexts, ILC, 'Fourth Report on State Responsibility, by Mr. Gaetano Arangio-Ruiz, Special Rapporteur' (12 and 25 May and 1 and 17 June 1992) UN Doc A/CN.4/444, para 112; WTO, 'United States: Standards for Reformulated and Conventional Gasoline—Report of the Appellate Body' (29 April 1996) WT/DS2/AB/RO 17; Lucius Conrad Caflisch and Antônio A Cançado Trindade, 'Les Conventions américaine et européenne des droits de l'homme et le droit international général' (2004) 108 Revue Générale de Droit International Public 5, 60.

[7] It is often argued that some substantial principles also form part of the 'general international law' that applies to all sub-systems. Examples include the prohibition of the use of force, the prohibition of genocide, or the obligation to respect fundamental human rights. These principles are often referred to as constituting part of *erga omnes* obligations (*Barcelona Traction, Light and Power Company, Limited (Belgium v Spain)* (Judgment) [1970] ICJ Rep 3, paras 33–34; *East Timor (Portugal v Australia)* (Judgment) [1995] ICJ Rep 90, para 29) or *jus cogens* (*Armed Activities on the Territory of the Congo (New Application: 2002) (Democratic Republic of the Congo v Rwanda)* (Judgment) [2006] ICJ Rep 6, para 64). Without addressing this issue here, it is worth noting the qualitative difference between norms that simply apply in all areas of international law, when parties have not provided special rules, and norms that *must* apply to all areas of international law, even in opposition to the agreed rules.

[8] *Pulp Mills on the River Uruguay (Argentina v Uruguay)* (Judgment) [2010] ICJ Rep 14, para 66.

[9] See Introduction, Section 4.

[10] The completeness of the system was already argued by Lauterpacht in 1933. See Hersch Lauterpacht, *The Function of Law in the International Community* (OUP 2011) 59.

[11] Vaughan Lowe, 'The Politics of Law-Making: Are the Method and Character of Norm Creation Changing?' in Michael Byers (ed), *The Role of Law in International Politics: Essays in International Relations and International Law* (OUP 2001) 207.

legal processes, in particular norm-creating: norms are derived from *within* the system and are not imposed or imported from outside. The complete system is autopoietic[12] and therefore able to create norms and obligations by itself, without reference to external sources, so as to fill the material gaps that will be detected as new concerns emerge and the sensibility of the international community ripens.[13]

The systemic nature of international law and its completeness make it possible to identify the norms that apply to new, uncategorized issues. In a complete legal system, conceptualizing normative responses to new concerns might be compared to synthesizing new compounds out of pre-existing substances. Legal rules are the 'substances' that can be mixed differently, according to the result that needs to be arrived at. The ingredients are existing legal norms (and, to a certain extent, legal instruments). These 'ingredients' need not all derive from the same category but may belong to different categories (the regimes of provenience). While it will usually be the case that mixtures will consist of 'ingredients' from the same category, it may also occur that ingredients belonging to different categories are mixed. This similitude cannot, however, be carried to the extremes, as the possibility to create new elements is arguably broader in law, rather than it is in chemistry. All the same, I think it provides a good analogy to the process of selecting and bringing together existing rules, instruments, and principles to address new issues and new concerns, which will be further discussed in Chapter 5.

3. The Conceptual Limitations of Thinking in Terms of Regimes

There is however a practical impediment to the synthesis of new sets of rules: the widespread and deeply embedded, though not always self-conscious, habit of thinking in terms of regimes.

Conceptual thinking in terms of regimes is today inherent in international law discourse.[14] The entire debate on fragmentation of international law could not

---

[12] 'An autopoietic system produces and reproduces its own elements by the interaction of its elements. According to *Niklas Luhmann*, the main representative of social autopoiesis, the decisive innovation in comparison to older theories of self-organization is that certain systems are capable not only of creating an autonomous order but of creating their own elements as well' Gunther Teubner, 'Introduction to Autopoietic Law' in Gunther Teubner (ed), *Autopoietic Law: A New Approach to Law and Society* (De Gruyter 1988) 1, 3.

[13] To equate the formal completeness of the system with its material completeness might indeed be 'an expression of intellectual inertia or of short-sightedness' since '[i]t is the idea that there do exist gaps in law—material gaps in the teleological sense as judged from the point of view of the general purpose of the law, and as distinguished from formal gaps identical with a break in the continuity of the legal order—it is this idea which has throughout the ages been a powerful and indispensable factor in the development of law, in enacting remedial legislation, in the daring application of general principles to altogether new facts of social development, in ingenious but indispensable "distinguishing" of cases, in creating fruitful frictions.' Lauterpacht (n 10) 94–95. Nor should the autopoietic nature of international law be interpreted as a closure of the system to external influences: '[t]he more the legal system gains in operational closure and autonomy, the more it gains in openness towards social facts, political demands, social science theories, and human needs' Teubner, 'Autopoietic Law' (n 12) 2.

[14] Regime thinking is transversal and informs different legal traditions, starting from textbooks which address discrete regimes such as human rights, the law of the sea, environmental law, and international criminal law; see James Crawford, *Brownlie's Principles of Public International Law* (8th edn,

have developed if it were not for international lawyers' instinctive division of international law into multiple regimes and the perception that these regimes were developing independently.[15] Whilst there is much room for discussion as to the nature of regimes generally speaking, and over the content of specific ones, not to mention terminological debates concerning the most appropriate term to designate distinct groups of rules, there is no serious contesting of the existence of specific regimes within international law. The concept of 'regime' is indeed particularly helpful for legal scholars and practitioners in addressing everyday issues. However, it presents some significant limitations when it comes to addressing new issues or issues that straddle across more than one well-established regime.

Regimes are helpful in that they set boundaries to legal thinking, making it easier to identify relevant rules and principles, instruments, and mechanisms. For example, if an issue is considered as falling within human rights law, then the normative answer is to be found in one among the limited range of human rights instruments, without there being the need to peruse every treaty adopted by the parties concerned. If these instruments do not provide any answer, or if the answer is not adequate in the light of the present societal concerns, then it will be for one of the human rights bodies to reconcile the situation by further development or change. Furthermore, if the individual affected has the fortune to be subject to the jurisdiction of a European or American State, they may have the option of initiating a case before one of the two regional human rights courts that hear complaints against contracting States in that respective region.

Regimes therefore save time and provide a relative degree of certainty as to the applicable rules and competent institutions. At the same time, the nature of regimes goes beyond a simple taxonomy of rules and institutions and includes a thinking habit, often endorsed in the principles of the regime. It is therefore the case that human rights lawyers will usually consider that the individual takes precedence, even when they address issues relating to other fields, such as investment law or the law of international organizations.[16]

Legal regimes, however, may end up imposing excessive constraints on legal thinking.[17] Creating automation, they establish gnoseological, albeit not legal, barriers

OUP 2012). One may indeed argue that regimes have always formed part of law, fulfilling cognitive, as well as didactic and taxonomic necessities. According to Pomponius, it was Quintus Mucius Scaevola who first divided law into branches: 'Quintus Mucius Publii filius pontifex maximus ius civile primus constituit generatim in libros decem et octo redigendo' (Digest 1.2.2.41).

[15] See the initial debate within the ILC Study Group on the fragmentation of international law, as summarized in ILC, 'Report of the International Law Commission—Fifty-fourth session' (29 April–7 June and 22 July–16 August 2002) UN Doc A/57/10, paras 497–98. Fragmentation however may also emerge within a single regime, due to the uneven ratification of a treaty and uncertainty as to the existence and the content of customary international law; see Wilfred C Jenks, 'The Conflict of Law-Making Treaties' (1953) 30 British Yearbook of International Law 403; Maurice H Mendelson, 'Fragmentation of the Law of the Sea' (1988) 12 Marine Policy 192.

[16] This is not necessarily wrong. However, there is the actual risk of this being argued axiomatically, rather than in the light of existing principles and rules.

[17] See the comments made by Richard Barnes, 'The International Law of the Sea and Migration Control' in Bernard Ryan and Valsamis Mitsilegas (eds), *Extraterritorial Immigration Control: Legal Challenges* (Martinus Nijhoff 2010) 103, 105–06, who points out that 'there is a tendency for people to

which may inadvertently limit recourse to rules and principles outside the strict limits of the 'regime'.[18] And while systemic conceptions may still allow for a reference to general international law,[19] they are often applied in a forward-and-backwards way between general international law and the specific regime, rather than encouraging a broader overview that explores laterally, beyond the limits of one regime into contiguous regimes. This one-way relationship is not mandated by logic or by law but is rather the product of mental habit. The systemic nature of international law, in fact, prevents regimes from developing into self-contained sets of rules and does not preclude 'lateral' interaction. Moreover, there is no logical obstacle to imagining lateral interactions between two or more specialized regimes. Nonetheless, it happens often in practice that lawyers familiar with one regime will not stray away from it to consider unfamiliar ones. When faced with an issue at the intersection of two regimes, the easy way out is to decide which regime will prevail and will therefore regulate the issue at hand.[20]

This limit becomes evident when one turns to people at sea. Empirical knowledge confirms that individuals at sea often suffer violations of their rights, as discussed in Chapter 1. Juridical cognizance reveals that there are a variety of legal rules—both procedural and substantive—which, in combination, provide for the safeguarding of human rights. Nevertheless, given the fact that the structure of legal competences and the scope of the rights and duties of States is different at sea, and that the physical circumstances at sea put people into situations that do not always sit comfortably within the paradigms that the drafters of human rights treaties envisaged, the law may apply incompletely or inefficiently or even incorrectly at sea.

A similar mind frame is sometimes exploited by States in an effort to avoid the legal consequences of their policies. In cases concerning the interception and return of boats carrying asylum seekers, States have often turned to a specific regime as being *the* appropriate one to deal with the issue, implying, sometimes rather openly, that other regimes do not have any role to play. In the *Haitian refugees* case, the US line of argument considered the interception of boats on the high seas as falling

be educated in specialist fields. There is thus a risk that they will lack an appreciation of the norms, values and structures that shape other areas of law' (ibid 105).

[18] Jenks' argument to consider the 'international statute book as a whole' is still valid today: 'it is important that there should develop in international and regional organizations and among Governments, and on the part of all who, in political, legal or technical capacities, are called upon to contribute to the formulation of law-making treaties, a habit of regarding the international statute book as a whole and attempting to judge of the value, proper scope, and detailed content of any proposed instrument not in isolation but in relation to the complex of law-making treaties on a wide range of intricately interrelated subjects of which it will form a part' (Jenks (n 15) 430).

[19] The so-called 'fall-back' on general international law.

[20] Oxman remarks: ' "Fields" appear to develop in isolation from each other. In law, this can produce an interesting dynamic when events force an intersection of fields dominated by separate guilds responsive to different needs, traditions, and policies. The typical response is to view this as a challenge requiring more precise jurisdictional or hierarchical lines between the fields, rather than as an opportunity for learning, adaptation and synthesis.' Bernard H Oxman, 'Human Rights and the United Nations Convention on the Law of the Sea' in Jonathan I Charney and Donald K Anton (eds), *Politics, Values and Functions: International Law in the 21st Century. Essays in Honor of Professor Louis Henkin* (Martinus Nijhoff 1997) 377. See also Koskenniemi Report (n 6) 11.

under the law of the sea rules on visit and exercise of jurisdiction; *ergo*, human rights law did not apply, since the former took precedence in this context.[21] In a similar vein, when faced with charges of human rights violations, Italy tried to describe its operations in the Mediterranean Sea targeting migrants and refugees sailing from Libya as 'salvage', rather than 'interdiction' operations. This denoted an attempt to argue that the legal regime pertaining to salvage operations, considered less cumbersome for the State, took prevalence over that concerning interdiction operations at sea.[22]

Similar attempts may be motivated, at least in part, by observing that international judges often need to examine cases through the lens of the specific regime to which they belong. While it is excessive to claim that '[i]n international law, every tribunal is a self-contained system',[23] it is true that the capacity of each court or tribunal to address certain issues and to apply a certain norm is constrained by the instrument that has created it.[24] Perhaps more surprisingly, these paradigms are apparent not only in the activities of courts and tribunals, but also in the contributions of legal scholars. Treatises on human rights ignore the peculiarities of the marine context, concentrating their analyses on the application of human rights on land[25] and even more specific works dealing with particular aspects of human rights law often do not consider the possibility of applying human rights treaties during activities carried out at sea.[26] For their part, law of the sea texts traditionally do not devote any

---

[21] *The Haitian Centre for Human Rights* et al *v United States* Case 10.675 (Report no 51/96 of 13 March 1997), para 156. It could be surmised that the prevalence might be due to the applicability of the *lex specialis* criterion. The Inter-American Commission on Human Rights did not accept this argument; see ibid para 157.

[22] *Hirsi Jamaa and Others v Italy* App no 27765/09 (Judgment (GC) of 23 February 2012) para. 95: 'In the Government's view, the legal system prevailing on the high seas was characterised by the principle of freedom of navigation. In that context, it was not necessary to identify the parties concerned. The Italian authorities had merely provided the necessary humanitarian assistance. Identity checks of the applicants had been kept to a minimum because no maritime police operation on board the ships had been envisaged'. The ECtHR did not accept this defence (*Hirsi* para 134).

[23] *Prosecutor v Tadic* (Decision on the Defence Motion for Interlocutory Appeal on Jurisdiction) ICTY-94-1 (2 October 1995) para 11.

[24] *The MOX Plant Case (Ireland v United Kingdom)* (Order 24 June 2003) para 19. See also Tullio Treves, 'Fragmentation of International Law: The Judicial Perspective' (2007) 23 Comunicazioni e Studi 821.

[25] To the point that three authoritative scholars have stated that '[h]uman rights are violated within individual states, not in outer space or on the high seas' (Henry J Steiner, Philip Alston and Ryan Goodman, *International Human Rights in Context* (3rd edn, OUP 2007) vi). A similar approach is included in other human rights textbooks, which do not refer to the many problems arising from the application of human rights at sea; eg Sarah Joseph and Adam McBeth, *Research Handbook on International Human Rights Law* (Edward Elgar 2010). A notable exception to this trend is provided by Guy S Goodwin-Gill and Jane McAdam, *The Refugee In International Law* (3rd edn, OUP 2007); the scope of the book however limits their discussion to protection afforded to asylum seekers travelling by sea.

[26] It is indicative that a 2010 collection of essays on the right to life (Christian Tomuschat, Evelyne Lagrange, and Stefan Oeter (eds), *The Right to Life* (Martinus Nijhoff 2010)) does not address at all the protection of life at sea or the positive obligations of States in this context. Similarly, recent publications on the extraterritorial application of human right treaties, including Fons Coomans and Menno T Kamminga (eds), *Extraterritorial Application of Human Rights Treaties* (Intersentia 2004) and Marko Milanovic, *Extraterritorial Application of Human Rights Treaties. Law, Principles, and Policy* (OUP 2011), while providing interesting constructions of extraterritorial jurisdiction, do not discuss in depth the application of human rights treaties at sea and the complexities created by the existence of areas

chapter to the rights of persons at sea, at most mentioning treaty-based regimes for the protection of workers.[27]

When it comes to the scholarly analysis of issues, reconstructing existing law on the basis of the rules that a judge would apply to a certain dispute often yields only a partial result, since the principle of consent requires that judges decide cases only if both parties have agreed to their jurisdiction, keeping within the boundaries set by the agreement. Due to jurisdictional constraints, judges will usually be faced with only one aspect of what in reality is a complex situation. The definition of a dispute itself, adopted by the Permanent Court of International Justice (PCIJ), focuses on '*a*' disagreement rather than multiple disagreements[28] and a basic skill of lawyers is to transform the blurred situations presented to them by clients into distinct legal disputes, to be submitted to the appropriate judge.[29] However, law is not only the means for upholding rights and redressing wrongs in court, but should also be a guide for action in everyday life.[30] Scholars in particular, who encounter neither the legal constraints faced by judges nor the political constraints that may hinder States, should not unnecessarily constrain their legal research by pigeon-holing new issues into already well-established categories.[31] On the contrary, they should explore with different 'mixtures' of rules, making the most of the systemic nature of international law.

4. From Conflict to Interaction

Action, which led to the unprecedented development of new instruments, procedures, courts, and institutional arrangements during the twentieth century, has caused an involute reaction and the proliferation of ontological and taxonomic studies, which address the new regimes and explore their nature and their place within the system of international law. Following the flourishing of new specialized regimes and the multiplication of instruments, rules, and procedures, international lawyers are now stepping into this luxurious superimposition of new rules like good

within and beyond national jurisdiction, as well as by the exercise of functional jurisdiction according to law of the sea provisions.

[27] Robin R Churchill and AV Lowe, *The Law of the Sea* (3rd edn, Manchester University Press 1999); Yoshifumi Tanaka, *The International Law of the Sea* (2nd edn, CUP 2015); Donald R Rothwell and Tim Stephens, *The International Law of the Sea* (Hart 2010).

[28] 'A dispute is a disagreement on a point of law or fact, a conflict of legal views or of interests between two persons' *Mavrommatis Palestine Concessions (Greece v Great Britain)* [1924] PCIJ Rep Series A No 2, 11.

[29] It is the more surprising to note that, with few exceptions, it is international courts and tribunals that have first combined the two fields; Irini Papanicolopulu, 'International Judges and the Protection of Human Rights at Sea' in Nerina Boschiero et al (eds), *International Courts and the Development of International Law* (Asser Press 2013) 535.

[30] Thus legal advisers have often to consider various fields when asked to assess the legality of their client's proposed activity.

[31] A similar point is made by Jeffrey L Dunoff, 'A New Approach to Regime Interaction' in Margaret A Young (ed), *Regime Interaction in International Law Facing Fragmentation* (CUP 2012) 136, 137–38.

gardeners, trimming the ends and pruning untoward branches, so as to produce a unified and well-ordered orchard.

This interaction of specialized legal regimes of international law is today addressed as a legal phenomenon,[32] as a societal challenge,[33] or as a logical operation.[34] The existence of more than one regime that addresses a particular issue—be it treaty-based or reconstructed through scholarly effort—and the need to produce a coherent and uniform set of rules have been approached in different ways. Scholars who have contributed to the growing body of literature that addresses the relationship between different regimes have mainly adopted one out of three models: the traditional 'conflict of norms' approach, the alternative 'conflict of laws' model, and the more recent 'regime interaction' model.

Firstly, the 'conflict of laws' approach borrows the technique used in domestic systems[35] and advocates its application to international law.[36] According to this approach, the regimes that compose international law should be considered as separate 'laws' and conflict would arise out of the incompatibility of the regimes, rather than of simple norms. Consequently, legal techniques should aim to establish which regime prevails, ruling out the possibility to apply norms belonging to the succumbing regime. Although a 'conflict of laws' approach could limit such conflicts and could produce more ordered outcomes, it does not appear appropriate to deal with regime conflict in international law. On the one hand, it is at odds with the systemic nature of international law, forcibly separating its components. On the other, it overlooks a basic difference between international law and domestic law systems. In its traditional application, 'conflict of laws' rules determine conflicts between complete normative systems, each of which consists of a number of sub-systems. Private international law rules determine, for example, the prevalence of Swiss law over Italian law, not the prevalence of environmental law over contract law. They settle conflict between bodies of law which address the same issue, not between bodies of law that address separate (although interlinked) issues. For these reasons, a 'conflict of laws' approach does not appear appropriate to address the relationship between discrete regimes of international law.

The alternative, 'conflict of norms' approach, is based upon the identification of potentially applicable rules of international law and, on the basis of tools provided by international law itself or by legal logic, settles the relationships between the rules either by combining the relevant rules or by operating a choice between them.[37] Traditionally conducted on the horizontal level, recent scholarly works tend

---

[32] When addressed as a legal phaenomenon, regime interaction is usually considered in the terms of conflict of treaties: eg Jenks (n 15); Elena Sciso, *Gli accordi internazionali confliggenti* (Cacucci 1986).

[33] Fischer-Lescano and Teubner (n 5).

[34] Jorge E Viñuales, *Foreign Investment and the Environment in International Law* (CUP 2012).

[35] Adrian Briggs, *The Conflict of Laws* (3rd edn, OUP 2013).

[36] Fischer-Lescano and Teubner (n 5). For a *sui generis* application of rules from conflict of laws see Dirk Pulkowski, *The Law and Politics of International Regime Conflict* (OUP 2014) 334–35, who proposes the use of the comparative impairment test.

[37] ILC Conclusions (n 3) paras 7–8. Joost Pauwelyn, *Conflict of Norms in Public International Law: How WTO Law Relates to Other Rules of International Law* (CUP 2003); Sciso (n 32). The need to compose normative conflicts so as to ensure the compatibility of treaty obligations is embedded in law. In 1932, Rousseau remarked that 'Parmi les problèmes juridiques qui se posent aujourd'hui avec

to explore ways of managing the relationship between rules through a hierarchical approach, which is seen both as a tool to achieve order and as an instrument to avoid unrestrained developments that do not 'fit into' the current social and normative imperatives.[38] Whilst means for addressing horizontal conflicts are well established in international law, such as the doctrines of *lex posterior* and *lex specialis*, the discourse concerning vertical interactions in international law is relatively recent and not well established. By way of example, *jus cogens* norms, obligations *erga omnes*, and Article 103 UN Charter are often identified as hierarchically superior norms.[39] Although treaties, various courts, and a significant portion of scholars have endorsed the concept of *jus cogens*, its content is still the object of debate. In any case, some fundamental human rights, such as the right to life, physical integrity, the freedom from slavery, and the prohibition of torture are generally considered as norms that bind all States and which cannot be derogated from. This type of approach does not necessarily envisage integrational strategies, since the hierarchically higher norm will constrain the applicability and content or even trump the lower, without the need to harmonize their content. In other cases, scholars have focused on minimizing conflict though harmonization of existing norms and the elaboration of tools that balance rules providing stable outcomes, thus advancing the predictability of international law.[40] Following the ILC approach to exclude institutional aspects from its consideration, this exercise is usually conducted within the notional boundaries set by the adjudication of international disputes.[41]

The two approaches discussed above are similar in their interest in conflicts, be they of norms or regimes, and repose on regime thinking. The third approach is concerned with 'regime interaction', and adopts a broader outlook by suggesting options to overcome the strict fences posed *de facto* by regime thinking, and to develop an interconnected system.[42] Despite all its different facets, regime interaction generally adopts a law-making perspective by expanding its field of research

---

le plus d'acuité, il n'en est peut-être pas de plus actuel que celui de la compatibilité des traités'; Charles Rousseau, 'De la compatibilité des normes juridiques contradictoires dans l'ordre international' (1932) Revue Général de Droit International Public 133, 133.

[38] The discourse on constitutionalization is, to a large extent, interested in these issues. Hierarchical hypotheses usually revolve around the primacy to be attributed to human rights (Erika De Wet and Jure Vidmar, *Hierarchy in International Law. The Place of Human Rights* (OUP 2012)) or to a few other rules that are usually referred to as exemplifying norms of *jus cogens* (Jan Klabbers, 'Setting the Scene' in Jan Klabbers, Anne Peters, and Geir Ulfstein (eds), *The Constitutionalization of International Law* (OUP 2009) 1). Peters argues for a 'international (constitutional) community' that will attribute primary importance to the individual, as the main actor: Anne Peters, 'Membership in the Global Constitutional Community' in Jan Klabbers, Anne Peters, and Geir Ulfstein (eds), *The Constitutionalization of International Law* (OUP 2009) 153, 261. cf Jonathan I Charney, 'The Implications of Expanding International Dispute Settlement Systems: The 1982 Convention on the Law of the Sea' (1996) 90 AJIL 69, 74: 'Hierarchy and coherence are laudable goals for any legal system, including international law, but at the moment they are impossible goals'.

[39] Koskenniemi Report (n 6) section E. Art 103 UN Charter will not be addressed here, as its examination goes beyond the scope of this study.

[40] ILC 'Conclusions' (n 3).

[41] Koskenniemi Report (n 6) 13. Pauwelyn, *Conflict of Norms* (n 37) 7.

[42] Margaret A Young, *Trading Fish, Saving Fish. The Interaction between Regimes in International Law* (CUP 2011) 13.

and by looking at techniques to overcome potential normative conflicts through the lens of inter-institutional cooperation and the participation of actors other than States in the process of making and applying the law.[43] This approach is oriented towards a continuous dialogue between regimes and rules (as well as the institutions that produce them and the actors that activate such institutions) in an effort to smooth over inconsistencies and find ways of upholding all interests involved, without necessarily prioritizing them. Regime interaction builds on the horizontal nature of international law and appears to account more for the practicalities of making international law, as opposed to merely adjudicating international law.

The 'conflict of norms' and 'regime interaction' approaches are not mutually exclusive but may rather be considered as addressing different dimensions of the challenge of regime interaction.[44] By focusing on different aspects, both approaches contribute elements to the solution of conflicts between international law regimes. At this stage, it is proposed that these two approaches can be combined within systemic thinking, so as to overcome the limitations posed by regime thinking.

5. Systemic Thinking as an Agent for Synthesis

As alluded to above, the shortcomings of regime thinking are especially exposed when it comes to identifying rules that apply to a new topic, in particular when this topic does not form the object of a dedicated treaty. In its strictest application, regime thinking might advocate the lack of any regulation altogether, since the topic under consideration does not provide the 'label' for any regime. Thus, since there is no treaty dedicated to 'people at sea', these people are not protected by law. One positive consequence of this negative conclusion might be the urge to regulate the topic, so as to remedy the lack of binding norms. In the meantime, however, and until dedicated regulation is adopted, a strict application of regime thinking would result in the clear lack of protection.

The absurdity of a similar conclusion has led to a broader understanding, which would allow for the application of the regime that more closely resembles the topic. Thus, people at sea who are also seafarers are protected by the Maritime Labour Convention (MLC) and other treaties that are addressed at this category. However, even with this looser application, regime thinking would still yield an unsuitable result. Even if it were to allow for the applicability of that single regime, it would

---

[43] James Harrison, *Making the Law of the Sea* (CUP 2011); Young, *Trading Fish* (n 42); Patricia Mallia, *Migrant Smuggling by Sea. Combating a Current Threat to Maritime Security through the Creation of a Cooperative Framework* (Martinus Nijhoff 2010); Pulkowski, *The Law* (n 36). Viñuales pushes such an approach further by distinguishing between normative conflicts (that involve two norms of international law) and legitimacy conflicts (which encompass conflicts between international law and domestic law); Viñuales (n 34) 28–29.

[44] Pulkowski, *The Law* (n 36) distinguishes between cases in which the management of conflicts can be pursued through legal interpretation (ibid 273) and cases in which the conflict of rules under different regimes needs to be settled by giving priority to one of the conflicting rules (ibid 318–19). For Pauwelyn, *Conflict of Norms* (n 37) 178, only conflicts of norms which cannot be 'interpreted away' are genuine conflicts.

still exclude other potentially applicable regimes which would result in a limited normativity. For example, if the 'people' aspect of the issue was to be considered as the relevant link to a regime, this would result in the application of human rights, to the exclusion of other legal regimes, such as law of the sea. Where human rights law did not provide any rights or remedies, people at sea would again not be subject to the protection of law.

Acting as an agent, systemic thinking addresses these drawbacks. It allows us to synthesize and apply normative replies to new issues that are more complete and articulated, and which better reflect both the richness of existing law and the peculiarities of societal interests underlying the new issue. This conclusion, of course, should not be read to deny the fact that, in some instances, even systemic thinking cannot yield results and it is necessary to admit a lack of regulation—which should be addressed through the adoption of new norms. This conclusion only means that those instances where a lack of regulation has to be admitted will be much reduced.

Systemic thinking can be described as a two-step process of identifying the applicable law, which requires us first to 'enter' into each legal regime that provides rules relevant for the issue under consideration, and then 'leave' these regimes and return to the system, so as to reconstruct a picture of regulation which is as complete as possible. In its application, systemic thinking therefore does not preclude the use of regime thinking, but considers the latter as only one part of a composite conceptual exercise, since regime thinking can be especially useful when you enter it but then leave it.

Furthermore, systemic thinking borrows elements from all three models illustrated in the previous section: 'conflict of laws', 'conflict of norms', and 'regime interaction'. From conflict of laws, it borrows the technique of legal characterization. This technique is however applied not only to identify the 'law' that regulates a certain issue, but also to single out the specific norms that can be used to regulate this issue. Conflicts of norms techniques are used to settle apparent and real conflicts between the norms thus identified. Finally, regime interaction is applied to the selected norms, so as to recognize the linkages between them and draw conclusions on the nature of the group of rules (as opposed to the single rules).

Going further, the first step consists in identifying the separate legal regimes that provide rules applicable to the issue under consideration and in assessing the respective contribution of each. Thinking in terms of regimes allows us to focus on intra-systemic issues and to elaborate in greater detail the solutions that are provided by specific regimes. While useful as a starting point, regime thinking eventually needs to be overcome lest it hinders a holistic approach to legal regulation. Once regime thinking has achieved its functions, it must be relinquished in favour of systemic thinking, which alone permits us to explore synergies and to make the most of the complete and autopoietic nature of international law. The second step contextualizes these preliminary findings within the system of international law, in order to identify conflicts and gaps but also to maximize interactions and linkages. As a result, systemic thinking may produce the identification of rules and principles that go beyond the ones originally identified by the creators of the specific regimes.

The systemic nature of international law and its completeness has a number of consequences when it comes to identifying the applicable law addressing new, uncategorized issues. First, a systemic conception of international law affects the determination of the applicable law, meaning that there is no preclusion to using rules deriving from any specialized regime, as long as these regimes are part of the system. Second, it mandates the use of the principle of systemic integration, which facilitates the migration of principles, concepts, and rules from one field to another. Third, it also mandates the application of the principle of harmonization, which encourages harmonious interaction and minimizes conflicts. Fourth, it informs the application of rules concerning the relationship between norms and mandates that conflicts be resolved on the basis of conflict-of-norms rules, allowing us to determine the hierarchical and other relationships that may exist between single norms, rather than as between regimes. Finally, the systemic approach promotes inclusiveness, since it results in an evaluation of the law that applies to the new issue against all major interests of the international community, rather than against those of a part of its actors only.

These five steps can be conceptualized as a three-pronged exercise, which results in the application of systemic thinking to the consideration of any issue of interest to the international community. Firstly, the relevant rules are identified, using the 'object' of regulation as the aggregating device. Secondly, these rules are combined by having recourse to the three principles that guide interaction of norms in international law: the principle of systemic integration, the principle of harmonization, and the conflict-of-norms rules. Thirdly, the result is checked on the basis of the inclusiveness test. Before applying this methodology to the focus of this book, 'people at sea', it would be useful to further reflect on the five consequences of systemic thinking.

5.1 Applicable norms

First and foremost, a systemic conception of international law means that there is no preclusion to using rules deriving from any specialized regime when formulating replies to questions on applicable law. All regimes may be resorted to, to the extent that they contain rules that are relevant for the issue at hand and that are applicable (*ratione personae, temporis, loci*, and *materiae*). Paraphrasing the order of the International Tribunal for the Law of the Sea (ITLOS) in the *Southern Bluefin Tuna* case, it can be affirmed that it is a commonplace of international law and State practice for more than one regime to bear upon a particular dispute,[45] and this statement holds true for issues that have not grown into disputes, as well. The criterion for identifying which rules are relevant and which are not is the 'object' of the regulation, that is, the aim that regulation is pursuing.[46] Different approaches may

---

[45] 'It is a commonplace of international law and State practice for more than one treaty to bear upon a particular dispute' *Southern Bluefin Tuna (New Zealand v Japan, Australia v Japan)* (2000) XXIII RIAA 1, para 52.
[46] See Chapter 5, Section 4.

be used in this respect; as will be discussed in Chapter 5, this book has opted for a 'human-centered' approach, according to which all rules that purport to protect the person, or can be used to protect the person, are relevant, even if they do not directly equip individuals with rights actionable against a State.[47]

When referring to the 'applicable law', it is necessary to avoid confusion between two different understandings of the phrase. In a narrow understanding, this phrase denotes the law that a tribunal may apply when addressing a dispute submitted to it by the parties. This need not be limited to the legal instrument that established the court. For example, the ITLOS, which was created by the United Nations Convention on the Law of the Sea (UNCLOS), applies the Convention 'and other rules of international law not incompatible with' the Convention when deciding cases submitted to it.[48] In a broader sense, the phrase 'applicable law' refers to the law that binds all subjects of the system and therefore the set of norms that any actor must comply with in any specific circumstance. The two do not always coincide.[49] On the one hand, a specific court or tribunal might encounter limitations in having recourse to norms deriving from regimes other than that which generated it. For example, the ITLOS might be prevented from referring to rules in other instruments that are incompatible with the UNCLOS. On the other, States and other international actors remain subject to all their legal obligations, even when in practice there is no competent tribunal to address their dispute.[50] By way of example, if a State is faced with a situation that involves both the protection of foreign investment and the protection of fundamental human rights, it will have to refer to both human rights law and international investment law in order to identify the legal rules that regulate its conduct, even if there is no human rights court and no investment tribunal that has jurisdiction to address an alleged breach.

Access to rules of the system deriving from different legal regimes may be possible in both cases. However, the ability of a court to introduce notions from other regimes may be impeded by the terms of the treaty conferring jurisdiction to it.[51] Therefore, when referring to the 'applicable law', I will refer to the broad understanding defined above.

---

[47] See Chapter 5, Section 5.   [48] Art 293 UNCLOS.

[49] This conclusion is common to both positivist and naturalist understandings of international law. Prosper Weil, 'Towards Relative Normativity in International Law?' (1983) 77 AJIL 413, 417, refers to 'a legal obligation that can be relied on before a court or arbitrator, the flouting of which constitutes an internationally unlawful act giving rise to international responsibility'. Ronald Dworkin, 'A New Philosophy for International Law' (2013) 41 Philosophy & Public Affairs 2, 14, imagines 'an international court with jurisdiction over all the nations of the world' where 'cases can be brought ... reasonably easily and ... effective sanctions are available to enforce the court's rulings'.

[50] *Legality of Use of Force (Serbia and Montenegro v Belgium)* (Preliminary Objections) [2004] ICJ Rep 279, para 128; *Application of the International Convention on the Elimination of All Forms of Racial Discrimination (Georgia v Russian Federation)* (Preliminary Objections) [2011] ICJ Rep 70, para 186.

[51] Tullio Treves, 'Human Rights and the Law of the Sea' (2010) 28 Berkeley Journal of International Law 1, 2.

5.2 The principle of systemic integration

Systemic thinking is expressed in the principle of systemic integration, which allows, and indeed may mandate, the migration of principles, concepts, and rules from one regime to another. According to a well-known phrase, systemic integration acts as the master-key, allowing the interpreter to have recourse to all the rules of the system—rules of general international law and those of specialized regimes.[52] Systemic integration operates during the identification of the applicable law, as described in the above section, during the interpretation of this law and during its application.

An expression of this principle is notoriously contained in Article 31(3)(c) Virenna Convention on the Law of Treaties (VCLT), requiring that 'any relevant rules of international law applicable between the parties' need to be taken into account when interpreting a treaty.[53] The deliberate use of a broad formulation ('any relevant rules') refers not only to the rules of the specific treaty but also to other rules of the regime, of general international law, and of other specialized regimes.[54] A significant limitation encountered by the principle of systemic integration endorsed in Article 31(3)(c) VCLT is that it presumes the existence of a norm, the interpretation of which will open the door to other norms of the system. It is therefore of little use if there is no applicable norm to interpret.[55] In contrast to the letter of Article 31(3)(c) VCLT, the European Court of Human Rights (ECtHR) has recently held that it can also take into account legal instruments that are not in force for the respective State, either because they have not entered into force or because they have not been ratified by it, as long as they express an emerging consensus.[56] There is, however, no evidence in State practice that this reading could be applied beyond the specific context of human rights, unless it is taken to refer to rules of customary law.

Systemic integration serves not only to ease interpretation, but also to provide additional guidance concerning the application of a norm.[57] In this way, it allows consideration of whether there are other rules in the system that constrain or exclude the applicability of the one under examination. In other words, systemic integration leads to an enlargement of the pool of rules against which the rule under examination needs to be measured when deciding if and how it can be applied. In *Al-Adsani*,

---

[52] Campbell McLachlan, 'The Principle of Systemic Integration and Article 31(3)(c) of the Vienna Convention' (2005) 54 ICLQ 279, 280–81.

[53] *Legal Consequences for States of the Continued Presence of South Africa in Namibia (South West Africa) notwithstanding Security Council Resolution 276 (1970)* (Advisory Opinion) [1971] ICJ Rep 16, para 53: 'an international instrument has to be interpreted and applied within the framework of the entire legal system prevailing at the time of the interpretation'. In the case of a multilateral instrument, reference to the parties should not be taken to require that all parties to the treaty that is being interpreted are also parties to the treaty that needs to be taken into consideration; it is sufficient that the parties to the dispute be parties to both treaties (Pulkowski, *The Law* (n 36) 289–92).

[54] *Oil Platforms (Islamic Republic of Iran v United States of America)* (Judgment) [2003] ICJ Rep 161, para 41. See also Pulkowski, *The Law* (n 36) 288.

[55] Pulkowski, *The Law* (n 36) 289.

[56] *Demir and Baykara v Turkey* App no 34503/97 (Judgment (GC) of 12 November 2008), paras 65–86.

[57] While 'interpretation' and 'application' of norms are sometimes compounded, the two acts are separate and not entirely coincident, the main difference being that 'interpretation' can never produce the non-application of a norm, while 'application' can.

the ECtHR used systemic integration to identify potential norms that would render the ECHR inapplicable.[58] In the *Oil Platforms* case, systemic integration was used by the International Court of Justice (ICJ) to import the entire regime prohibiting the use of force in order to evaluate compliance with a norm contained in a treaty of friendship, commerce, and navigation. Although the Court referred to the 'interpretation' of the obligations contained in the Iran/US treaty, what it did in practice was to evaluate the facts of the case against both this treaty and the regime on the use of force so as to eventually rule in favour of the pre-eminence of norms contained in the latter.[59]

Systemic integration is facilitated by the introduction of triggering provisions in the text of treaties. Triggering provisions could be divided into two main categories. The first includes those provisions that make express reference to other regimes, such as Article 311 UNCLOS. The second category, while not containing any express reference, includes those provisions that employ broad terms or terms which belong to another regime, effectively engaging these other regimes. For example, reference to 'jurisdiction' under human rights treaties brings into play notions of jurisdiction to be found in other regimes.[60] Reference to general principles, such as 'sovereignty' or 'good faith', and the use of generic expressions such as 'applicable rules and regulations' perform the same function. However, even when such provisions are not inserted into treaties, the principle of systemic integration may be applied.

5.3 The principle of harmonization

Whereas systemic integration tells us that we need to take into account norms coming from all sorts of different regimes, as long as they belong to the system of international law, the principle of harmonization tells us what to do with the norms. In fact, the potential existence of more than one norm—or more than one regime—that address any one issue paves the way to possible conflicts and fragmentation.[61] In its basic formulation, the principle of harmonization—or the presumption against conflict as it has been termed in the past[62]—requires that every effort be made to interpret and to coordinate applicable rules so as to avoid conflict.[63] This may be

---

[58] *Al-Adsani v The United Kingdom* App no 35763/97 (Judgment of 21 November 2001) para 55; see also *Hirsi* (n 22) para 171. In the *Al-Adsani* judgment, the ECtHR used the principle of systemic integration to introduce the law of State immunity into the case, which concerned a claim for the violation of human rights, in order to identify a possible conflict between norms belonging to the two systems (*Al-Adsani*, paras 55–56). The reference to Art 31(3)(c) VCLT does not sound convincing, since it was called to decide upon the applicability of a treaty provision to a specific factual set of circumstances, rather than to interpret the norm; McLachlan (n 52) 305–06.

[59] *Oil Platforms* (n 54) para 43. Interpretation is often extended to include not only the clarification or determination of the content of a legal rule, but also the determination of its application. However, the two are separate.

[60] See Chapter 3, Section 2.3.

[61] Fragmentation may therefore ensue as between general international law and specialized regimes, or between two or more specialized regimes. Koskenniemi Report (n 6) 47–56.

[62] Jenks, (n 15) 427–28.

[63] 'It is a generally accepted principle that when several norms bear on a single issue they should, to the extent possible, be interpreted so as to give rise to a single set of compatible obligations' ILC Conclusions (n 3) para. 4. A rare instance of the incorporation of the principle of harmonization into

achieved by choosing, among many different meanings, the one that allows co-existence of two norms; by construing a norm so that it does not impede the application of another norm; or by incorporating principles from other regimes that mitigate the adverse effects of norms on some of the affected addressees.

Harmonization achieves the best results when it is applied at the law-making stage. Those negotiating new legal instruments or updating existing ones are best placed to examine the compatibility of proposed formulations vis-à-vis existing rules and to take action either to curb new texts to fit with existing rules, or to supersede old regulation by new rules that expressly modify previous norms.[64] States, international organizations, and other actors are continuously engaged in a process of harmonization of diverging interests, and their crucial role in promoting harmonization has been emphasized.[65]

However, political and other considerations may not always yield this optimal result and may make it necessary to use the principle of harmonization after the norm has come into existence, during its interpretation and application to specific situations. The application of this principle requires a balancing act that results in the preservation of all norms, rather than a choice between one among the many potentially applicable norms.[66] While it will not settle all issues, harmonization allows us to do away with apparent conflicts and therefore to reduce cases of incompatibility between norms.[67] The principle of harmonization however encounters two limitations. Firstly, it is certainly not a panacea insofar as it will not solve real conflicts of norms, since it does not have an overriding character.[68] Furthermore, it requires the exercise of discretion and some caution in its application. The principle of harmonization is a procedural criterion, silent as to the underlying aim which will guide the interpreter, and these aims need to be extrapolated from the general principles underlying the system.

5.4 Consequences for the solution of normative conflicts

A systemic approach to all of the relevant norms allows for a fuller and more comprehensive application of rules settling the relationship between norms including, if necessary, their hierarchy. An examination of the relevant norms which does not consider each specialized regime as part of the international law system will inevitably lead to a comparison between regimes, rather than norms.[69] As a consequence,

a treaty text is to be found in Art 20 Convention on the Protection and Promotion of the Diversity of Cultural Expressions (adopted 20 October 2005, entered into force 18 March 2007) 2440 UNTS 311. For an application of the principle of harmonization in an effort to coordinate the different regimes that apply to the interdiction of irregular migrants at sea, see Natalie Klein, 'A Case for Harmonizing Laws on Maritime Interceptions of Irregular Migrants' (2014) 63 ICLQ 787.

[64] Jenks (n 15) 429–33.   [65] Young, *Trading Fish* (n 42).
[66] Koskenniemi Report (n 6) 37–40; Rousseau (n 37) 153.
[67] See Pauwelyn, *Conflict of Norms* (n 37) 178 on the distinction between genuine and apparent conflicts.
[68] Jenks (n 15) 429.
[69] This distinction is clearly illustrated in Joost Pauwelyn, 'Bridging Fragmentation and Unity: International Law as a Universe of Inter-Connected Islands' (2004) 25 Michigan Journal of International Law 903.

any conflict will need to be solved on the basis of rules governing a conflict of laws, rather than those concerning a conflict of norms. This will eventually result in the norms of one regime being discharged *in toto* in favour of those of another regime,[70] or being admitted only subject to those of the regime which are considered applicable.[71] Instead, applying the systemic approach allows us to focus on the norms and to determine the hierarchical and other relationships between single norms, rather than between regimes. Relationships between regimes are thus transformed into relationships between single sets of norms.[72]

This approach will certainly increase cases of conflict and will add complexity. By requiring a careful evaluation of the specific circumstances surrounding each pair of norms under examination, this approach may produce a different balancing. This in turn may bring a lack of absolute criteria, resulting in norms deriving from different systems being given priority according to the case. This inconsistency comes as a natural consequence of the present state of the international community and should not be considered as an excessive price to pay. It allows us to collect and to give due regard to all norms that are useful for a more comprehensive regulation of the emerging issue and minimizes the subsequent contestation of adopted solutions.

5.5 Inclusiveness

Eventually, by incorporating all the basic principles of international law and by blending norms of various origins, the systemic approach encourages a holistic evaluation of the law that applies to the new issue, since each regime of international law is the product of a certain set of actors and reflects specific, partial interests. Accordingly, recourse to the systemic approach means that the group of rules thus collected will be measured against all major interests of the international community, rather than against those of a part of its actors only. If the actors that interpret or apply international law were to be asked to choose one among the many regimes potentially applicable, they would give undue priority to some underlying interests and would silence all others. Systemic integration, while sacrificing some formal

---

[70] This is the conclusion of Ralf Michaels and Joost Pauwelyn, 'Conflict of Norms or Conflict of Laws?: Different Techniques in the Fragmentation of Public International Law' (2012) 22 Duke Journal of Comparative & International Law 349, who reject balancing as a harmonization technique and advocate the applicability of 'inter-systemic conflict-of-laws rules' to solve conflict between branches of international law by selecting the regime that 'is more appropriate to be applied to the particular fact pattern' (ibid 368–69). While the authors expressly reject basing their finding on the systemic or otherwise nature of international law (ibid 350), they make unproven assumptions concerning the alleged impact of the lack of a (fictional) coherent legislative intent in international law (ibid 367). These assumptions on one hand tint their conclusion as to the applicable rule (conflict of laws or conflict of norms rules) and on the other do not appear to take into due regard the often similar situation that is produced in domestic legal systems, wherein the substantial provisions of legal texts may be drafted by specialized commissions and their adoption reposes on contextual political considerations or the causal interaction of different pressure groups, rather than uniform, consistent, and continuative intent to ensure the coherence of the normative system.

[71] As suggested by Fischer-Lescano and Teubner (n 5).

[72] These sets may include principles or other norms. Once principles are harmonized, the conflict between single norms can be solved more easily.

coherence for the sake of inclusiveness, is to be preferred because it allows contrasting hegemonic tendencies.[73]

This conclusion is in line with the horizontal and accumulative mode of international law-making, based on the absence of a single legislator and the existence of multiple actors who pursue diverging aims in a variety of fora. It would be at odds with either the conceptual need for inclusiveness and democracy or with the actual practice of States and other international actors to operate a clear-cut choice between different and sometimes opposite interests and to attribute to a single regime—and thereby to a single set of actors—the regulation of an emerging issue. For example, it would be dismissive of many interests to only select the facilitation of trade *or* the protection of the environment *or* human rights as the applicable regime, discharging the remaining two.[74] All of these aims are noteworthy and are endorsed by large sectors of the international community. Even if the end result might eventually be perceived as not entirely balanced, a systemic approach to international law is likely to result in consideration being given to all interests and all actors.

6. Selecting the Rules

It is now pertinent to turn to the application of systemic thinking to the subject matter of this book, 'people at sea'. Consequently, it is first necessary to identify the rules that (may) apply to this subject matter, so as to proceed to their comprehensive evaluation during the second step. In other words, the reconstruction of the law that applies to people at sea needs first to turn to the discrete regimes of international law that are potential sources of regulation, in order to identify these regimes and ascertain which of their norms are relevant. The specific criterion that will be adopted is the 'human-oriented' approach identified in the Introduction, which requires us to take into consideration any rule that has a direct bearing on people at sea. Rules may create rights and duties for individuals or groups; they may impose duties on States or other actors to undertake (or abstain from undertaking) conduct which directly impacts upon individuals or groups; and they may attribute rights to States or other actors to undertake such conduct. It is worth repeating that the human-oriented approach mandates the consideration not only of rules that have been drafted for people at sea, but also of those that may apply to them, on the basis of their scope, even if they have not been drafted with people at sea in mind, and even if traditionally they have not been applied to people at sea.

There are numerous legal rules that apply to people at sea, which are to be found in a number of international law regimes. As the phrase 'people at sea' intuitively reveals, the law of the sea and human rights law are of primary importance. Other

---

[73] Martti Koskenniemi, 'Hegemonic Regimes' in Margaret A Young (ed), *Regime Interaction in International Law* (CUP 2012) 305, 324, sees '[r]egime interaction as political contestation'.

[74] See Young, *Trading Fish* (n 42). This conclusion is not altered depending on the criterion used to operate the choice, which can be a collision rule, as argued by Pauwelyn, 'Bridging Fragmentation' (n 69) or a substantive rule, as advanced by Fischer-Lescano and Teubner (n 5) 1021.

specialized regimes are also relevant. International labour law may be significant, particularly for those people who work at sea. Consular law may provide a handful of significant rules, in particular concerning diplomatic protection and the right of the State of nationality to be informed. Refugee law contains a paramount principle for the protection of aliens at sea, the prohibition of *refoulement*. Technical rules and regulations concerning the safety of vessels and the enforcement of common standards, included in maritime law treaties, contribute to the overall picture, since they have a direct bearing upon the protection of people at sea.

7. Delving into the Regimes

An examination of the law that applies to people at sea requires that we delve into each of these regimes, so that we may assess the applicability and limitations of various legal rules that emanate from different legal regimes, in order to aggregate and map the relevant rules. This analysis will also allow the identification of those characteristics and peculiarities which may facilitate or hinder interaction, as well as assessing the openness of the overall regime to external elements. Only afterwards will it be possible to exit the regimes and return to the system of international law for a conceptual appraisal of the law that regulates persons at sea.

7.1 The law of the sea

The law of the sea, as traditionally understood, includes 'the rules and principles that bind States in their international relations concerning maritime matters'.[75] Initially developed to strengthen arguments in favour of the freedom of navigation against claims for the territorialization of the oceans, it has now developed into a complex and well-articulated regime that addresses issues as diverse as the protection of the marine environment, the fight against piracy, the protection of underwater cultural heritage, the exploitation of the resources of the seabed, and the conduct of scientific research.[76]

Structurally, the law of the sea presents an advanced framework of legal regulation, wherein the UNCLOS codifies much of the pre-existing custom and sets the principles for the development of most of the law to follow.[77] The central role of the UNCLOS within the law of the sea is reinforced by its designation as the 'constitution for the oceans'.[78] The law of the sea, however, also includes many other

---

[75] Churchill and Lowe (n 27) 1.

[76] Tullio Scovazzi, 'The Evolution of International Law of the Sea: New Issues, New Challenges' (2000) 286 Recueil des Cours 39 provides a captivating account of the historical evolution of the discipline. The significance of the ten-year long Third United Nations Conference on the Law of the Sea on the development of the law of the sea in its present form is discussed in Tullio Treves, 'Codification du droit international et pratique des Etats dans le droit de la mer' (1990) 223 Recueil des Cours 9.

[77] David Freestone (ed), *The 1982 Law of the Sea Convention at 30: Successes, Challenges and New Agendas* (Martinus Nijhoff 2013).

[78] 'A Constitution for the Oceans', Remarks by Tommy TB Koh, President of the Third United Nations Conference on the Law of the Sea <http://www.un.org/depts/los/convention_agreements/

treaties that address specific aspects at the global, regional, or bilateral level.[79] Many maritime law treaties dealing with the safety of navigation, the training of crews, or the protection of the marine environment can also be considered as forming part of the law of the sea.[80] The regime is enhanced by a complex institutional structure, where new institutions (the International Seabed Authority, the Commission on the Limits of the Continental Shelf, and the ITLOS) have been created alongside existing ones (UN, Food and Agriculture Organization (FAO), International Labour Organization (ILO), and International Maritime Organization (IMO)). Finally, it is completed by a disputes settlement system that may produce binding outcomes.[81]

The quasi-constitutional nature of the UNCLOS is further reflected when assessing the content of this regime. From a normative perspective, the law of the sea contains two separate sets of rules which are conceptually and ontologically different. The first includes those provisions that can be defined as 'structural',[82] whilst the second includes all substantial rules.[83] Structural rules specific to the law of the sea are much more complex than on land, where the basic rule, at least up to now, has been the exclusivity of State sovereignty.[84] Their complexity derives from the fact that apart from a narrow band of territorial waters, the seas are not subject to the exclusive sovereignty of one State to the exclusion of all others. Rather, they are divided into a number of maritime zones, each accommodating jurisdictional rights of more than one State through a shifting paradigm.[85] Structural law of the sea rules,

texts/koh_english.pdf> accessed 17 August 2017. Rainer Lagoni, 'Commentary' in Alex G Oude Elferink (ed), *Stability and Change in the Law of the Sea: The Role of the LOS Convention* (Martinus Nijhoff 2005) 49, 49–51, provides a concise summary of some misrepresentations that the use of this designation may produce.

[79] A collection of relevant treaties may be found in AV Lowe and Stefan Talmon, *The Legal Order of the Oceans: Basic Documents on the Law of the Sea* (Hart 2009).

[80] Emmanuel Roucounas, 'Facteurs privés et droit international public' (2002) 299 Recueil des Cours 9, 183–84.

[81] Information on the instruments and institutions making up the law of the sea are available in the website of the United Nations Division for Oceans Affairs and the Law of the Sea (DOALOS) at <http://www.un.org/depts/los/index.htm> accessed 17 August 2017.

[82] I avoid speaking of procedural rules, since this expression may bring into the mind of the reader rules concerning law-making, such as sources of law, procedures through which new norms are adopted, or the organs or institutions to which this function is devolved. Philip Allott, 'Power Sharing in the Law of the Sea' (1983) 77 AJIL 1, 17, considers that sea areas have a 'structural character'.

[83] Shirley V Scott, 'The LOS Convention as a Constitutional Regime for the Oceans' in Alex G Oude Elferink (ed), *Stability and Change in the Law of the Sea: The Role of the LOS Convention* (Martinus Nijhoff 2005) 9, 15–16, considers that only the former can be properly considered parts of the UNCLOS 'constitutional regime'.

[84] Although challenges to sovereignty and its absoluteness are gathering momentum in international legal discourse and the practice of global governance institutions, it is still very much the case that any regulation applicable within a State's territory still needs to be mediated through one, and one only, State: the State having sovereignty (Jean L Cohen, *Globalization and Sovereignty* (CUP 2012)). The prominence of sovereignty results in particular from debates relating to instances where sovereignty itself runs the risk of being set aside, as in the case of failed States and States against which an intervention is being discussed. For instance, the territorial integrity of the State has been consistently affirmed in Security resolutions concerning Somalia (eg UNSC Res 2158 (29 May 2014) UN Doc S/RES/2158, second preambular para) and Syria (eg UNSC Res 2139 (22 February 2014) UN Doc S/RES/2139, second preambular para).

[85] Maria Gavouneli, *Functional Jurisdiction in the Law of the Sea* (Martinus Nijhoff 2007).

therefore, allocate power among States to rule—that is, to regulate and enforce—in the different zones and for different purposes.[86] Such rules include those concerning the existence and breadth of maritime zones, as well as those that assign jurisdiction to the flag State, the coastal State, the port State, and occasionally to other States. Notably, these provisions are merely about power rather than the way in which this power should be used,[87] and they do not contain normative standards that should apply to the treatment of people. The latter aim is achieved through the adoption of substantial rules, which require States to put into practice specific conduct, that has a certain aim or that needs to be carried out in a prescribed way. For example, under Article 56(1)(a) UNCLOS, the coastal State has sovereign rights over the resources in its exclusive economic zone. This provision, however, does not contain any indication on how these rights have to be exercised, what limitations they incur, or what other rules of international law need to be complied with in the exercise of the sovereign rights over resources. Similarly, Article 33(1)(b) UNCLOS attributes to the coastal State the right to punish, within its contiguous zone, infringements of its customs, fiscal, immigration, or sanitary laws and regulations committed in its territory or territorial sea, but does not mention what forms punishment may take, what procedure needs to be followed, or what safeguards apply to persons involved.

If examined through the lens of 'people at sea', the law of the sea presents two features that characterize its contribution: the State-centeredness of this regime and the widely permissory nature of its rules. These two features will be examined in the following subsections, before turning to a preliminary assessment of the contribution of the law of the sea to the protection of people at sea.

7.1.1 *The permissory nature of law of the sea rules*

A distinct characteristic of much international law of the sea is the permissory nature of its rules.[88] Building on the material and legal fact that most of the sea cannot be subjected to the sovereignty of a State to the exclusion of all other States, the basic purpose of this branch of law has been to allocate power among States in a space that was open to dual or multiple utilization by more than one State at the same time.[89] According to this paradigm, the law of the sea is full of rules that allow States to undertake a specific activity at sea. The State enjoys the right to navigate, the right to exploit seabed resources, the right to fish, and the right to conduct scientific

---

[86] As Allott (n 82) 10, has noted, the UNCLOS 'is a massive structure of powers' which are carefully 'fettered' by power modifiers. In this respect, Allott distinguishes between a 'freedom', which 'implies the absence of legal control' and a 'power', which 'implies the absence of unfettered discretion' (ibid 26).

[87] According to Allott (n 82) 10, '[p]owers are a sort of delegated legislative function'.

[88] Use is made here of the deontic modalities discussed in Julius Stone, *Legal System and Lawyers' Reasonings* (Stanford University Press 1968) 187 et seq. The assumption is that the law of the sea (and international law) are closed legal systems. However, the same conclusion would be reached, for the purposes of the present discussion, if the systems were considered as open. In the latter case, the norms would be termed 'allowable' (ibid 197).

[89] The Spanish and Portuguese claims to exclusive rights over oceans were contested by Grotius so successfully that even today we still consider that most of the sea is not subject to the sovereignty of any State.

research. When rights are exclusive, they are matched by a correspondent prohibition on all other States. The right of the flag State to exercise exclusive jurisdiction over vessels flying its flag and navigating on the high seas is thus matched by the prohibition imposed upon all other States to exercise jurisdiction.[90]

The evolution of international law from rules that simply allow the co-existence of States to rules that also facilitate the cooperation of States to achieve societal interests has shown the limits of this approach. The attribution of rights often proved insufficient to promote compliance with practices that would minimize adverse effects to common goods, be they the marine environment, the safety of navigation, or the conservation of living resources.[91] Rights were therefore paired with duties in an effort to balance the requirements of States with those of the international community. For example, the sovereign rights over living resources in the exclusive economic zone and the freedom to fish on the high seas were checked by the obligation to ensure the conservation of fish stocks.[92] Similarly, the freedom of navigation was qualified by the obligation to protect the marine environment from ship-source pollution.[93] In some instances, these new duties address the right itself rather than the modalities for its exercise, by rendering it necessary to exercise the pre-existing right (which of course ceases to be such). The right of the flag State to exercise jurisdiction over vessels flying its flag suffered a particularly severe attack following the spreading of open registries and flags of convenience. As traditionally understood, the flag State had the right to exercise exclusive jurisdiction over vessels flying its flag when the vessels were navigating beyond the territorial sea. It was probably considered that it would be in the interest of the flag State to ensure that its vessels were safe and that the master and crew met with humane treatment. Experience challenged this assumption, often resulting in grave incidents that exposed the unwillingness of some States to exercise their jurisdiction. In response to numerous disasters, new rules were elaborated that mandate the exercise of jurisdiction by the flag State to ensure the safety of vessels, the protection of the marine environment, and the security of navigation.[94] The fundamental changes between the text of Article 10 Convention on the High Seas (HSC) and Article 94 UNCLOS illustrate the depth and intensity of such transformation.[95]

---

[90] Art 92(1) UNCLOS.

[91] The tragedy of the commons was often cited as a reason for imposing duties on States and fishers. For a critical perspective see Fikret Berkes, 'Fishermen and "The Tragedy of the Commons"' (1985) 12 *Environmental Conservation* 199.

[92] Art 117 UNCLOS.   [93] Art 211 UNCLOS.

[94] Notably, the first Convention for the Safety of Life at Sea (SOLAS) was adopted in response to the *Titanic* disaster, which caused the loss of more than 1,500 lives due to an accident of navigation and lack of safety equipment; Convention for the Safety of Life at Sea (adopted 20 January 1914). The adoption of the International Convention for the Prevention of Pollution from Ships as amended by the 1978 Protocol (adopted 17 February 1978, entered into force 2 October 1983) (MARPOL) was a response to the 1967 *Torrey Canyon* disaster, in which the Liberian-flagged oil tanker ran aground while entering the English Channel and spilled the entire cargo of 120,000 tons of crude oil into the sea. The Convention for the Suppression of Unlawful Acts Against the Safety of Maritime Navigation (adopted 10 March 1988, entered into force 1 March 1992) 1678 UNTS 201 (SUA Convention) was adopted following the highjacking of the *Achille Lauro* cruise ship in 1985.

[95] Art 30 Convention on the High Seas (adopted 29 April 1958, entered into force 30 September 1962) 450 UNTS 11 (HSC) and Art 92(1) UNCLOS.

As these examples illustrate, it is only recently that the language of duties has found widespread use in law of the sea instruments. This has often happened to the detriment of their universal acceptance, since States were sometimes precluded from accepting the new treaties that embody the change.[96] Nonetheless, the normative paradigm of duties has insinuated itself into the structure of the law of the sea and there is no turning back, as it is becoming generally accepted that rights entail duties and responsibilities. The statement by Anderson that '[i]n today's world, freedoms of the high seas are freedoms under the law' can indeed be extended to all other rights and freedoms.[97]

7.1.2 *The State-centeredness of the law of the sea*

It is a truism to say that the law of the sea, one of the oldest and most developed fields of international law, is State-centered. Certainly up to a great extent, the law of the sea has been designed *by* States *for* States.[98] Over the last five centuries, it has been shaped through State practice, producing rules of custom that still apply today. From the twentieth century onwards, it has usually been developed through treaties negotiated by States and then ratified by them. It is symptomatic that the ultimate expression of this field of law, the United Nations Convention on the Law of the Sea, was not based on a text elaborated by an international organization or an NGO but was created through the direct interaction of States' representatives, in order to 'accommodate the interests and needs of all States'.[99] In other words, even in today's multi-actor world, the law of the sea still provides a particularly strong example of Westphalian law-making procedures.[100]

Furthermore, normative discourse pertaining to the law of the sea is deeply rooted in the idea of the State. Traditional rights, such as the freedom of navigation, the right of innocent passage, and the freedom of fishing are overwhelmingly attributed to the State.[101] The same happens with legal obligations: it is States that are burdened with duties, such as the obligation to protect the marine environment and to

[96] As of 18 August 2017, the Agreement for the Implementation of the Provisions of the United Nations Convention on the Law of the Sea of 10 December 1982 relating to the Conservation and Management of Straddling Fish Stocks and Highly Migratory Fish Stocks (adopted 4 August 1995, entered into force 11 December 2001) 2167 UNTS 3 (FSA), which implements and augments the duties of States concerning the protection of the living resources on the high seas, has been ratified by eighty-six parties, as opposed to the 168 parties of UNCLOS.

[97] David Anderson, 'Freedoms of the High Seas in the Modern Law of the Sea' in David Freestone, Richard Barnes, and David Ong (eds), *The Law of the Sea: Progress and Prospects* (OUP 2006) 327.

[98] Much could be said, in this respect, from a feminist critical perspective. For a general overview of international law through this lens see Hilary Charlesworth, Christine Chinkin, and Shelley Wright, 'Femminist Approaches to International Law' (1991) 85 AJIL 613.

[99] As indicated by the UN General Assembly in the resolution that convened the Third United Nations Conference on the Law of the Sea, which produced the UNCLOS; UNGA Res 2750 (XXV) (17 December 1970) UN Doc A/RES/2750(XXV)C, eight preambular para.

[100] As incorporated in *The Case of the S.S. Lotus (France v Turkey)* PCIJ Rep Series A No 10 (*Lotus*).

[101] Although this is generally so, there are instances in which rights have been apparently attributed to individuals; *Eritrea v Yemen* (Award of the Arbitral Tribunal in the First Stage—Territorial Sovereignty and Scope of the Dispute) (1998) para 526 and *Eritrea v Yemen* (Award of the Arbitral Tribunal in the Second Stage—Maritime Delimitation) (1999) paras 101–03.

conserve marine living resources.[102] Even when the subject/actor materially bound by the obligation is the individual, the law of the sea imposes the obligation upon the State to ensure that the individual complies with what is required.[103] Article 98 UNCLOS illustrates the point. In stating that '[e]very State shall require the master of a ship flying its flag . . . to render assistance to any person found at sea in danger of being lost', this provision concentrates on the duty of the State, not that of the individual. Although its aim is to ensure that masters comply with the duty to save life at sea, from a strictly legal perspective one must conclude that this provision does not impose any obligation upon individuals, but instead only upon States. In a similar vein, the UNCLOS does not prohibit individuals from engaging in piracy and it does not criminalize acts of piracy, but rather, it provides that States shall cooperate in the repression of piracy.[104] Perhaps even more importantly, the creation of obligations pertaining to the law of the sea is generally due to other States, often pursuant to a synallagmatic understanding of international law based upon horizontal State relationships.

This deeply rooted characteristic, in conjunction with the 'personification' of the ship borrowed from maritime law,[105] often results in the drafting of rules that set aside the individual. Individuals are substituted not only by States but also by ships, even in cases when it is evident that it is the individual that is concerned. Article 230(3) UNCLOS thus provides that 'In the conduct of proceedings in respect of such violations committed by a foreign vessel which may result in the imposition of penalties, recognised rights of the accused shall be observed'. In this provision, mention of the 'recognised rights of the accused' seems at odds with the personification of the vessel, which is referred to as having committed the violation and might hence be considered as being the accused. The phrase 'persons charged with violations will enjoy the recognised rights of the accused', or a similar wording actually mentioning those persons involved in the allegedly unlawful pollution of the marine environment, would have made the content of the provision clearer.

Having established this point, it should be noted however, that the pervasiveness of State-centered discourse should not be equated with a disregard of individuals' needs. State-centeredness can actually be rather neutral, since States usually pursue interests that transcend their existence. The focus on States, therefore, can be seen as affecting the drafting techniques for the production of legal rules, rather than their content. For example, we can examine the interest to protect human life. This interest can be identified in the right to life of an individual, but also in a rule that prohibits a State from killing individuals and even in a rule that imposes on a State the duty to take measures to avoid that private actors kill the individual. The legal consequences of different drafting techniques are self-evident and need not be

---

[102] See respectively Art 192 UNCLOS and Art 117 UNCLOS.
[103] Roucounas (n 80) 180.
[104] 'All States shall cooperate to the fullest possible extent in the repression of piracy on the high seas or in any other place outside the jurisdiction of any State' (Art 100 UNCLOS).
[105] Robert Force, AN Yiannopoulos, and Martin Davies, *Admiralty and Maritime Law*, vol 2 (Beard Books 2008) 183.

touched upon here.[106] What matters is that the interest behind all these rules is the same: that people are not killed.

The focus on States as the recipients of international norms has not prevented them from developing rules that aim at the protection of persons at sea. Although the UNCLOS 'is not ordinarily considered a human rights instrument', it 'also addresses traditional human rights preoccupations with the rule of law, individual liberties and procedural due process'.[107] Notably, the duty to save life at sea and the detailed regulation concerning the safety of vessels,[108] as well as the prohibition of corporal punishment (if only for fisheries law violations)[109] have as their object and purpose the protection of the life and physical integrity of people at sea. Furthermore, some of the powers attributed to States, such as the right to apprehend pirates, the right to visit ships used for the slave trade, and the right to interdict vessels engaged in drug trafficking all have the *de facto* aim of the protection of the rights of individuals.[110]

Recent treaties are indeed showing a shift towards a more human-oriented approach (and wording). The 2005 Convention for the Suppression of Unlawful Acts Against the Safety of Maritime Navigation (SUA Convention)[111] is particularly detailed in its human rights guarantees. Apart from provisions aiming at ensuring contact with national authorities,[112] the safety of life at sea,[113] and the protection of human dignity,[114] it also obliges States to provide for effective remedies against unlawful action by State authorities,[115] fair treatment of persons taken into custody,[116] and prior informed consent for the transfer of a person detained or serving a sentence from one State to another for the purposes of providing evidence.[117] Furthermore, the SUA Convention is probably the first law of the sea treaty to contain a non-prejudice clause safeguarding human rights in general.[118]

---

[106] Consequences may also include effectiveness, since a rule that envisages the right to life as a right actionable in front of a court may be more effective for upholding this right in practice.

[107] Bernard H Oxman, 'Human Rights and the United Nations Convention on the Law of the Sea' (1998) 36 Columbia Journal of Transnational Law 399, 401–02.

[108] On the safety of life at sea see Art 98 UNCLOS. Safety of vessels is pursued mainly through the SOLAS and, for fishing vessels, the Torremolinos Protocol of 1993 relating to the Torremolinos International Convention for the Safety of Fishing Vessels (adopted 2 April 1993).

[109] Art 73(3) UNCLOS. In this case, as well as in the case of pollution of the marine environment, the UNCLOS generally gives priority to monetary penalties, rather than imprisonment.

[110] Art 105 UNCLOS; Art 110(1)(b) UNCLOS; Art 17 United Nations Convention against Illicit Traffic in Narcotic Drugs and Psychotropic Substances (adopted 20 December 1988, entered into force 11 November 1990) 1582 UNTS 165 (Convention against Illicit Traffic in Drugs).

[111] Convention for the Suppression of Unlawful Acts Against the Safety of Maritime Navigation (adopted 10 March 1988), as amended by the 2005 Protocol (adopted 14 October 2005, entered into force 28 July 2010) 1678 UNTS 222 (SUA Convention).

[112] Art 7(3) SUA Convention.   [113] Art 8*bis* (10)(a)(i) SUA Convention.

[114] Art 8*bis* (10)(a)(ii) SUA Convention.   [115] Art 8*bis* (10)(b) SUA Convention.

[116] Art 10(2) SUA Convention.   [117] Art 12*bis* (1)(a) SUA Convention.

[118] 'Nothing in this Convention shall affect other rights, obligations and responsibilities of States and individuals under international law, in particular the purposes and principles of the Charter of the United Nations and international human rights, refugee and humanitarian law' (Art 2*bis* (1) SUA Convention).

In all these cases, it is doubtful whether the obligation of the State is matched by a correspondent right of the person involved to be rescued or to be protected. From a formalistic point of view, these are all obligations which are owed to other States, rather than to individuals. At most, these rules can be seen as incorporating *erga omnes* obligations, which are owed to the international community as a whole, or, to the extent that they do not reflect custom, as *erga omnes partes* obligations.[119] In conclusion, under the law of the sea, it is States that have the rights (and obligations) while people may at most be considered as the material beneficiaries of legal regulation. Even when it has had at heart human concerns, the law of the sea has spoken the language of State duties and not of individual rights.

7.1.3 *The contribution of the law of the sea*

People are evidently not at the center of the law of the sea and careful reading is often required to isolate the handful of relevant provisions. The reasons for this difficulty are twofold. On the one hand, law of the sea and maritime treaties protect human rights only incidentally. Safeguards for humans are generally only a condition for the exercise of authority by the State and seem subordinate, in importance if not in legal standing, to the latter. For example, States are attributed the right to impose penalties for illegal fishing in the exclusive economic zone but these penalties 'may not include imprisonment, in the absence of agreements to the contrary by the States concerned, or any other form of corporal punishment', so as to safeguard personal integrity.[120] By the same token, the right of the coastal State to try persons allegedly having caused pollution of the marine environment is qualified by the requirement to respect the recognized rights of the accused and, except in the case of a wilful and serious act of pollution in the territorial sea, to impose monetary penalties.[121]

This practice has now been generalized and it is becoming usual for recent treaties that regulate enforcement action by States against vessels to contain a safeguard provision, aiming at protecting human life and the dignity of the persons on board the intercepted vessel. Thus, the 1995 Fish Stocks Agreement provides that the 'inspecting State shall require its inspectors to observe generally accepted international regulations, procedures and practices relating to the safety of the vessel and the crew'.[122] Similar wording is included in treaties concerning the fight against drug trafficking,[123] people

---

[119] Art 48 Draft Articles on Responsibility of States for Internationally Wrongful Acts. See also *Reservations to the Convention on the Prevention and Punishment of the Crime of Genocide* (Advisory Opinion) [1951] ICJ Rep 15, 23; *Questions relating to the Obligation to Prosecute or Extradite (Belgium v Senegal)* (Judgment) [2012] ICJ Rep 422, paras 68–69.

[120] Art 73(3) UNCLOS.   [121] Art 230 UNCLOS.

[122] Art 21(10) FSA. See also Art 22(1) FSA.

[123] Art 17(5) Convention against Illicit Traffic in Drugs. Art XV (2) of the Supplementary Arrangement between the Government of the United States of America and the Government of the Republic of Panama for Support and Assistance from the United States Coast Guard for the National Maritime Service of the Ministry of Government and Justice, signed in Panama on 5 February 2002 (Lowe and Talmon (n 79) 45), provides also that the parties 'shall observe the norms of courtesy, respect and consideration for the persons on board the suspected vessel'.

smuggling,[124] and security of navigation.[125] On the other hand, the UNCLOS and most of the other law of the sea provisions do not attribute any right directly to individuals, but rather impose duties upon States to protect and respect specific rights or to undertake action towards this end. The duty to protect life at sea enshrined in Articles 98 and 146 UNCLOS is an expression of the more general positive obligation of States to protect the right to life of individuals.[126]

A special feature that distinguishes law of the sea treaties is the fact that they usually contain a specific obligation for a State taking action against a vessel to allow the master, crew, or other persons on board to contact the flag State or, in some cases, the State of nationality.[127] These provisions can be considered as specific applications of the general right to consular information, notification, and assistance, which all foreign individuals enjoy under Article 36(1) of the Vienna Convention on Consular Relations.[128]

Apart from these provisions, it is indeed possible to consider that many activities regulated under the UNCLOS are of benefit for individuals or groups, as Oxman has perceptively argued.[129] It is however difficult to extrapolate subjective rights for individuals from generic provisions concerning, for example, the common heritage of mankind, the duty not to pollute the marine environment, or the freedom of all States to fish on the high seas.

In conclusion, the law of the sea, notwithstanding all its peculiarities, does contribute to the protection of people at sea in three ways. Firstly, it consolidates the rule of law insofar as it applies on the seas through its structural provisions. Secondly, it provides detailed regulation of the duties of States concerning the protection of human life, safety, and security. Thirdly, it provides a few specific provisions that address human concerns at sea and provides for the respect of fundamental human rights by States while acting at sea.

7.2 International human rights law

International human rights law provides substantive standards for the treatment of individuals by the State and contains institutional and procedural solutions for upholding such standards.[130] In legal terms, substantive standards are couched as

---

[124] Art 9(1)(a) Protocol against the Smuggling of Migrants by Land, Sea and Air Supplementing the United Nations Convention against Transnational Organized Crime (adopted 15 November 2000, entered into force 28 January 2004) 2241 UNTS 480 (Smuggling Protocol).
[125] Art 8bis (10)(a)(iv) SUA Convention.   [126] Chapter 4, Section 4.2.
[127] Art 8bis (10)(a)(viii) SUA Convention.
[128] *LaGrand (Germany v United States of America)* (Judgment) [2001] ICJ Rep 466, para 77.
[129] Oxman, 'Human Rights' (n 107).
[130] Most human rights treaties create supervisory mechanisms. In the case of global instruments, these mechanisms are rather weak, as they do not act as judicial bodies and cannot take decisions that are binding upon States, even in cases in which they can hear complaints brought by individuals. Nonetheless, they may play a relevant role as a forum for the discussion of human rights issues and the elaboration of statements intending to clarify the content and extent of States' duties to protect human rights. Stronger supervisory mechanisms are provided by three regional conventions, all of which have created an independent international Court that can hear claims brought by individuals against States and can adjudicate with binding force. The European Court of Human Rights (ECtHR) and the Inter-American Court of Human Rights (IACtHR), in particular, have produced abundant case law and

rights of the individual, which can be claimed against the State, and duties of the State, which are owed to the individual, as well as to the other States or the international community (*erga omnes partes* or *erga omnes* obligations).[131] Human rights law has thus allowed individuals to acquire international standing and to secure (albeit limited) action against the State at the international level.[132]

The 1948 Universal Declaration of Human Rights (UDHR)[133] is generally considered the starting point for the development of modern international human rights law, which was soon followed by binding treaties at the regional and, although at a later stage, at the global level. This body of law is today complemented by a significant number of binding decisions and soft law instruments which have helped to clarify, contextualize and, in some cases, develop the general standards contained in treaties.[134] Importantly, the duty to respect basic human rights is imposed by customary international law, as the ICJ has noted more than once.[135] The right to life, the prohibition of torture, and freedom from slavery are generally considered to be peremptory rules of customary international law, although there is lack of agreement on the nature of other human rights norms.[136]

International and regional human rights treaties contain bills of rights applicable to all individuals and which establish the duty for States to protect these rights.[137]

have played a prominent role in the development of this field. For a comparative perspective on the relevance of the two Courts for the development of human rights, by two scholars sitting on the bench, see Caflisch and Cançado Trindade (n 6).

[131] UNHRC, 'General Comment No. 31—The Nature of the General Legal Obligation Imposed on States Parties to the Covenant' (26 May 2004) UN Doc CCPR/C/21/Rev.1/Add. 13 (General Comment 31) para 2. *Belgium/Senegal* (n 119) paras 68–69.

[132] As described, among others, by Anne Peters, *Beyond Human Rights. The Legal Status of the Individual in International Law* (CUP 2016) and Antonio Augusto Cançado Trindade, *The Access of Individuals to International Justice* (OUP 2011).

[133] UNGA Res 217 (III) (10 December 1948) UN Doc A/RES/217(III).

[134] On human rights, generally, see Steiner, Alston, and Goodman (n 24); Walter Kalin and Jorg Kunzli, *The Law of International Human Rights Protection* (OUP 2009); Joseph and McBeth, *Research Handbook* (n 24).

[135] *Corfu Channel (United Kingdom of Great Britain and Northern Ireland v Albania)* (Judgment) [1949] ICJ Rep 4, para 22; *Barcelona Traction, Light and Power Company, Limited (Belgium v Spain)* (Judgment) [1970] ICJ Rep 3, paras 33–34.

[136] The ILC was not able to solve the issue, hence the mention of both human rights and 'other obligations under peremptory norms of general international law' in Art 50(1) Draft Articles on State Responsibility. See also the ILC Commentary to this provision in ILC, *Yearbook of the International Law Commission* vol II, Part Two (2001) 132–33. Similarly, in the *Belgium/Senegal* case, the ICJ simply stated that the obligations contained in the CAT are *erga omnes partes*, without examining their nature as jus cogens.

[137] At the regional level, treaties follow the same patterns as global treaties and may provide protection of human rights generally, or of some specific rights, or of a specific group of people. The (European) Convention for the Protection of Human Rights and Fundamental Freedoms (adopted 4 November 1950, entered into force 3 September 1953) 213 UNTS 221, as amended (ECHR), the American Convention on Human Rights (adopted 11 November 1969, entered into force 18 July 1978) 1144 UNTS 123 (ACHR), the African Charter on Human and People's Rights (adopted 22 June 1981, entered into force 21 October 1986) 1520 UNTS 217 (ACHPR), and the Arab Charter on Human Rights (adopted 15 September 2004 entered into force 15 March 2008) [2005] 12 Int'l Hum Rts Rep 893 (ArCHR) contain bills of rights and combine social, economic, cultural, civil, and political rights. Although these are regional treaties that bind only States belonging to a specific geographic area, they are of general interest as they may be invoked also by individuals who do not have the nationality of the parties and they may operate also outside the parties' territory.

Human rights include the right to life;[138] the prohibition of torture;[139] the prohibition of slavery;[140] the right to personal liberty;[141] the right to fair trial;[142] the freedom of thought, conscience, and religion;[143] the freedom of movement;[144] the freedom of opinion, assembly, and association;[145] the right to work;[146] the right to social security;[147] the right to adequate standards of living;[148] the right to health;[149] and cultural rights.[150] Specific rights and the procedural steps to ensure their guarantees are effective have been further elaborated in dedicated treaties[151] and ad hoc treaties are dedicated to groups that are particularly vulnerable to suffer violations of some of their rights and therefore need to be specifically protected.[152]

Human rights treaties also provide, generally in rather broad terms, that States have the duty to protect these rights.[153] Wording of the exact obligation varies from one treaty to the other, as well as the detail into which the obligations of States are described. It is now generally accepted that States have both negative and positive obligations or, in other words are under the duty to 'respect', to 'protect', and to 'fulfil' human rights obligations.[154] Human rights provisions addressed to States are

[138] Art 6 International Covenant on Civil and Political Rights (adopted 16 December 1966, entered into force 23 March 1976) 999 UNTS 171 (ICCPR); Art 4 ACHR; Art 4 ACHPR; Art 5 ArCHR; Art 2 ECHR. Christian Tomuschat, Evelyne Lagrange, and Stefan Oeter (eds), *The Right to Life* (Martinus Nijhoff 2010).
[139] Art 7 ICCPR; Convention against Torture and Other Cruel, Inhuman or Degrading Treatment or Punishment (adopted 10 December 1984, entered into force 26 June 1987) 1465 UNTS 85 (CAT); Art 5 ACHR; Art 5 ACHPR; Art 8 ArCHR; Art 3 ECHR.
[140] Slavery Convention; Art 8 ICCPR; Art 6 ACHR; Art 5 ACHPR; Art 10 ArCHR; Art 4 ECHR.
[141] Art 9 ICCPR; Art 7 ACHR; Art 6 ACHPR; Art 14 ArCHR; Art 5 ECHR.
[142] Art 14 ICCPR; Art 7 ACHPR; Art 8 ACHR; Arts 12 and 13 ArCHR; Art 6 ECHR.
[143] Art 18 ICCPR; Art 8 ACHPR; Arts 12 and 13 ACHR; Art 30 ArCHR; Art 9 ECHR.
[144] Art 12 ICCPR; Art 12 ACHPR; Art 22 ACHR; Art 26 ArCHR; Art 2 Prot 4 ECHR.
[145] Arts 19, 21 and 22 ICCPR; Arts 9, 10 and 11 ACHPR; Arts 13, 15, and 16 ACHR; Arts 24(6) and 32 ArCHR; Arts 10 and 11 ECHR.
[146] Arts 6 and 7 International Covenant on Economic, Social and Cultural Rights (adopted 16 December 1966, entered into force 3 January 1976) 993 UNTS 3 (ICESCR); Art 15 ACHPR; Art 34 ArCHR.
[147] Art 9 ICESCR; Art 36 ArCHR.   [148] Art 11 ICESCR; Art 38 ArCHR.
[149] Arts 12 and 7(b) ICESCR; Art 10 ACHR; Art 16 ACHPR; Art 39 ArCHR.
[150] Art 15 ICESCR; Art 17 ACHPR; Art 42 ArCHR.
[151] The Slavery Convention (adopted 25 September 1926, entered into force 9 March 1927) 60 LNTS 253; the Convention on the Prevention and Punishment of the Crime of Genocide (adopted 9 December 1948, entered into force 12 January 1951) 78 UNTS 277; the CAT.
[152] Convention relating to the Status of Refugees (adopted 28 July 1951, entered into force 22 April 1954) 189 UNTS 137 (Refugee Convention), the Convention on the Elimination of All Forms of Racial Discrimination (adopted 7 March 1966, entered into force 4 January 1969) 660 UNTS 195 (CERD), the Convention on the Elimination of All Forms of Discrimination against Women (adopted 18 December 1979, entered into force 3 September 1981) 1249 UNTS 13 (CEDAW), the International Convention on the Protection of the Rights of All Migrant Workers and Members of their Families (adopted 18 December 1990, entered into force 1 July 2003) 2220 UNTS 3 (Migrant Workers Convention), the Convention on the Rights of the Child (adopted 20 November 1989, entered into force 2 September 1990) 1577 UNTS 3, and the Convention on the Rights of Persons with Disabilities (adopted 13 December 2006, entered into force 3 May 2008) 2515 UNTS 3.
[153] The scope of States' duties is generally determined through recourse to the notion of 'jurisdiction'. See Chapter 3, Section 2.3.
[154] General Comment 31 (n 131) paras 6 and 7. In the case of positive obligations, they include both obligations of conduct and obligations of result; CESCR, 'General Comment No. 3—The nature of States parties' obligations' (1 January 1991) UN Doc E/1991/23 (General Comment 3) para 1; Kalin and

always obligatory. This means that derogations of human rights need to be specifically worded in the treaty and that States cannot avoid their human rights duties, even if they are allowed some discretion in compliance under the margin of appreciation doctrine.[155]

Stemming from the aspiration to ensure universal validity, human rights are often drafted in absolute terms: they apply to all people, everywhere at all times.[156] The UDHR refers to 'all human beings', 'everybody', and 'no one', and the rights provided in Articles 1–28 do not generally contain spatial or temporal limitations.[157] While spatial and temporal limitations inherent to treaties constrain conventional human rights,[158] the aspiration of these instruments remains universal and is reflected in language similar to that of the UDHR. This approach means that no human rights instrument either mentions people at sea or contains provisions that take into account the peculiarities of the marine environment and the special needs of people who are therein. All the same, there is nothing in the text and context of human rights treaties to preclude the applicability of rights listed therein to people at sea, as has often been done by international courts and scholars alike.[159] It can therefore be safely concluded that all human rights treaties and customary norms apply to people at sea as a general rule.

Although the applicability of human rights at sea cannot be seriously questioned, this branch of law presents two characteristics that may create interpretative dilemmas concerning both the scope and the content of States' obligations towards persons

Kunzli (n 134) 96–97. The African Commission on Human and Peoples' Rights (ACommHPR) has considered that 'all rights, both civil and political rights and social and economic, generate at least four levels of duties for a State that undertakes to adhere to a rights regime, namely the duty to *respect, protect, promote*, and *fulfil* these rights'; ACommHPR, *Social and Economic Rights Action Center (SERAC) and Center for Economic and Social Rights (CESR) v Nigeria*, Communication No 155/96 (2001), para 44 (emphasis added).

[155] One notable exception to the binding nature of legal obligations deriving from human rights concerns Art 5(1)(c) CAT, according to which the State of the nationality of the victim may establish its jurisdiction over acts of torture 'if that State considers it appropriate'. The obligatory nature of human rights duties may allow some discretion in determining how to comply with them, as recognized under the margin of appreciation doctrine. *Handyside v The United Kingdom* App no 5493/72 (7 December 1976) paras 48–49 and more recently *Vinter and Others v The United Kingdom* Apps nos 66069/09, 130/10 and 3896/10 ((GC) 9 July 2013); Andrew Legg, *The Margin of Appreciation in International Human Rights Law: Deference and Proportionality* (OUP 2012).

[156] In 1948 the UDHR mentioned 'the inherent dignity and . . . the equal and inalienable rights of all members of the human family' and set the aim 'to secure their universal and effective recognition and observance' (Preamble, UDHR).

[157] The only limitation, to be found at the end of the UDHR Preamble, refers to 'the peoples of Member States themselves and . . . the peoples of territories under their jurisdiction'.

[158] In particular the rule that treaties bind only States that have accepted them (Arts 26 and 34 Vienna Convention on the Law of Treaties (adopted 23 May 1969, entered into force 27 January 1980) 1155 UNTS 331 (VCLT)), that they are not retroactive (Art 28 VCLT) and that they apply only on the territory of the parties (Art 29 VCLT). The latter rule is often tempered through reference to 'jurisdiction' to determine the scope of State obligations. See Chapter 3, Section 2.3.

[159] *Corfu Channel* (n 135) 22; *Medvedyev and Others v France* App no 3394/03 (Judgment (GC) of 29 March 2010) para 81; *Hirsi* (n 22) para 178; *The Haitian Centre for Human Rights* et al *v United States* Case 10.675 (Report no 51/96 of 13 March 1997) para 169. See also Oxman, 'Human Rights' (n 107); Treves, 'Human Rights' (n 51); Sophie Cacciaguidi-Fahy, 'The Law of the Sea and Human Rights' (2007) 19 Sri Lanka Journal of International Law 85.

at sea. The human-centric nature of much human rights law may hinder the identification of the precise obligations that bind States, as norms focus on rights of individuals, rather than duties of States. Further complexity results from the fact that human rights law was drafted having situations on land in mind, and the application of its rules and principles at sea may require a rethinking of some operative rules, so as to ensure the right balance between rights and duties while taking into account the natural and legal peculiarities of maritime space. These issues are explored in the next sections, before moving to a preliminary assessment of the contribution of human rights law to the protection of people at sea.

7.2.1 Human rights law as a right-centered regime

While 'human' is the politically charged part of the phrase 'human rights', it is the 'rights' aspect that is most relevant for lawyers. The basic purpose of human rights law is to attribute subjective rights to the individual, that is rights that can be claimed and enforced against an identified State.

Human rights were born in the Western legal tradition in order to protect individuals from the absolute power of sovereigns by reversing the traditional relationship, in terms of rights and duties, between the sovereign and its subjects. Since their inception, in addition to duties for the State, bills of rights were couched in terms of rights for citizens. The French Declaration of the Rights of Man and of the Citizen thus contained provisions stating that '[n]ul homme ne peut être accusé, arrêté ni détenu que dans les cas déterminés par la Loi, et selon les formes qu'elle a prescrites'[160] and that '[n]ul ne doit être inquiété pour ses opinions'.[161] The USA Bill of Rights provides that 'the right of the people to be secure in their persons, houses, papers, and effects, against unreasonable searches and seizures, shall not be violated'[162] and that 'in all criminal prosecutions, the accused shall enjoy the right to a speedy and public trial, by an impartial jury'.[163] Twentieth century human rights treaties stuck to the rhetoric of rights underlying the national declarations, and provided lists of the rights and liberties of the individual.[164] In contrast to this, the obligations of the State were usually dealt with in rather generic provisions, often to be found in a part other than those listing rights.[165]

---

[160] Art 7 (French) Declaration of the Rights of Man and of the Citizen.

[161] Art 10 (French) Declaration of the Rights of Man and of the Citizen.

[162] Amendment IV (USA) Bill of Rights.   [163] Amendment VI (USA) Bill of Rights.

[164] This paragraph is concerned with rights (of the individual) as opposed to duties (of the State). However, the rights-centered approach has also been criticized as avoiding or unduly formulating the duties of individuals themselves. The ECHR, eg, does not mention any duty of individuals, as opposed to the ACHR and the ACHPR, which contain an article and a section, respectively. The tension between the rights and duties of individuals themselves is beyond the scope of this paragraph. See briefly Gerhard Hafner, 'Some Thoughts on the State-Oriented and Individual-Oriented Approaches in International Law' (2013) 14 Austrian Review of International and European Law 27; and in detail Joseph Raz, *Ethics in the Public Domain: Essays in the Morality of Law and Politics* (Clarendon Press 1995), in particular Chapter 2 'Liberating Duties'.

[165] Thus, Art 2 ICCPR provides that 'Each State Party to the present Covenant undertakes to *respect* and to *ensure* to all individuals within its territory and subject to its jurisdiction the rights recognised in the present Covenant, without distinction of any kind, such as race, colour, sex, language, religion,

The focus on 'rights' when drafting treaties and the 'right-centered' formulation of many provisions is not devoid of problematic aspects.[166] Although it is generally possible to identify a corresponding duty imposed upon a State for every right of an individual, it is also true that the description of duties is not well-developed in most human rights instruments. Also, the provisions concerning rights and those referring to duties are often found in separate parts of a legal instrument, requiring an interpretative effort to match the right of a certain individual with the corresponding duty pending on an identified State to undertake a particular action.[167] Misalignment may result in three problems: identification of the duty bearer, clarification of the content of the obligation, and, more generally, coping with preventive action. The first is closely linked with the grounding on land of human rights, and will be discussed in the following section; the remaining two issues will be examined here.

The focus on rights often results in a *de facto* indeterminacy of the content of a State's duty. Of course, the existence of human rights means that the State has to avoid conduct that would infringe upon individuals' rights. In many cases, however, compliance with obligations under human rights law may require a complex set of actions that extend well beyond negative conduct. Social and economic rights provide many meaningful examples. As the Committee on Economic, Social and Cultural Rights (CESCR) has noted, Article 2 ICESCR requires States to adopt steps that 'should be deliberate, concrete and targeted as clearly as possible towards meeting the obligations recognised in the Covenant'.[168] However, what is the exact content of the duty which corresponds to the right to social security[169] or to the right to an adequate standard of living?[170] This issue is also present with respect to civil and political rights. The right to life, for example, certainly means that State agents must not kill individuals, but is it enough for a State not to kill an individual to fulfil its obligation, or is something more required? The issue assumes great practical importance in the case of rescued people who were saved at sea, when disembarkation and the duties of the master of the vessel are blurred. Furthermore, what is the exact content of the duty correlative to the right not to be subject to inhuman and degrading treatment? If a fisherman is regularly beaten while the fishing vessel on which he works is out at sea fishing, what action is the State required to undertake? Should it provide for remedies once (and if) the fisherman disembarks on its shore? Should it send State agents to control what happens on board the vessel? Should it send State officials to enforce the rights of the fisher? Or, as a last resort,

political or other opinion, national or social origin, property, birth or other status' (emphasis added). The provision then specifies that this shall be done through the adoption of 'laws or other measures' (Art 2(2) ICCPR) and that adequate procedural measures shall be adopted concerning effective remedies, hearing by an authority determined by law and effective enforcement (Art 2(3) ICCPR).

[166] The relationship between rights and duties is at the core of much human rights and, more generally, legal discourse. An even superficial examination of the jurisprudential debates on the issue is beyond the scope of this chapter (and indeed of this book).

[167] This issue becomes particularly relevant when one turns to positive obligations.

[168] General Comment 3 (n 154) para 2.   [169] Art 9 ICESCR.

[170] Art 11(1) ICESCR.

should it prohibit fishing entirely?[171] These are key questions and indeed most decisions by international judges and a great part of soft law instruments adopted by international bodies have been devoted to clarifying the exact content of a State's duties.[172]

Furthermore, the dangers that the sea presents often require States to take preventive action at a time when it is not yet possible to identify any person having the right to claim compliance with a duty imposed upon the State. For example, an effective way to protect human life at sea consists in the supervision of the construction of ships, so as to ensure that they are seaworthy and that they are supplied with all necessary safety equipment. However, these issues are preliminary to the voyage of the vessel and take place at a stage when it is not possible to know the individual whose right to life may be affected by poor safety. In many cases, the identification of the person claiming the right endangered by State conduct will be possible only when harm has already occurred. Although an injured person or the relatives of a drowned person may be able to claim a State's responsibility and exercise their right to compensation, this is, however, cold comfort and only a partial and unsatisfactory way of fulfilling the obligation to protect life at sea.

7.2.2 The territorial grounding of human rights

A necessary prerequisite to the application of human rights is the identification, from among all States, of the State that bears the duty to protect them. In this respect, international human rights law was developed to attribute rights to individuals who were within the territory of a sovereign that had agreed to respect them. The use of rights rhetoric as a normative technique generally works well on land, where there is always one 'sovereign' who is considered as having the 'default' duty to protect all of these rights. Citizens and other individuals within the territory of a State will naturally address claims for the protection of their rights to that State. In other words, human rights law was grounded on land, and not the sea. As a consequence, the sea was—rightly or wrongly—for centuries considered as a lawless extension of water.[173]

While certainly not a lawless environment, the seas still present a legal framework that is different from land and the rights rhetoric generates a number of problems in the complex jurisdictional framework that applies to marine spaces.[174] In this context, even when it may be relatively easy to recognize the rights enjoyed by an

---

[171] In all these cases, it also remains to establish whether State action should be *proprio motu* or should be prompted by the request of the interested party, or of other actors.

[172] See Chapter 4.

[173] In 1915, Marsden still recalled the 'centuries of lawlessness upon the seas'; Reginald Godfrey Marsden, *Documents Relating to Law and Custom of the Sea*, vol I (Navy Records Society 1915) viii.

[174] Another area of complexity concerns the extraterritorial applicability of human rights obligations within the territory of another State. If agents of State A act in the territory of State B, can State A be held accountable for violating human rights obligations that it has accepted? In this case, the complexity is due to the existence of the sovereignty of State B. See Chapter 3.

individual, the identification of the State that has to ensure these rights may become a major issue. Let us take, for example, the case of a national of State A working on board a fishing vessel flying the flag of State B which is licensed to fish in the exclusive economic zone of State C. If this person is not allowed to leave the vessel and is regularly beaten whenever he tries to disembark, there is a clear violation of a number of human rights, including the prohibition of forced labour, the right to personal integrity, the right not to be subject to torture or inhuman treatment, and the right to the freedom of movement. But which is the State that has failed its duty to secure these rights? Is it the flag State, the coastal State, or the State of nationality? Or is it, perhaps, all three States? Human rights law alone does not provide any clear-cut answer to these questions. It is only an integrated reading of international human rights norms and law of the sea norms that may ensure a comprehensive answer to these issues, as will be discussed in Chapter 3.[175]

7.2.3 *The contribution of human rights law*

While it is trite to underline the relevance of human rights law for the protection of persons, it is worth highlighting three aspects in particular: it provides basic substantial and uniform standards of treatment; it grants rights and liberties to individuals directly; and it imposes correspondent duties on States.

However, these positive contributions do not come without a price. Examples above illustrate the limits encountered by human rights law in its effort to ensure the protection of people at sea and demonstrate that the effective protection of these persons cannot be based solely on human rights provisions, but must also include detailed duties for States. Although the applicability of human rights at sea cannot be seriously questioned, the absence of dedicated provisions may create interpretative dilemmas concerning both the scope and the content of States' obligations towards persons at sea, which may require some rethinking so as to adapt States' duties to the harsh natural conditions and complex overlap of jurisdiction that characterizes marine space.

7.3 Technical regimes

A different but significant role is played by two other regimes, namely labour law and maritime law.[176] These two regimes can be considered part of human rights law and the law of the sea, respectively, but I prefer to deal with them separately so as to concentrate on their distinctive contribution to the law concerning persons at sea. While the content of these regimes that is particularly relevant for the protection of people at sea has been expounded in Chapter 1, it seems apt to add a few general considerations on their role in framing the legal framework that applies to people at sea.

---

[175] See Chapter 3, Section 7.
[176] The content of these regimes has been presented in Chapter 1.

In contrast to human rights law and the law of the sea, which comprise general principles, these two regimes are chiefly composed of detailed and rather technical instruments that set rules specifying and clarifying the duties of States with regard to the pursuance of specific aims. In a synallagmatic relationship, both are governed by the general principles mentioned above and at the same time complement—and in many instances render enforceable—the rules deriving from the other two fields. However, the limited scope of these regimes, and of the legal instruments that contain them, while often being the key to their successful adoption, is also their most significant limitation. Taken by themselves, they produce fragmentation, thus consolidating regime thinking whilst hindering systemic thinking.

7.4 A preliminary assessment

The sections above have examined the principal specialized legal regimes of international law that provide rules that apply to people at sea and that contain States' obligations towards these people. The analysis has highlighted the individual contributions of each regime and at the same time has expounded those characteristics that may constitute an obstacle to the value or effectiveness of existing rules. Before leaving the regimes to return to the overall system, it is useful to highlight some elements that will be used in subsequent analysis.

First, there are some terms that are used interchangeably in different regimes. Of these, 'jurisdiction' is probably the most relevant. Identical words used in different instruments may prove potentially dangerous for a sound understanding of the applicable law, but are also highly suggestive of novel associations not previously imagined. In these cases, it is necessary to investigate whether the same meaning is attributed to the term in different contexts or whether there are peculiar nuances particular to a single regime. Furthermore, one should also consider whether a common understanding of the term could be advanced, or whether this is hindered by formal obstacles, such as the presence of definitions in legal instruments. For example, while 'jurisdiction' is a broad term, a provision that refers to 'the power to adopt laws and regulations', or to 'legislative jurisdiction' only, would limit the possibility to transfer meaning from one regime to another.

Second, all regimes regulate the conduct of States and all confer obligations that bind States. There is great variety, however, as to the content of these obligations, their scope, and the detail into which they are drafted, even when they avowedly aim to address the same issue. The protection of human life at sea illustrates the point, with its accumulation of similar, though not identical, legal norms. All States are under the duty to protect the right to life as endorsed by human rights treaties. Similarly, customary law of the sea places all States under the general duty to save life at sea. Furthermore, States have many detailed obligations concerning the safety of ships, as provided in the SOLAS and other treaties. Additionally, States have duties concerning the safety of navigation in their maritime zones, provided by both custom and treaties, such as the International Convention on Maritime Search and Rescue (SAR Convention). How are all these duties to be read? Are they independent duties? Do they have the same content? Do they pursue the same aim through different content? Do they complete each other? Do they exclude each other? These are all questions that need to be addressed in order to avoid gaps and to maximize efficiency of the system.

Third, there are a number of rights (of individuals and of States) and duties (generally of States) which are disjointed, but which could present some overlaps or the potential for interaction. For example, there are logical nexuses between the right to personal liberty, the safeguards usually accompanying any arrest of persons who commit illegal acts, and the duties of a State to enforce legal instruments designed to combat illegal acts. However, these nexuses are often latent and are not fully exploited in legal instruments. As a consequence, the questions posed above remain valid also for these examples.

8. Back to the System

All instances mentioned above show that the factual circumstances surrounding the presence of people at sea require that existing rules be interpreted and applied in ways that often go beyond those that their drafters had in mind. For example, human rights have been drafted having in mind situations on land. However, since individuals may clearly also suffer violations of their rights at sea, human rights now need to be interpreted and applied so as to ensure the protection of people at sea as well as on land. Similarly, norms concerning the distribution of power among States, in the form of jurisdictional rules, were developed so as to determine the State that might exercise certain rights over a person. Now however, these norms also apply for determining the State that has the obligation to protect a person, and are therefore instrumental in identifying the duties of a State. In all these cases, it is necessary to explore the inter-systemic potential of norms to adapt to and be applied in different contexts, while maintaining their fundamental intra-systemic characteristics. Regime thinking does not allow such an operation.

It is therefore time to return to the system of international law for a comprehensive appraisal of the law that applies to people at sea. Making use of the systemic approach presented above, the rest of the volume will engage in an appraisal of the added value of the co-existence of all rules and regimes recalled in Chapter 1 and in the above sections within one legal system. Four questions could be posed that determine any evaluation of the effects of interaction. Firstly, what is the general framework of reference against which the law that applies to people at sea is identified, interpreted, and applied? Is this the framework of human rights, that of the law of the sea, or a composite one? Secondly, are there any devices for facilitating the systemic integration of legal instruments and rules belonging to separate regimes? Thirdly, is there any particular general principle that guides the development and interpretation of the law which is specific to this issue? Fourthly, is the interaction between discrete regimes affecting the structure of legal norms? The first two issues will be dealt with here, while the second two, which relate to the substantial content of the applicable rules, will be addressed in Chapter 4.

8.1 The framework of reference

The description of any set of legal rules rests on assumptions, often implicitly made, concerning a certain framework of reference. Indeed, a 'system' or 'regime' will provide the background concepts upon which the set of rules will be carved and the guiding principles against which these rules will be assessed.[177] At the same time, the existence of a framework of reference does not preclude the existence of norms that will apply only to specific cases. These norms are however constructed as exceptions to the generally applicable standard, and not as general rules themselves.

A lack of consideration and analysis of this consequence has tainted the development of a legal discourse addressing the applicability of human rights at sea and, more generally, the protection of people at sea. The conceptualization of rules that apply to persons at sea has so far mostly been conducted adopting a partial approach, which limits any inquiry into the rules that apply to a specific category of persons, often in conjunction with a limited functional scope of enquiry. For instance, scholars have considered the extent to which human rights apply during interdiction operations at sea,[178] or whether and how they apply to captured pirates,[179] or to migrants rescued at sea.[180] This approach is unsatisfactory for present purposes, since the rules applicable to a specific case would appear to materialize according to the point of view adopted. While differences in treatment may be grounded in the existence of well-developed, or less-developed, legal instruments, the conclusion that is often reached is that people outside the regime most beneficial to them enjoy fewer rights. It is perhaps no surprise that experienced scholars have opted for a non-committal approach which highlights mutual interactions, rather than arguing in favour of the prevalence of one field and the subsequent subsumption of rules deriving from other regimes into the former.[181]

The preliminary assessment of the specialized legal regimes carried out above shows that two legal regimes play a major role in framing the rules on people at sea: international human rights law and the law of the sea. The former provides the basic substantial standards for the treatment of persons. The latter distributes power

---

[177] *Georges Pinson (France) v United Mexican States* (1928) V RIAA 327, para 12.

[178] Douglas Guilfoyle, *Shipping Interdiction and the Law of the Sea* (CUP 2009) 266–71; Efthymios Papastavridis, *The Interception of Vessels on the High Seas* (Hart 2014) 73–80.

[179] Robin Geiss and Anna Petrig, *Piracy and Armed Robbery at Sea: The Legal Framework for Counter-Piracy Operations in Somalia and the Gulf of Aden* (OUP 2011) 101–16; Mihaela Ailincai, 'Piraterie et droits de l'homme au sein du Conseil de l'Europe' in Constance Chevallier-Govers and Catherine Schneider (eds), *L'Europe et la lutte contre la piraterie maritime* (Pedone 2015) 227; Cesare Pitea, 'Azioni di contrasto alla pirateria e Convenzione europea dei diritti umani: questioni di attribuzione e di applicazione extraterritoriale' (2015) 9 Diritti Umani e Diritto Internazionale 489; Tullio Treves and Cesare Pitea, 'Piracy, International Law and Human Rights' in Nehal Bhuta (ed), *The Frontiers of Human Rights. Extraterritoriality and Its Challenges* (OUP 2016) 89.

[180] Mark Pallis, 'Obligations of States towards Asylum Seekers at Sea: Interactions and Conflicts Between Legal Regimes' (2002) 14 International Journal of Refugee Law 329; Barnes (n 17); Klein (n 63).

[181] Works by Oxman and Treves, in particular, provide knowledgeable hints at the potential of applying systemic thinking to the interaction between human rights and the law of the sea; Oxman, 'Human Rights' (n 107); Treves, 'Human Rights' (n 51). See Chapter 5, Section 6.

among States in different maritime zones and therefore determines the State that has the correspondent obligation to ensure respect of the applicable law, including human rights. Both regimes are essential, although neither is sufficient, by itself, to ensure the achievement of the overall aim of legal regulation in this field. It would therefore be incorrect to consider that either one is *the* appropriate regime for dealing with persons at sea, albeit mediated by rules and concepts deriving from the other. Unless the entire allocation of jurisdiction achieved by law of the sea rules is introduced into human rights law, or unless all human rights rules (as interpreted and applied by human rights bodies) are ushered into the law of the sea, neither regime will contain all rules that are required to deal with the particular issues that are discussed in this book.

This book proposes a different stance, based on the systemic nature of international law. Having identified the regimes that contribute to the regulation of 'people at sea', and having collated the specific rules that regulate this topic, it is submitted that these rules need to be interpreted and applied against the background comprised of principles of general international law, the law of the sea, and international human rights law. These include principles that were originally developed within one or the other regime and which now need to be applied beyond the original intentions of their makers. Any existing rule and any proposal to develop new regulation must be measured against the general principles that derive from both law of the sea and human rights law. These are basic notions concerning the treatment of people and the responsibilities of the State, as endorsed in human rights, and the distribution of power between States at sea, as crystallized in the law of the sea. Furthermore, it could be argued that the friction between the law of the sea and international human rights law has resulted in the production of a further, new principle, which is independent from either regime and which is proper to the law that relates to people at sea. According to this principle, States are under a duty to protect people at sea and to undertake positive action in this respect. Since it pertains to the substantial content of the applicable law, this principle will be discussed in Chapter 4.

8.2 Integrational devices and rules on conflict

Having established the general framework against which rules concerning people at sea are to be applied, it is now time to turn to the rules themselves. How do these norms interact? What rules, if any, regulate this intercourse? These are the questions that will be addressed in the following paragraphs.

The basic premise is that the relationship between rules of international law cannot be settled in advance, since any balancing needs to take into account the elements of the particular case. However, it is possible to identify some general rules that will assist in this task. The principle of systemic integration and the principle of harmonization, discussed above, serve both the purpose of reducing conflicts, by eliminating apparent conflicts. In the case of real conflicts, further rules of general international law apply, with a view towards settling the conflict and identifying the rule that will eventually apply.

From a conceptual perspective, the possibility that one regime entirely rules out the application of another cannot be sustained in the face of the systemic nature of international law. Notwithstanding their peculiarities and the characteristics that distinguish them from each other, all legal regimes contain rules that can be subsumed, in the end, within the loose category of rules of international law. The provisions of an international human rights treaty, as well as those of maritime treaties and those contained in instruments that can be traced back to other specialized legal regimes, not to mention custom, belong at the same time to their specific (sub) regime and are part of the wider regime of public international law. This conclusion is supported by the source of the rules, their use by States and other international actors, the relevance that is given to them by domestic courts, as well as their use by all international courts and tribunals that are asked to settle disputes 'on the basis of international law'.

8.2.1 *Rules on conflict*

Long before discussion of the proliferation of legal instruments and the ensuing threat to the integrity of the system began, States realized that the increase in treaty-making would require relationships between treaties to be regulated. Two types of rules were therefore developed. On the one hand, it became settled practice to introduce specific rules on conflict in legal instruments during the drafting stages.[182] Such rules regulate the relationship between the treaty to which they belong and other treaties, which can be identified by name or, more generally, by date of conclusion or subject matter. While these provisions do not necessarily settle all issues, they are very helpful in discussing relationships between legal provisions. On the other hand, general rules on the relationships between treaties were developed, which apply in the absence of a specific rule contained within a treaty concerning that treaty's relationship with other instruments. Whilst the provisions of the VCLT prima facie regulate the relationship between treaties, they are generally considered as regulating also that between legal norms.[183] The latter include general principles such as *lex posterior* and *lex specialis*, as well as hierarchical principles including *jus cogens* and *erga omnes* obligations.[184] General rules on the relationship between norms have been extensively discussed in legal doctrine[185] and will not be further expounded here. Specific provisions introduced into relevant treaties will however be further discussed in the following subsections.

---

[182] For example Art 103 United Nations Charter.

[183] ILC Conclusions (n 3) para 3: 'When seeking to determine the relationship of two or more norms to each other, the norms should be interpreted in accordance with or analogously to the VCLT and especially the provisions in its articles 31–33 having to do with the interpretation of treaties'. For the applicability of Arts 31–33 VCLT to the interpretation of the ECHR see *Demir and Baykara* (n 56) para 65.

[184] For an articulated discussion of the use of these norms and principles see ILC Conclusions (n 3).

[185] Koskenniemi Report (n 6); Pauwelyn, *Conflict of Norms* (n 37); Pulkowski, *The Law* (n 36).

8.2.1.1 The UNCLOS

Article 311 of the UNCLOS addresses conflicts by providing rules concerning different types of treaties.[186] Firstly, the UNCLOS prevails over the 1958 Geneva Conventions.[187] Secondly, the UNCLOS permits *inter se* modifications—that is, treaties agreed by some of its parties—subject to three conditions. The modification must not prevent effective execution of the object and purpose of the UNCLOS, it must not affect the application of its basic principles, and it must not affect the rights and obligations of third States.[188] Thirdly, parties cannot amend the principles of Article 136 relating to the common heritage of humanity.[189] Fourthly, Article 311 addresses the relationships between the UNCLOS and other pre-existing or subsequently enacted treaties. In this respect, Article 311 distinguishes treaties expressly provided for in UNCLOS provisions from all other treaties.

On the one hand, all treaties which are expressly preserved or permitted by specific provisions are not affected by the conclusion of the UNCLOS.[190] Notably, this provision applies both to treaties predating the UNCLOS, as well as to treaties concluded afterwards.[191] Among many other provisions, Article 146 requires the adoption of effective measures to protect human life and requires the Authority to 'adopt appropriate rules, regulations and procedures to supplement existing international law *as embodied in relevant treaties*'.[192] Similarly, Article 94(3)(b) of the UNCLOS provides that when regulating the 'manning of ships, labour conditions and the training of crews', flag States shall take into account 'the applicable international instruments'. On the basis of these norms, it can be concluded that all labour and human rights treaties that are relevant will supersede the Convention. But reference to other norms of international law is to be found also in some of the fundamental provisions allocating power at sea. The UNCLOS provides that '[t]he sovereignty over the territorial sea is exercised subject to this Convention and to other rules of international law',[193] and that '[f]reedom of the high seas is exercised under the

---

[186] Generally on the interaction between the UNCLOS and other international law regimes Alan Boyle, 'Further Development of the 1982 Convention on the Law of the Sea: Mechanisms for Change' in David Freestone, Richard Barnes, and David Ong (eds), *The Law of the Sea: Progress and Prospects* (OUP 2006) 40.

[187] Art 311(1) UNCLOS.

[188] Art 311(3) UNCLOS. According to Art 311(4) UNCLOS, there is a duty of notification in this respect.

[189] Art 311(6) UNCLOS. The discussion of this norm, including whether Art 136 UNCLOS is part of *jus cogens*, is beyond the scope of this book. See Harrison (n 43) 133–34; Kemal Baslar, *The Concept of the Common Heritage of Mankind in International Law* (Martin Nijhoff 1998).

[190] Art 311(5) UNCLOS.

[191] Myron H Nordquist, Shabtai Rosenne, and Louis B Sohn (eds), *United Nations Convention on the Law of the Sea, 1982: A Commentary,* vol V (Martinus Nijhoff 1989) 243 '[a]lthough doubts were expressed as to the necessity for this paragraph, its presence has the effect of precluding any argument of possible inconsistency between the *lex generalis* of article 311 and the *lex specialis* of the other articles'.

[192] Emphasis added. References to other treaties are common in UNCLOS. Art 73(3) UNCLOS safeguards agreements between two or more States that allow for imprisonment for violation of the laws and regulation of the coastal State concerning fishing in its exclusive economic zone. Art 92(1) and Art 110(1) preserves treaties that attribute jurisdiction, including enforcement jurisdiction, over vessels sailing on the high seas to States other than the flag State. For other examples see Nordquist, Rosenne, and Sohn (n 191) para 311.8.

[193] Art 2(3) UNCLOS.

conditions laid down by this Convention and by other rules of international law'.[194] Reference to 'other rules of international law' in these provisions arguably includes reference to duties vis-à-vis persons provided under human rights law, labour law, and refugee law.[195] These duties could therefore be considered as prevailing over the UNCLOS provisions.

On the other hand, the notion of 'all other treaties' has a somewhat ambiguous meaning. According to Article 311(2) of the UNCLOS:

> This Convention shall not alter the rights and obligations of States Parties which arise from other agreements compatible with this Convention and which do not affect the enjoyment by other States Parties of their rights or the performance of their obligations under this Convention.

At first sight, this provision might be taken to provide for the prevalence of obligations contained in other instruments.[196] However, the reference to 'agreements compatible' with the UNCLOS seems to point to the opposite direction: that the UNCLOS prevails over all agreements that are not compatible with it, or which prejudice the rights and duties deriving from the UNCLOS.[197] Furthermore, the language used in this provision demands a determination of the level of analysis. Does compatibility refer to the two norms or to the two treaties? While both readings are possible, the reference to the 'object and purpose' in the following paragraph seems to point towards an assessment of the compatibility between the treaties, rather than their provisions, or at least between the provision of the other treaty and the UNCLOS as a unitary instrument. As long as the other treaty does not go against the object and purpose of the UNCLOS, its provisions will prevail.

However, if the treaty or one of its provisions frustrates the objectives of the UNCLOS, the latter will prevail. This conclusion requires an assessment of the 'object and purpose' of the UNCLOS, as this needs to be taken into account lest it invalidates other agreements. In the case of a sizeable and complex treaty such as the UNCLOS, it is difficult to identify a single object and scope. Multiple interests were advanced during the negotiations and while it is certain that navigation, access to resources, and the protection of the marine environment were key aspects of the negotiating process, they cannot be considered as representing the entire object and scope of the UNCLOS.[198] Furthermore, any of the other issues that were debated and agreed upon by the drafters cannot be done so either. Rather, the object of the UNCLOS is a broader one: providing a stable jurisdictional framework and the consolidation of the rule of law at sea.[199] This objective is not subject-specific, but

---

[194] Art 87(1) UNCLOS.   [195] Klein (n 63) 807.   [196] See Art 30(2) VCLT.

[197] In this sense, see Nordquist, Rosenne, and Sohn (n 191) 243.

[198] The UNCLOS Preamble refers to the 'desirability of establishing through this Convention, with due regard for the sovereignty of all States, a legal order for the seas and oceans which will facilitate international communication, and will promote the peaceful uses of the seas and oceans, the equitable and efficient utilization of their resources, the conservation of their living resources, and the study, protection and preservation of the marine environment'.

[199] The UNCLOS Preamble opens by mentioning 'the desire to settle, in a spirit of mutual understanding and cooperation, *all issues* relating to the law of the sea and aware of the historic significance of this Convention as an important contribution to the maintenance of peace, justice and progress for all peoples of the world' (emphasis added). The fact that it was a package deal, achieved through a balancing

embraces all issues relating to the law of the sea. As a consequence, agreements that further the rule of law and respect the division of jurisdictional competences established within the UNCLOS should be considered compatible with this Convention for the purposes of Article 311(2) and their provisions may prevail over those of the UNCLOS.[200] In this sense, one could well say that the UNCLOS is 'a living instrument, capable both of change in order to accommodate new challenges and of construing novel associations of existing provisions, both in the text itself and in other international conventions, to support the evolving needs of the international community'.[201]

8.2.1.2 Human rights treaties

Human rights treaties do not contain provisions similar to Article 311 of the UNCLOS. They do however contain provisions which aim to establish that the human rights recognized in them are a minimum, and that further protection may derive from other treaties. For example, the International Covenant on Civil and Political Rights (ICCPR) provides that:

There shall be no restriction upon or derogation from any of the fundamental human rights recognized or existing in any State Party to the present Covenant pursuant to law, conventions, regulations or custom on the pretext that the present Covenant does not recognize such rights or that it recognizes them to a lesser extent.[202]

Similarly, Article 53 of the European Convention on Human Rights (ECHR) safeguards 'any of the human rights and fundamental freedoms which may be ensured under the laws of any High Contracting Party or under any other agreement to which it is a Party'.[203]

More detail about the relationship with other instruments and norms is provided by the African Charter on Human and Peoples' Rights (ACHPR). It is thereby established that the (African) Commission 'shall draw inspiration from international law on human and peoples' rights'[204] and that it shall also take into consideration, in

of different interests and the sacrifice of some individual positions in order to obtain a binding legal instrument, strengthens the conclusion that there is no single substantial issue that could be considered as its main object. The remark of the president of UNCLOS III at the closing of the negotiation that 'we celebrate human solidarity and the reality of interdependence which is symbolised by the United Nations Convention on the Law of the Sea' goes in the same direction, as do the declarations of States during the signature of the final text (Tommy TB Koh, 'A Constitution for the Oceans' <http://www.un.org/depts/los/convention_agreements/texts/koh_english.pdf>).

[200] Alex Oude Elferink, *Stability and Change in the Law of the Sea: The Role of the LOS Convention* (Martinus Nijhoff 2005).

[201] Gavouneli (n 85) 146. Of course, to say simply that the UNCLOS is a 'living treaty' does not answer queries as to '*how* it evolves, *who* controls these processes, and what limits there are, or should be, to the scope each category of actors have to grow and change it' (Jill Barrett, 'The UN Convention on the Law of the Sea: A "Living" Treaty?' in Jill Barrett and Richard Barnes (eds), *Law of the Sea. UNCLOS as a Living Treaty* (BIICL 2016) 3, 8, emphasis in the original). On the issue see also Richard Barnes, 'The Continuing Vitality of UNCLOS' in Jill Barrett and Richard Barnes (eds), *Law of the Sea. UNCLOS as a Living Treaty* (BIICL 2016) 459.

[202] Art 5(2) ICCPR. See also, with identical content, Art 5(2) ICESCR.

[203] See also Art 29(b) ACHR.

[204] Art 60 ACHPR. In particular the ACHPR mentions 'provisions of various African instruments on human and peoples' rights, the Charter of the United Nations, the Charter of the

a subsidiary manner, 'other general or special international conventions', 'customs generally accepted as law, general principles of law', and lastly 'legal precedents and doctrine'.[205]

Apart from express provisions in the relevant instruments, human rights bodies have examined the relationship between human rights instruments and norms, and other international law instruments and norms. The ECtHR has repeatedly recalled the rule of Article 31(3)(c) of the VCLT, underlying that the ECHR should be interpreted in the light of other international law norms, including other treaties and general principles of international law.[206] The ECtHR has furthermore developed a series of principles concerning the interpretation and application of the ECHR, also in the context of other sources of international law: the Convention must be interpreted and applied 'in a manner which renders its rights practical and effective, not theoretical and illusory' and 'in such a way as to promote internal consistency and harmony between its various provisions';[207] account should be taken of 'any relevant rules and principles of international law applicable in relations between the Contracting Parties';[208] and account should also be taken of the 'living' nature of the ECHR as well as of the development of other rules of international law.[209] Thus, in considering any issue raised under the ECHR, the Court has maintained that it must take into account 'the international law background to the legal question before it',[210] which notably comprises not only instruments that are legally binding for the States appearing before it, but also soft law instruments,[211] or even unratified treaties.[212]

There is thus much room for introducing provisions of other treaties, including law of the sea, maritime and labour treaties, in the interpretation and application of the ECHR. The one aspect that has not been clarified by the ECtHR so far is the exact relevance of other international law provisions. In this respect, the jurisprudence of the ECtHR is far from consistent and has raised concerns because of its

Organization of African Unity, the Universal Declaration of Human Rights, other instruments adopted by the United Nations and by African countries in the field of human and peoples' rights as well as from the provisions of various instruments adopted within the Specialized Agencies of the United Nations' (ibid).

[205] Art 61 ACHPR.

[206] *Golder v The United Kingdom* App no 4451/70 (Judgment of 21 February 1975) para 35; *Demir and Baykara* (n 56) paras 69–71. On the use of the principle of systemic integration enshrined in Art 31(3)(c) VCLT see Cesare Pitea, 'Interpreting the ECHR in the Light of "Other" International Instruments: Systemic Integration or Fragmentation of Rules on Treaty Interpretation?' in Nerina Boschiero, Tullio Scovazzi, Cesare Pitea, and Chiara Ragni (eds), *International Courts and the Development of International Law. Essays in Honour of Tullio Treves* (Asser Press 2013) 545; Magdalena Forowicz, *The Reception of International Law in the European Court of Human Rights* (OUP 2010).

[207] *Demir and Baykara* (n 56) para 66.   [208] ibid para 67.   [209] ibid para 68.

[210] ibid para 76. See also ibid para 85, according to which '[t]he Court, in defining the meaning of terms and notions in the text of the Convention, can and must take into account elements of international law other than the Convention'. Reference to 'must' is very strong and clearly marks the necessity to take into account other international law norms.

[211] ibid para 74.   [212] ibid para 78.

potential to undermine, rather than strengthen, the coherence of international law as a system.[213]

8.2.1.3 Other treaties

Rules on conflict are often inserted in other treaties that bear upon people at sea. These rules usually operate in three different ways. First, they may consist of non-prejudice clauses safeguarding the application of earlier or later treaties, such as Article 4 United Nations Agreement for the Implementation of the Provisions of the United Nations Convention on the Law of the Sea of 10 December 1982 relating to the Conservation and Management of Straddling Fish Stocks and Highly Migratory Fish Stocks (FSA),[214] which provides for the prevalence of the UNCLOS over the FSA itself. Safeguard clauses may also refer to entire regimes, as in the case of Article 19(1) Smuggling Protocol and Article 2*bis*(1) SUA Convention, according to which norms of human rights law, refugee law, and international humanitarian law prevail over the treaty.

Second, they may refer more generally to a certain regime, stating that the provisions of the treaty must be interpreted or applied 'in accordance with' that regime. For example, the SUA Convention requires the State that is taking action against a vessel at sea to 'take due account of the need not to interfere with or to affect: (i) the rights and obligations and the exercise of jurisdiction of coastal States in accordance with the international law of the sea'.[215] Similarly, the Smuggling Protocol provides that the parties shall cooperate in preventing and suppressing the smuggling of people 'in accordance with the international law of the sea'.[216]

Third, legal instruments may refer more generally to one or more instruments or legal regimes, without however formally establishing relationships of precedence. References to this effect are usually found in the preamble of the relevant treaty. The MLC Preamble recalls that the UNCLOS 'sets out a general legal framework within which all activities in the oceans and seas must be carried out and is of strategic importance as the basis for national, regional and global action and cooperation in the marine sector, and that its integrity needs to be maintained'.[217]

---

[213] Giorgio Gaja, 'Does the European Court of Human Rights Use Its Stated Methods of Interpretation?' in *Divenire sociale e adeguamento del diritto: Studi in onore di Francesco Capotorti*, vol 1 (Giuffré 1999) 213. Contra see Pitea, 'Interpreting' (n 206).

[214] United Nations Agreement for the Implementation of the Provisions of the United Nations Convention on the Law of the Sea of 10 December 1982 relating to the Conservation and Management of Straddling Fish Stocks and Highly Migratory Fish Stocks (adopted 4 August 1995, entered into force 11 December 2001) 2167 UNTS (FSA).

[215] Art 8*bis*(10)(c)(ii) SUA Convention.

[216] Art 7 Smuggling Protocol. See also Art 9(3)(a) Smuggling Protocol and Art 17(1) Convention against Illicit Traffic in Drugs.

[217] Maritime Labour Convention (adopted 23 February 2006, entered into force 20 August 2013) (MLC), eigth preambular para. The Work in Fishing Convention (No 188) (adopted 14 June 2007, entered into force 16 November 2017) (Work in Fishing Convention) simply 'recalls' the UNCLOS (eleventh preambular para). Similarly, the Agreement on Port State Measures to Prevent, Deter and Eliminate Illegal, Unreported and Unregulated Fishing (adopted 22 November 2009, entered into force 5 June 2016) 'recalls' the UNCLOS 'relevant provisions' (tenth preambular para).

Clearly, whenever a provision expressly indicates that the treaty which contains it or another treaty will prevail, then this will be so. At the same time, while not formally defining relationships between legal instruments and norms, cross-references of a different type strengthen the systemic reading of the instruments and may *de facto* suggest hierarchical relationships. Phrases such as 'general legal framework' or 'in accordance with' suggest that the regime or treaty thus made reference to will prevail on the norms of the instrument at hand, or at least will guide the interpretation and application of this instrument.

8.2.2 *Generally accepted international rules and standards*

Furthermore, in a few but significant instances, the UNCLOS paves the way for the incorporation of standards deriving from other instruments through reference to 'international rules and regulations' or 'generally accepted international rules and standards'.[218] These include—mostly technical—'standards, regulations, rules, procedures and practices'.[219] They thus comprise technical treaties dealing, for example, with safety and labour issues, but are not limited to them. In fact, generally accepted international rules and standards can be found in a number of treaties, decisions, and non-binding instruments[220] adopted by the United Nations, the IMO, and other international organizations.

From a practical point of view, the adoption of these standards was dictated by practical necessity in order to avoid the chaotic situation that would arise if States were to adopt their own standards relating to seagoing vessels.[221] As a consequence, they are generally followed by the shipping industry, which often takes an active part in developing them. From a legal point of view, these standards have assumed particular relevance following the incorporation in the UNCLOS of a reference to them in a significant number of provisions.[222] While the wording of these provisions varies and is not always consistent,[223] their objective is common: to oblige States to follow the standards that are generally accepted in a number of fields, at least as

---

[218] Catherine Redgwell, 'Mind the Gap in the GAIRS: the Role of Other Instruments in LOSC Regime Implementation in the Offshore Energy Sector' (2014) 29 IJMCL 600, 603. Different terms are used throughout the UNCLOS; this difference in terminology, however, does not affect States' obligations to comply with them (DOALOS, *The Law of the Sea: Obligations of States Parties Under the United Nations Convention on the Law of the Sea and Complementary Instruments* (United Nations 2004) 2).

[219] DOALOS (n 218) 2.

[220] According to the ILC, these standards may include 'regulations which are a product of international cooperation, without necessarily having been confirmed by formal treaties' (ILC, 'Commentary to the articles concerning the law of the sea' in *Yearbook of the International Law Commission*, vol II (1956) 281). See Harrison (n 43) 174.

[221] Churchill and Lowe (n 27) 265.

[222] For a partial list see IMO, 'Implications of the United Nations Convention on the Law of the Sea for the International Maritime Organization' (30 January 2014) IMO Doc LEG/MISC.8 (IMO Implications).

[223] For a detail of the different wording used see DOALOS (n 218) 2–3.

a minimum.[224] Among these fields, navigation is the one that provides the most articulated reference to these standards.

Unlike references to functional regimes in safeguard clauses, in these instances there is no indication of the legal regime where the rules and standards are to be found or to the institutional setting where these are adopted.[225] As a consequence, these rules of reference allow for a wide reading and may be used to incorporate into the UNCLOS regulation that is adopted elsewhere. While this mechanism has been sparingly used, its potential for a 'humanisation' of the UNCLOS provisions is as noteworthy as it is welcome. Furthermore, since it is the role of these standards to allow for the 'facilitating, strengthening and updating [of] the [UNCLOS] in the light of legal and technical developments since its conclusion',[226] they are particularly useful in bringing the UNCLOS up to date with the requirements under human rights and labour law, including the positive obligations provided by these two fields.

8.2.3 *Notional linkages between regimes*

A final tool that allows for communication between different instruments belonging to separate regimes includes devices that encourage interaction by establishing notional linkages between two or more regimes. Differing from the other tools addressed above, in this case there is no explicit provision that makes reference to another instrument belonging to a different regime. Rather, the aim is achieved through norms drafted using general concepts that derive their content from other fields. These concepts operate as a vehicle for conveying content from one regime to another.[227]

Some examples will illustrate how this tool operates in practice. Most human rights treaties refer to 'jurisdiction' in order to determine the scope of States' obligations, thus opening the door to multiple provisions of the law of the sea that attribute jurisdiction to the State.[228] Article 230(3) of the UNCLOS mentions 'recognised rights of the accused', a phrase that requires references to human rights law for its interpretation. Reference to 'human life' itself in Article 146 of the UNCLOS openly paves the way for the application of the right to life under human rights law and all of its consequences.

The relevance of reference to shared notions for the harmonization of international law has been recognized by the ILC:

---

[224] A collateral issue is whether generally accepted international standards need to be compatible with the UNCLOS, as mandated by Art 311(2) UNCLOS or whether they should be considered as compatible, under Art 311(5) UNCLOS.

[225] The IMO claim of a special place (IMO Implications (n 222) 7) should not be interpreted to mean that other institutions may not have a significant role.

[226] Redgwell (n 218) 603. 'One of the functions of GAIRS is therefore to harmonise the LOSC with existing instruments and replace the (generally unsatisfactory) *lex generalis* with explicit treaty rules (*lex specialis*) on the treaty relationship' (ibid 617).

[227] See also Pulkowski, *The Law* (n 36) 245, according to whom this is due to the spreading of legal doctrine.

[228] See Chapter 3.

certain multilateral treaty notions or concepts, though perhaps not found in treaties with identical membership, are adopted nevertheless widely enough so as to give a good sense of a "common understanding" or a 'state of the art' in a particular technical field without necessarily reflecting formal customary law.[229]

Importantly, as the ILC has emphasized, it is not necessary that the legal instrument, which explains the content of the notion, is in force for the State or States against which it is invoked. It is sufficient that it is 'widely adopted' and that it provides a sense of 'common understanding'.[230]

This tool may appear very similar to the use of generally accepted international rules and standards. The difference is that, while the reference to generally accepted international rules and standards is rendered mandatory by its inclusion in specific UNCLOS provisions, reference to other notions allows for a wider freedom in determining whether and how much relevance should be given to concepts from other treaties or regimes. Indeed, it can be argued that the former simply represents a codification, at the treaty level, of the latter. While this codification strengthens the legal validity of referring to generally accepted international rules and standards, as the use of such rules and standards is indeed required by hard law provisions, at the same time it does not detract from the validity of recourse to notions found in other treaties for the purpose of providing meaning and eventually, strengthening the cohesion of the system.

8.2.4 An assessment

In the light of the rules of conflict and the rules of reference described above, it is possible to draw some general conclusions concerning the interaction between the legal regimes that regulate 'people at sea'. While the detailed definition of relationships will depend upon the specificities of the case, it is possible to illustrate some typical cases of vertical and horizontal interaction.

Preliminarily, it is worth stressing that human rights law and the law of the sea are both 'open' regimes. The legal instruments incorporating most of their rules contain an array of legal devices that support a systemic approach to their interaction and permit a generally smooth intercourse. This is achieved by rules on conflict, reference to notions incorporated in another treaty or used in another regime, and the reference to generally accepted standards.

Turning to vertical relationships, there are two categories of norms that hold a particularly strong position. Human rights law provides a basic threshold of behaviour that must be complied with in all cases in which State action impacts people at sea.[231] As such, they can be derogated from only if the possibility of derogation is provided for in the human right norm itself and only to the extent that this is

---

[229] Koskenniemi Report (n 6) 239.
[230] McLachlan (n 52) 315, refers to 'a rather elaborate law dictionary'.
[231] De Wet and Vidmar (n 38). See however the note of caution by Andrea Bianchi, 'Human Rights and the Magic of *Jus Cogens*' (2008) 19 EJIL 491, 506, who suggests that 'one of the major threats posed to the concept of *jus cogens* is the tendency by some of its most fervent supporters to see it everywhere'.

allowed. According to the principle of harmonization, States are required to enact their rights and obligations in a manner that safeguards human rights norms, even if this may result in more onerous conditions being imposed.[232] If every effort towards harmonization fails, the human rights obligations will eventually trump other obligations. This relationship of strength is particularly relevant when State power is delegated to another actor, as the challenges encountered by States in the handling of pirates apprehended off the coast of Somalia illustrate.[233] In a highly diversified world where States may provide different levels of protection of human rights, it becomes necessary for States to take into account the existence or otherwise of substantial and procedural guarantees in other States before delegating their jurisdiction, lest they violate their own human rights duties.

A particular degree of strength is also attributed to structural provisions of the law of the sea that allocate power, in the form of spatial and functional jurisdiction. These rules are not *jus cogens*, since they can be suspended or modified by States by agreement and their *erga omnes* character is also a matter of debate. At the same time, their aim to provide a stable framework of reference, the fact that they have emerged as the result of a long and careful negotiation and the circumstance that they are generally preserved in all successive legal instruments, which build upon this framework, point towards a special status for these rights. The right to exercise jurisdiction can be transferred from one State to another, but only within the limits of the consent from the former and only temporarily. Thus, the State that has initial jurisdiction can always claim back its original right. As a consequence, any other rule that deals with the exercise of State jurisdiction needs to comply with these rules, either by upholding them or by building on the consent of the State to relinquish its jurisdiction. Other rules that do not constitute law of the sea structural rules do not share this important status, and therefore do not share their strength. As a consequence, they can be affected more easily by rules from other regimes, for example those concerning the protection of specific interests.

For the remainder, the relationships between rules applicable to people at sea are horizontal and need to be addressed through the usual tools. Human rights law often provides minimum levels of protection and States are not only free but also encouraged to adopt treaties and other instruments that will provide for a better protection. Enhanced protection may be the result of more strict standards that define and give flesh to otherwise generic provisions, or they may be the outcome of institutionalized cooperation which ensures enforcement of human rights obligations in practice. Treaties that provide detailed regulation fleshing out basic obligations under human rights law, such as the MLC, are to be read as additional to human rights treaties and their more detailed obligations will prevail against the general undertakings in human rights treaties. More generally, all provisions that aim to apply, strengthen, or enforce human rights will take precedence over less significant

---

[232] This duty is often spelt out in the relevant legal instruments, eg Art 19 Smuggling Protocol and Art 2*bis*(1) SUA Convention.
[233] Treves 'Human Rights' (n 51) 13; Douglas Guilfoyle, 'Counter-Piracy Law Enforcement and Human Rights' (2010) 59 ICLQ 141, 141–42.

and weaker commitments, according to the *lex specialis* principle. This holds true even if the provisions are not included in treaties identified as belonging to the human rights regime. Thus, the positive obligation enshrined in Article 98(2) of the UNCLOS will prevail over readings of the right to life that take into account only negative duties.

9. Chance Encounter or Regular Interaction? *Renvoi*

A question that arises at this point concerns the ontological nature of the interaction between general international law, the law of the sea, and international human rights law. Is it just an occasional interaction, to be recognized, analysed, and settled on a case-by-case basis, when the need arises? Or is it a more regular intercourse, which derives its solutions from some stable basic principles? International practice, so far, seems to point to the first conclusion, since the relationships between the law of the sea and other regimes are generally examined in the light of a specific issue that comes to the forefront. This is true whether it be the management of flows of refugees, the upsurge in piracy, or the enforcement of human rights standards on board vessels licensed to fish in the exclusive economic zone. This solution, however, might be due to contingent reasons and the heavy workload of the organizations that have played a prominent role in addressing all of these issues. Furthermore, the possibility for action might be restricted by the mandate of each international organization, since all have a limited mandate with the exception of the United Nations.

Contingent reasons, however, do not provide answers to conceptual problems, which need to be addressed on their own merits. It seems however better to leave this analysis aside until after the main elements of the law that applies to persons at sea have been examined. Chapters 3 and 4 will therefore address the scope, nature, and content of States' obligations to protect persons at sea. It is only after this overview is concluded that a more informed discussion of the ontological problem will take place in Chapter 5.

3

The Scope of State Duties

1. Why Scope Matters

International law rules identified in the previous chapters may give States the power, or may impose on them the duty, to protect people at sea. It would, however, be excessive and impractical to require that all such powers and duties apply to all States, all the time, everywhere, and with respect to all people. It would be excessive as it would not take into account the fact that action taken by one State or several States is often sufficient to ensure effective protection. It would be impractical because it would overlook the limited means and personnel at the disposal of States. If a State were obliged to patrol all seas continuously it would disperse its efforts over a vast area without necessarily achieving more effective or more comprehensive protection.[1]

As such, there may be situations in which a State does not owe a duty to a specific individual. If a national of State A sails on board a vessel flying the flag of State B, which is intercepted by a military vessel of State C on the high seas (or in the exclusive economic zone of State D) it would be absurd to consider that State E has to comply with the obligation to protect the right to life of this person. The issue would rather be which of the other State(s)—A, B, C, or D—bears such a duty. It is therefore necessary to identify the scope of norms that attribute these rights and duties, so as to define when, where, and to whom they apply.[2]

Aspects of scope are sometimes incorporated in the text of substantial norms. For example, Article 94 of the United Nations Convention on the Law of the Sea (UNCLOS)[3] confines the scope of the flag State's obligations to the master and crew of vessels that are flying its flag. In many cases, however, the norm does not expressly

---

[1] The 'policy behind the rule' is often the need to ensure that normative solutions are effective, practicable, and workable, as argued by Marko Milanovic, *Extraterritorial Application of Human Rights Treaties. Law, Principles, and Policy* (OUP 2011) 66.

[2] Norms referred to in this chapter are norms of international law which establish duties of States towards people at sea, and which can be owed either to the people themselves or to another State. A different issue relates to norms that establish duties owed to people on the basis of national laws, for example labour laws. In the latter case, and whenever the existence of international elements requires to establish which, among many separate national laws, will apply, it is private international law (or conflict of laws) to establish the applicable law. See, with respect to the law that regulates maritime labour, Zanobetti Pagnetti, *Il rapporto internazionale di lavoro marittimo* (Bononia University Press 2008) and more generally Sergio M Carbone, *Conflits de Lois en Droit Maritime* (Martinus Nijhoff 2010).

[3] United Nations Convention on the Law of the Sea (adopted 10 December 1982, entered into force 16 November 1994) 1833 UNTS 397 (UNCLOS).

International Law and the Protection of People at Sea. Irini Papanicolopulu. © Irini Papanicolopulu, 2018. Published 2018 by Oxford University Press.

provide for its scope or does not refer to scope at all. For example, Article 7 of the Protocol against the Smuggling of Migrants by Land, Sea and Air Supplementing the United Nations Convention against Transnational Organized Crime (Smuggling Protocol), which contains the obligation for States to prevent and suppress the smuggling of migrants by sea, does not define the scope of this obligation. In other cases, the norm makes reference to general concepts, such as 'jurisdiction' as in the case of Article V(1) of the Maritime Labour Convention (MLC). Yet in other cases, the norm just makes a generic reference to international or domestic law.

In all dubious cases where scope cannot be defined by reference to the substantial norm, it is necessary to turn to the overall system. International law, in fact, provides general principles that supplement and complete ambiguous norms. These principles may be referred to when there is no indication as to the scope of a particular norm. In most cases, scope is closely linked with the notion of jurisdiction. According to this connection, a State has rights and bears duties towards people when they come within that State's jurisdiction. In order to determine the scope of rights and duties discussed in this book, it is therefore necessary to establish when a State has 'jurisdiction' over a person who is at sea, and what might limit this jurisdiction.

Jurisdiction creates a reciprocal link between a State and an individual. On the one hand, it provides a basis for the exercise of power by the State, since the State will have the right to impose rules and regulations on individuals under its jurisdiction. On the other hand, it empowers individuals, who may therefore require that the State not only respect their rights but also protect them by undertaking all positive measures necessary to promote the rights of individuals who are under its jurisdiction. Jurisdiction must therefore be considered in its dual capacity to empower both States and individuals towards each other. The first relationship is reflected in the notion of jurisdiction under international law, while the second constitutes the basis of the notion of jurisdiction under human rights law. As will be argued later, the former is in fact a component of the latter.[4]

Identifying the scope of State duties towards people at sea presents a number of challenges. First, there is no uniform framework for identifying the State that has jurisdiction over a person at sea. This is due to the fact that duties that bind States may be found in different legal regimes and may make use of jurisdictional links deriving from general international law, for example the nationality of a person; from human rights law, for example exercise of *de facto* control over a person; or from the law of the sea, for example the nationality of a vessel. Second, human rights instruments and most literature on the issue of jurisdiction over persons has considered this topic from a dry-land perspective, without fully taking into consideration the specialty of the sea.[5] Third, scholarly works that have analysed the obligations due by States to people at sea generally, or to specific groups, have focused on the content of the obligation, rather than on its scope. In a few cases, some discussion of the relevant scope

---

[4] See Section 2.3.
[5] For example Milanovic (n 1) 60, according to whom '[i]nternational law is a territorial system.'

has been undertaken with respect to specific rights or duties.[6] There is, however, no general treatment of the topic and the specific analyses just mentioned might be called into doubt in the absence of general criteria to identify the scope of obligations. In fact, one might question whether a case-by-case analysis of scope that is detached from any general framework would be productive or whether it would be merely self-serving. Fourth, normative instruments and scholarly works that analyse jurisdiction at sea focus on space and objects—that is the maritime zones, the vessels, and more recently platforms—without considering people.[7]

All of these challenges are different manifestations of a single problem: the lack of norms specifically dedicated to delimiting the jurisdiction of States over persons at sea. This regrettable void demands the development of a dedicated conceptual framework that will provide guidance in determining scope. In doing so, it is necessary to interpret and combine rules on jurisdiction deriving from general international law and its specialized regimes, so as to identify the State or States that have jurisdiction over a person at sea, which will eventually define the scope of States' obligations towards these people.

The present chapter will set out to fill this gap and develop a conceptual framework within which to locate the principles determining the scope of State duties towards people at sea. Scope is usually determined by referring to the concept of jurisdiction. This chapter will therefore begin by providing a brief overview of what jurisdiction is often taken to mean in public international law, so as to dispense with some misconceptions and to provide a working understanding of the concept. It will first focus on general international law rules for the allocation of jurisdiction among States before turning to the notion of jurisdiction as developed within human rights law. This shift in perspective is necessary to argue that jurisdiction under international law (*de jure* jurisdiction) in fact constitutes one facet of jurisdiction under human rights law, which also includes the *de facto* exercise of power by a State upon an individual (*de facto jurisdiction*). Having established what is meant by 'jurisdiction' in this work, it will then be possible to discuss whether common analyses of jurisdiction duly take into account the specificities of the sea.

2. Jurisdiction in International Law

Broadly speaking, jurisdiction is a manifestation of the power to rule.[8] The term therefore refers to the powers not only of States, but also of their organs. At the same

---

[6] Urfan Khaliq, 'Jurisdiction, Ships and Human Rights Treaties' in Henrik Ringbom (ed), *Jurisdiction over Ships* (Martinus Nijhoff 2015) 324; Efthymios Papastavridis, 'European Convention on Human Rights and the Law of the Sea: the Strasbourg Court in Unchartered Waters?' in Malgosia Fitzmaurice and Panos Merkouris (eds), *The Interpretation and Application of the European Convention of Human Rights: Legal and Practical Implications* (Martinus Nijhoff 2013) 117.

[7] An otherwise excellent analysis of these rules is provided in Maria Gavouneli, *Functional Jurisdiction in the Law of the Sea* (Martinus Nijhoff 2007).

[8] On jurisdiction in international law, see generally Frederick Alexander Mann, 'The Doctrine of International Jurisdiction Revisited after Twenty Years' (1984) 186 Recueil des Cours 9; Cedric Ryngaert, *Jurisdiction in International Law* (OUP 2008); Ian Brownlie, *Principles of Public International Law* (OUP 2008) 299; A Vaughan Lowe and Christopher Staker, 'Jurisdiction' in Malcolm D Evans

time, the notion of 'jurisdiction' denotes the power of national and international courts, meaning the scope of the competence of a tribunal to rule on cases submitted to it.[9] The International Court of Justice (ICJ) has jurisdiction in all cases submitted in accordance with Articles 35 and 36 of its Statute, while the International Tribunal for the Law of the Sea (ITLOS) has jurisdiction in the cases provided for by Article 288 UNCLOS. The notion of 'jurisdiction' is however, widely understood under international law as the power of a State to rule, and it is this meaning that will be adopted in this chapter.

While 'jurisdiction' is a basic concept of international law, there is no commonly agreed definition of the term. The reason may well be that this word does not have a unique meaning, but may signify different and sometimes conflicting concepts. In reconstructing its meaning, three fields are of relevance: general international law, which provides the basic principles; the law of the sea, which contains rules specifically applicable in the maritime environment; and international human rights law, which has developed its own conception of jurisdiction. The rules in each field will be examined in turn, before discussing the jurisdiction of States over persons at sea.

2.1 General rules on jurisdiction

In the post-Westphalian world, the starting point for any discussion of jurisdiction is still that States are sovereign and do not recognize any authority above them. This means that, in principle, each State has absolute jurisdiction and can regulate any conduct, wherever it takes place, and whatever the nationality of the subjects involved.[10] A literal application of this principle would, however, generate countless cases of overlapping jurisdiction, causing the international community to collapse into utter confusion and endless disputes. In response to this threat, States have developed rules on jurisdiction with the dual purpose of confining a State's power within established material and notional boundaries, and of allocating the power to prescribe or enforce certain conduct among States, so as to avoid or at least minimize cases in which more than one State may regulate the same activity.[11] As Higgins has noted, '[w]ithout that allocation of competences, all is rancour and chaos'.[12]

(ed), *International Law* (OUP 2010) 313; Carlo Focarelli, *Trattato di Diritto Internazionale* (UTET 2015) 685–715.

[9] This, more restrictive, meaning is the original meaning in Roman law, which distinguished between *jurisdictio* and *imperium*. A restrictive understanding of the term jurisdiction is still used in civil law systems.

[10] *The Case of the S.S. Lotus (France v Turkey)* PCIJ Rep Series A No 10, 19. While this conclusion was put into question in *Arrest Warrant of 11 April 2000 (Democratic Republic of the Congo v Belgium)* (Judgment) [2002] ICJ Rep 3, international practice does not yet seem to have superseded the findings of the PCIJ in the *Lotus* case; see James Crawford, *Brownlie's Principles of Public International Law* (8th edn, OUP 2012) 458.

[11] Ryngaert (n 8); Lowe and Staker (n 8) 314. Exclusivity is such by reference to other States, while there is no presumption that individuals will be subjected to the jurisdiction of only one State (Crawford (n 10) 457).

[12] Rosalyn Higgins, *Problems and Process: International Law and How We Use It* (Clarendon Press 1994) 56.

Jurisdiction thus entails the power of States to create and impose rules. This power stems directly from sovereignty[13] and may assume three different forms, reflecting the separation of powers within a State. Firstly, *legislative* (or prescriptive) jurisdiction is the power of a State to create legal norms regulating conduct. Secondly, *enforcement* jurisdiction is the power of a State to apply its rules through coercive action directed against persons and objects.[14] Finally, *adjudicative* jurisdiction is the power of a State to decide, through its judges, on the interpretation and application of legal rules, including those concerning the consequences of unlawful action. Adjudication may be seen as a *sub-generis* of prescriptive jurisdiction, if one considers that the competence of courts is stated in legal instruments adopted by States in their exercise of legislative jurisdiction,[15] or as an aspect of enforcement jurisdiction, since it puts into effect the general and abstract rules that are contained in laws. Despite these considerations, it can also be seen as separate. Judges of a State may decide a case applying rules adopted by another State and sometimes a lawful arrest does not mean that the courts of that State will have the power to hear the case.[16]

The allocation of jurisdiction may take place on the basis of different links between a State and a person. The *territorial* principle attributes jurisdiction to a State over persons located and activities taking place in its territory. The *personality* principle attributes jurisdiction to a State over persons that are nationals of that State, even when these persons are in the territory of another State or in an area over which no State exercises rights.[17] For example, a State may prohibit its citizens from committing a certain crime even when they sail on the high seas. The *passive personality* principle permits States to regulate activities that negatively impact on their nationals or their territory. For example, a State may prosecute terrorists that have taken its citizens hostage, even when the action occurred in the territory of another State or on board a vessel flying the flag of another State. The *protective* principle permits a State to exercise its jurisdiction in cases when an activity threatens the essential interests of that State. For example, a State may prosecute individuals who smuggle migrants into its territory, even when the smugglers themselves do not enter into that territory, for example, because they abandon the migrants on the high seas and sail elsewhere.[18] Finally, the *universal* principle allows States to exercise their jurisdiction with respect to specific acts, disregarding location and nationality, as in

[13] *Lotus* (n 10) 19. Mann (n 8) 20, considers that sovereignty is linked to territory.

[14] Enforcement jurisdiction at sea may be divided into the power to visit a ship ('boarding and searching') and the power to arrest the ship and the persons on board ('seizure'); Douglas Guilfoyle, *Shipping Interdiction and the Law of the Sea* (CUP 2009) 9.

[15] Lowe and Staker (n 8) 317; Mann (n 8) 67. See, for a contrary argument, Tullio Treves, *La giurisdizione nel diritto penale internazionale* (CEDAM 1973) 20.

[16] Private international law regulates the 'when' and 'how' of this.

[17] I consciously avoid speaking of areas beyond national jurisdiction at this point, as this would be a tautology.

[18] Tribunale di Crotone, Decision of 12 September 2001, n 1118, which applied Art 6 of the Italian Penal Code, according to which a crime is considered as having been committed in the territory of the State if the event, which is the consequence of the crime, took place therein.

the case of piracy, when every State can seize the pirate vessel and arrest the pirates on board, even in the absence of any link between the pirates and the State itself.[19]

2.2 Jurisdiction under the law of the sea: The special character of marine spaces

General rules of international law concerning jurisdiction are premised upon a territorial vision. The creation of nation States that exercised (or at least claimed to exercise) full authority and control over a geographically defined portion of the Earth led to the emergence of 'sovereignty' as a concept that 'organizes global political space'.[20] Accordingly, the notion of jurisdiction emerged in close connection with our understanding of sovereignty, and was therefore linked to the territory of a State.[21]

This conception still forms the basis of contemporary discourse on jurisdiction: on land, the dominant principle is still territoriality, according to which a State has general and exclusive jurisdiction over its territory and all persons and activities therein, while, as a rule, it cannot exercise jurisdiction outside these boundaries.[22] To quote Lapradelle, territory is a framework wherein public power is exercised.[23] This is of course a general principle which provides for exceptions. Legislative jurisdiction by the territorial sovereign may indeed co-exist with the legislative jurisdiction of other States. For example, individuals may continue to be bound by their national laws even when abroad. The enforcement jurisdiction of the State over its territory, however, is generally exclusive, since territorial jurisdiction is directly linked with and stems from sovereignty and may be subject to limitations in exceptional cases only. Accordingly, no State may lawfully enforce laws and regulations on the territory of another State, unless expressly authorized by the sovereign State.[24]

This paradigm, however, does not sit comfortably when we consider the seas, where no State is capable of exercising full control over vast expanses of waters, as the ineffective claims of Spain and Portugal since the late fifteenth century illustrate.[25] In response to this factual difference between land and sea, 'nationality' was

---

[19] As Lowe and Staker (n 8) 326–27 point out, universal jurisdiction is indeed composed of two separate strands, ie the wish to punish heinous crimes and the need to assert jurisdiction in cases that otherwise would go unpunished. Universal jurisdiction should be kept separate from so-called 'treaty based quasi-universal jurisdiction' which requires States to exercise mandatory prescriptive jurisdiction over individuals that have committed a certain crime if they happen to be within their territory (Crawford (n 10) 469–70).

[20] Janice E Thomson, *Mercenaries, Pirates, and Sovereigns: State-Building and Extraterritorial Violence in Early Modern Europe* (Princeton University Press 1996) 13–14.

[21] On the historical evolution and the general acceptance of territoriality as the basis for jurisdiction see Ryngaert (n 8) 47–55.

[22] Crawford (n 10) 456; Andrew Clapham, *Brierly's Law of Nations: An Introduction to the Role of International Law in International Relations* (OUP 2012) 168.

[23] *Nationality Decrees Issued in Tunis and Morocco* (Speech by MA De Lapradelle) [1923] PCIJ Rep Series C No 2, 106: 'le territoire n'est ni un objet, ni une substance, mais un cadre. Quel cadre? Le cadre dans lequel s'exerce la puissance publique. Quelle puissance publique? La puissance publique la plus haute, car c'est la plus haute qu'on qualifie de puissance souveraine'.

[24] *Lotus* (n 10) 18.

[25] Tullio Scovazzi, 'The Evolution of International Law of the Sea: New Issues, New Challenges' (2000) 286 Recueil des Cours 39.

selected as providing the necessary link to a State, and therefore as the general crite-rion to allocate jurisdiction. According to the nationality rule, a vessel and all per-sons on it were subject to the general jurisdiction of the flag State, to the exclusion of all other States. A limited space for territorial jurisdiction was however allowed, in the form of sovereignty by the coastal State over its territorial sea, a narrow belt of waters adjacent to its shores.

The initial dichotomy territory–flag, according to which the coastal State had exclusive jurisdiction over its 'maritime territory' (what we call the territorial sea today) while the flag State had exclusive jurisdiction over vessels navigating beyond that zone, came to an end in the twentieth century. The expansion of coastal States' power, on the one hand, and the necessity to regulate activities having the general interest in mind, on the other, have eroded this principle at a greater pace than on land. At least since the beginning of the twentieth century, there is no marine space where a single State, be it the coastal State or the flag State, enjoys exclusive jurisdic-tion to the exclusion of all other States. Rather, in most maritime areas, States enjoy certain rights and duties, often limited functionally to allow for the simultaneous exercise of rights by other States.[26]

Indeed, one of the primary aims of the modern law of the sea has been to allocate jurisdiction between States engaged in activities at sea. In doing so, the law of the sea has made use of the general principles of international law, adapting them to the maritime space. The criteria used are the territorial principle, according to which a State has jurisdiction in a certain maritime zone such as the territorial sea or the exclusive economic zone, and the nationality principle, according to which a State has jurisdiction over a vessel that has its nationality. In addition, the desire to check the expansion of coastal State jurisdiction—what is usually referred to by the deni-gratory phrase 'creeping jurisdiction'—has promoted the use of the functional cri-terion which has been incorporated into many law of the sea norms.[27] Accordingly, the functional principle attributes jurisdiction to a State with respect to a certain activity, for example fishing or oil exploitation. The functional approach character-izes most rules relating to the exclusive economic zone, including the rights of the coastal State and those of third States.[28]

Today, in order to determine whether a State has the right to regulate conduct or to enforce its laws and regulations at sea, one has to consider not only the maritime zone within which the activity has taken place and the flag of the ship, but also the scope of the purposed regulation. For instance, a State may arrest a vessel flying another flag stationed in its exclusive economic zone if it fishes without licence,[29]

---

[26] Gavouneli (n 7) 6.
[27] This is very much an ongoing process, as new concerns about security are driving States to try and enlarge their jurisdictional competence vis-à-vis foreign-flagged vessels on the high seas to counter the threat of terrorism at sea and piracy. This effort is putting into question the balance achieved by the UNCLOS, which is based on the assumption that the exclusive jurisdiction of the flag State on the high seas will be matched by the 'genuine link' required by Art 91 UNCLOS and a genuine effort by the flag State to control its vessels; Neil Brown, 'Jurisdictional Problems Relating to Non-Flag State Boarding of Suspect Ships in International Waters: A Practitioner's Observations' in Clive R Symmons (ed), *Selected Contemporary Issues in the Law of the Sea* (Martinus Nijhoff 2011) 69.
[28] Respectively, Art 56 UNCLOS and Art 58 UNCLOS.   [29] Art 73(1) UNCLOS.

but not if it is laying submarine cables.[30] This is not to say that the same paradigm may not operate on land. In the latter case, however, there is a presumption that a State can legislate and enforce rules concerning any conduct taking place on its territory, which does not exist at sea outside the narrow belt of the territorial sea.

Further complexity is added to this composite pattern if one turns from custom to treaty. Treaty rules often provide additional grounds for the exercise of jurisdiction, or aim to allocate jurisdiction differently from the general (customary) rule. These rules mainly utilize traditional linking criteria to provide mandatory jurisdiction by more than one State, and cannot therefore be considered as changing the principles in this field. In most cases, in fact, these treaties either require the consent of the State having primary jurisdiction—usually the flag State—or refer to the States that would in any case be allowed to exercise legislative jurisdiction and simply make the exercise of this jurisdiction compulsory.[31]

A category of treaty-based jurisdictional rules that is typical to the law of the sea comprises treaties on port State control. These instruments allow (or in some circumstances require) the State, within the ports of which a vessel is voluntarily present, to exercise its jurisdiction also with respect to events that have taken place outside the territory of the State.[32] Port State control derives from the combination of two principles: the capacity of the State to legislate with respect to acts that take place outside its territory, and the inherent right of States to exercise their enforcement and adjudicative jurisdiction vis-à-vis ships and people in their territory.

This complex and fragmented jurisdictional framework poses particular challenges in order to determine the State that can or must exercise its jurisdiction over an individual at sea.[33] In the first place, law of the sea rules that allocate jurisdiction do so with reference to the ship or maritime zone, not to the person, and require the interpreter to ascertain whether, and to what extent, the jurisdiction also extends to the people on board the vessel or within the zone. Secondly, many law of the sea rules are functionally limited. Individuals, however, cannot be fragmented when it comes to protecting human rights and this may make it more complex to establish whether a specific State has the obligation to protect the rights of a person, say, on board a ship flying its flag.

2.3 Jurisdiction under human rights law: *De jure* and *de facto*

The notion of jurisdiction discussed so far is what may be termed 'lawful' jurisdiction, or alternatively, 'jurisdiction under the law'. There is however also (at least) one other meaning attributed to the word which is relevant to the discussion in this chapter. This additional meaning derives from international human rights law and

---

[30] Art 58(1) UNCLOS.

[31] This issue relates to the relationship between rights and duties and will be discussed in Chapter 4.

[32] See, eg International Convention for the Prevention of Pollution from Ships (MARPOL), Maritime Labour Convention (MLC).

[33] Or even a 'delinquent vessel'; see Ivan Shearer, 'Problems of Jurisdiction and Law Enforcement Against Delinquent Vessels' (1986) 35 ICLQ 320.

may be found in the jurisprudence of human rights bodies, when they consider jurisdiction as the trigger for the application of the substantive provisions of human rights instruments and eventually of the administrative mechanisms designed to ensure compliance with substantive obligations. In determining their scope, almost all human rights instruments refer to individuals under the jurisdiction of a State.[34] In fact, the notion of jurisdiction used to determine the scope of human rights obligations is wider than the one usually endorsed by international law. Although the concept is still under development, judicial decisions provide evidence that this is a composite notion, that partly adopts the notion as it is understood under general international law, whilst at the same time partly consisting of an autonomous, human-rights-specific, component.

Jurisdiction in this context includes two different aspects of the exercise of power. The first aspect refers to the power attributed by a rule of international law to a State to act in a specific situation, for example the right of the coastal State to arrest a vessel that is seriously and wilfully polluting its territorial sea.[35] It is not relevant, as far as the inquiry into the existence of jurisdiction is concerned, whether the State actually makes use of this power or not. The second aspect refers to the actual exercise of power by the agents of a State over a person, whether permitted by a rule of international law or not, for example in the case of a vessel that is boarded and the persons on board are arrested. In this case, the *act* is sufficient to create 'jurisdiction', independent of the existence of a legal basis. This dual criterion for the determination of jurisdiction serves the purpose of avoiding a gap in protection in those situations where the State takes action outside a legal framework with the aim of avoiding the applicability of human rights treaties.[36]

This dual notion has been incorporated into European Court of Human Rights (ECtHR) jurisprudence under the two headings of *de jure* jurisdiction and *de facto* jurisdiction.[37] The Human Rights Committee (HRC) seems to have in mind the

---

[34] Art 1 (European) Convention for the Protection of Human Rights and Fundamental Freedoms (adopted 4 November 1950, entered into force 3 September 1953) 213 UNTS 221, as amended (ECHR); Art 2 International Covenant on Civil and Political Rights (adopted 16 December 1966, entered into force 23 March 1976) 999 UNTS 171 (ICCPR). For an overview of other jurisdictional clauses see Milanovic (n 1) 11–12.

[35] Arts 220(2) and 19(2)(h) UNCLOS.

[36] *Case of Issa and Others v Turkey* App no 31821/96 (Judgment of 16 November 2004) para 71: 'Article 1 of the Convention cannot be interpreted so as to allow a State party to perpetrate violations of the Convention on the territory of another State, which it could not perpetrate on its own territory.'

[37] Following a period of uncertainty due to contradictory pronouncements, recent decisions have settled the issue: see *Al-Saadoon and Mufdhi v United Kingdom* App no 61498/08 (Decision of 30 June 2009) para 88; *Al-Skeini and Others v The United Kingdom* App no 55721/07 (Judgment (GC) of 7 July 2011) para 136; *Hirsi Jamaa and Others v Italy* App no 27765/09 (Judgment (GC) of 23 February 2012) para 81. It is open to discussion whether the *Al-Skeini* judgment represents a change in direction or rather an effort in conceptualizing and clarifying an otherwise confused series of cases. The latter point is made in Irini Papanicolopulu, 'La nozione di giurisdizione ai sensi dell'art. 1 della Convenzione Europea dei Diritti Umani nella recente giurisprudenza della Corte Europea dei Diritti Umani' in Tullio Scovazzi, Irini Papanicolopulu, and Sabrina Urbinati (eds), *I diritti umani di fronte al giudice internazionale. Atti della giornata di studio in memoria di Carlo Russo* (Giuffre 2009) 83. For a different perspective see Milanovic (n 1) 53.

same distinction when it differentiates 'power' and 'effective control'.[38] In discussing these two aspects, I will follow the ECtHR and will call the former '*de jure* jurisdiction' and the latter '*de facto* jurisdiction'.[39]

On the one hand, *de jure* jurisdiction could be defined as the power, conferred upon a State by a legal rule, to legislate and enforce laws, and to adjudicate legal disputes, which coincides with the notion usually referred to in scholarly writing, discussed above. In order to determine whether there is *de jure* jurisdiction, it is necessary to identify a rule of international law that allows or mandates a State to exercise its power. The customary or conventional origin of the rule and the basis of jurisdiction—territorial, personal, or other—do not matter in this respect.[40]

De facto jurisdiction, on the other hand, includes all those situations in which a State *acts* using its power, and is often linked to the extraterritorial exercise of jurisdiction.[41] Here, the relevant issue for determining the existence of 'jurisdiction' is the actual exercise of legislative or enforcement power by a State, rather than an abstract right to do so. The exercise of power will usually take the form of control over a territory,[42] control over the premises or the vessel where an individual happens

---

[38] UNHRC, 'General Comment No. 31—The Nature of the General Legal Obligation Imposed on States Parties to the Covenant' (26 May 2004) UN Doc CCPR/C/21/Rev.1/Add. 13 (General Comment 31) para 10. As Khaliq (n 6) 343 notes, ' "power" as a term is not clarified but as it is distinguished from "effective control" to avoid a tautology it logically follows that power refers to legal powers; namely those of prescription and enforcement'.

[39] The two are clearly distinguished by the ECtHR in dealing with the *Al-Saadoon* case; *Al-Saadoon* (n 37) paras 87–88. See also *Hirsi* (n 37) para 81. .

[40] *Hirsi* (n 37) para 75. Interestingly, the Court seems to admit also the relevance of domestic legislation in this respect.

[41] *Legal Consequences of the Construction of a Wall in the Occupied Palestinian Territory* (Advisory Opinion) [2004] ICJ Rep 136, para. 111; *Application of the International Convention on the Elimination of All Forms of Racial Discrimination* (*Georgia v Russian Federation*), (Order of 15 October 2008) 109. Much legal literature is devoted to the issue of extraterritorial jurisdiction; see among many others, Pasquale De Sena, *La nozione di giurisdizione statale nei trattati sui diritti dell'uomo* (Giappichelli 2002); Rick Lawson, 'Life After Bankovic: On the Extraterritorial Application of the European Convention on Human Rights' in Fons Coomans and Menno T Kamminga (eds), *Extraterritorial Application of Human Rights Treaties* (Intersentia 2004) 83; Guy S Goodwin-Gill, 'The Extra-territorial Reach of Human Rights Obligations: A Brief Perspective on the Link to Jurisdiction' in Laurence Boisson de Chazournes and Marcelo Kohen (eds), *International Law and the Quest for its Implementation: Liber Amicorum Vera Gowlland-Debbas* (Brill 2010) 293; Sarah Miller, 'Revisiting Extraterritorial Jurisdiction: A Territorial Justification for Extraterritorial Jurisdiction under the European Convention' (2010) 20 EJIL 1223; Ralph Wilde, 'Compliance with Human Rights Norms Extraterritoriality: Human Rights Imperialism?' in Laurence Boisson de Chazournes and Marcelo Kohen (eds), *International Law and the Quest for its Implementation: Liber Amicorum Vera Gowlland-Debbas* (Brill 2010) 319; Milanovic (n 1); Samantha Besson, 'The Extraterritoriality of the European Convention on Human Rights: Why Human Rights Depend on Jurisdiction and What Jurisdiction Amounts to' (2012) 25 Leiden Journal of International Law 857.

[42] Control over a territory, as applied by the ECtHR, includes military occupation (*Loizidou v Turkey* App no 15318/89 (Judgment (GC) (Preliminary Objections) of 23 March 1995) para 62; *Cyprus v Turkey* App no 25781/94 (Judgment (GC) of 10 May 2001) para 77; *Al-Skeini* (n 37) para 149) and cases in which a State provides support to a separatist regime. In the *Ilaşcu* case, the Court considered that the 'effective authority, or at the very least . . . the decisive influence' of the Russian Federation on the separatist regime in Transdnistria was sufficient to establish the jurisdiction of Russia (*Ilaşcu and Others v Moldova and the Russian Federation* App no 48787/99 (Decision (GC) (Admissibility) of 4 July 2001) paras 392–94).

to be,[43] or control over the person itself, when the applicant is under the 'continued and uninterrupted control exercised by' the State's agents.[44] In all these cases, the State is exercising 'jurisdiction' as far as human rights treaties are concerned.

De facto control does not necessitate that the State's action be formally qualified as 'enforcement', as long as, in the light of the actual circumstances of the case, the individuals concerned are under the control of State organs. In other words, any assessment of the existence of jurisdiction is 'objective' and factual, and does not depend upon the labelling given by the State to its action, or the invocation of motives other that the wish to exercise State power.

This is illustrated in cases relating to the interception of migrants and asylum seekers at sea. In the *Marine I* case, which concerned the interception of a boat of migrants by the Spanish authorities off the Mauritanian coast, the Committee Against Torture (CAT) stated that Spain 'maintained control over the persons on board the *Marine I* from the time the vessel was rescued and throughout the identification and repatriation process' that took place in Mauritania.[45] In the *Hirsi* case, Italy had argued that there was no exercise of jurisdiction, since the only aim of the push-back operations under the scrutiny of the Court was to come to the rescue of the boats transporting migrants and asylum seekers from the Libyan shore to Italy, and not to conduct a maritime police operation. Therefore, its agents were not exercising absolute and exclusive control over the applicants to engage Italy's jurisdiction under Article 1 of the (European) Convention for the Protection of Human Rights and Fundamental Freedoms (ECHR).[46] The ECtHR strongly rejected this line of argument,[47] holding that:

The Court observes that in the instant case the events took place entirely on board ships of the Italian armed forces, the crews of which were composed exclusively of Italian military personnel. In the Court's opinion, in the period between boarding the ships of the Italian

---

[43] *Al-Saadoon* (n 37) para 87.

[44] *Hirsi* (n 37) para 80. Also *Ocalan v Turkey* App no 46221/99 (Decision [GC] of 12 May 2005); *Issa* (n 36) para 71; *Andreou v Turkey*, App no 5653/99 (Decision of 3 June 2008) ('even though the applicant sustained her injuries in territory over which Turkey exercised no control, the opening of fire on the crowd from close range, which was the direct and immediate cause of those injuries, was such that the applicant must be regarded as "within [the] jurisdiction" of Turkey within the meaning of Article 1'); *Isaak and Others v Turkey* App no 44587/98 (Decision (Admissibility) of 28 September 2006); *Solomou and Others v Turkey* App no 36832/97 (Judgment of 24 June 2008) para 45 and paras 50–51; *Pad and Others v Turkey* App no 60167/00 (Decision of 28 June 2007) para 54.

[45] CAT: *JHA v Spain* 323/2007 (Decision of 21 November 2008) CAT/C/41/D/323/2007, para 8.2. See also *The Haitian Centre for Human Rights* et al *v United States* 10.675 (Report 51/96, 13 March 1997).

[46] (European) Convention for the Protection of Human Rights and Fundamental Freedoms (adopted 4 November 1950, entered into force 3 September 1953) 213 UNTS 221, as amended (ECHR). *Hirsi* (n 37) para 65.

[47] This was most probably in part also due to the declarations by members of the Italian government in the aftermath of the operation, eg the declarations of Roberto Maroni, Minister of the Interior, to the Italian Parliament on 14 May 2009 at <http://www.camera.it/_dati/leg16/lavori/stenografici/sed177/pdfs005.pdf>, 25 May 2009 at <http://www.senato.it/service/PDF/PDFServer/BGT/00424000.pdf>, and on 27 May 2009 at <http://www.camera.it/_dati/leg16/lavori/stenografici/sed183/pdfs002.pdf>. Regrettably, these declarations were reiterated after the *Hirsi* judgment <http://www.repubblica.it/solidarieta/immigrazione/2012/02/23/news/l_italia_condannata_per_i_respingimenti-30366965>.

armed forces and being handed over to the Libyan authorities, the applicants were under the continuous and exclusive de jure and de facto control of the Italian authorities. *Speculation as to the nature and purpose of the intervention* of the Italian ships on the high seas *would not lead the Court to any other conclusion.* [48]

Consequently, the reasons for which persons come under the control—and therefore the jurisdiction—of the organs of a State do not affect the existence of jurisdiction in the meaning of Article 1 of the ECHR. As the ECtHR makes clear, there is no place for subjectivity when determining the existence of *de facto* jurisdiction, and this conclusion may be extended to the application of any human rights instrument.

3. The Challenges of Determining Jurisdiction over People at Sea

Having illustrated the general rules on jurisdiction under international law, the law of the sea, and international human rights law, it is now time to address their application, or not as the case may be, to people at sea, in order to determine the scope of States' obligations towards them. This undertaking presents a number of challenges.

First, some norms only contain an indication as to their scope, whilst others do not provide any suggestion and it is for the interpreter to determine their scope. Second, and linked to the first issue, there is no general principle that would guide the interpreter when determining which State or States exercise jurisdiction over a specific person. There is no rule such as that espoused under Article 1 of the ECHR, for example, that would apply specifically at sea. There is also no general rule similar to Article 92 UNCLOS, according to which ships on the high seas are subject to the exclusive jurisdiction of the flag State.

In order to identify the State that has jurisdiction over a person at sea, it is therefore necessary to interpret and apply, combining them if necessary, the specific rules pertaining to the law of the sea attributing jurisdiction to States at sea, and the general principles of international law, as well as the specific principles of international human rights law in cases where there is a human right at issue. This combination needs to take into account the principle of systemic integration. General rules of international law, law of the sea rules, and human rights rules need to be interpreted so as to allow for the effective coordination of these rules with each other and—to the extent possible—the drawing of the complete picture.

4. Direct Attribution of Jurisdiction over a Person

In some cases, a provision of the UNCLOS or of another treaty directly and expressly establishes that a State has jurisdiction over a person. This can be done *expressis verbis,*

---

[48] *Hirsi* (n 37) para 81 (emphasis added). The Court, rightly, does not exclude the relevance of motives in examining the substantial allegations of the applicants.

by mentioning the word 'jurisdiction', as in the case of Article 94(2)(b) UNCLOS, which requires the flag State to

> assume *jurisdiction* under its internal law over each ship flying its flag and its *master, officers* and *crew* in respect of administrative, technical and social matters concerning the ship.[49]

More often, the norm refers to the activity that displays the exercise of jurisdiction, authorizing in certain cases the State to 'adopt laws and regulations', 'arrest', or 'conduct investigations'. Thus Article 27 UNCLOS, concerning the exercise of enforcement jurisdiction by the coastal State on board foreign ships exercising the right of innocent passage through its territorial sea, provides:

> The criminal jurisdiction of the coastal State should not be exercised on board a foreign ship passing through the territorial sea to *arrest* any *person* or to *conduct any investigation* in connection with any crime committed on board the ship during its passage, save only in the following cases.[50]

The right to arrest and conduct investigations stems directly from enforcement jurisdiction. Similarly, Article 105 UNCLOS on the exercise of jurisdiction with respect to piracy expressly provides that any State may '*arrest* the persons and *seize* the property on board' a pirate ship.[51] In both cases, the rules make it clear that the State mentioned in them has the right to exercise enforcement jurisdiction.[52]

The principle constituting the basis for the attribution of jurisdiction over the person also varies. In some cases it is the nationality of the person, in other cases the nationality of the vessel, in yet other cases the need to protect an essential interest of the State.

The nationality of the person may play a role when it comes to people exploiting resources. The nationality of both physical and juridical persons is at the basis of the regime applicable to activities of exploitation and exploration of the resources of the International Seabed Area ('the Area'), in particular concerning liability and compensation, provided for in Article 139 UNCLOS, and adjudicative jurisdiction, provided for by Article 235(2) UNCLOS. According to these provisions, nationals of a State directly engaged in activities in the Area, as well as those effectively controlling companies engaged in the activities mentioned, are subject to the jurisdiction of the State of nationality with respect to their activities in the International Seabed Area.[53]

---

[49] Emphasis added. According to Myron H Nordquist, Shabtai Rosenne, and Satya N Nandan (eds), *United Nations Convention on the Law of the Sea, 1982: A Commentary. Volume III* (Martinus Nijhoff 1995) 146, '[b]y necessary extension paragraph 2(b) [of article 94] also applies to all persons on board a ship, whether legally or not (e.g., stowaways)'.

[50] Emphasis added.   [51] Emphasis added.

[52] See also Art 62(4)(a) UNCLOS on the exercise of legislative jurisdiction, Art 97(1) UNCLOS and Art 109(4) for the exercise of enforcement jurisdiction and Art 109(3) UNCLOS for the exercise of judicial jurisdiction.

[53] See further the provisions of Annex III, Art 4(4) UNCLOS, and the clarifications and guidelines furnished by the Seabed Disputes Chamber of the International Tribunal for the Law of the Sea in the case concerning *Responsibilities and Obligations of States Sponsoring Persons and Entities with Respect to Activities in the Area* (Advisory Opinion of 1 February 2011) in particular para 218.

A further case for 'nationality' would seem to be included in the provisions regulating fishing on the high seas. For example, Article 117 UNCLOS requires the State to:

take, or to cooperate with other States in taking, such measures for their respective *nationals* as may be necessary for the conservation of the living resources of the high seas.[54]

Similar provisions are included in Article 7 of the United Nations Agreement for the Implementation of the Provisions of the United Nations Convention on the Law of the Sea of 10 December 1982 relating to the Conservation and Management of Straddling Fish Stocks and Highly Migratory Fish Stocks (FSA),[55] and are contained in regional fisheries agreements.[56] These provisions could be interpreted to mean that nationals of a State fishing on the high seas are subject to the jurisdiction of that State insofar as fishing activities are concerned, regardless of the flag of their vessel.

A similar conclusion, however, has to be assessed in order to ascertain whether this was the understanding of the drafters of these articles, as their drafting history shows. In the case of the Convention on Cooperation in the Northwest Atlantic Fisheries, the relevant provisions make it clear that it is indeed the State of nationality of the persons that is under the duty to adopt measures.[57] However, in the case of the UNCLOS a different conclusion has to be reached.[58] The use of the term 'nationals' dates back to the draft articles prepared by the International Law Commission (ILC), which were eventually used as the basis for the text of the four Geneva Conventions. The Convention on Fishing and Conservation of the Living Resources of the High Seas, in particular, refers to the rights of States 'for their nationals to engage in fishing on the high seas',[59] as well as to the measures that a State may adopt 'for its own nationals'.[60] These provisions were based upon Articles 49 and 51 of the ILC draft. It is however clear from the commentary to the provisions that 'the term "nationals" denotes fishing boats having the nationality of the State concerned, irrespective of the nationality of the members of their crews',[61] and

---

[54] Emphasis added.

[55] Agreement for the Implementation of the Provisions of the United Nations Convention on the Law of the Sea of 10 December 1982 relating to the Conservation and Management of Straddling Fish Stocks and Highly Migratory Fish Stocks (adopted 4 August 1995, entered into force 11 December 2001) 2167 UNTS 3 (FSA).

[56] For example Art X(1)(g) and (h) of the Convention on Cooperation in the Northwest Atlantic Fisheries (adopted 24 October 1978, entered into force 1 January 1979) 1135 UNTS 369, as amended (NAFO Convention). On the substantial obligations of the flag State see *Request for an advisory opinion submitted by the Sub-Regional Fisheries Commission* (Advisory Opinion of 2 April 2015).

[57] Art X(g) NAFO Convention, eg, provides that each State party '*without prejudice to the jurisdiction of the flag State* [shall], to the greatest extent possible, take actions or cooperate with other Contracting Parties, to ensure that its nationals and fishing vessels owned or operated by its nationals conducting fishing activities comply with the provisions of this Convention and with the conservation and management measures adopted by the Commission' (emphasis added).

[58] Nordquist, Rosenne, and Nandan (n 49).

[59] Art 1(1) Convention on Fishing and Conservation of the Living Resources of the High Seas (adopted 29 April 1958, entered into force 20 March 1966) 559 UNTS 285 (Fishing Convention).

[60] Art 3 Fishing Convention.

[61] ILC, 'Articles concerning the Law of the Sea with commentaries' in *Yearbook of the International Law Commission*, vol II (1956) 286.

there is nothing to indicate that this understanding changed in the course of the negotiations for the 1958 Geneva Conventions or the UNCLOS itself.

The nationality of the offender is also relevant to assert jurisdiction over persons committing certain illegal activities and crimes. According to Article 97(1) UNCLOS, the State of nationality has exclusive jurisdiction, together with the flag State, to institute penal or disciplinary proceedings against the master or any other person at the service of the ship in the event of 'collision or any other incident concerning a ship on the high seas'. The State of nationality of the offender has jurisdiction over the person in the case of unauthorized broadcasting,[62] offences relating to the illegal trafficking of narcotic drugs and psychotropic substances,[63] migrant smuggling,[64] and offences against the safety of maritime navigation.[65]

The passive personality principle, while not used in the UNCLOS, is endorsed in various treaty provisions concerning the prevention and repression of crimes at sea. Thus a State may exercise jurisdiction over an individual engaged in migrant smuggling or in unlawful acts against maritime navigation when the victims of such conduct are nationals of that State.[66] Furthermore, there have been cases in which the protective principle was used to assert jurisdiction.[67]

In other cases, jurisdiction is based upon the nationality of the vessel on which the person is working or is located, as in the case of flag State jurisdiction over the master and crew provided by Article 94 UNCLOS. The jurisdiction of the flag State over persons on board its vessels is also expressly provided in the case of unauthorised broadcasting,[68] offences relating to the illegal trafficking of narcotic drugs and psychotropic substances,[69] migrant smuggling,[70] and offences against the safety of maritime navigation.[71]

---

[62] Art 109(3)(c) and (4) UNCLOS.

[63] Art 4(1)(b)(i) United Nations Convention against Illicit Traffic in Narcotic Drugs and Psychotropic Substances (adopted 20 December 1988, entered into force 11 November 1990) 1582 UNTS 165 (Convention against Illicit Traffic in Drugs). As Art 17 Convention against Illicit Traffic in Drugs makes clear, the jurisdiction of the State of nationality does not include the right to enforce its legislation against its nationals in the high seas (and allegedly in areas subject to the jurisdiction of other States), if on board a vessel flying the flag of another State. Guilfoyle (n 14).

[64] According to the combined reading of Art 15(2)(b) United Nations Convention against Transnational Organized Crime (adopted 15 November 2000, entered into force 29 September 2003) 2225 UNTS (TOC Convention) and Art 1(2) Protocol against the Smuggling of Migrants by Land, Sea and Air Supplementing the United Nations Convention against Transnational Organized Crime (adopted 15 November 2000, entered into force 28 January 2004) 2241 UNTS 480 (Smuggling Protocol).

[65] Art 6(1)(c) of the Convention for the Suppression of Unlawful Acts Against the Safety of Maritime Navigation (adopted 10 March 1988), as amended by the 2005 Protocol (adopted 14 October 2005, entered into force 28 July 2010) 1678 UNTS 222 (SUA Convention).

[66] Respectively, Art 15(2)(c) TOC Convention and Art 6(2)(b) SUA Convention.

[67] Sean D Murphy, 'Extraterritorial Application of U.S. Law to Crimes on Foreign Vessels' (2003) 97 AJIL 183.

[68] Art 109(3)(a) and (4) UNCLOS.

[69] Art 4(1)(a)(ii) Convention against Illicit Traffic in Drugs.

[70] According to the combined reading of Art 15(1)(b) TOC Convention and Art 1(2) Smuggling Protocol.

[71] Art 6(1)(a) SUA Convention.

Yet in other cases, the basis for establishing jurisdiction is the territorial principle, as in the case of criminal jurisdiction over persons on board a ship in the territorial waters of a State, according to Article 27 UNCLOS. Finally, in the case of piracy, jurisdiction over the pirates is based on the universality principle. Article 105 UNCLOS contains one of the rare instances in which adjudicative jurisdiction with respect to a specific crime (piracy) is expressly mentioned.

When it comes to determining jurisdiction, the cases just described are the simplest ones. Provisions establishing whether one or more States have jurisdiction over a person are to be considered as *lex specialis* and will therefore prevail over general international law principles. The relevant person is subject to the jurisdiction of the State only if and to the extent that the norm so provides. If jurisdiction is general, then it is correct to presume that its exercise may concern any issue. If it is functional, it can be exercised only within the limits and subject to the conditions provided for by the relevant rule.

As these rules constitute *lex specialis* norms, they cannot be applied by way of analogy. They may however play a role in identifying the jurisdictional link between a person and a State in other cases, as far as they reflect general principles which are well accepted by international law and the law of the sea.[72]

Norms expressly attributing jurisdiction over a person need to be read together with the general principles of international law and law of the sea. The latter may be useful in interpreting the content of the State's right in case of doubt. Doubts may arise, in particular, with respect to three separate aspects: whether a person falls under the scope of the rule on jurisdiction (definitional issues); the type of jurisdiction envisaged; and the absence of an identifiable link in the substantial norm. Each of these issues will be discussed in the following subsections.

4.1 How to define the person or group

There can be no doubt that a legal provision that generally refers to a 'person' should be considered applicable to any human being. This is the case of Article 98(1)(a) UNCLOS concerning the duty to save life at sea.[73]

Conversely, rules that specify *ratione personae* or *ratione materiae* the type and content of the State's powers should be interpreted accordingly. In limiting jurisdiction *ratione personae*, norms will usually refer to a specific category of people, such as the 'master and the crew',[74] the master or 'any other person in the service of the ship',[75] 'pirates',[76] or 'fishermen'.[77] In some cases, norms may circumscribe the group of people by reference to the activity in which they engage, for example a 'national of other States fishing in the exclusive economic zone',[78] or a 'person

---

[72] Section 5.

[73] Other norms referring expressly to a 'person' include those on activities that render passage through the territorial sea non-innocent (Art 19(2)(g) UNCLOS); norms on the exercise of criminal jurisdiction (Art 27(1) UNCLOS; Art 27(5) UNCLOS); and civil jurisdiction (Art 28(1) UNCLOS) in the territorial sea.

[74] Art 94(2)(g) UNCLOS.   [75] Art 97(1) UNCLOS. See also Art 109(3)(c) UNCLOS.

[76] Art 105 UNCLOS.   [77] Art 62(4)(a) UNCLOS and Art 119(3) UNCLOS.

[78] Art 62(4) UNCLOS.

engaged in unauthorised broadcasting'.[79] In all of these cases, the persons mentioned fall under the jurisdiction of the State or States referred to in the relevant rules, while every other individual that cannot be included in the group is excluded from the scope of the rule. Definitions are therefore paramount, as they may make the difference between effective protection or lack thereof. At the same time, reliance on a literal interpretation of a term may not always provide guidance, as nouns and adjectives may be attributed with special meanings in legal texts which may differ from the more commonly understood interpretations.

When the relevant treaties provide definitions, these will be applied to delimit the scope. The MLC defines a 'seafarer' as 'any person who is employed or engaged or works in any capacity on board a ship to which this Convention applies'.[80] Notably, this would oblige State parties to apply the provisions of the MLC to any person engaged in 'work' on a ship flying their flag, including those people undertaking work that does not have any maritime characteristic, such as pianists on a cruise ship.[81] The 2007 Work in Fishing Convention provides that the word fisher 'means every person employed or engaged in any capacity or carrying out an occupation on board any fishing vessel, including persons working on board who are paid on the basis of a share of the catch but excluding pilots, naval personnel, other persons in the permanent service of a government, shore-based persons carrying out work aboard a fishing vessel and fisheries observers'.[82]

In other cases, although no definition is provided, the meaning of a specific term can be deduced from the context. The term 'pirate' used in Article 105 UNCLOS, for example, can only mean a person in dominant control of a vessel[83] used for the activities mentioned in Article 101 UNCLOS.

In the absence of a definition or of other rules that may point to the meaning of a specific term, interpretation may become more difficult. The UNCLOS, in particular, does not contain any definition of terms that are used throughout the Convention, such as 'master', 'crew', or 'fishermen'. In these cases, reference to other treaties may provide useful, albeit not binding, guidance. For example, the MLC definition of a 'seafarer' could be used to determine who belongs to the 'crew' of a vessel, as provided for in Article 94 UNCLOS. Any person falling outside the group will therefore not be subject to the State's power envisaged by that provision.

In practice however, there are cases in which the groups are loosely defined and difficulties may arise when determining which persons are included and which are not. An example is provided by the case of persons engaged in bunkering activities for fishing vessels in the exclusive economic zone of a State. Are these persons to be equated with fishers, and therefore subject to the enforcement jurisdiction of the coastal State according to Article 73(1) UNCLOS? Are they also able to avail themselves of the prompt release procedure provided by Article 73(2) UNCLOS and the safeguards of Article 73(3), or not? The ITLOS, while initially refusing to take a

---

[79] Art 109(3) and (4) UNCOS.   [80] Art II(1)(f) MLC.
[81] Moira McConnell, Dominick Devlin, and Cleopatra Doumbia-Henry (eds), *The Maritime Labour Convention, 2006. A Legal Primer to an Emerging International Regime* (Martinus Nijhoff 2011).
[82] Art 1(e) Work in Fishing Convention.   [83] Art 103 UNCLOS.

position on the characterization of bunkering,[84] later clarified that 'the regulation by a coastal State of bunkering of foreign vessels fishing in its exclusive economic zone is among those measures which the coastal State may take in its exclusive economic zone to conserve and manage its living resources'.[85] It could therefore be argued that the provisions of Article 73 UNCLOS also apply to people involved in bunkering activities, since this provision refers to laws and regulations adopted in conformity with the Convention.

In conclusion, three different types of situations may be envisaged. In the first, a definition in the legal text will clarify which persons are included. In the second case, absent such a definition, a working definition will have to be developed, in accordance with rules on interpretation. Definitions of the same or similar terms included in other legal instruments may be adopted by analogy, or may at least point towards a specific meaning. Thirdly, if this evidence is not conclusive, a different meaning may be used if there is sufficient reason to do so.

4.2 Determining the type of jurisdiction

A provision may specify whether the jurisdiction attributed to a State is legislative, enforcement, or judicial, and may pose conditions and limits to its exercise. In particular, a legal rule may establish that the jurisdiction of a State over a person has a limited scope. Whereas the enforcement jurisdiction attributed by Article 27(1) UNCLOS concerns any criminal act, as long as it sorts the effects described in letters (a), (b), and (c), the legislative jurisdiction provided for by Article 6 of the Convention for the Suppression of Unlawful Acts against the Safety of Maritime Navigation (SUA Convention) concerns only the specific crimes described in its Articles 3, 3*bis*, 3*ter*, and 3*quater*.

There may be some doubts when the rule does not specify the type of jurisdiction— legislative, enforcement, or judicial—to be exercised. In this case, general principles relating to territorial jurisdiction and nationality jurisdiction, as applied to maritime zones and vessels and installations respectively, will have to come into play.

Doubts may also arise when the norm mentions some, but not all, acts attaching to a certain type of jurisdiction. This is mostly the case of enforcement jurisdiction, which may take different forms, from a basic right of visit to the more pervasive right of arrest and detention. It seems possible to surmise that mention of more invasive acts may implicitly include less invasive acts. However, the opposite conclusion, that a mention of a less invasive right, for example the right of visit mentioned in Article 110 UNCLOS, would exclude the existence of a more pervasive right is not always correct. This issue is particularly relevant in cases dealing with the lawfulness of enforcement measures undertaken against vessels and their crew. In the *Medvedyev* case, for example, the French authorities intervened against a Cambodian-flagged vessel on the high seas, based upon the authorization provided by the Cambodian

---

[84] *The M/V 'Saiga' (No 2) (Saint Vincent and the Grenadines v Guinea)* (Judgment of 1 July 1999) ITLOS Reports 1999, 10 para 138.

[85] *The M/V 'Virginia G' case (Panama/Guinea-Bissau)* (Judgment of 14 April 2014) para 217.

authorities to 'intercept, inspect and take legal action'.[86] The ECtHR, seized of the case, maintained that the authorization given did not include the arrest of the persons on board and their detention pending transfer to the judge for trial.[87]

4.3 Absence of a clear jurisdictional link

A peculiar problem is posed by Article 113 UNCLOS, which imposes a duty on every State to establish as a punishable offence any damage caused to submarine cables and pipelines located beneath the high seas, if the injury is caused by a person subject to its jurisdiction.[88] However, the provision does not specify how the jurisdiction over the person is to be determined, nor is there any indication in other rules of the UNCLOS.[89]

The reason may be historical. The content of Article 113 was taken from Article 27 of the Convention on the High Seas.[90] This provision was itself first proposed by the ILC, drawing upon the text of Article 2 of the 1884 Convention for the Protection of Submarine Telegraph Cables.[91] The 1884 Convention went on to identify, in Article 8, the States that had jurisdiction to adjudicate. The latter provision was not included in the successive codification of the rules in the Convention on the High Seas or the UNCLOS, with the result that there is now no indication as to which States have jurisdiction in this particular case.

We therefore have a direct reference to the jurisdiction of a State over a person, without however any indication as to what this State is. In this case, two approaches are possible. According to the first, it would be necessary to resort to other international law provisions in order to determine which State has jurisdiction over the person. Since however both the Convention on the High Seas and the UNCLOS are silent on this point, it seems preferable to check national legislation in order to determine whether a specific person—who in this case could be a juridical, as well as a physical, person—is subject to the jurisdiction of the State.[92]

---

[86] *Medvedyev and Others v France* App no 3394/03 (Judgment (GC) of 29 March 2010) para 10.

[87] ibid para 99, according to which 'the fate of the crew was not covered sufficiently clearly by the note and so it is not established that their deprivation of liberty was the subject of an agreement between the two States'. See however *Medvedyev, Joint partly dissenting opinion of Judges Costa, Casadevall, Bîrsan, Garlicki, Hajiyev, Šikuta and Nicolaou*, according to whom 'it is scarcely possible to dissociate the crew from the ship itself when a ship is boarded and inspected on the high seas' (para 7).

[88] Similarly, Art 114 UNCLOS provides for the duty of every State to arrange that the owners of a cable or pipeline, if they are persons subject to its jurisdiction, who damage another cable or pipeline, shall bear the costs for the repair.

[89] Nordquist, Rosenne, and Nandan (n 49) 267.

[90] Convention on the High Seas (adopted 29 April 1958, entered into force 30 September 1962) 450 UNTS 11 (HSC).

[91] Convention for the Protection of Submarine Telegraph Cables (adopted 14 March 1884). See ILC, *Articles concerning the Law of the Sea with commentaries*, in *Yearbook of the International Law Commission*, vol II (1956) 294.

[92] For example, s 12(3)(f) of the General Civil Penal Code of Norway provides that Norwegian laws applies with respect to acts envisaged by Art 113 UNCLOS on the basis of the nationality/residence principle; text available at <http://www.un.org/Depts/los/LEGISLATIONANDTREATIES/PDFFILES/NOR_penal_code.pdf> accessed 31 January 2012.

4.4 Conclusion

The overview of rules on jurisdiction of States over people at sea shows that there are rules that provide guidance. These rules, however, apply only to the cases they regulate and do not form a coherent framework within which to locate the State that has jurisdiction in every single case. Consequently, they cannot be applied, without further elaboration, to cases outside those expressly regulated.

5. Other Means for Determining Jurisdiction

All rules concerning the identification of the State having jurisdiction over a person at sea discussed in the previous section expressly refer to persons, either generally or by distinguishing a specific category, such as seafarers, fishers, or pirates. While the use of similar provisions is increasing, they still do not address all situations and are to be considered rather as *lex specialis* rules which either confirm or derogate from the general rules concerning the jurisdiction of States at sea. Reference to the latter is therefore necessary in order to determine the State that has jurisdiction over a person in all other cases. Many law of the sea provisions have been worded so that they do not directly establish the jurisdiction of a State over a person, but instead determine that a State will have jurisdiction over the ship or structure on which the person is located, or over the activity in which the person is engaged, or over the effects of the conduct of a person.[93]

The fact that the UNCLOS and other law of the sea treaties often do not mention persons at all makes it necessary to turn our attention to the general principles on jurisdiction in order to identify the State that may or must exercise jurisdiction over a person. With very few exceptions, people at sea are usually found either on a ship or on a platform. The main difference between the two is that, while a ship travels across the seas and from time to time reaches land, platforms are usually fixed in a certain location. Consequently, the rules referred to could be divided into two main groups. The first group comprises those rules relating to jurisdiction over the vessel on which the person is located, while the second group includes those rules relating to jurisdiction over a platform. The following sections will discuss these two groups of norms.

5.1 Vessels

The first category includes those rules widely known and accepted under the law of the sea that distribute jurisdiction between the flag State, coastal State, and port

---

[93] This might be due to a latent desire to keep people—and all the problems arising out of their presence—out of the law of the sea picture. In some cases the avoidance of any mention of the word 'persons' (or similar terms) is brought to the extremes. Art 230(3) UNCLOS, eg, recognizes the applicability of 'rights of the accused' for 'violations committed by a foreign vessel'. Violations of anti-pollution laws and regulations are however more likely to be committed by persons on board, ie the master and crew of the vessel, rather than by the vessel itself.

State, as well as other States, depending on where the ship sails and what activity it is engaged in.[94] It is indeed logical to consider that if a State has jurisdiction to regulate a specific vessel or a specific activity undertaken by the vessel, then it also has jurisdiction over the persons on the vessel who are conducting or are somehow involved in the activity.

For example, in its territorial sea the coastal State may exercise enforcement jurisdiction to prevent passage which is not innocent in nature.[95] Since the loading or unloading of a person contrary to the coastal State's laws renders passage non-innocent, therefore triggering the applicability of Article 25 UNCLOS, the coastal State will be able to enforce its legislation not only with respect to the vessel, its master, and its crew, but also with respect to any person involved in the unlawful activity. This is equally true for the exercise by the coastal State of the rights provided for in Article 33 in the contiguous zone. Even though there is no mention of persons or even ships in this provision, it is evident that the coastal State may adopt enforcement action to prevent or punish infringement of its customs, fiscal, immigration, or sanitary laws and regulations with respect not only to vessels, but also to persons, be they on board the vessel, found on another structure, or in the water. Likewise, the jurisdiction attributed to the coastal State with respect to the exploitation of resources or the protection of the marine environment in its exclusive economic zone includes measures adopted with respect to persons engaging in these activities. There is no doubt, therefore, that enforcement measures envisaged by Article 73(1) UNCLOS apply not only to vessels, but also to the persons on board the vessel, as the reference to the crew of captured vessels in Article 73(2) UNCLOS confirms.

5.1.1 Flag

It is a well-established rule of customary international law that a vessel is subject to the jurisdiction of its flag State.[96] Flag State jurisdiction includes both legislative and enforcement jurisdiction and is general, in the sense that it concerns any aspect of the vessel and any activity it is engaged in. This jurisdiction becomes exclusive on the high seas, with the few exceptions provided by custom or treaty.[97] Under the UNCLOS, the following exceptions to exclusive flag State jurisdiction exist: piracy,[98]

---

[94] These rules are illustrated and discussed in Gavouneli (n 7). See also Dolliver Nelson, 'Maritime Jurisdiction' in Rüdiger Wolfrum (ed), *Max Planck Encyclopedia of Public International Law* (OUP 2012).

[95] Art 25 UNCLOS.

[96] Art 94 UNCLOS. See also, among many others, Art 6(1)(a) SUA Convention; Art 8(1) Smuggling Protocol. Outside law of the sea instruments see Art 5(1) Convention against Torture and Other Cruel, Inhuman or Degrading Treatment or Punishment (adopted 10 December 1984, entered into force 26 June 1987) 1465 UNTS 85 (CAT) on jurisdiction over offences committed on a vessel flying the flag of the State.

[97] Art 92(1) UNCLOS. The exclusive jurisdiction of the flag State on the high seas is also provided by a rule of customary international law; see *Lotus* (n 10) 25: 'It is certainly true that—apart from certain special cases which are defined by international law—vessels on the high seas are subject to no authority except that of the State whose flag they fly. In virtue of the principle of the freedom of the seas, that is to say, the absence of any territorial sovereignty upon the high seas, no State may exercise any kind of jurisdiction over foreign vessels upon them (sic).'

[98] Art 105 UNCLOS.

unauthorized broadcasting,[99] slavery,[100] right of visit,[101] hot pursuit and constructive presence.[102] These exceptions can be considered as part of international customary law, while most exceptions in other instruments are treaty-based.

Although it is not expressly stated in the UNCLOS, the flag State's jurisdiction extends also to the persons on board the ship. As the ITLOS has noted:

the ship, everything on it, and every person involved or interested in its operations are treated as an entity linked to the flag State.[103]

It is worth noting that this has been recognized not only by judges routinely dealing with the law of the sea, but also by international tribunals dealing with other fields of international law. Thus, for example, the ECtHR has noted that the jurisdiction of a State extends also to 'cases involving the activities of its diplomatic or consular agents abroad and on board craft and vessels registered in, or flying the flag of, that State'.[104]

Even though the link between the flag State and the vessel is often described in terms of 'nationality', as in Article 91 UNCLOS, the jurisdiction exercised in this case is qualitatively different from jurisdiction over nationals and sometimes may be described better in territorial terms.[105] Like territorial jurisdiction, flag State jurisdiction is general in nature. It therefore extends to any aspect of life on board the vessel, not only to those issues relating to navigation or the conduct of maritime activities such as fishing.[106]

This is particularly relevant in the case of activities other than navigation. The wish to avoid the restrictions placed upon certain activities by national laws may prompt individuals or companies to 'relocate' to the seas activities that are traditionally carried out on land. From the well-established activity of food processing on board fishing vessels or factory ships,[107] the presence of casino ships off the coasts of California in the 1920s,[108] and the radio station ships broadcasting music in the North Sea in the 1970s,[109] and more recently with the plans for vessels to provide

---

[99] Art 109 UNCLOS.   [100] Art 110(1)(b) UNCLOS.   [101] Art 110 UNCLOS.

[102] Art 111 UNCLOS.   [103] *Saiga* (n 84) para 106.

[104] *Banković and Others v Belgium and 16 Other Contracting States* App no 52207/99 (Decision (GC) of 12 December 2001) para 73. See also *Haitian Centre for Human Rights* (n 45).

[105] The ILC has made the distinction in its commentary on Art 18 of the Draft Articles on Diplomatic Protection, concerning protection of ships' crews; ILC, 'Report of the International Law Commission—Fifty eighth session' (1 May–9 June and 3 July–11 August 2006) UN Doc A/61/10, 94. See also Malcolm Shaw, *International Law* (CUP 2008) 656.

[106] Khaliq (n 6) 330.

[107] For example the *MV Nisshin Maru*, the 8145 gross tonnage mother vessel of the Japanese whaling fleet.

[108] O Shane Balloun, 'The True Obstacle to the Autonomy of Seasteads: American Law Enforcement Jurisdiction over Homesteads on the High Seas' (2012) 24 University of San Francisco Maritime Law Journal 409, 412–13.

[109] N March Hunnings, 'Pirate Broadcasting in European Waters' (1965) 14 ICLQ 410; JC Woodliffe, 'Some Legal Aspects of Pirate Broadcasting in the North Sea' (1965) 12 Netherlands International Law Review 365; Horace Robertson, 'The Suppression of Pirate Radio Broadcasting: A Test Case of the International System for Control of Activities Outside National Territory' (1982) 45 Law and Contemporary Problems 71.

office space for start-up companies or data storage space,[110] the relocation of activities usually carried out on land to the seas that do not actually require a marine environment is a recurrent phenomenon.

The destination of the vessel, however, does not impact the jurisdiction of the flag State, which remains general notwithstanding the activity pursued on board. Therefore, people on board are still subject to the full jurisdiction of the flag State, regardless of their reason for being on board and the duration of their stay. On the one hand, this conclusion is further strengthened by the fact that the MLC treats all people working on board vessels equally, thus reinforcing the idea that the vessel should be considered as a unique whole for the purpose of regulating the activities of people on board. On the other hand, if flag State jurisdiction was to be limited to some aspects only, this would result in a lack of protection for other aspects. For example, if the flag State did not have jurisdiction to address common crime on board a vessel, a murder that happened on board would not be subject to control by the flag State and, therefore, would be potentially subject to control by no State. For example, if a murder took place on the high seas and the persons involved were both nationals of the flag State, in the absence of any other linking factor no other State could exercise its jurisdiction. In conclusion, the flag State may exercise its legislative and enforcement jurisdiction against people on board vessels independent of the object of this action.

In this respect, legislative jurisdiction is general and may be exercised at any time. This includes cases when the ship is outside the maritime areas of the flag State, for example on the high seas or in the ports of another State. Conversely, enforcement jurisdiction encounters some spatial limitations, as the flag State can enforce its laws and regulations against its vessels when they sail in its maritime zones and on the high seas, but not when they are in the territorial sea or internal waters of another State. Therefore, the flag State cannot arrest a person on board a vessel flying its flag when the vessel is docked in a foreign port, or when the vessel is sailing in the territorial sea of another State. Unless its national legislation empowers the master of a vessel to act as State agent and arrest a person on board the vessel, the flag State will have to wait until the vessel reaches its own ports or, at least, until it leaves the territorial waters of the third State.

5.1.1.1 Delegation of flag State jurisdiction

According to a well-established rule of international law, the flag State may authorize other States to exercise jurisdiction over its vessels, including when they sail on the high seas.[111] The delegation[112] of flag State authority follows the same rules as the original authority: it includes both legislative and, when applicable, enforcement

---

[110] On the so-called Google ships see Stephen Swanson, 'Google Sets Sail: Ocean-Based Server Farms and International Law' (2011) 43 Connecticut Law Review 709.

[111] *United States v Perez-Oviedo* 281 F3d 400, 403 (3d Cir 2002). See Charles Doyle, 'Extraterritorial Application of American Criminal Law' (CRS Report 15 February 2012) 6.

[112] The use of the term 'delegation' should be understood to mean that, while a State other than the flag State may lawfully exercise jurisdiction over a ship and the persons on board, the delegating State still retains its jurisdiction and may intervene directly at any moment.

jurisdiction. It is indeed becoming common in treaties on cooperation in criminal matters to provide that the flag State may authorize other States to intervene against ships flying its flag.[113] This delegation of authority may also happen on a case-by-case basis. It does not need to be communicated in any particular way and it may even take the form of an exchange of notes.[114]

Having said that, in order to be valid, the authorization must be explicit and it should specify the actions that the intervening State may undertake. Any act falling outside the scope of the authorization is prohibited and would constitute a violation of flag State jurisdiction. The issue was raised in the *Medvedyev* case decided by the ECtHR. In that case, France had sought and obtained the consent by Cambodia to board the *Winner*, a Cambodian-flagged vessel suspected of being engaged in drug smuggling. The note produced by Cambodia authorized the French authorities 'to intercept, inspect and take legal action against the ship'.[115] The Court's reading of this authorization was rather restrictive. It considered that the sole object of the agreement was the ship and that consequently, 'the fate of the crew was not covered sufficiently clearly by the note and so it is not established that their deprivation of liberty was the subject of an agreement between the two States that could be considered to represent a "clearly defined law" within the meaning of the Court's case law'.[116]

This reading seems excessively restrictive and not in line with the jurisprudence of the ITLOS and other law of the sea tribunals, which have tended to consider the ship and its crew as a whole.[117] Furthermore, it was criticized by a significant number of judges of the ECtHR, who considered that 'it is scarcely possible to dissociate the crew from the ship itself when a ship is boarded and inspected on the high seas', and that therefore the authorization by Cambodia included the crew of the *Winner*.[118] The jurisprudence of the ECtHR needs however to be taken into account and indicates that the delegation of authority to board vessels by a State other than the flag State should be worded carefully, so as to include all possible action as well as whether such action may be taken against any person on board the vessel.

5.1.1.2 Flagless vessels
There is no general rule on flagless vessels—that is, vessels that are not registered in any State or that sail under the flags of two or more States, using them according to

---

[113] Art 8(2) Smuggling Protocol; Art 8*bis*(5)(b) SUA Convention; for a general authorization see Art 5(2) Treaty to Combat Illicit Drug Trafficking at Sea (Italy-Spain) (adopted 23 March 1990, entered into force 7 May 1994) 1776 UNTS 229.

[114] *Medvedyev* (n 86) paras 96–97; for an example of such notes see Amedeo Antonucci, Irini Papanicolopulu, and Tullio Scovazzi (eds), *L'immigrazione irregolare via mare nella giurisprudenza italiana e nell'esperienza europea* (Giappichelli Editore 2016) document n 23.

[115] *Medvedyev* (n 86) para 10.

[116] ibid 99. The Court also considered that the authorization did not meet the foreseeability requirement of Art 5(1) ECHR either; ibid 100.

[117] Section 5.1.

[118] *Joint Partly Dissenting Opinion of Judges Costa, Casadevall, Bîrsan, Garlicki, Hajiyev, Šikuta, and Nicolaou*, 7.

convenience[119]—in the UNCLOS. The only provision that mentions these ships provides for the right of visit of all States, which includes sending a boat under the command of an officer, the checking of documents, and further examination on board the ship.[120] This provision however does not regulate the exercise of legislative or adjudicative jurisdiction or other consequences of enforcement jurisdiction, such as seizure and arrest.

If vessels generally are subject to the jurisdiction of the flag State, it would seem reasonable to consider either that flagless vessels do not fall under the jurisdiction of any State, or that they are subject to the jurisdiction of all States. Both possibilities, however, would produce an unsatisfying result. As will be discussed in Chapter 4, jurisdiction not only implies the right of the State to regulate activities on board the ship, but also its duty to afford protection to those on board. If a lack of flag were to be equated to a lack of jurisdiction, it would leave people on board flagless vessels without protection. It is this likely consequence that has prompted people conducting criminal activities to make use of flagless vessels. People smugglers employ flagless vessels to transport migrants and asylum seekers, in an effort to elude control by any State while navigating the seas beyond the coastal States' maritime zones,[121] while those engaged in illegal, unreporting and unregulated (IUU) fishing also use flagless vessels for the same reasons.[122] At the same time, opting for the opposite conclusion, that is, that flagless vessels would be subject to the jurisdiction of all States, would also produce unwelcome results. Those vessels that were navigating without a flag while pursuing lawful activities could be overwhelmed by the control of many States.

State practice seems to point towards the acceptance of the right of States to intervene and take action against flagless vessels. In the first place, a number of decisions by national courts has upheld the principle that flagless vessels—sometimes considered as international pariahs—enjoy the protection of no State and are therefore subject to the control of any State. This conclusion has been reached in the case of vessels engaged in drug trafficking,[123] migrant smuggling,[124] and IUU fishing.[125] As the

---

[119] Art 92(2) UNCLOS. See Tribunale di Lecce, decision n. 20 of 11 January 2012. See also Myron H Nordquist, Shabtai Rosenne, and Louis B Sohn (eds), *United Nations Convention on the Law of the Sea, 1982: A Commentary*, vol V (Martinus Nijhoff 1989) para 92.6(a), on ships that conceal their identity.

[120] Art 110 UNCLOS.

[121] Efthymios Papastavridis, *The Interception of Vessels on the High Seas* (Hart 2014) 264–66.

[122] Zoe Scanlon, 'Taking Action against Fishing Vessels without Nationality: Have Recent International Developments Clarified the Law?' (2017) 32 IJMCL 54.

[123] *United States v Ibarguen-Mosquera* 634 F3d 1370, 1378–379 (11th Cir 2011) (internal citations omitted) ('In determining whether an extraterritorial law comports with due process, appellate courts often consult international law principles ... In the past we have held that [these] ... principles have no applicability in connection with stateless vessels because such vessels are international pariahs that have no internationally recognized right to navigate freely on the high seas. Indeed, the law places no restrictions upon a nation's right to subject stateless vessels to its jurisdiction'); *United States v Suerte*, 291 F3d 366, 375 (5th Cir 2002) ('[T]o the extent the Due Process Clause may constrain the MDLEA's extraterritorial reach, that clause does not impose a nexus requirement, in that Congress has acted pursuant to the Piracies and Felonies Clause') Doyle (n 111) 6.

[124] Corte di Cassazione, decision of 28 February 2014, n. 720; Corte di Cassazione, decision of 23 May 2014, n. 36052.

[125] See the decisions cited in Scanlon (n 122) 58–60.

Italian Court of Cassation has noted, freedom of navigation is a right attributed to States, and not to ships or persons on board. It follows that individuals may enjoy freedom of navigation, and the protection from control by other States, only if their ship is linked to a State through the flag.[126]

This conclusion is strengthened by the express provision of the right to intervene against flagless vessels in treaties dealing with security threats at sea. The Smuggling Protocol provides that any State may board and search a vessel that is suspected of being 'engaged in the smuggling of migrants by sea and is without nationality or may be assimilated to a vessel without nationality'.[127] Furthermore, if 'evidence confirming the suspicion is found, that State Party shall take appropriate measures in accordance with relevant domestic and international law'.[128] The intervening State may therefore exercise enforcement, legislative, and adjudicative jurisdiction. Some uncertainty might arise from the reference to international law at the end of this provision. If this were interpreted as a cross reference to Article 110 UNCLOS, then there is not much that could be done apart from inspecting the vessel. However, Article 8(7) of the Smuggling Protocol, in making reference to action undertaken *after* the inspection has taken place, points to enforcement and adjudication, which necessarily presupposes the previous exercise of legislative action. This interpretation, furthermore, is more in line with the object and scope of the Protocol to take action against smuggling of migrants. If action were to be confined to inspection, then the aim of the Protocol would be frustrated as smugglers would escape arrest and prosecution by the intervening State by simply using flagless vessels. It is therefore in line with the text and the object and scope of the treaty to interpret the notion of 'relevant domestic and international law' in Article 8(7) of the Smuggling Protocol as a reference to the rules on the use of force in the arrest of ships and individuals[129] and those on the deprivation of liberty and its safeguards under human rights law.[130]

Similarly, both the Smuggling Protocol and the Convention against Illicit Traffic in Drugs seem to equate flagless vessels to vessels flying the flag of the State intervening, in that they provide the same rights and duties of States towards both categories of vessels.[131] The same approach is followed by the FSA[132] and measures adopted by regional fisheries organizations.[133]

A detailed framework for intervention is provided by the Strasbourg Agreement on Illicit Traffic by Sea,[134] which seems to link the right to intervene against a flagless vessel with the existence of an interest of the intervening State. According to it, a

---

[126] The conclusion of the Italian Court of Cassation cannot however be interpreted to mean that vessels flying no flag are prevented from accessing the seas. It should only be taken to mean that they are subject to the jurisdiction of any State.

[127] Art 8(7) Smuggling Protocol.   [128] ibid.   [129] *Saiga* (n 84) paras 155–58.

[130] *Medvedyev* (n 86) para 80. See, more extensively, Chapter 4, Section 4.1.

[131] Respectively Art 8(1) Smuggling Protocol and Art 17(2) Convention against Illicit Traffic in Drugs.

[132] Art 21(17) FSA.   [133] Scanlon (n 122) 61–63.

[134] Agreement on Illicit Traffic by Sea, implementing Article 17 of the United Nations Convention against Illicit Traffic in Narcotic Drugs and Psychotropic Substances (adopted 30 January 1995, entered into force 1 May 2000) 2136 UNTS 79 (Agreement on Illicit Traffic by Sea).

State that encounters a flagless vessel suspected of being engaged in the illicit trafficking of drugs may inform other States which 'appear most closely affected'. The latter may exercise their jurisdiction against the flagless vessel and may determine what action to undertake, provided they communicate the results of such action to the State that has provided the information in the first instance.[135] While this is not specifically mentioned, it would seem to logically follow that if the State encountering the flagless vessel appears closely affected by the illicit traffic, it can also take direct action against the trafficking vessel.

In conclusion, it seems in line with international practice to consider that any State may exercise its jurisdiction with respect to a flagless vessel if there is a sufficiently strong jurisdictional link between the vessel and the intervening State.[136] The linking criteria of international law, in particular the nationality principle (of those on board, be they the actors or victims of illicit conduct) and the protective principle (aiming at protecting the intervening State against a security threat, be it people smuggling, drugs trafficking, or other) seem particularly appropriate to establish a connection between a State, on one hand, and a vessel and the people on board, on the other. Furthermore, in the case of activities that are deemed to constitute a general threat to security, a State may be considered to have a genuine concern not only if the activity of the vessel is directly aimed at its territory—for example, the vessel transports migrants to its territory—but also when the activity is considered a general threat, as in the case of drug trafficking or other illicit trafficking by sea. In the latter case, the existence of international treaties qualifying the threat as such and making international collaboration compulsory appears to provide a sufficiently strong basis for the exercise of jurisdiction.

5.1.2 *Maritime zone and activity*

In addition to the jurisdiction of the flag State, which follows the vessel wherever it is navigating, people on a ship may also be subject to the jurisdiction of other States depending on the maritime zone in which the ship is sailing and the activity in which it is engaged.

---

[135] Art 5 Agreement on Illicit Traffic by Sea:

'1. A Party which has reasonable grounds to suspect that a vessel without nationality, or assimilated to a vessel without nationality under international law, is engaged in or being used for the commission of a relevant offence, shall inform such other Parties as appear most closely affected and may request the assistance of any such Party in suppressing its use for that purpose. The Party so requested shall render such assistance within the means available to it.

2. Where a Party, having received information in accordance with paragraph 1, takes action it shall be for that Party to determine what actions are appropriate and to exercise its jurisdiction over any relevant offences which may have been committed by any persons on board the vessel.

3. Any Party which has taken action under this article shall communicate as soon as possible to the Party which has provided information, or made a request for assistance, the results of any action taken in respect of the vessel and any persons on board.'

[136] For a similar conclusion see Corte di Cassazione, decision n. 36052 of 23 May 2014.

Under customary international law, the coastal State has sovereignty over the internal waters and territorial sea off its coasts and enjoys functional jurisdiction in the contiguous zone, the exclusive economic zone, and the continental shelf.[137] These jurisdictional rights derive from title attached to the land territory, according to the well-established principle that 'the land dominates the sea'.[138]

In all these cases, the sovereignty and jurisdiction of the coastal State should be considered to extend also to the persons that are in each maritime zone. Therefore, the coastal State will have jurisdiction over persons on board ships sailing in its territorial sea and, to the extent that they engage in the activities envisaged by Articles 33 and 54 UNCLOS, over persons on board ships sailing, respectively, in its contiguous zone and in its exclusive economic zone. Additionally, States will have jurisdiction over people on board vessels navigating above their continental shelf, if they participate in the exploration and exploitation of the resources of this maritime zone.[139]

The application of the general principles on spatial and functional jurisdiction to people at sea, however, raises some issues. A source of potential confusion derives from the peculiar application of the 'territorial' principle in the law of the sea. On the one hand, the division of the sea into maritime zones determines the allocation of jurisdiction on the basis of the zone (the 'territory') in which persons find themselves. The sovereignty of the coastal State over the territorial sea and its jurisdiction in the exclusive economic zone express this principle. On the other hand, unlike land, jurisdiction at sea is seldom all-inclusive but rather, it encounters limitations. It is therefore necessary to carve out the exceptions to the general jurisdiction enjoyed by the coastal State over persons in its territorial sea and, conversely, to identify the extent of the functional jurisdiction it can exercise over persons in its contiguous zone, exclusive economic zone, and continental shelf.

5.1.2.1 The limits of general jurisdiction

The jurisdiction enjoyed by the coastal State over its internal waters and territorial sea is general, including any aspect that can be submitted to regulation. The attention devoted to delimiting and minimizing the actual exercise of jurisdiction by the coastal State over ships and other activities taking place in its territorial sea, as contained in Part II UNCLOS, provides confirmation of the existence of such general right.

However, there are exceptions to it in the territorial sea. A specific qualification of the jurisdiction of the coastal State derives from the right of innocent passage.[140] While the right of innocent passage does not automatically exclude the

---

[137] It has been noted that the distribution of jurisdiction 'is not infused with a coherent theory' (DP O'Connell, *The International Law of the Sea*, vol II (Clarendon Press 1984) 733).

[138] *North Sea Continental Shelf (Federal Republic of Germany v Denmark)* [1969] ICJ Rep 3, para 96. See also *Grisbadarna (Norway v Sweden)* 11 RIAA 147, 159; *Fisheries (United Kingdom v Norway)* [1951] ICJ Rep 116, 133; *Dispute between Argentina and Chile concerning the Beagle Channel* 21 RIAA 53, 80.

[139] Art 77 UNCLOS.   [140] Art 17 UNCLOS.

power of the coastal State to adopt laws and enforce them,[141] its power is significantly limited by Articles 27 and 28 UNCLOS, which tend to narrow the cases in
which a coastal State should exercise its criminal and civil jurisdiction with respect
to people on board foreign vessels exercising the right of innocent passage in its
territorial sea.[142] According to Article 27(1) UNCLOS, the:

criminal jurisdiction of the coastal State should not be exercised on board a foreign ship
passing through the territorial sea to arrest any person or to conduct any investigation in
connection with any crime committed on board the ship during its passage, save only ... if
the consequences of the crime extend to the coastal State; if the crime is of a kind to disturb
the peace of the country or the good order of the territorial sea; if the assistance of the local
authorities has been requested by the master of the ship or by a diplomatic agent or consular
officer of the flag State; or if such measures are necessary for the suppression of illicit traffic in
narcotic drugs or psychotropic substances.

According to Article 28(1) UNCLOS, the 'coastal State should not stop or divert
a foreign ship passing through the territorial sea for the purpose of exercising civil
jurisdiction in relation to a person on board the ship'.

The use of 'should' in both provisions indicates that these constraints on the jurisdiction of the coastal State are only applicable to the extent that the State accepts
them.[143] It is true, however, that these norms are generally applied and that coastal
States do not, as a rule, exercise their criminal and civil jurisdiction over persons sailing in ships exercising the right of innocent passage in their territorial sea.

Nevertheless, these constraints upon the jurisdiction of the coastal State imposed
by Articles 27 and 28 UNCLOS encounter some limitations. In the first place,
Article 27(2) provides that the limits posed by the preceding paragraph 'do not affect
the right of the coastal State to take any steps authorized by its laws for the purpose
of an arrest or investigation on board a foreign ship passing through the territorial
sea after leaving internal waters'. The coastal State therefore enjoys full jurisdiction
over people on board vessels departing from its shores.

Secondly, Articles 27 and 28 UNCLOS are included in Part II, Section 3 ('Innocent
Passage in the Territorial Sea'), Subsection B ('Rules Applicable to Merchant Ships
and Government Ships Operated for Commercial Purposes'). They therefore relate
only to vessels that are exercising the right of innocent passage, as defined in Articles
18 and 19 UNCLOS. If passage is not 'passage' according to the UNCLOS definition, or if it is not innocent, the full sovereignty and jurisdiction of the coastal State
revert. In fact, some activities that would allow the intervention of the coastal State,
such as illegal fishing or pollution of the marine environment, are included in the
activities listed in Article 19(2) which render passage non-innocent. These activities

---

[141] Art 21 UNCLOS.
[142] The extent and limits to enforcement jurisdiction in the territorial sea are discussed in Shearer,
'Problems of Jurisdiction' (n 33).
[143] A further element in favour of this conclusion derives from the history of the provision. During
the 1930 Hague Conference for the Codification of International Law, a proposal to extend the right of
innocent passage to persons and merchandise was not accepted, as it would exclude the possibility for
coastal States to arrest an individual on board. See comment to draft Art 6 in League of Nations Doc
C.230.M.117.1930.V (2 May 1930) 8.

therefore re-establish the full power of the State over a vessel, and it may exercise its full unimpeded jurisdiction over any person engaged in any activity listed in Article 19 (2) UNCLOS.

At the same time, Article 19(2) UNCLOS leaves out activities that, while not constituting a threat to the coastal State, may negatively impact the persons on board, such as potential violations of their human rights. It is true that an argument could be made that violations of human rights, in particular if they are gross and protracted, would be prejudicial to the peace and good order of the coastal State and would therefore render passage non-innocent, as provided in Article 19(1) UNCLOS. The argument however is yet to be made in legal proceedings and does not seem to have been tested in practice so far.

Even more problematic from the perspective of the protection of people at sea is the limitation posed by Article 27(5) UNCLOS. According to this provision 'the coastal State may not take any steps on board a foreign ship passing through the territorial sea to arrest any person or to conduct any investigation in connection with any crime committed before the ship entered the territorial sea, if the ship, proceeding from a foreign port, is only passing through the territorial sea without entering internal waters'. This provision, which was included to avoid undue interference by the coastal State with the right of innocent passage of vessels that are just crossing the territorial sea,[144] may produce particularly unwelcome effects in the case of gross violations of human rights.

Consider, for example, the case of a vessel where its crew are systematically subjected to inhuman and degrading treatment that may amount to torture, which happens to enter the territorial sea of a State. The coastal State would be barred from intervening, even if the vessel is in its 'territory' and members of the crew have contacted the local authorities and have asked for help, if the inhuman treatment stops just before entering its territorial waters and recommences as soon as the vessel has passed through them.[145] It is true that the coastal State may always ask for the authorization of the flag State to intervene, but the outcome will be uncertain as the latter may not only refuse authorization (evidently breaching its human rights obligations) but it may also simply avoid responding to the request. A solution might be to refer to the *jus cogens* nature of some duties deriving from human rights, such as the prohibition of torture and the prohibition of slavery, that would make them prevail on the content of Article 27(5) UNCLOS.

5.1.2.2 The extent of functional jurisdiction

In contrast to the territorial sea, wherein the coastal State enjoys general jurisdiction, jurisdiction in the other maritime zones is functional and extends only to those matters covered by relevant norms.[146] For example, a State cannot exercise enforcement jurisdiction over a person on board a vessel flying a foreign flag and navigating in

---

[144] Nordquist, Rosenne, and Nandan (n 49).

[145] One may question whether the coastal State will have any interest to intervene. This may happen not only if there is a link with the perpetrator or the victim, but also in case the State considers that a claim might be brought against it in front of an international tribunal.

[146] Gavouneli (n 7) 68–69.

its contiguous zone if the purpose of such exercise does not fall within the matters referred to in Article 33 UNCLOS.

Jurisdiction over a person, therefore, derives from jurisdiction over the activity in which the person is engaged. This basis for jurisdiction is often combined with other criteria and serves to better define their scope, as in the case of enforcement of fishing laws against fishers in the exclusive economic zone.[147] The coastal State may enforce its laws because the fishers are in its exclusive economic zone and because they are engaged in fishing. Where one of the two elements appears to be lacking, there would be no possibility to undertake action against these persons.

This concept of 'function' (or 'activity'), while being a useful tool for allocating jurisdiction between States, presents some difficulties in its application to people. The content and limitations of functional jurisdiction are often unclear and this may cause uncertainty as to whether a State can legislate or enforce laws against people in a given circumstance.

The case of the foreign chartered fishing vessels licensed to fish in New Zealand's exclusive economic zone is particularly demonstrative of the limits of functional jurisdiction.[148] In a number of cases, serious physical, verbal, and contractual abuses were documented on board these vessels.[149] However, there was much uncertainty as to whether the coastal State could intervene on board vessels which were fishing in its exclusive economic zone but were flying the flag of another State. On the one hand, fishing in the exclusive economic zone is subject to the legislative and enforcement jurisdiction of the coastal State.[150] On the other, the primary responsibility for regulating social matters belongs to the flag State.[151]

Arguably, the law of the sea does not preclude coastal States from exercising jurisdiction over fishing vessels in conjunction with the flag State while these vessels are engaged in fishing under a licence in their maritime zones. Although labour and social matters do not figure in the list of Article 62(4) UNCLOS, the use of '*inter alia*' when introducing the list testifies to its open character and to the possibility of adopting regulations in further fields. In this case, the uncertainty as to the existence of jurisdiction has caused the government of New Zealand to change its legislation and promote the reflagging of all foreign chartered vessels.[152]

This example also illustrates the relevance of legal characterization for the purposes of determining whether there is functional jurisdiction. Do labour and social matters concerning fishing vessels fall under 'fishing' in Article 62 UNCLOS?

---

[147] Art 73 UNCLOS.
[148] Christina Stringer, Glenn Simmons, and Daren Coulston, 'Not in New Zealand's Waters Surely? Labour and Human Rights Abuses Aboard Foreign Fishing Vessels' (2011) New Zealand Asia Institute Working Paper Series 11-01 <http://docs.business.auckland.ac.nz/Doc/11-01-Not-in-New-Zealand-waters-surely-NZAI-Working-Paper-Sept-2011.pdf> accessed 21 August 2017.
[149] Report of the Ministerial Inquiry into the use and operation of Foreign Charter Vessels (2012) <https://www.mpi.govt.nz/document-vault/4008>.
[150] Art 73 UNCLOS.
[151] Art 94 UNCLOS, in combination with Art 58(2) UNCLOS.
[152] Ministry for Primary Industries, 'Briefing on the Management of Foreign Charter Vessels in New Zealand' (4 February 2013) <http://www.fish.govt.nz/NR/rdonlyres/25D4468F-1F4B-4F7A-92EB-4DE3691279C5/0/B12458forrelease.pdf> accessed 30 March 2013.

While 'labour law' is apparently a separate field from 'conservation of marine living resources,' and while the protection of workers' rights falls more easily within the first category, it is nonetheless evident that the presence of workers on fishing vessels is instrumental and closely linked to fishing activities.

In other cases, the inclusion of activities not expressly mentioned within the ones that characterize functional jurisdiction has been accepted without raising any issues. For example, in the *Drieman* case, decided by the ECtHR, the Court considered that the conviction of and the adoption of other measures by Norway against members of a non-governmental organization interfering with whaling in the Norwegian exclusive economic zone 'were all measures which the respondent State had taken in the exercise of its jurisdiction in the sense of Article 1 of the Convention, and thus were capable of engaging its responsibility under the Convention', and that 'the measures taken against the applicants' conduct in obstructing whaling could reasonably be viewed as having been taken for the prevention of disorder or crime or for the protection of the rights and freedoms of others'.[153] The ECtHR implicitly characterized measures to protect fishers as measures relating to the exercise of sovereign rights with respect to marine living resources, recognized in Article 56 UNCLOS. Similarly, in the *Arctic Sunrise* case, the arbitral tribunal, also citing the preparatory work of the ILC on the Geneva Conventions, concluded that the rights of the coastal State over the continental shelf include the right to take enforcement action to support legislation relating to matters included in Article 70 UNCLOS.[154]

5.1.3 Port State

A *sui generis* form of jurisdiction is that of the port State, which combines territorial and extraterritorial elements.[155] On the one hand, port State jurisdiction is based on the territorial principle, according to which a State has full sovereignty, and therefore jurisdiction, over its territory, including its ports.[156] Therefore, any ship which is voluntarily in the ports of the State and any persons on board it are subject to the jurisdiction of that State. On the other hand, this jurisdiction can be exercised with respect to acts which have been performed before the ship entered into the port and, often, when the ship was navigating on the high seas, beyond the port State's maritime zones. As a result, the port State may exercise jurisdiction over a person with respect to acts that this person has committed while he or she was outside the maritime zones of the port State.

Port State jurisdiction is provided by treaties with respect to safety and security,[157] environmental,[158] and labour[159] issues, as well as the conservation of

---

[153] *Drieman and Others v Norway* App no 33678/96 (Decision of 4 May 2000).
[154] *Arctic Sunrise (The Kingdom of the Netherlands v The Russian Federation)* PCA Case no 2014-02 (Award (merits) of 14 August 2015) paras 283–84.
[155] Robin Churchill, 'Port State Jurisdiction Relating to the Safety of Shipping and Pollution from Ships—What Degree of Extra-territoriality' (2016) 31 IJMCL 442.
[156] AV Lowe, 'The Right of Entry into Maritime Ports in International Law' (1977) 14 San Diego Law Review 597.
[157] Art 219 UNCLOS; Reg 19 SOLAS.   [158] Art 6 MARPOL.
[159] Art V(4) MLC. See Laura Carballo Piñeiro, 'Port State Jurisdiction over Labour Conditions: a Private International Law Perspective on Extra-territoriality' (2016) 31 IJMCL 531.

resources.[160] The special element of this form of jurisdiction, as it has developed through State practice, is that it allows States to legislate, enforce, and adjudicate with respect to acts committed elsewhere, in other States' maritime zones or on the high seas. Port State control refers not only to the conditions existing when the ship enters the port of the State, but it may indeed target activities that have occurred outside the ports, and even the territorial waters. Thus, for example, a State may validly exercise its enforcement jurisdiction against a vessel in its ports for discharges on the high seas[161] and may consequently take action against any person involved in such discharge.

The admissibility of this form of jurisdiction is now generally accepted[162] and is not considered to violate the territorial principle.[163] It would therefore seem possible that a State could adopt legislation which would be applicable to persons on board any ship going beyond what is provided under the port State control regime.[164] The power to implement such legislation would, in fact, repose not on jurisdiction allocated under law of the sea rules, but rather on the territorial jurisdiction that a State enjoys over any person who happens to be within that State's territory, even if for a limited time period and even if the conduct against which the State is acting has taken place elsewhere. This legislation could be enforced in favour or against the person in question, not because this person is part of the crew of a ship visiting a port of the State, but because this person is present on the territory of the State.[165]

5.2 Structures and installations

In addition to ships, people at sea may be found on artificial islands, structures, and installations, that is, manmade objects that float in the waters—but are not considered as ships under current maritime law—or are fixed to the seabed. The number of platforms and other fixed or floating installations is constantly increasing. These objects may vary in size, composition, and use and it is difficult, if not impossible, to provide a general definition. What connects oil rigs, fishing platforms, scientific stations, and rocket launching platforms is that, despite their very different purposes,

---

[160] For example under the Agreement on Port State Measures to Prevent, Deter and Eliminate Illegal, Unreported and Unregulated Fishing (adopted 22 November 2009, entered into force 5 June 2016) (PSCA).

[161] Art 218(1) UNCLOS.

[162] Erik Jaap Molenaar, 'Port State Jurisdiction: Toward Comprehensive, Mandatory and Global Coverage' (2007) 38 ODIL 225; Judith Swan, 'Port State Measures—from Residual Port State Jurisdiction to Global Standards' (2016) 31 IJMCL 395.

[163] Brownlie (n 8) 479.

[164] Khaliq (n 6) 330 considers that a port State may exercise jurisdiction over a foreign vessel 'where acts or conditions which amount to human rights abuses are criminal acts in the domestic law of that state' or when they 'amount to crimes which are of universal jurisdiction' (ibid 331).

[165] Robin R Churchill and Alan Vaughan Lowe, *The Law of the Sea* (3rd edn, Manchester University Press 1999) 68. For a different point of view Natalie Klein, *Maritime Security and the Law of the Sea* (OUP 2011) 69–73.

they are not 'ships' in legal terms when they operate. In fact, in more than one case, the same object may have a double nature.[166] Structures can be distinguished from ships because they are relatively fixed and do not sail in the waters, as ships do. Thus, it is the relative stability that distinguishes these objects. Therefore, in order to determine which rules apply to an object at sea—whether rules on ships or those on platforms—it is necessary to consider whether the object, at a given time, navigates or not.

This distinction is particularly relevant in the case of self-propelling structures, such as mobile offshore drilling units (MODUs). While MODUs are navigating to their destination, they are to be considered as ships and are therefore subject to the rules on jurisdiction over ships. Once they have reached their destination and have been anchored to the seabed, they then become subject to the rules on structures.

A final preliminary point concerns language used in different normative provisions. While Articles 60 and 80 UNCLOS refer to 'artificial islands, structures and installations', the Convention does not define these terms. Nor does it define the term 'devices' used in provisions on marine scientific research.[167] Devices used for different purposes may include buoys, floats, gliders, platforms, and unmanned vehicles, both tethered (ie connected to a ship with a cable) and autonomous, as well as other floating and submerged structures and devices that are introduced into the marine environment. Their dimensions, their use, and the period of time during which they are deployed in the sea vary. What are relevant for the purpose of the present discussion are, however, only those objects that may host people on them. In this respect, the fact that the UNCLOS uses a variety of terms to define these objects, joined with the fact that some articles distinguish between vessels and other objects,[168] necessarily leads to an interpretation that includes within its scope all objects that are used to conduct any activity at sea[169] which are not, in fact, 'vessels'.[170]

---

[166] Vaughan Lowe, 'Ships' in Tullio Scovazzi, Nerina Boschiero, Cesare Pitea, and Chiara Ragni (eds), *International Courts and the Development of International Law: Essays in Honour of Tullio Treves* (Asser Press 2013) 291.

[167] For example Art 258 UNCLOS.   [168] For example Art 248 UNCLOS.

[169] Equipment having dual uses is discussed in Tullio Treves, 'Military Installations, Structures and Devices on the Seabed' (1980) 74 AJIL 808.

[170] Florian HTh Wegelein, *Marine Scientific Research* (Martinus Nijhoff 2005) 135. This conclusion however leaves some ambiguities, since there is no general definition of 'vessel'; Lowe, 'Ships' (n 166). The distinction between a vessel and something that is not one may become problematic, eg in cases of objects linked with a vessel, as well as in the case of unmanned underwater vehicles. A possible criterion would consist in distinguishing between what is to be considered as an accessory to a vessel, eg towed arrays or Expendable Bathythermographs (XBTs) that remain connected with a vessel that is navigating, and what is to be considered as a separate item, eg remotely operated gliders and other vehicles: Wegelein (n 170) 140–41.

5.2.1 Structures in coastal zones

It seems generally accepted that structures in the coastal State's maritime zones, including the territorial sea, the exclusive economic zone, and the continental shelf, are subject to the jurisdiction of that State.

If the jurisdiction of the flag State is *sui generis*, the exclusive jurisdiction of the coastal State over artificial islands, installations, and structures in its exclusive economic zone and on its continental shelf reposes on the territorial principle. Article 60(2) UNCLOS, concerning structures in a State's exclusive economic zone, states that:

The coastal State shall have *exclusive* jurisdiction over such artificial islands, installations and structures, *including* jurisdiction with regard to customs, fiscal, health, safety and immigration laws and regulations.[171]

The jurisdiction that the coastal State exercises over artificial islands, installations, and structures in its exclusive economic zone and continental shelf is general and exclusive. It includes all persons on board, and it may consist of its legislative, enforcement, or adjudicatory competences.

The broad language of the provision, the fact that specific normative areas are provided by way of example, and the fact that the jurisdiction of the State is exclusive, all point to a general competence of the State, both *ratione materiae* and *ratione personae*. In this respect, jurisdiction exercised by the coastal State over platforms can be considered as a similar manifestation of jurisdiction to that exercised by a State over ships flying its flag, which is not limited functionally but can impact any aspect of life that takes place on board and is not restricted to activities having a linkage with navigation. Thus, the jurisdiction of the coastal State extends to the persons on board the platform or other structure, similarly to what happens for vessels. This has been confirmed by the Court of Justice of the European Union (CJEU) in a series of cases involving workers on platforms. In the *Salemink* case, relating to the applicability of European Union (EU) legislation on social security to a person employed on a platform on the Dutch continental shelf, the CJEU referred to the rights of the coastal State on its continental shelf and its exclusive jurisdiction over platforms thereon in order to establish the applicability of EU legislation.[172]

The jurisdiction of the coastal State over a platform includes both legislative and enforcement jurisdiction. In that regard, the ILC commented in 1956 that 'installations are under the jurisdiction of the coastal State for the purpose of maintaining order and of the civil and criminal competence of its courts' and there is no evidence to show that a new rule has since developed.[173]

---

[171] Emphasis added. The same regime applies to artificial islands, installations, and structures on the continental shelf, on the basis of the cross-reference in Art 80 UNCLOS.

[172] Case C-347/10 *Salemink* [2012] paras 34–35. See also Case C-347/10 *Salemink* [2012], Opinion of AG Villalon, paras 33–36, who also pointed out that the Commission, Greece and Spain considered that the coastal State had jurisdiction.

[173] ILC, *Yearbook of the International Law Commission*, vol II (1956) 299.

Finally, jurisdiction is exclusive. Exclusiveness certainly relates to enforcement jurisdiction exercised on the platform. The 2005 Protocol for the Suppression of Unlawful Acts Against the Safety of Fixed Platforms Located on the Continental Shelf provides confirmation of the exclusivity of enforcement jurisdiction. However, limited legislative jurisdiction may be exercised by other States having a link with the persons, for example by the State of nationality.

Furthermore, it is debatable whether the coastal State still enjoys exclusive jurisdiction in the safety zone around the installation.[174] According to Article 60 UNCLOS, a State may establish reasonable safety zones around artificial islands, installations, and structures 'in which it may take appropriate measures to ensure the safety both of navigation and of the artificial islands, installations and structures'.[175] This provision allows the coastal State to take, in the safety zone, appropriate measures relating both to normative and enforcement actions, but only within the limits of ensuring the safety of navigation and of the object itself. These rights of the coastal State go beyond its rights in the exclusive economic zone at large.[176] It seems more in accordance with the content and purpose of its rights, which are to ensure that activities carried out on the installation do not happen in a legal vacuum, to consider that the jurisdiction of the coastal State may extend in the safety zone only if it relates to activities of the installation and not, for example, to activities happening on a vessel passing by, unless the vessel were to interfere with the activities of the platform. In the *Arctic Sunrise* case, the arbitral tribunal considered that Russia, the coastal State, had the right to exercise enforcement action against vessels that would enter the 500 metres safety zone established around an oil rig.[177]

5.2.2 Structures on the high seas

The placement of structures on the high seas are one of the scenarios in which international law does not provide any rule to determine the State that has jurisdiction. For example, the UNCLOS does not mention platforms on the high seas, nor is there any indication as to whether a State can exercise its jurisdiction over persons which are on such a platform.

In some cases, a State may acquire jurisdiction by applying the general rules of jurisdiction illustrated above. For example, the State of nationality of the persons on board will have jurisdiction if the platform is used for fishing,[178] while the State of nationality of the persons on board or of the person owning it or controlling the company that owns it will have jurisdiction if the platform is used to explore mineral resources in the Area.[179] Other activities may however still remain outside these rules, for example if the platform is used to temporarily host persons being

---

[174] Klein (n 165) 103.
[175] Art 60(4) UNCLOS. The safety zone needs to be explicitly created by the coastal State (*Arctic Sunrise* (n 154) para 248) and its breadth shall not exceed 500 metres, as established by Art 60(5) UNCLOS.
[176] *Arctic Sunrise* (n 154) para 211.   [177] ibid para 250.   [178] Art 117 UNCLOS.
[179] Art 139 UNCLOS.

smuggled, or to store weapons or drugs trafficked illegally. With respect to the latter case, an analogy may be drawn with flagless vessels. When a person is on board a flagless vessel, Article 110 provides the possibility for a State to *visit* a vessel which does not fly a flag, although it does not provide any independent basis for the exercise of jurisdiction over the vessel or over the persons on board, other than those permissible factors already provided by other rules of the UNCLOS, such as the nationality of the vessel or piracy.[180] The same conclusion could be reached with respect to platforms on the high seas used for any activity.

In order to allow a State to control activities and to ensure that they do not hinder the exercise of rights enjoyed by other States, and that they comply with international rules, including those concerning human rights, it is conceivable that in those cases, and until generally accepted rights and obligations under international law come into existence, a State may exercise its jurisdiction based on the nationality, the universality, the passive personality, or any other appropriate principle. For example, there is no doubt that a State can legislate and can enforce its laws and regulations with respect to platforms used by its nationals, be they physical or juridical persons, albeit there might be some uncertainty as to the extent of the State's powers if nationals of other States were also on board the platform. It might also be considered entirely reasonable for a State to exercise criminal jurisdiction in situations where the victim of an illegal act committed by one of the persons on the platform is a national of that State. Universality of jurisdiction, possibly in the qualified form of comprising the *aut dedere aut iudicare* principle, could operate to prevent and punish conduct that is condemned under global treaties, such as the slave trade and human trafficking, threats to safety and security, pollution of the marine environment, or inhuman working and living conditions.

A specific situation of interest concerns installations used for scientific research at sea.[181] Article 262 UNCLOS indirectly refers to the registration of scientific installations and equipment. It is clear from the text that States can register installations and equipment and that international organizations can own scientific research installations and equipment not registered in a State. It could therefore be considered that, if a specific installation is registered in a State, then this State may exercise jurisdiction with respect to the installation itself and the people on board.[182]

---

[180] Guilfoyle (n 14) 16–18.

[181] Other special cases concern ice islands, see FM Auburn, 'International Law and Sea-Ice Jurisdiction in the Arctic Ocean' (1973) 22 ICLQ 552, and artificial islands, see Craig Walker, 'Jurisdictional Problems Created by Artificial Islands' (1973) 10 San Diego Law Review 638 and Robert B Krueger, Myron H Nordquist, and Robert P Wessely, 'New Technology and International Law: The Case of Deepwater Ports' (1977) 17 Virginia Journal of International Law 597.

[182] Rules on registration are however far from clear. The 1993 IOC Draft Convention on Ocean Data Acquisition Systems, Aids and Devices (Second Revision) IOC Doc. IOC-XVII/INF.1 (1993) (Draft ODAS Convention) contained the requirement to register all ODAS and the detailed regime of the registration system, as well as the assimilation to vessels of registered ODAS and the exclusive jurisdiction of the registering State over them. The 1993 Draft ODAS Convention, however, was not adopted and although the issue is currently being discussed in the context of the IOC, views of States seem still irreconcilable and no agreement has been reached; IOC, Advisory Body of Experts on the Law of the Sea: Report of the Ninth Session (2009).

Finally, it would seem appropriate that the exercise of jurisdiction by a State, generally the State of nationality, over people on a platform on the high seas should be considered as general, that is including any aspect and any activity. If jurisdiction were only functional, there could be cases in which no State could claim jurisdiction and therefore the people on the platform would not benefit from the legal protection following the existence of the power by a State over them.

6. The Relationship between Jurisdictional Grounds: Exclusive and Priority Jurisdiction

The existence of multiple rules, based on different linking criteria, to identify the State that has jurisdiction over a person at sea may determine situations of multiple and overlapping jurisdictions.[183] Thus, for example, the jurisdiction of the flag State of a fishing vessel co-exists with that of the coastal State while the vessel is fishing in the latter's exclusive economic zone. Similarly, jurisdiction of the flag State co-exists with that of the State of nationality of the persons on board the vessel. The overlapping of multiple jurisdictions is not unique to the sea, but may happen on land, where multiple jurisdictional competences are managed, rather than avoided.[184]

The potential existence of multiple jurisdictions raises the issue of the relationship between them. If more than one State has jurisdiction to intervene against a person, or to regulate the conduct of that person, is there a rule that regulates which jurisdiction—and therefore which State—prevails? The case of the *Enrica Lexie*, presently pending before a UNCLOS Annex VII arbitral tribunal, illustrates the issue. The facts of the case are not entirely clear, but it seems that the dispute stems from an incident involving an Indian flagged fishing vessel, two fishermen of which were killed, and an Italian flagged commercial vessel, the *Enrica Lexie*, among the crew of which were two Italian marines, who allegedly killed the fishermen. Both Italy and India claim they have jurisdiction to try the two marines. On the one hand, Italy refers to the nationality principle, since both the vessel and the marines have Italian nationality. Furthermore, on the basis of Article 97 UNCLOS, Italy claims that its jurisdiction is exclusive, since it is able to claim to be both the flag State and the State of nationality of the person involved in the maritime incident. On the other hand, India refers to the passive personality principle, since the victims were Indian nationals, and the territorial principle, since the incident took place in the Indian exclusive economic zone and the marines were arrested upon entering an Indian port.

While there is no generally applicable rule to this effect, there is a tendency to defer to the jurisdiction of the flag State. In some cases, this situation is set out in rules of positive law. In the first place, there are cases in which a norm may make it

---

[183] For the case of jurisdiction over fishers see Raymond Goy, 'Le Pêcheur Devant le Juge Pénal en Droit International' in Giuseppe Cataldi (ed), *La Méditerranée et le Droit de la Mer à l'Aube du 21e Siècle* (Bruylant 2002) 113.
[184] Brownlie (n 8) 457.

clear that a State *cannot* exercise jurisdiction over a person. This is usually achieved by expressly stating that only one, or a specific number of States, have *exclusive* jurisdiction. On the basis of the already mentioned Article 97(1) UNCLOS, insofar as criminal jurisdiction in matters of collision between vessels is concerned, there is no doubt that no State can exercise jurisdiction over the master and crew of the vessel involved in the incident, apart from the flag State and the State of nationality.[185] Similarly, on the basis of Article 92 UNCLOS, only the flag State has jurisdiction on vessels flying its flag on the high seas; therefore, all other States are prevented from exercising jurisdiction. Limitations may be accompanied by exceptions. Taking as an example flag State jurisdiction, its exclusivity on the high seas is restrained by the norms that allow, amongst others, every State to exercise enforcement jurisdiction over pirates[186] or that allow every State to visit a ship that is engaged in the slave trade.[187]

In other cases, jurisdiction of the flag State prevails over that of other States, but it does not exclude the latter completely. As a consequence, any State that has a jurisdictional link may, for example, prosecute a certain vessel and the persons on board. If, however, the flag State decides to prosecute, then its action prevails over that of the other States. This is, for example, the case of the situations described in Article 228 of the UNCLOS, on proceedings concerning the pollution of the marine environment, which sets criteria for the suspension of proceedings and restrictions on the institution of proceedings, favouring the exercise of jurisdiction by the flag State of the polluting vessel. The preferential jurisdiction of the flag State is also explicitly provided for in the Agreement on Illicit Traffic by Sea.[188]

For the remaining cases, jurisdictional overlapping is usually managed in accordance with the independent and the cumulative principles, rather than the subsidiary principle.[189] A further element to take into account concerns the reasonableness of the exercise of jurisdiction, in the light of the circumstances of the particular case.[190]

In conclusion, the well-established rule that allocates jurisdiction over people on board ships to the flag State, also when the ship is navigating far from its coasts and in the maritime zone of another State, may in fact prevent the exercise of jurisdiction by any State. It is questionable whether the flag State will take much interest in what is happening on board the vessel, and even if it wanted to intervene, it lacks enforcement jurisdiction. Enforcement rests in fact with the coastal State, but the latter might prefer not to exercise jurisdiction, lest it be considered that it is in breach of the right of innocent passage. Perhaps the best solution would be for the flag State to ask for the intervention of the coastal State, as envisaged in Article 27(1)(c) UNCLOS.

---

[185] A different issue, and one raised in the *Enrica Lexie* case, concerns the characterization of an event as an 'incident of navigation'.

[186] Art 105 UNCLOS.   [187] Art 110(1)(b) UNCLOS.

[188] Art 3(4) Agreement on Illicit Traffic by Sea.   [189] Crawford (n 10) 477.

[190] ibid; Ryngaert (n 8) ch 5.

7. The Relevance of Jurisdictional Grounds to Determine the Applicability of Human Rights Obligations at Sea

Jurisdiction under international human rights law, in particular *de jure* jurisdiction, is based upon the existence of rules of international law that attribute jurisdiction to a State. All rules illustrated in the preceding sections are examples of such rules. It follows that in all cases in which the law of the sea or general international law provides that a State has jurisdiction over a person, a maritime zone, a vessel or a platform, then that State is obliged to observe its human rights obligations towards that person or persons in that zone or indeed those on the vessel or platform.[191]

International practice clearly supports this conclusion. Flag State jurisdiction is indeed routinely referred to as one of the established cases of extraterritorial jurisdiction of States, even in cases adopting a narrow reading of the extraterritorial application of human rights obligations.[192] Similarly, 'territorial-like' jurisdiction over maritime zones is so much embedded in the practice of States, that it is not raised as a preliminary exception in human rights litigation. In the *Drieman* case, which concerned the arrest by the coastal State of persons that had allegedly violated its legislation concerning fisheries in its exclusive economic zone, the ECtHR simply acknowledged the fact that 'the applicants' convictions and sentence to pay fines and the confiscation of the first applicant's dinghy were all measures which the respondent State had taken *in the exercise of its jurisdiction* in the sense of Article 1 of the Convention, and thus were capable of engaging its responsibility under the Convention'.[193] In the *Salemink* case, concerning the applicability of social security norms to a person working on an oil rig on the continental shelf of the Netherlands, an EU Member State, the CJEU considered that 'work carried out on fixed or floating installations positioned on the continental shelf, in the context of the prospecting and/or exploitation of natural resources, is to be regarded as work carried out in the territory of that State for the purposes of applying EU law'.[194] Similar considerations apply to jurisdiction of the port State.[195]

---

[191] Irini Papanicolopulu, 'A Missing Part of the Law of the Sea Convention: Addressing Issues of State Jurisdiction over Persons at Sea' in Clive Schofield, Seokwoo Lee, and Moon-Sang Kwon (eds), *The Limits of Maritime Jurisdiction* (Martinus Nijhoff 2014) 387.

[192] *Banković* (n 104) para 59; *Markovic and Others v Italy* App no 1398/03 (Decision [GC] of 14 December 2006) para 49; *Assanidze v Georgia* App no 71503/01 (Decision [GC] of 8 April 2004) para 137; *Medvedyev* (n 86) para 65; *Hirsi* (n 37) para 77. See also Khaliq (n 6) 345, who notes, with respect to communications to the Human Rights Committee, that 'no state has objected to the admissibility of a communication on the basis that a state's obligations under the [ICCPR] do not extend to vessels flying their flag'.

[193] *Drieman* (n 153) 8, emphasis added.

[194] *Salemink* (n 172) para 35. The Court added that '[a] Member State which takes advantage of the economic rights to prospect and/or exploit natural resources on that part of the continental shelf which is adjacent to it cannot avoid the application of the EU law provisions designed to ensure the freedom of movement of persons working on such installations' (ibid para 36).

[195] Although sometimes this link may not be used. In a recent case, a section of the ECtHR was called upon to determine whether the port State had jurisdiction according to Art 1 ECHR over stowaways on board a vessel that had entered into one of its ports. The ECtHR preferred to assert the existence

At the same time, and in application of *de facto* jurisdiction, a State will be under the duty to respect and protect the rights of people who are under its control, or who are on board vessels or platforms under the control of that State.[196] The exercise of *de facto* jurisdiction at sea usually takes the form of enforcement action by one State against a vessel flying a different flag, in its own maritime zones or on the high seas. In the *Rigopoulos* and *Medvedyev*[197] cases, both of which concerned the interdiction and arrest of vessels engaged in drug trafficking on the high seas by a State other than the flag State, the respondent States, Spain and France, did not contest the existence of jurisdiction under Article 1 ECHR, thus implicitly confirming that undertaking police enforcement measures against a foreign vessel and crew is sufficient to bring the latter within a State's jurisdiction for the purposes of the ECHR.[198] Furthermore, in the *Medvedyev* case, the ECtHR considered that boarding a vessel and taking action against the persons on board constitutes the exercise of full and exclusive control and thus triggers the *de facto* jurisdiction of the intervening State.[199]

In light of the special characteristics of the marine environment, it is not necessary that a vessel be boarded for *de facto* jurisdiction to come into play.[200] Manoeuvring in a way that compels the targeted vessel to stop or change its course may amount to 'control' and may be sufficient to bring the individuals on board the targeted vessel within the control of the State. In the *Xhavara* case, concerning the sinking on the high seas of the *Kater I Rades*, an Albanian vessel engaged in migrant smuggling, as a result of the collision with the Italian Navy vessel *Sibilla*, the ECtHR considered that persons on board the *Kater I Rades* were brought within the jurisdiction of Italy as a consequence of the collision caused by the Italian vessel.[201] Physical contact between the two vessels is not a requirement either. In the *Women on Waves* case, the ECtHR considered the (unlawful) *de facto* jurisdiction exercised by a Portuguese navy vessel over a Dutch vessel navigating outside the territorial waters of Portugal, thus implying that there was jurisdiction despite the fact that the two vessels had not made any physical contact.[202]

The decisions mentioned in the preceding paragraphs provide evidence that the notion of jurisdiction under international human rights treaties includes both *de jure* and *de facto* jurisdiction. *De jure* and *de facto* jurisdiction are not necessarily mutually exclusive. They are based on different elements—the first on the existence

of jurisdiction upon the State's 'exercise of its sovereign powers to control the entry of aliens into its territory' (*Kebe and Others v Ukraine* App no 12552/12 (Decision of 12 January 2017) paras 75–76).

[196] Papastavridis (n 6) 122.

[197] Gianmatteo Breda and Jean Paul Perini, 'Legal Issues Surrounding Maritime Counterdrug Operations and the Related Question of Detention as Highlighted in the *Medvedyev and Others v. France* Decision of the European Court of Human Rights' (2008) 47 Military Law and the Law of War Review 167, 171.

[198] *Medvedyev* (n 86) para 50.   [199] ibid paras 66–67.

[200] Papastavridis (n 6) 123 considers that there is jurisdiction in cases in which there is 'a ship-to-ship operation prior to boarding, which involves limited use of force' while there is no jurisdiction in cases of shadowing or surveillance.

[201] *Xhavara and Others v Italy and Albania* App no 39473/98 (Decision of 11 January 2001) para 1.

[202] *Women on Waves and Others v Portugal* App no 31276/05 (Judgment of 3 February 2009) para 43.

of a norm, the second on the existence of conduct. Both may operate within the territory of a State *and* beyond, in areas which are either under the sovereignty of another State or are not subject to the sovereignty of any State, as in the case of maritime zones beyond the territorial sea. Furthermore, both forms of jurisdiction have a significant role to play in ensuring the protection of people at sea. On one hand, *de facto* jurisdiction will come into play when States undertake police or other enforcement operations at sea, as in the case of the fight against drug trafficking or the arrest of pirates. In such cases, the intervening State will be under the obligation to ensure that the conduct of such operations complies with human rights requirements, independently from the existence of a legal basis for its intervention. On the other hand, *de iure* jurisdiction, in particular that of the flag State, will be essential in ensuring protection of the human rights of people on board vessels that navigate beyond the territorial sea of the flag State. When a vessel is navigating on the high seas, it is extremely unlikely that any State shall intervene and check what is happening on board the vessel, thus establishing *de facto* jurisdiction. Consequently, it is only through recourse to the *de iure* jurisdiction of the flag State that a human rights body will be able to identify a State that has the duty to protect the human rights of those on board. Otherwise, a legal vacuum would arise, which would be contrary both to the letter and the purpose of human rights instruments.

It has been argued that only *de facto* jurisdiction should be relevant for the application of human rights treaties outside the boundaries of a State, that is extraterritorially. Under this argument, jurisdiction 'is a question of fact, of actual authority and control. Despite its name, it is not a legal competence, and it has absolutely nothing to do with that other notion of jurisdiction in international law which delimits the municipal legal systems of states'.[203] I do not agree with this conclusion as far as the sea is concerned.[204] I agree that the actual exercise of power over a person or a place is sufficient to establish jurisdiction. However, I also argue that the existence of *de jure* jurisdiction—of a rule that attributes jurisdiction to a State over a ship, a platform, or a maritime zone—is also sufficient to meet the threshold for the applicability of international human rights treaties. This conclusion is supported by international practice, the decisions of international courts, systemic considerations, and policy concerns.

It is beyond doubt that the practice of States and international organizations has always considered that the existence of *de jure* jurisdiction is sufficient to trigger human rights obligations. The case of ships is paradigmatic. It is well known that commercial vessels are rarely under the actual control of State organs, as most of the time they navigate far away from the coasts (and the patrol vessels) of their State of nationality. Nevertheless, this has not impeded flag States from being held liable for the violations of human rights that have happen on them, as numerous cases have

---

[203] Milanovic (n 1) 53. The author concludes that one should completely disregard the 'legal' notion of jurisdiction, in favour of a purely factual one and that the application of human rights treaties 'should never depend on naked title over a territory, but on actual power exercised over it' (Milanovic (n 1) 61).

[204] I also have some doubts about its applicability to land as well, but this is beyond the scope of this book.

demonstrated. The flag State is routinely referred to as the State having jurisdiction over people on board, in accordance with the well-accepted law of the sea principle.[205] Furthermore, human rights bodies have consistently confirmed the argument advanced here. The Committee Against Torture, in its General Comment, has supported the view that 'a State party's jurisdiction includes any territory where the State party exercises, directly or indirectly, in whole or in part, de jure or de facto effective control, in accordance with international law'.[206]

In a systemic perspective, it must be kept in mind that the law of the sea and international human rights law are both branches of public international law. They are sub-regimes or sub-systems within the more general system of international law, and they are certainly not self-contained, but share the general notions which are essential to the functioning of public international law. The development of an entirely autonomous notion of jurisdiction under the sub-regime 'human rights law' would constitute an exception to the generally accepted notion of jurisdiction in international law. As a consequence, this development cannot be presumed but needs to be proved. International practice, in the form of judicial pronouncements, State conduct, and soft and hard law instruments of international organizations, illustrated above, has so far provided evidence that a specific notion has developed alongside the general notion, but not that the specific notion has taken the place of the general one. The insistence of the ECtHR on the 'international law' notion of jurisdiction, both in cases adopting a narrow approach and also in those adopting a broad approach to extraterritorial jurisdiction, corroborates the point and operates a fair balance between considerations of effectiveness and considerations of universality.

Additionally, an interpretation of 'jurisdiction' in human rights instruments that would exclude *de iure* jurisdiction would go against a systemic reading of human rights instruments in light of law of the sea instruments, in particular provisions of the latter, such as Article 94 UNCLOS, which *oblige* States to exercise their jurisdiction with respect to people on board vessels flying their flag. Such interpretation would be contrary to the principle of harmonization and would cause unnecessary fragmentation.[207]

Finally, from a policy perspective, it has been maintained that an understanding of extraterritorial jurisdiction which relies solely on the actual exercise of control over the persons or the ship, would allow us to balance the requirements of universality and effectiveness.[208] This argument has some worth if we consider the possibility of one State exercising extraterritorial jurisdiction over persons or places situated in the territory of another State. In that case, the exercise of jurisdiction by the first

---

[205] This principle was applied in *Bakanova v Lithuania* App no 11167/12 (Judgment of 31 May 2016) para 63. See also the cases mentioned in n 192.

[206] CAT, 'General Comment No. 2 on implementation of Article 2 of the Convention by States parties' in Official Documents of the General Assembly, sixty-third session, Supplement No 44 (A/63/44), annex VI, para 16. See also CAT, 'Communication No. 368/2008' UN Doc A/HRC/15/21 para 67: 'The international human rights treaties accepted by each of these States at the time of the incident under investigation were applicable on the relevant vessels'; Conclusions and recommendations of the Committee against Torture concerning the second report of the United States of America, CAT/C/USA/CO/2, 25 July 2006.

[207] See also Khaliq (n 6) 340–41.   [208] Milanovic (n 1) 219.

State would constitute an exception and a curtailment of the general jurisdiction by the territorial State. As such, it should not be over-expanded. In addition, even if the acting State were to be found not to have exercised jurisdiction, individuals would not be devoid of any protection, since the obligation to protect and enforce human rights would return to the default State, the territorial sovereign.

However, it should be kept in mind that jurisdiction at sea is almost always 'extra-territorial', since only the territorial sea is State territory, while the contiguous zone, exclusive economic zone, and high seas are not. If applied to these areas, the theory illustrated above would exclude the operation of human rights provisions in almost all cases, since it is rarely the case that a State has actual control over what is happening in its maritime zones, let alone on the high seas. Instead of furthering the protection of human rights at sea, it would allow for the worst forms of human exploitation, without actually helping in any way to consolidate the reign of human rights on land. A negation of the flag State's 'general' jurisdiction under international law would mean that at sea there is no 'default' State entrusted with the protection of human rights, to which the individual could turn to in order to complain for the violation of his or her rights.[209] This conclusion is both abhorrent to reason and useless in practice, since it does not serve any purpose.

An additional consideration only strengthens this conclusion. The act of granting the flag to a vessel or the authorization to construct and operate a platform or installation is a *voluntary* act of the State. States are neither obliged by law, nor coerced by factual circumstances, to grant their flag to any vessel. If they decide to do so, they exercise a right provided by customary international law. This right, however, comes with some duties, first and foremost the obligation to effectively exercise jurisdiction over the vessel, now enshrined in Article 94 UNCLOS. States are well aware of this when they evaluate what conditions they should set for the granting of their flag to vessels. They cannot pick and choose, taking only the right to grant the flag without accepting the ensuing obligation to exercise jurisdiction. It is therefore not possible to neglect human rights obligations *in toto* by simply claiming that it is not possible to exercise effective control over all ships that fly a State's flag.[210]

In light of the foregoing considerations, it is appropriate to conclude that 'jurisidction' for the purposes of establishing the applicability of human rights instruments to people at sea and therefore the existence of States' duties towards them, includes not only *de facto*, but also *de iure* jurisdiction. Any other conception would be against the actual practice of States and international bodies, would be contrary to reason, and would result in bad policy.

---

[209] Khaliq (n 6) 343.
[210] A different issue is the extent to which human rights obligations have to be fulfilled by the State. This will be considered in Chapter 4, Section 3.

8. Distinguishing Lawful Jurisdiction from the Lawful Exercise of Jurisdiction

There is a final point worthy of some consideration before bringing to a close the discussion of jurisdiction of States over persons at sea and the consequent scope of States' duties towards them. The evaluation of whether jurisdiction exists according to the law should not be confused with the evaluation of the modalities through which it is exercised. Lawful jurisdiction may in fact be exercised in violation of rules of international or national law. For example, if a State arrests a vessel fishing illegally in its exclusive economic zone and its courts impose penalties on the owner and master, it is exercising its lawful jurisdiction according to Article 73 UNCLOS. If, however, the arrest is conducted using excessive force, then there is a breach of the rules concerning the use of force in enforcement actions.[211] In the same way, if the penalties decided by the national court include corporal punishment, then the exercise of jurisdiction is unlawful, not because the State does not have the power to enforce its fishing laws, but because of the modalities adopted to do so, which are in violation of Article 73(3) UNCLOS.

The opposite may also be true, since there can be instances in which enforcement, for example an arrest, is carried out in conformity with legal requirements but without having *de jure* jurisdiction. In the *Medvedyev* case, the ECtHR was asked to evaluate the circumstances of the arrest, carried out by the French armed forces on the high seas, of a Cambodian vessel carrying drugs. On the basis of the fact that France had not obtained the prior consent of the Cambodian government, the Chamber concluded that the arrest was not in conformity with international law.[212] However, when called to evaluate the modalities of the arrest, the Chamber considered that the actions carried out by the French forces were in conformity with the requirements under international human rights law and other applicable rules.

What has created some confusion is the fact that, while *de jure* jurisdiction is always lawful, *de facto* jurisdiction may be lawful or unlawful. It is lawful when it stems from a rule conferring *de jure* jurisdiction upon the State. On the flip side of the coin, exercise of a power without valid permission under international law would amount to unlawful exercise of *de facto* jurisdiction and would be unlawful. If we consider the example of a vessel interdicted on the high seas, if the reason for boarding the foreign vessel is that it is engaged in piracy, then the exercise of enforcement jurisdiction is lawful, since this is permitted under Article 105 UNCLOS. If, on the other hand, the vessel is boarded because it transports drugs, and assuming that there is no consent from the flag State for this operation, then the action is unlawful but still consists in the *de facto* exercise of enforcement jurisdiction. Finally, it is worth noting that the notion of unlawful exercise of jurisdiction is not exclusive

---

[211] *Saiga* (n 84) para 155.
[212] *Medvedyev and Others v France* App no 3394/03 (Judgment of 10 July 2008) para 62. The decision was confirmed by the Grand Chamber of the Court, though on different grounds; *Medvedyev* (n 86) para 102.

to international human rights law, since the situation just described and the qualification given to it are well accepted in the law of the sea.[213] What is unique to international human rights law, however, is that it is now the established rule that both forms of jurisdiction trigger the applicability of human rights.

9. Conclusions

The analysis carried out in this chapter has shown that a general principle concerning the identification of the State that has jurisdiction over a person at sea does not exist. At the same time, it is usually possible to identify such a State through the application of the relevant rules of international law, the law of the sea, and international human rights law concerning the exercise of jurisdiction over persons, ships, and other objects at sea. Jurisdiction over people at sea is often functionally and spatially qualified, and a State may or may not have jurisdiction with respect to a person depending on the maritime zone in which the person is and on the activity that this person is engaged in.

A State will have jurisdiction, and will therefore have the right to impose rules upon a person and to enforce them in all cases where this is provided by international law. Since most of the sea is not subject to the sovereignty of any one State, the 'default' jurisdiction is that of the flag State, with respect to vessels, and that of the coastal State, with respect to platforms and installations in the latter's maritime zones. In these cases, the jurisdiction of the State is general and includes all subject matters. Nationality of the person may also operate as a criterion for the attribution of 'default' legislative jurisdiction, although the enforcement of any laws will be possible only within much stricter limits.

There are however many other cases in which States other than those mentioned have jurisdiction to legislate, enforce, and adjudicate with respect to persons who are at sea. The jurisdiction of the coastal State and, increasingly, of the port State are widely used in the law of the sea. In the case of particularly serious crimes, the number of States that may exercise jurisdiction is further enlarged.

If examined through a taxonomic lens, there are two different modalities for the attribution of jurisdiction. In the first case, jurisdiction is general and concerns all matters. This jurisdiction may be based on the territorial principle, as in the case of persons in the territorial sea of a State or on platforms or other structures in its exclusive economic zone or on its continental shelf, or on the flag State principle, in the case of persons on board a vessel flying the flag of a State. In all these cases, the State may regulate and enforce laws relating to any aspect, whether they are linked to the vessel and its navigation, or not. Exceptions to this general jurisdiction cannot

---

[213] In the *Arctic Sunrise* case, the Arbitral Tribunal stated that '[t]o assess the lawfulness of measures taken by a coastal State in response to protest actions within its EEZ, the Tribunal considers it necessary to determine whether: (i) the measures had a basis in international law; and (ii) the measures were carried out in accordance with international law, including with the principle of reasonableness' (*Arctic Sunrise* (n 154) para 222).

be presumed, but will have to be proven on a case-by-case basis. In other words, the person that wants to challenge the exercise of jurisdiction will have to point to the rule containing the exception.

In the second case, jurisdiction is limited and functional, as is the case when a State other than that having general competence is attributed with jurisdiction for specific matters. Examples include the jurisdiction over nationals fishing or exploring mineral resources in areas beyond national jurisdiction. This category is expanding, as more and more treaties attribute jurisdiction for specific matters to States other than the flag State of a vessel. In these cases, the burden of proof is inverted. It is the State wishing to exercise its power over the person that will have to identify the rule that allows it to exercise its legislative, enforcement, or judicial jurisdiction with respect to the person. In the absence of such a rule a display of power will be unlawful.

De jure jurisdiction is paramount when determining the duty to comply with human rights obligations, as these obligations need to be fulfilled in all cases in which international law attributes jurisdiction. In addition, human rights have to be protected in all cases in which a person finds himself or herself under the actual authority and control of a State and its organs. The exercise of *de facto* jurisdiction does not depend on the existence of *de jure* jurisdiction, although the two may co-exist. As a consequence, *de facto* jurisdiction triggers the applicability of human rights obligations even if the conduct which brings the individual within the State's power does not depend on a valid basis for the exercise of *de jure* jurisdiction and is therefore unlawful.

Finally, the distinction between general jurisdiction and functionally limited jurisdiction will also have a role to play in identifying the human rights obligations of States vis-à-vis people at sea. With general jurisdiction in mind, a State will have the duty to protect and promote all human rights of the person, since every aspect of the person's activities falls under its potential control. In the case of functionally limited jurisdiction, however, a State will have the duty to protect the human rights of the person only to the extent that this is possible—or allowed—by the type of jurisdiction it exercises, as will be discussed in the next chapter.[214]

---

[214] Chapter 4, Section 5.

4

The Content of State Obligations

1. Introduction

Having determined where we should look for rules of international law that protect people at sea, as well as what the scope of such rules are, it is now time to turn to the content of the rules. The rapid development of public international law has resulted in a constant increase of legal instruments and rules in this field, as well as in many others. An exposition of the substantial content of all the rules that pertain to the duties of States towards people at sea, while unquestionably useful for any potential interpreter who is called upon to digest and apply the law, would be particularly extensive and would go far beyond what is possible in a book of this size. It is therefore not the aim of this book to provide a detailed account of all the duties of States, nor to assess the exact extent to which each human or labour right applies at sea.[1]

While practical examples will be used to illustrate the discussion, this chapter rather sets out to identify and discuss some common aspects of the legal obligations of States owed towards people at sea. This is achieved by developing a conceptual framework for the identification of the content of rules on States' duties towards people at sea. This exercise serves a dual purpose. On the one hand, a framework of reference may be of use to those who intend to carry out further analytical and codificatory work, exploring the substantive content of rules and discussing their precise content and limits. On the other hand, a framework of reference, which clarifies the types of content and the reach of rules, may serve as a basis for the development of new, effective, and coherent rules.

This chapter first argues that a new general principle is emerging, which requires States to act and protect people at sea. The chapter then explores the nature of the duties that stem from this principle and the extent to which an extensive range of positive obligations accompany negative ones. It then turns to the tension between comprehensiveness and severability and scrutinizes the usefulness of these different approaches for the protection of people at sea. The chapter ends discussing the structural change in the content of norms relating to the powers that States exercise at sea. In this respect, it is argued that the widespread acceptance of human rights and the development of detailed regulation providing for the exercise of mandatory

---

[1] These are however relevant issues and it is hoped that others will take up the challenge and provide in-depth analyses.

International Law and the Protection of People at Sea. Irini Papanicolopulu. © Irini Papanicolopulu, 2018. Published 2018 by Oxford University Press.

legislative and enforcement jurisdiction is actually transforming the rights attributed to States under the traditional law of the sea into duties that they must adhere to.

2. The General Principle

This section seeks to address one overarching and fundamental question, namely, whether there is a general principle that should guide State action towards people at sea. The analysis of existing legal instruments, in Chapters 1 and 2, has shown that both hard and soft law instruments do not yet contain an explicit general statement to this effect.[2] However, it is now argued, the numerous specific obligations that States have accepted—under the law of the sea, international human rights law, labour law, and maritime law, among others—cannot be considered as isolated cases anymore. They have to be viewed as the expression of a general principle, which requires States to protect people at sea and to take all reasonable measures necessary to ensure that this objective is achieved.

While they are generally considered as a sub-genus of customary international law,[3] general principles of international law can be considered to include 'abstractions from a mass of rules' that 'have been so long and so generally accepted as to be no longer *directly* connected with state practice'.[4] It is a fundamental argument of this book that a general principle of international law, the requirement for States

---

[2] The United Nations Convention on the Law of the Sea (UNCLOS) does not contain any principle which, in a manner similar to Art 192 UNCLOS, would state that 'States have the obligation to protect people at sea and to ensure their rights'. Apparently, the only attempt to introduce some general rules concerning protection of the rights of individuals was made in a Soviet proposal. In its proposal, the Soviet Union suggested that some principles that had been drafted with respect to the enforcement of environmental measures should be taken out to form a separate part of the convention, entitled 'General Safeguards' (UN Doc A/CONF.62/RCNG/1 (19 May 1978) 112–13). The suggestion was set aside for apparently systematic reasons: 'The suggestion to have a new Part XIV bis is beyond the terms of reference of the Third Committee, for it covers matters relating to general safeguards, mainly concerning navigation and other uses of the sea and not merely protection and preservation of the marine environment.' (ibid 102). The absence of a part on persons could be read in two opposite ways. On one hand, this might be interpreted as marking the indifference of States for persons. On the other hand, it could also be construed to signify that persons are so important that they permeate the entire convention and that every provision can be traced back to the need to protect these persons and further their interests.

[3] Antonio Cassese, *Diritto internazionale* (10th edn, Editoriale Scientifica 2014) 49; Jean Combacau and Serge Sur, *Droit International Public* (11th edn, LGDJ 2014) 111; Attila M Tanzi, *Introduzione al diritto internazionale contemporaneo* (3rd edn, CEDAM 2010) 118. Others however consider them as principles of domestic law common to States: Francesco Salerno, *Diritto internazionale. Principi e norme* (CEDAM 2008) 188; for an acceptance of both theories Hugh Thirlway, 'The Sources of International Law' in Malcolm D Evans (ed), *International Law* (OUP 2010) 104–05; Enzo Cannizzaro, *Corso di diritto internazionale* (Giuffrè Editore 2011) 108; Beatrice I Bonafe and Paolo Palchetti, 'Relying on General Principles in International Law' in Catherine Brölmann and Yannick Radi (eds), *Research Handbook on the Theory and Practice of International Law-Making* (Edward Elgar 2016) 161.

[4] Ian Brownlie, *Principles of Public International Law* (7th edn, OUP 2008) 19 (emphasis in the original). In a similar sense, Vaughan Lowe, *International Law* (OUP 2007) 87 and Bonafe and Palchetti (n 3) 163, who speak about '*a process of abstraction* based on precise and existing legal rules' (emphasis in the original). Brownlie includes both procedural principles (eg consent, reciprocity, finality of awards, good faith) and substantial principles (equality of States, freedom of the high seas) under this rubric (Brownlie (n 4) 19).

to protect people at sea, is crystallizing. Although this principle is not yet spelt out expressly in legal instruments, it is implied in the numerous obligations that States have accepted, and serves to inform both the application of existing rules and the development of new ones.

As the following sections will discuss, this principle is conceptually based on essential assumptions underlying the international legal system and is the natural and logical response to the commonly held presumption that there is no law, and therefore no protection, that generally applies to people at sea. The principle has been developed through the adoption of international instruments and the decisions of international courts, and is today reinforced by normative developments and the application of existing instruments by international actors.

2.1 The case for a general principle

The emergence of a principle mandating the protection of people at sea is conceptually grounded in two fundamental principles of international law, one old and one new: sovereignty and its consequences, on one hand, and the obligation to respect and protect human rights, on the other.

As Max Huber stated in 1928, sovereignty as a right entails a correspondent duty, the duty to take measures to protect other States and people within a State's territory.[5] Although this statement refers to sovereignty in respect of land territory, it could comfortably be extended to rights enjoyed by States at sea. It would be contrary to any current idea of law to suggest that the rights enjoyed by States at sea are intended to be merely self-serving and do not aim at promoting societal interests.[6] As a result, Max Huber's statement supports a reading of the rights enjoyed by States at sea which sees these rights as instrumental for the protection of humans. It follows that the right to exercise jurisdiction over a vessel, structure, or person entails the positive duty 'to assure ... at all points the minimum of protection of which international law is the guardian'.[7] This general principle finds expression in numerous detailed norms, such as those stating the duties of the flag State and those imposing obligations on the coastal State within its maritime zones.

As to the 'minimum protection', its meaning has been shaped throughout the twentieth century by the introduction of human rights in international law discourse

---

[5] 'Territorial sovereignty cannot limit itself to its negative side, i.e. to excluding the activities of other States; for it serves to divide between nations the space upon which human activities are employed, in order to assure them at all points the minimum of protection of which international law is the guardian' (*The Island of Palmas Case (or Miangas) (United States of America v The Netherlands)* (1928) II RIAA 829, 839.

[6] Such an allegation is refuted by the United Nations Convention on the Law of the Sea (adopted 10 December 1982, entered into force 16 November 1994) 1833 UNTS 397 (UNCLOS) itself, which considers that 'the codification and progressive development of the law of the sea achieved in this Convention will contribute to the strengthening of peace, security, cooperation and friendly relations among all nations in conformity with the principles of justice and equal rights and will promote the economic and social advancement of all peoples of the world, in accordance with the Purposes and Principles of the United Nations as set forth in the Charter' (UNCLOS, Preamble).

[7] *Island of Palmas* (n 5) 839.

and their rapid establishment as fundamental and inescapable legal norms.[8] It is now well established that the protection of human beings is one of the fundamental aims of the international community[9] and that the promotion and protection of human rights 'is a matter of priority for the international community' which forms the content of a positive legal obligation.[10]

The duty to protect human rights is a fundamental assumption of international law generally.[11] What is interesting to note, however, is that the protection of people at sea may require States to adopt actions that go beyond those required with respect to land, in order to take into account the special characteristics of the sea. The inherently dangerous nature of the marine environment and the legal and practical complexities characterizing maritime activities boost the positive obligations of States which are owed towards people at sea.

2.2 The concept of 'considerations of humanity'

The groundwork for the assumption that there is a general principle of international law mandating the protection of people at sea was laid by the International Court of Justice (ICJ) in the *Corfu Channel* case. In that case, the Court and the parties all recognized the existence of the obligation of the coastal State to warn ships passing through its territorial waters of the presence of any sea mines. In the absence of any applicable treaty, the Court grounded this legal obligation as follows:

on certain general and well-recognized principles, namely: elementary considerations of humanity, even more exacting in peace than in war; the principle of the freedom of maritime communication; and every State's obligation not to allow knowingly its territory to be used for acts contrary to the rights of other States.[12]

The first principle, 'elementary considerations of humanity', is what interests us here. The ICJ was in fact faced with a paradoxical situation, whereby the laws of war were more protective of persons than the laws of peace. While the former included a treaty that imposed obligations on States laying minefields,[13] the latter did not contain any such provision or any other provision aimed at the protection of persons from harm. The Court avoided the illogical conclusion that people are more

---

[8] Art 50 draft Articles on the Responsibility of States for Internationally Wrongful Acts.
[9] Art 1(3) Charter of the United Nations (adopted 26 June 1945, entered into force 24 October 1945) (UN Charter).
[10] 'Vienna Declaration and Programme of Action' World Conference on Human Rights (25 June 1993) UN Doc A/CONF.157/23, Preamble (Vienna Declaration) para 1. On positive obligations in international human rights law see Section 3.1.
[11] *South West Africa (Liberia v South Africa)* (Second Phase, Dissenting Opinion of Tanaka) [1966] ICJ Rep 250, paras 294–99. It is true, however, that there are divergences, also marked, concerning the exact extent of this duty. In particular, it has been argued that only grave breaches of human rights can be sanctioned by the international community as such (Antonio Cassese, *Diritto internazionale. Problemi della comunità internazionale* (Il Mulino 2004) 89).
[12] *Corfu Channel (United Kingdom of Great Britain and Northern Ireland v Albania)* (Judgment) [1949] ICJ Rep 4, 22.
[13] Convention (VIII) relative to the Laying of Automatic Submarine Contact Mines (adopted 18 October 1907, entered into force 26 January 1910).

protected during wartime than during peacetime through reference to 'considerations of humanity' as a principle that should guide the determination and application of more specific obligations binding upon States. With this statement, the ICJ re-established the natural order and recognized that there does exist a legal obligation, binding upon States during peacetime, to take measures to protect persons from harm at sea, as well as on land.[14]

The *Corfu Channel* judgment is particularly significant for two reasons. On the one hand, it can be considered to have expressed the concerns underlying early treaties regulating human activities at sea, namely the need for the creation of a safe and secure environment for people.[15] On the other, it can be considered as the first expression of a more generalized intent of the international community as a whole to elaborate normative standards that would flesh out specific duties binding upon States as far as the protection of persons at sea is concerned. At a time when the United Nations (UN) Charter had just entered into force and international human rights treaties did not yet exist, 'considerations of humanity' were 'related to human values already protected by positive legal principles which, taken together, reveal certain criteria of public policy and invite the use of analogy'.[16]

The term coined by the ICJ was taken up some decades later by the International Tribunal for the Law of the Sea (ITLOS) when deciding its first case on the merits. In the *Saiga* case, the Tribunal had been called upon to assess, among other issues, the lawfulness of the enforcement measures carried out by Guinea against the *M/V Saiga*, an oil tanker flying the flag of Saint Vincent and the Grenadines.[17] In a celebrated passage, the Tribunal, which sought to identify rules that apply to the use of force in law enforcement activities at sea, concluded by referring to the general obligation to take into account considerations of humanity:

In considering the force used by Guinea in the arrest of the Saiga, the Tribunal must take into account the circumstances of the arrest in the context of the applicable rules of international law. Although the Convention does not contain express provisions on the use of force in the arrest of ships, international law, which is applicable by virtue of article 293 of the Convention, requires that the use of force must be avoided as far as possible and, where force is unavoidable, it must not go beyond what is reasonable and necessary in the circumstances. Considerations of humanity must apply in the law of the sea, as they do in other areas of international law.[18]

---

[14] It is worth noting that the existence of a legal obligation was well accepted also by both parties to the dispute. Note, in particular, that Counsel for Albania stated that 'if Albania had been informed of the operation [of laying the minefield] before the incidents of October 22nd, and in time to warn the British vessels and shipping in general of the existence of mines in the Corfu Channel, her responsibility would be involved' (*Corfu Channel* (n 12) 22).

[15] Art 1 Convention for the Safety of Life at Sea (adopted 20 January 1914) stated the purpose to ensure the safety of life at sea.

[16] Brownlie (n 4) 27.

[17] *The M/V 'Saiga' (No 2) (Saint Vincent and the Grenadines v Guinea)* (Judgment of 1 July 1999) ITLOS Reports 1999 10.

[18] ibid para 155.

What the Tribunal did not clarify, however, was what exactly those 'considerations of humanity' were. Nor did it explain what consequences flow from them. For some judges, the expression seemed to point towards international human rights law,[19] thus possibly introducing into the picture specific norms that regulate the duties of States towards persons. Others seemed to consider it a pre-legal factor, which would arguably adapt the existing rules towards a more human-oriented content in a *lex ferenda* perspective, without however having any practical consequences on the *lex lata*.[20]

The trend towards a general reference to 'considerations of humanity' by individual judges or the Tribunal as a whole was consolidated in the following cases, in particular those considering prompt release claims and those involving the arrest of or other forcible acts against persons.[21] The ITLOS however also referred to different, yet similar, concepts. In the *Tomimaru* case, for example, it considered that the confiscation of a vessel should not 'be taken through proceedings inconsistent with international standards of due process of law'.[22] In the *Louisa* case, the ITLOS went further than ever before when it affirmed that 'States are required to fulfil their obligations under international law, in particular human rights law, and that considerations of due process of law must be applied in all circumstances'.[23] The statement in the *Louisa* case is all the more impressive since it was not required in the logic of the judgment and shows the concern of the ITLOS to keep in mind the wider picture, and not just the specific United Nations Convention on the Law of the Sea (UNCLOS) provisions it is called to apply from time to time. The ITLOS had in fact just mentioned that it did not have jurisdiction to decide the case. Notwithstanding this conclusion, it also considered that 'it cannot but take note of the issues of human rights'[24] raised and thus went on to make the statement just reported.

Somewhat unexpectedly, 'considerations of humanity' were not expressly mentioned by the ITLOS in its Order on provisional measures in the *Arctic Sunrise* case. This is somewhat of a surprise due to the fact that the case was greatly concerned with the arrest and detention of the crew of a vessel, the *Arctic Sunrise*, and thus had a direct bearing on the protection of individuals' rights. The Netherlands claimed that

---

[19] *The M/V 'Saiga' (No 2) (Saint Vincent and the Grenadines v Guinea)* (Judgment of 1 July 1999, Separate Opinion of Mensah) para 20. 'Human rights' are also expressly mentioned in *Juno Trader (Saint Vincent and the Grenadines v Guinea-Bissau)* (Judgment of 18 December 2004, Joint Separate Opinion of Mensah and Wolfrum) para 3, and *Juno Trader (Saint Vincent and the Grenadines v Guinea-Bissau)* (Judgment of 18 December 2004, Separate Opinion of Treves) para 5.

[20] *The M/V 'Saiga' (No 2) (Saint Vincent and the Grenadines v Guinea)* (Judgment of 1 July 1999, Dissenting Opinion of Ndiaye) para 90, according to whom 'humanitarian considerations may inspire rules of law ... are not, however, rules of law in themselves'.

[21] *The 'Juno Trader' Case (Saint Vincent and the Grenadines v Guinea-Bissau)* (Prompt Release, Judgment of 18 December 2004) para 77. See also *The 'Juno Trader' Case (Saint Vincent and the Grenadines v Guinea-Bissau)* (Prompt Release, Judgment of 18 December 2004, Separate Opinion of Treves) para 1; *The 'Juno Trader' Case (Saint Vincent and the Grenadines v Guinea-Bissau)* (Prompt Release, Judgment of 18 December 2004, Joint Separate Opinion of Mensah and Wolfrum) paras 3–4.

[22] *The 'Tomimaru' Case (Japan v Russian Federation)* (Prompt Release, Judgment of 6 August 2007) para 76.

[23] *The M/V 'Louisa' Case (Saint Vincent and the Grenadines v Kingdom of Spain)* (Merits, Judgment of 28 May 2013) para 155.

[24] ibid para 154.

the arrest and detention were in violation of both law of the sea and international human rights law standards, the latter point in particular being argued extensively, and that the vessel and crew should be released upon the posting of a bond.[25] The case was therefore very similar to the prompt release cases in which the Tribunal had referred to the 'considerations of humanity' to remind the parties of their duties beyond those in the UNCLOS. There are however two differences that may have warranted a diverse treatment of the issue. The first one is that here the Tribunal was requested to prescribe only provisional measures pending the constitution of the arbitral Tribunal and that it had therefore adopted a very strict approach to its juris-diction.[26] The second is that the ITLOS eventually ordered the immediate release of the persons involved, thereby making it superfluous to indicate how they had to be treated, since they were to be set immediately free.[27]

A recent case decided by ITLOS, the *Enrica Lexie (provisional measures)* case, saw the return of the concept of 'considerations of humanity'.[28] This time, however, a further development can be noted. Until this case, in fact, the reliance upon the notion had been univocal. Considerations of humanity were invoked by one party only, that which was taking up the rights of its people against allegedly unlawful action exercised by the other State. In the *Enrica Lexie* case, the situation was dif-ferent, since both parties used the 'considerations of humanity' argument to invoke protection for their people against the acts of the other State and its organs.[29]

Considerations of humanity have been invoked not only by the ITLOS but also by arbitral tribunals adjudicating a dispute on the basis of the UNCLOS (Annex VII Tribunals). In the *Guyana/Suriname* case, the arbitral Tribunal recalled the state-ment in the ITLOS *Saiga* decision, although it did not elaborate on it.[30] In the *Arctic Sunrise* case, the Arbitral Tribunal similarly recalled the *Saiga* statement when discussing the applicability of international human rights law.[31] In both cases, the passage was cited when attempting to ascertain the rules regulating law enforce-ment activities at sea, in particular the use of force and, in the *Arctic Sunrise* case, the deprivation of personal liberty. Thus, the reference to 'considerations of humanity'

---

[25] *The Arctic Sunrise Case (Kingdom of the Netherlands v Russian Federation)* (Provisional Measures, Order of 22 November 2013) para 33.

[26] *The Arctic Sunrise Case (Kingdom of the Netherlands v Russian Federation)* (Provisional Measures, Order of 22 November 2013, Joint Separate Opinion Wolfrum and Kelly) para 2.

[27] Similar considerations may also have prevented any mention of 'considerations of humanity' in the *Ara Libertad* case, which was also concerned with provisional measures pending the constitution of an Annex VII Tribunal.

[28] *The 'Enrica Lexie' Incident (Italy v India)* (Provisional Measures, Order of 24 August 2015) para 133.

[29] ibid paras 94 and 99. This double invocation shows that considerations of humanity are not a pana-cea and cannot by themselves provide the solution to all cases involving individuals. 'Considerations of humanity', in fact, does not by itself alone allow the judge to operate a balancing of the different 'humans' and their interests involved in the case. Only a direct reference to human rights law, which also contains balancing mechanisms, could help settle the issue. See further Irini Papanicolopulu, 'Considerations of Humanity in the Enrica Lexie Case' (2015) QIL—Questions of International Law <http://www.qil-qdi.org/considerations-of-humanity-in-the-enrica-lexie-case> accessed 23 August 2017.

[30] *Guyana v Suriname* (Award of 17 September 2007) para 405.

[31] *Arctic Sunrise (The Kingdom of the Netherlands v The Russian Federation)* PCA Case no 2014-02 (Award (merits) of 14 August 2015) para 191.

served the purpose of protecting the weak party, that is, the persons against whom force had been used or threatened.

In conclusion, this overview of the jurisprudence of international courts shows that 'considerations of humanity' is a concept that is well represented in judicial language dealing with law of the sea matters, albeit somewhat ambiguously. On the one hand, considerations of humanity have been the shorthand for the introduction of human rights norms and principles into law of the sea cases, in particular such fundamental civil rights as the right to life, the right to personal freedom, and the right to due process. On the other hand, the invocation of 'considerations of humanity' would appear to be a call for the application of extra-legal concepts, in particular a humanitarian perspective vis-à-vis the protection of people, which does not however necessarily find its expression in concrete legal rules.

2.3 Proving the existence and content of the principle

The ambiguities in the language of international judges, just illustrated, require us to conduct a more thorough examination of international practice to prove that the principle requiring States to protect people at sea is not only the logical consequence of the two principles of sovereignty and of the protection of human rights, but that it is actually emerging in the international field.[32] The starting point for this analysis is the assumption that the protection of people at sea is indeed a goal of the entire international community.

This intent can be identified in numerous international treaties and other instruments[33] that contain duties for States to take measures to protect the safety of life at sea and the physical integrity of people at sea; to adequately train those who work at sea so as to ensure both their own safety and that of other persons who depend on them; to create living and working conditions that comply with minimum standards; to allow the enjoyment of economic and social rights; and to protect the fundamental rights of any person that might be subject to enforcement activity or that might be a victim of criminal activity. Although in the past it might have been possible to consider all these duties as a piecemeal approach to regulation, their present number, detail, density, and comprehensiveness are all significant elements to prove that today they cannot but be considered as the expression of a general principle, according to which States have the legal obligation to protect people at sea.

First, the number of treaties that include either a general obligation to protect specific categories of people or a set of more specific obligations on how to achieve this result is significant and constantly increasing. It is now the rule that legal

---

[32] As Massimo Iovane, 'L'influence de la multiplication des juridictions internationales sur l'application du droit international' (2017) 383 Recueil des Cours 233, 435 notes 'C'est la réaction à l'égard de l'arrêt, de l'avis consultatif ou de l'ordonnance qui établira si tous ces critères ont été respectés et si l'innovation apportée au droit existant a, par conséquent, bien réussi. Cette réaction peut provenir des juridictions supérieures, des parties au litige, et de la communauté internationale dans son ensemble.'

[33] As Roberto Ago, *Scienza giuridica e diritto internazionale* (Giuffre 1950) 82 notes, manifestations of practice usually vary and may assume one among a number of forms.

instruments addressing people at sea and their activities make some reference to the need to take into account the human element, and to protect the rights of the individuals involved.[34]

Second, most of these instruments contain secondary norms addressing issues of enforcement, responsibility and adjudication, and other forms of compliance control. These provisions consolidate the substantial obligations of States and work towards their maximum normative density.

Third, provisions are to be found in all sorts of legal instruments, adopted within the most diverse institutional forums and expressing the particular interests of different communities. They are included in treaties concerning labour standards, the safety of navigation, illicit trafficking by sea, and the regulation of fishing, as well as in the UNCLOS. Legal instruments are adopted by the UN and its specialized agencies dealing with labour issues (International Labour Organization (ILO)), maritime issues (International Maritime Organization (IMO)), food and agriculture (Food and Agriculture Organization (FAO)), and refugees (United Nations High Commissioner for Refugees (UNHCR)) as well as regionally.

Fourth, evidence of the existence of an obligation to protect people at sea can be found in all abovementioned fields, even where there are still no hard law instruments yet in place—as in the case of migration by sea—or where the existing instruments have not entered into force—as in the case of fishing vessel safety.

Finally, in the absence of a specific norm dealing with the particular issue, or to simply reinforce a State's existing obligations, the case law of international tribunals has often endorsed and referred to the principle. Similar to what has occurred with treaties, this endorsement of the substance of the principle, albeit not an express enunciation, is common to judicial organs belonging to different regimes. Following the steps of the ICJ in the *Corfu Channel* case, reference to 'considerations of humanity' is routinely employed by the ITLOS, while the European Court of Human Rights (ECtHR) has more than once affirmed that the high seas cannot be considered as an area outside the reach of the law where persons are not afforded any protection.[35]

All these elements, taken together, prove that a general principle obliging States to protect people at sea exists, or is at least emerging. This statement, however, does not settle all issues. Like all general principles of law, this principle raises a number

---

[34] See, among many other, Art 2*bis*(1) Convention for the Suppression of Unlawful Acts Against the Safety of Maritime Navigation (adopted 10 March 1988), as amended by the 2005 Protocol (adopted 14 October 2005, entered into force 28 July 2010) 1678 UNTS 222 (SUA Convention); Art 10 Agreement on Port State Measures to Prevent, Deter and Eliminate Illegal, Unreported and Unregulated Fishing (adopted 22 November 2009, entered into force 5 June 2016) (PSCA); UNSC Res 1816 (2 June 2008) UN Doc S/RES/1816, para 11; UNSC Res 2240 (9 October 2015) UN Doc S/RES/2240, paras 10 and 12; UNGA Res 71/257 (23 December 2016) UN Doc A/RES/71/257, para 148; UNGA Res 71/`123 (7 December 2016) UN Doc A/RES/71/123, para 109; IMO, UNHCR and ICS, 'Rescue at Sea. A Guide to Principles and Practice as Applied to Refugees and Migrants' (January 2015) <http://www.imo.org/en/MediaCentre/HotTopics/seamigration/Documents/UNHCR-Rescue_at_ Sea-Guide-ENG-screen.pdf> accessed 22 August 2017.
[35] *Medvedyev and Others v France* App no 3394/03 (Judgment (GC) of 29 March 2010) para 81; *Hirsi Jamaa and Others v Italy* App no 27765/09 (Judgment (GC) of 23 February 2012) para 178.

of problems bearing on the scope, extent, and content of States' obligations ensuing from it. A critical aspect of the operation of the principle, tied to its indeterminate content, relates to the wide range of formulations used in the various instruments. While in many cases different language can be considered to mean effectively the same thing, in some cases variation in the formulation of relevant provisions may point towards duties that are quantitatively and qualitative different.

At a minimum, it is submitted that this principle would oblige States to comply with fundamental human rights and to always consider the needs of people when taking action that may affect them, independent of whether the action is directed towards them or affects them only incidentally. While the right to life will be one of the most prominent rights that come into play, the general principle by no means is limited to the protection of the sole right to life. Freedom from slavery, physical integrity, freedom from torture are all rights that must be protected under the general principle, as well as any other right which is capable of being affected while a person is at sea. This statement, however, necessitates a number of qualifications. First, this principle would go beyond what is required under international human rights law, in that it would oblige States to take preventive measures even when it is not possible to identify the specific individual or individuals possessing the right. Second, the existence of this principle would not necessarily require States to guarantee all human rights to all people at sea in the same way. Apart from issues pertaining to the severability of human rights,[36] regional variations in the interpretation and application of human rights standards may come into play and may produce treatment that is somewhat different. Third, the principle would nonetheless require that State action be effective. Effectivity is identified as a requirement under both the law of the sea and human rights law and is a necessary corollary to the protection of people, lest the latter prove futile in practice.[37]

Finally, the existence of the principle undoubtedly impacts on the elaboration, interpretation, and application of legal norms. As a criterion of public policy, it promotes and informs the elaboration of new legal norms. The influence of this principle has been felt both during the adoption of new instruments and during the updating of existing ones. The influence of the duty to protect people at sea can be seen in the adoption of legal instruments that aim directly at the protection of people, as well as in the introduction of protective or non-prejudice clauses into instruments that deal with other matters. The adoption of the Maritime Labour Convention (MLC) and the Work in Fishing Convention are strong examples of the principle influencing the adoption of instruments.[38] The same principle has led to the modification of existing instruments in order to bring them in line with

---

[36] Section 5.

[37] For example, Art 1 Maritime Labour Convention (adopted 23 February 2006, entered into force 20 August 2013) (MLC) requires States 'to give complete effect to its provisions' and to ensure 'effective implementation' of the Convention. In *Hirsi* (n 35) para 175, the ECtHR noted that 'it is essential that the Convention is interpreted and applied in a manner which renders the guarantees concrete and effective and not theoretical and illusory'.

[38] Cases in which clauses mandating protection have been inserted in treaties addressing other issues are illustrated in Chapter 1, Section 4.2.

existing obligations concerning the protection of persons, as the 2005 modifications to the Convention for the Suppression of Unlawful Acts Against the Safety of Maritime Navigation (SUA Convention) particularly illustrate. While the original 1988 Convention did not refer to human rights, the 2005 version has been amended to take human rights, refugee law, and international humanitarian law into account, which is also a result of the UN debates concerning the relationship between measures to combat terrorism and the respect for fundamental human rights.[39] The duty to protect people at sea and the flagrant non-compliance with this principle demonstrated by Australia in the case of the *Tampa* has prompted modifications to binding instruments, such as Annex V to the Safety of Life at Sea Convention (SOLAS) and the International Convention on Maritime Search and Rescue (SAR Convention), in addition to the adoption of soft law instruments, in the form of Guidelines on the Treatment of Persons Rescued at Sea.[40] The UN Security Council, with its binding resolutions concerning piracy off the coasts of Somalia, has consistently required States that undertake action to ensure that such action complies with international human rights law.[41]

As an international law norm, the duty to protect persons at sea impacts on the interpretation and application of other rules of international law in accordance with Article 31(3)(c) of the Vienna Convention on the Law of Treaties (VCLT).[42] It may therefore provide general guidance in the absence of other, more detailed, regulation, in particular in the application of rules concerning State action against people. It may also supersede older regulation that does not take into account the human element. Finally, it could also be used to apply other general standards, such as the 'due regard' principle required by a number of UNCLOS provisions.[43]

In light of all these considerations, it would be particularly significant if the general principle were explicitly mentioned by international actors. International organizations, in particular, would be in the best position to express such principle. For example, the principle could be recognized by the UN General Assembly in its annual resolution on oceans and the law of the sea.

---

[39] See 2005 SUA Protocol, Preamble, para 12.

[40] IMO, 'Guidelines on the Treatment of Persons Rescued at Sea' Res MSC.167(78) (20 May 2004) IMO Doc MSC 78/26/Add.2 (IMO Guidelines). The *Tampa* incident involved the rescue of over 400 asylum seekers by the Norwegian cargo vessel, the *MV Tampa*, and Australia's refusal to allow the vessel into its port and subsequent forcible boarding of the vessel. On the *Tampa* case see, among many others, Penelope Mathew, 'Australian Refugee Protection in the Wake of the Tampa' (2002) 96 AJIL 661; Donald R Rothwell, 'The Law of the Sea and the MV Tampa Incident: Reconciling Maritime Principles with Coastal State Sovereignty' (2002) 13 Public Law Review 118; Cecilia Baillet, 'The Tampa Case and Its Impact on Burden Sharing at Sea' (2003) 25 Human Rights Quarterly 741; Matteo Fornari, 'Soccorso di profughi in mare e diritto d'asilo: questioni di diritto internazionale sollevate dalla vicenda della nave Tampa' (2002) 57 Comunità Internazionale 61.

[41] See, eg, UNSC Res 2020 (22 November 2011) UN Doc S/RES/2020, paras 13-15.

[42] Tullio Treves, 'Human Rights and the Law of the Sea' (2010) 28 Berkeley Journal of International Law 1, 6.

[43] For example, Art 27(4), Art. 56(2), and Art 58(3) UNCLOS. Treves, 'Human Rights' (n 42) 6, suggests that in assessing which, between two incompatible uses of the sea, should be privileged, one could take into account the fact that one activity would entail less risk for human life than the other.

3. Substantiating Obligations

The existence of a general principle mandating the protection of people at sea facilitates the task of the interpreter and the policy-maker. Both are provided with guidance concerning the aims of their actions and with a yardstick that may check the solutions adopted. Yet general principles alone cannot determine conduct, as their purpose is to supplement and complement existing duties contained in binding rules of international law. As a consequence, some degree of elaboration is needed to flesh out this general principle and provide the concrete mechanisms to uphold the rights of people and to allow States to fulfil their obligations.

It is therefore now necessary to turn our attention to the specific duties that bind States. At the outset, it can be noted that these duties include both obligations to abstain from conduct that would harm people at sea, and obligations to undertake action to promote the protection of these people. In particular, States will have to abstain from any act that would violate an individual's rights whenever they are taking action against a person, for example when undertaking enforcement measures. Conversely, States will be required to undertake action to ensure that the rights of individuals are respected by both State authorities and by private actors, such as the owner or operator of a vessel, the master, or the operator of a platform. In other words, States' duties are both positive and negative in nature. It follows that responsibility may stem for both acts and omissions, as provided in Article 2 of the Draft Articles on State Responsibility. The general principle itself requires an proactive approach and therefore mandates States to take positive action to protect people.

Interestingly, both sets of obligations, positive and negative, may be identified in international human rights law, the law of the sea, and other fields of international law, albeit the conceptualization of positive obligations has mainly been carried out for the purposes of international human rights law.[44] A significant degree of assistance in substantiating and expounding State obligations is provided in the jurisprudence of international judicial and quasi-judicial bodies. These bodies, over time, have clarified the scope of positive obligations and have specified what type of conduct is required to comply with them and to ensure full enjoyment of all human rights.[45] Furthermore, in recent years, a cross-fertilization among different legal fields has been promoted both by human rights and by law of the sea bodies. Human rights bodies have been concerned with the application of human rights at

---

[44] Alastair Mowbray, *The Development of Positive Obligations under the European Convention on Human Rights by the European Court of Human Rights* (Hart 2004); Sandra Fredman, *Human Rights Transformed: Positive Rights and Positive Duties* (OUP 2008); Riccardo Pisillo Mazzeschi, 'Responsabilité de l'État pour Violation des Obligations Positives Relatives aux Droits de l'Homme' (2008) 333 Recueil des Cours 175.

[45] Paul Tavernier, 'La Cour européenne des Droits de l'Homme et la Mer' in *La mer et son droit: mélanges offerts á Laurent Lucchini et Jean-Pierre Quéneudec* (Pedone 2003) 575; Efthymios Papastavridis, 'European Convention on Human Rights and the Law of the Sea: the Strasbourg Court in Unchartered Waters?' in Malgosia Fitzmaurice and Panos Merkouris (eds), *The Interpretation and Application of the European Convention of Human Rights: Legal and Practical Implications* (Martinus Nijhoff 2013) 117.

sea, while law of the sea tribunals have addressed, albeit often incidentally, human rights issues when deciding law of the sea cases. Their decisions therefore provide invaluable guidance that can facilitate the concretization of duties owed towards people at sea.

3.1 The conceptualization of negative and positive duties in human rights law

Human rights were born in the Western legal tradition in order to protect individuals from the absolute power of sovereigns.[46] Initially, human rights were mostly negative in nature. In that context, the existence of human rights meant that the State had to avoid conduct that would infringe upon individuals' civil liberties.[47] Hence, States had a negative obligation to abstain from conduct which would violate human rights. For example, the State, among others entities, had the duty not to torture, not to take life, and not to take personal freedom arbitrarily. More generally, the State had to refrain from interfering with all the rights and liberties bestowed upon individuals.

As the field developed, it became apparent that in many cases abstention or inaction by the State was not sufficient to ensure enjoyment of a specific right. Taking as an example the right to life, it is not sufficient for the State to abstain from killing individuals. If individuals subject to the jurisdiction of the State are to enjoy their right to life to the full extent, the State must also take steps to prevent them being killed, it must investigate their killings and it must punish those responsible, so as to avoid further killings.[48] Thus the ECtHR has held that a State is responsible for a violation of Article 2 of the (European) Convention for the Protection of Human Rights and Fundamental Freedoms (ECHR)[49] if:

> the authorities knew or ought to have known at the time of the existence of a real and immediate risk to the life of an identified individual or individuals from the criminal acts of a third party and that they failed to take measures within the scope of their powers which, judged reasonably, might have been expected to avoid that risk. [50]

As a consequence, and in addition to those duties already framed in terms of positive obligations, most negative obligations assimilated a positive aspect, requiring States to act both before violations occurred, in order to prevent them, and after the violations had taken place, in order to punish them.[51] The right to

[46] Walter Kalin and Jorg Kunzli, *The Law of International Human Rights Protection* (OUP 2009) 21–25.
[47] Christian Tomuschat, *Human Rights. Between Idealism and Realism* (3rd edn, OUP 2014) 138.
[48] HRC, *Baboeram* et al *v Suriname*, Communications Com nos 146/1983 and 148–154/1983 (Decision of 1985); *Velásquez Rodríguez v Honduras* Judgment (Merits) Inter-American Court of Human Rights Series C No 4 (29 July 1988).
[49] (European) Convention for the Protection of Human Rights and Fundamental Freedoms (adopted 4 November 1950, entered into force 3 September 1953) 213 UNTS 221, as amended (ECHR).
[50] *Osman v the United Kingdom* App no 87/1997/871/1083 (Judgment (GC) of 28 October 1998) para 116.
[51] Dinah Shelton and Ariel Gould, 'Positive and Negative Obligations' in Dinah Shelton (ed), *The Oxford Handbook of International Human Rights Law* (OUP 2013) 563, 575. It should be noted that the

life,[52] the right not to be tortured, and the right to personal freedom all are now recognized as requiring positive action by States for their full enjoyment. At the same time, the need to take positive action was particularly felt with the recognition and creation of social, economic, and cultural rights. Their fulfilment cannot be achieved if States do not take active steps to guarantee these rights.[53]

Three types of positive obligations thus developed under international human rights law.[54] The first and oldest type includes obligations that stem from economic, social, and cultural rights, which require the State to take action to fulfil those rights.[55] For example, Article 2(1) of the International Covenant on Economic, Social and Cultural Rights (ICESCR)[56] provides that:

Each State Party to the present Covenant undertakes to take steps, individually and through international assistance and co-operation, especially economic and technical, to the maximum of its available resources, with a view to achieving progressively the full realization of the rights recognized in the present Covenant by all appropriate means, including particularly the adoption of legislative measures.

As the Committee on Economic, Social and Cultural Rights (CESCR) has noted, Article 2 of the ICESCR requires States to take steps that 'should be deliberate, concrete and targeted as clearly as possible towards meeting the obligations recognized in the Covenant'.[57]

The second and widest type of positive obligations comprise those that require the State 'to take some positive action in order to ensure the effective enjoyment of the right protected' which may be necessary in respect of either civil and political rights

terminology used to designate these duties is not uniform. While the ECtHR generally refers to positive obligations, the IACHR and the UN human rights bodies often refer to obligations of due diligence; see, eg, *Velásquez Rodríguez* (n 48) para 79; UN Human Rights Committee, 'General Comment No 31' (26 May 2004) UN Doc CCPR/C/21/Rev.1/Add.13, para 8; UN Committee on the Elimination of Discrimination against Women, 'General Recommendation No 28' (16 December 2010) UN Doc CEDAW/C/GC/28, para 13. It is generally considered that the two terms are synonyms; it has however also been argued that not all positive obligations are also due diligence obligations (Pisillo Mazzeschi (n 44) 284).

[52] Benedetto Conforti, 'Reflections on State Responsibility for the Breach of Positive Obligations: The Case-Law of the European Court of Human Rights' (2003) XIII The Italian Yearbook of International Law 3.

[53] Let us consider, eg, the right to instruction. This right requires the State to act and ensure that individuals have access to schooling and education. It has however been pointed out that there may be a limit to the extent of positive obligations deriving from the impact that compliance by a State with its positive obligations would produce on classical freedoms of the individual which require abstention by the State (Christian Tomuschat, 'Human Rights: Tensions between Negative and Positive Duties of States' (2009) 14 Austrian Review of International and European Law 19).

[54] Silvia Borelli, 'Positive Obligations of States and the Protection of Human Rights' (2006) 15 Interights Bulletin 101.

[55] Tomuschat, *Human Rights* (n 47) 139.

[56] International Covenant on Economic, Social and Cultural Rights (adopted 16 December 1966, entered into force 3 January 1976) 993 UNTS 3 (ICESCR).

[57] UN Committee on Economic, Social and Cultural Rights, 'General Comment No 3' in 'Compilation of General Comments and General Recommendations Adopted by Human Rights Treaty Bodies' (27 May 2008) UN Doc HRI/GEN/1/Rev.9 (Vol I), para 2.

or economic, social, and cultural rights.[58] Thus, Article 6(1) of the International Covenant on Civil and Political Rights (ICCPR),[59] in requiring that the right to life 'shall be protected by law', clearly indicates that the State must act and adopt laws that protect the right to life.

Turning to the third type of positive obligations, these are essentially procedural obligations, which require the State to investigate any alleged violation of a human right, sanction any such violation, and bring those responsible to justice.[60] This is, for example, the case in respect of any violation of the prohibition of torture. According to the ICCPR, '[n]o one shall be subjected to torture or to cruel, inhuman or degrading treatment or punishment'.[61] This provision seems to point towards a negative obligation, which imposes on States the duty not to torture individuals. Torture, however, may also occur at the hands of private actors, and it is the duty of States, as international bodies have clearly recognized, to try and prevent this from happening, both by preventive action and also by taking action after the violation has occurred.[62] Positive procedural obligations may also require the State to set up an administrative framework that adequately protects human rights, for example by setting up controls for businesses that are often used as a cover for the violation of specific human rights, such as the freedom from human trafficking.[63]

A significant feature of positive obligations is the fact that they affect the duties of States, not only with respect to action carried out by their organs, but also by acts carried out by private persons. As the Humn Rights Committee has noted:

the positive obligations on States Parties to ensure Covenant rights will only be fully discharged if individuals are protected by the State, not just against violations of Covenant rights by its agents, but also against acts committed by private persons or entities that would impair the enjoyment of Covenant rights in so far as they are amenable to application between private persons or entities.[64]

[58] Borelli (n 54) 102: 'in relation to some civil and political rights, the fact that positive action is mandated is, if not explicit in the language of the provision in question, at the least very clearly derivable from its text'.

[59] International Covenant on Civil and Political Rights (adopted 16 December 1966, entered into force 23 March 1976) 999 UNTS 171 (ICCPR).

[60] Shelton and Gould (n 51) 569. It has been argued that, contrary to the first two types of positive obligations, which are derived from the language of the relevant provision, the third type includes obligations to act which are not to be derived from the text of human rights provisions, but are rather implied in their objective, which is to ensure the effective enjoyment of human rights; Shelton and Gould (n 51) 570–71.

[61] Art 7 ICCPR. See also Art 3 ECHR.

[62] For the duty of the State to take positive action also with respect of the violation of human rights of one individual by another individual see *Osman* (n 50) para 115; on the applicability of this principle to Art 3 ECHR see *Opuz v Turkey* App no 33401/02 (Judgment of 9 June 2009) para 159 and recently *Talpis v Italy* App no 41237/14 (Judgment of 2 March 2017) para 100.

[63] *Rantsev v Cyprus and Russia* App no 25965/04 (Judgment of 7 January 2010) paras 284–85; see also *L.E. v Greece* App no 71545/12 (Judgment of 21 January 2016) paras 65–66.

[64] UN Human Rights Committee, 'General Comment No 31' (n 51) para 8. On the relevance of this aspect for the protection of human rights at sea see Urfan Khaliq, 'Jurisdiction, Ships and Human Rights Treaties' in Henrik Ringbom (ed), *Jurisdiction over Ships* (Martinus Nijhoff 2015) 324, 345–47.

3.2 Positive duties under the law of the sea and the 'due diligence' standard

Positive obligations are not unique to international human rights law, but are also common under the law of the sea. The duty of the flag State to 'assume jurisdiction under its internal law over each ship flying its flag and its master, officers and crew in respect of administrative, technical and social matters concerning the ship', provided by Article 94(2)(b) UNCLOS, is an example of a positive obligation. The same is true of the two obligations provided by Article 98 UNCLOS, to require masters to save life at sea and to organize search and rescue facilities, as well as the duty to take effective measures to prevent and punish the transport of slaves in vessels flying a State's flag, provided in Article 99 UNCLOS.

Similar to what happens in respect of positive obligations under human rights law, positive obligations under the law of the sea are usually drafted in quite generic terms. Furthermore, in many cases the State is required not to achieve a certain result, but rather to take measures to ensure that the result is achieved by someone else. For example, under Article 94(3) UNCLOS, the flag State is required to 'take such measures for ships flying its flag as are necessary to *ensure* safety at sea',[65] while Article 146 UNCLOS requires 'necessary measures [to] be taken to *ensure* effective protection of human life' with respect to activities in the International Seabed Area.[66] As a consequence, and in a manner that resembles international human rights law jurisprudence, law of the sea rules have had to be interpreted by international judicial bodies, in order to clarify their content and scope.

In this respect, international judges have developed and applied the concept of 'due diligence' to frame in more specific terms the content of positive obligations by States in the context of the UNCLOS and other law of the sea treaties.[67] The obligation of 'due diligence' was actually first defined by the ICJ, in the context of environmental law, as:

> an obligation which entails not only the adoption of appropriate rules and measures, but also a certain level of vigilance in their enforcement and the exercise of administrative control applicable to public and private operators, such as the monitoring of activities undertaken by such operators, to safeguard the rights of the other party.[68]

The ITLOS has followed this precedent, for example, when its Seabed Disputes Chamber affirmed that 'the "due diligence" obligation "to ensure" requires the sponsoring State to take measures within its legal system and that the measures must be "reasonably appropriate" ',[69] further adding that a State's obligation 'to ensure':

---

[65] Emphasis added.

[66] Emphasis added. The passive voice used in the article does not provide any indication as to who should take these measures.

[67] On due diligence obligations generally see Joanna Kulesza, *Due Diligence in International Law* (Brill | Nijhoff 2016).

[68] *Pulp Mills on the River Uruguay (Argentina v Uruguay)* [2010] ICJ Rep 14, para 197.

[69] *Responsibilities and Obligations of States Sponsoring Persons and Entities with Respect to Activities in the Area* (Seabed Disputes Chamber, Advisory Opinion of 1 February 2011) (*SDC Opinion*) para 120.

is not an obligation to achieve, in each and every case, the result that the sponsored contractor complies with the aforementioned obligations. Rather, it is an obligation to deploy adequate means, to exercise best possible efforts, to do the utmost, to obtain this result.[70]

While initially adopted with respect to the protection of the environment, there is nothing to prevent the use of the concept of 'due diligence' beyond the narrow field of environmental protection. This concept is capable of being applied to any activity which requires the State to ensure that a certain result is reached by other actors, as the ITLOS has made clear. The 2011 Advisory Opinion, in fact, relates to all duties provided under the UNCLOS,[71] including Article 146 on the protection of human life. In 2015, the ITLOS extended the concept to cover duties of the flag State vis-à-vis its vessels fishing in the exclusive economic zone of another State.[72] Consequently, this concept applies in all those cases in which a treaty provision or rule of customary international law requires a State 'to ensure'.[73] Furthermore, the notion of a 'due diligence' obligation seems an appropriate way to describe the standard of conduct required by States that are requested to 'take effective measures',[74] or 'to give complete effect'.[75]

These 'due diligence' obligations are variable and their content may change over time, in light of new scientific or technological knowledge, but also in respect of the risks involved in the specific activity.[76] If transposed to the field of protection of rights of humans at sea, this changing content might also depend, for example, on the acquisition of new elements concerning the capacity of a State to prevent torture from occurring, or to avoid the *refoulement* of refugees. Additionally, 'due diligence' obligations are engaged, time and again, to introduce further obligations upon States to regulate the conduct of private actors under their jurisdiction.[77] These obligations are therefore particularly significant in the case of flag States, which must ensure that vessels under their jurisdiction—as well as, it is implied, the people on board—comply with international standards.

One final point to be noted concerns the elements necessary for the identification of a breach of a 'due diligence' obligation. As a general rule, the responsibility of a State will be triggered once the private actor that should have been controlled by the State has breached its own duty. Additionally, it is also possible to argue that a State may be responsible for a breach of a due diligence obligation to prevent a private actor carrying out certain conduct, even if the private actor does not actually perform that conduct. In other words, for the State to be responsible, it would be sufficient that it fails to adopt measures to prevent the negative consequences, without

---

[70] ibid para 110.   [71] ibid para 104.

[72] *Request for an Advisory Opinion Submitted by the Sub-Regional Fisheries Commission (SRFC)* (Advisory Opinion of 2 April 2015) (*SRFC Opinion*) para 149.

[73] Among others, Art 94(3) UNCLOS, Art 139 UNCLOS, and Art 146 UNCLOS.

[74] Art 99 UNCLOS.   [75] Art I MLC.   [76] *SDC Opinion* (n 69) para 117.

[77] ibid para 112: 'The expression "to ensure" is often used in international legal instruments to refer to obligations in respect of which, while it is not considered reasonable to make a State liable for each and every violation committed by persons under its jurisdiction, it is equally not considered satisfactory to rely on mere application of the principle that the conduct of private persons or entities is not attributable to the State under international law'.

the need to prove that this omission has actually produced harmful consequences, damage in particular.[78] In this respect, due diligence obligations are different from obligations pertaining to prevention envisaged by Article 14(3) of the ILC Draft Articles on Responsibility of States for Internationally Wrongful Acts.[79] As a consequence, the number of actual violations of the underlying standard of conduct does not matter.[80]

3.3 The contribution of technical regimes and generally accepted standards

An issue with positive obligations under international human rights treaties, but also under the UNCLOS, is the generic language used by these instruments. The provisions mentioned above are indeed important when identifying the standard to be respected by States, which can no longer maintain that they have only to abstain from certain conduct to respect human rights. At the same time, however, their stringent wording and the absence of specific guidance on how the aims set by positive obligations are to be achieved leaves much uncertainty for States that bona fide wish to comply with them. This is even more so, if one considers that positive obligations are relative rather than absolute, leaving a broad discretion to the State as to the manner of implementation.[81] As the ECtHR has found, a positive obligation 'must be interpreted in a way which does not impose an impossible or disproportionate burden on the authorities'.[82]

Positive obligations are also provided under most maritime safety treaties and labour treaties. All SOLAS provisions that require States to ensure that vessels are safe and that the master and crew are adequately trained contain positive obligations of States. Maritime safety and security treaties and labour treaties can thus be set against human rights treaties and the UNCLOS. While the latter only provide general positive duties, often identifying the aim that must be reached but not the exact steps that must be undertaken, maritime safety and security treaties and labour treaties contain specific guidance to States. The provisions of these treaties are in fact often so detailed that they leave little room for further action by States. When the guidance is particularly detailed, both in stating the aim to be achieved and in detailing the steps that must be followed, it is possible to argue that a State that applies the requirements set down in those provisions in practice complies with its positive obligations under human rights law.

---

[78] ibid para 210, which does not require damage for responsibility to arise under general international law—as opposed to the requirement for damage envisaged in Art 139 UNCLOS (described ibid para 176). See also *SRFC Opinion* (n 72) para 146, according to which the responsibility of the flag State for the breach of a due diligence obligation does not depend on the actual conduct of the private actor that should have been regulated by the flag State's regulations. See also *Certain Activities carried out by Nicaragua in the Border Area (Costa Rica v Nicaragua)* and *Construction of a Road in Costa Rica along the San Juan River (Nicaragua v Costa Rica)* [2015] (Judgment of 16 December 2015, Separate Opinion Donoghue) para 9.

[79] James Crawford, *State Responsibility. The General Part* (CUP 2013) 227–28.

[80] *SRFC Opinion* (n 72) para 150.   [81] Shelton and Gould (n 51) 567.

[82] *Osman* (n 50) para 116.

More generally, when concretizing the content of positive obligations, rules which are usually referred to as 'generally accepted international rules and standards' may play an important role.[83] As a result of their mention in the UNCLOS and due to the fact that they are widely accepted and followed in practice, generally accepted international rules and standards should be used in fleshing out States' positive duties towards people at sea.

Let us consider, for example, the right to rest. The UNCLOS only hints at this right when it refers to the duty of the flag State to take measures concerning, inter alia, 'labour conditions'.[84] An express recognition of this right is found in the ICESCR, according to which:

The States Parties to the present Covenant recognize the right of everyone to the enjoyment of just and favourable conditions of work which ensure, in particular: ... Rest, leisure and reasonable limitation of working hours and periodic holidays with pay, as well as remuneration for public holidays.[85]

This provision identifies the right ('the right to work'), as well as a specific supplementary right, the right to rest. The same right is recognized in the MLC, which extensively regulates hours of work and hours of rest in Regulation 2.3.[86] Clearly,

---

[83] Chapter 2, Section 8.2.2.   [84] Art 94(3)(b) UNCLOS.   [85] Art 7(d) ICESCR.
[86] The Regulation provides as follows: 'Standard A2.3—Hours of work and hours of rest. 1. For the purpose of this Standard, the term: (a) hours of work means time during which seafarers are required to do work on account of the ship; (b) hours of rest means time outside hours of work; this term does not include short breaks. 2. Each Member shall within the limits set out in paragraphs 5 to 8 of this Standard fix either a maximum number of hours of work which shall not be exceeded in a given period of time, or a minimum number of hours of rest which shall be provided in a given period of time. 3. Each Member acknowledges that the normal working hours' standard for seafarers, like that for other workers, shall be based on an eight-hour day with one day of rest per week and rest on public holidays. However, this shall not prevent the Member from having procedures to authorize or register a collective agreement which determines seafarers' normal working hours on a basis no less favourable than this standard. 4. In determining the national standards, each Member shall take account of the danger posed by the fatigue of seafarers, especially those whose duties involve navigational safety and the safe and secure operation of the ship. 5. The limits on hours of work or rest shall be as follows: (a) maximum hours of work shall not exceed: (i) 14 hours in any 24-hour period; and (ii) 72 hours in any seven-day period; or (b) minimum hours of rest shall not be less than: (i) ten hours in any 24-hour period; and (ii) 77 hours in any seven-day period. 6. Hours of rest may be divided into no more than two periods, one of which shall be at least six hours in length, and the interval between consecutive periods of rest shall not exceed 14 hours. 7. Musters, fire-fighting and lifeboat drills, and drills prescribed by national laws and regulations and by international instruments, shall be conducted in a manner that minimizes the disturbance of rest periods and does not induce fatigue. 8. When a seafarer is on call, such as when a machinery space is unattended, the seafarer shall have an adequate compensatory rest period if the normal period of rest is disturbed by call-outs to work. 9. If no collective agreement or arbitration award exists or if the competent authority determines that the provisions in the agreement or award in respect of paragraph 7 or 8 of this Standard are inadequate, the competent authority shall determine such provisions to ensure the seafarers concerned have sufficient rest. 10. Each Member shall require the posting, in an easily accessible place, of a table with the shipboard working arrangements, which shall contain for every position at least: (a) the schedule of service at sea and service in port; and (b) the maximum hours of work or the minimum hours of rest required by national laws or regulations or applicable collective agreements. 11. The table referred to in paragraph 10 of this Standard shall be established in a standardized format in the working language or languages of the ship and in English. 12. Each Member shall require that records of seafarers' daily hours of work or of their daily hours of rest be maintained to allow monitoring of compliance with paragraphs 5 to 11 inclusive of this Standard. The records shall be in a standardized format established by the competent authority taking into account any available guidelines of the International

the Provisions of the MLC are much more detailed, in identifying exactly the number of hours of work and rest, the maximum periods of uninterrupted work that the seafarer may be requested to carry out, as well as the exceptions, for example in case work is required for the immediate safety of the ship, persons on board, or cargo, or for the purpose of providing assistance to other ships or persons in distress at sea. The only margin of discretion left to the State consists in determining the exact number of hours of work, or hours of rest, keeping within the parameters identified in the MLC. As such, the MLC provisions leave very little for the State to determine. It follows that the State that complies with the requirement of Regulation 2.3 MLC may reasonably be considered in compliance with the worker's right to rest during work.[87]

Similar considerations may be advanced with respect to the right to a safe working environment. According to Article 7(b) ICESCR, favourable conditions of work must include safe and healthy working conditions. The entire SOLAS could be considered as a practical application of this duty, together with other maritime safety treaties, such as the Convention on the International Regulations for Preventing Collisions at Sea (COLREG)[88] and the International Convention on Standards of Training, Certification and Watchkeeping for Seafarers (STCW). In fact, the SOLAS regulates how ships must be built up to the exact dimensions, but also how they must be equipped and conducted, in order to ensure that they are safe. Given that the ship is the working space for seafarers, a ship which is safe according to the SOLAS requirements could also be considered to comply with the requirements of Article 7(b) ICESCR.

As a consequence, provisions in maritime law and labour law instruments and, more broadly, all relevant generally accepted international rules and standards,

---

Labour Organization or shall be in any standard format prepared by the Organization. They shall be in the languages required by paragraph 11 of this Standard. The seafarers shall receive a copy of the records pertaining to them which shall be endorsed by the master, or a person authorized by the master, and by the seafarers. 13. Nothing in paragraphs 5 and 6 of this Standard shall prevent a Member from having national laws or regulations or a procedure for the competent authority to authorize or register collective agreements permitting exceptions to the limits set out. Such exceptions shall, as far as possible, follow the provisions of this Standard but may take account of more frequent or longer leave periods or the granting of compensatory leave for watchkeeping seafarers or seafarers working on board ships on short voyages. 14. Nothing in this Standard shall be deemed to impair the right of the master of a ship to require a seafarer to perform any hours of work necessary for the immediate safety of the ship, persons on board or cargo, or for the purpose of giving assistance to other ships or persons in distress at sea. Accordingly, the master may suspend the schedule of hours of work or hours of rest and require a seafarer to perform any hours of work necessary until the normal situation has been restored. As soon as practicable after the normal situation has been restored, the master shall ensure that any seafarers who have performed work in a scheduled rest period are provided with an adequate period of rest.'

[87] The MLC is certainly relevant for States that have ratified this treaty. It is however possible to argue that the MLC is now one of the 'generally accepted international regulations' recalled in Art 94(5) UNCLOS and therefore binding, as a standard, for all UNCLOS parties—or, if Art 94(5) is considered as reflecting customary international law, for all States; see Irini Papanicolopulu, 'Seafarers as an Agent of Change of the Jurisdictional Balance' in Henrik Ringbom (ed), *Jurisdiction over Ships. Post-UNCLOS Developments in the Law of the Sea* (Martinus Nijhoff 2015) 301.

[88] Convention on the International Regulations for Preventing Collisions at Sea (adopted 10 October 1962, entered into force 15 July 1977) 1050 UNTS 16, as amended (COLREG).

are accessory when identifying positive duties under human rights treaties or the UNCLOS. In this manner, these technical instruments could also be used by human rights bodies to assess the compliance of a State with its positive obligations to protect specific human rights. This is particularly important because human rights treaties, as already mentioned, are generic in their wording and rarely specify how exactly the State must act to comply with its positive obligations under them. Importantly, human rights bodies are not new to the use of non-binding standards developed by technical bodies.[89] While international human rights bodies have contributed greatly to the understanding of treaty provisions through their interpretative guidance in their decisions and judgments, there are still ambits of uncertainty, in particular concerning activities at sea, which are not often brought to the attention of these bodies. This shortcoming not only allows States to seize upon ambiguities and a lack of clarity to avoid complying with human rights, but it may also generate hesitation amongst States that honestly wish to fulfil their human rights obligations but are not sure how to do so. Technical instruments thus fill this gap.

4. State Obligations at Sea: A Practical Illustration

Negative and positive obligations are therefore promoted by all legal fields that are relevant for people at sea. This could on the face of it be considered sufficient to ensure the protection of people at sea but there are, however, more issues to take account of. Recent years have witnessed the development of legal regulations concerning human activities at sea that combine duties arising under human rights with those that derive from the law of the sea, with a view towards ensuring a comprehensive protection for people. This is rendered conceptually possible by the systemic nature of international law, and practically feasible by the willingness of international judges to 'intrude' into fields other than their own in order to better elaborate States' duties.

As it is clearly an impossible undertaking to explore each and every situation in which people at sea need to be protected, two examples have been selected to demonstrate this point. The first one relates to protection afforded during law enforcement activities. This is a field in which the rather generic content of human rights duties of States has been clarified in a more precise way, while taking into account the specificities of the sea. The second one relates to the protection of human life at sea which, as this book seeks to argue, is a field which has not yet been expounded by the judiciary to its full potential. Ultimately, these issues exemplifies the advantages of a combined reading of human rights and law of the sea duties in terms of the protection of persons.

---

[89] For example, the ECtHR has often referred to the standards developed by the European Committee for the Prevention of Torture and Inhuman or Degrading Treatment or Punishment in order to evaluate whether prison overcrowding falls short of the guarantees of Art 3 ECHR; see, among others, *Belousov v Russia* Apps nos 2653/13 and 60980/14 (Judgment of 4 October 2016) para 98.

4.1 The protection of personal liberty at sea

International law provides many substantial rights and duties that relate to persons at sea. Nonetheless, even a hopeless optimist would concede that these alone cannot really make a difference if there is a lack of enforcement mechanisms. Thus, much modern international law, including the law of the sea, has focused on ways to strengthen the enforcement of legal rules at sea. Law enforcement, however, may in turn impact on fundamental human rights, including the right to life, personal liberty, and prohibition of torture.[90]

This is also recognized in the UNCLOS. The most elaborate UNCLOS provisions in terms of the protection of individuals are in fact those addressing the consequences of the exercise of enforcement jurisdiction in the case of fisheries and the pollution of the marine environment.[91] These provisions essentially envisage three types of requirements:[92] the release of vessels upon the posting of a reasonable bond; the prohibition of imprisonment, corporal punishment, and other non-monetary penalties; and notice to the flag State of the arrest and action taken pursuant to it. The provisions, however, are silent as to the actual moment of the arrest. It is therefore necessary to turn to other rules in order to establish when personal liberty at sea may be restricted and what conditions States are asked to comply with.

During law enforcement activities at sea, three specific moments deserve particular attention. The first relates to the actual moment of arrest of the vessel and the people on board when it is more likely that the right to life may be engaged, in addition to questions surrounding the legal justification of a restriction to personal liberty.[93] The second includes all the time during which the people are being transported to their destination when issues of restriction of personal liberty, including the duration and conditions of detention, as well as judicial supervision, come into play. The third includes the moment when the persons are handed over to someone else, be they the competent authorities of the arresting State or those of a different State; at this moment, the protection from torture and other inhuman and degrading treatment and the corollary duty of *non-refoulement* are paramount.

Focusing first on the moment when a vessel is intercepted at sea, it is evident that any enforcement action undertaken by the intercepting State may involve some use of force.[94] The use of force may in turn create the need to consider the protection

---

[90] Chapter 1, Section 3.5.

[91] Respectively, Art 73 and Arts 226, 230, and 231 UNCLOS. According to Bernard H Oxman, 'Human Rights and the United Nations Convention on the Law of the Sea' (1998) 36 Columbia Journal of Transnational Law 399, 422, these provisions 'were in a significant measure a response to concerns about the treatment of foreign ships and crew members by various states, including detention policies, trial practices and prison conditions in different parts of the world'.

[92] Oxman (n 91).

[93] For different types of boarding see Efthymios Papastavridis, *The Interception of Vessels on the High Seas* (Hart 2014) 67–68.

[94] In *Fisheries Jurisdiction (Spain v Canada)* [1998] ICJ Rep 432, para 84, the ICJ noted that 'Boarding, inspection, arrest and *minimum use of force* for those purposes are all contained within the concept of enforcement of conservation and management measures according to a "natural and reasonable" interpretation of this concept' (emphasis added). See also Papastavridis, *The Interception* (n 93) 69. Of course, use of force in this context should not be confused with use of force prohibited by Art 2(4) United Nations Charter; see Enrico Milano and Irini Papanicolopulu, 'State Responsibility in Disputed

granted to people by the right to life, even in cases when the persons involved are not actually killed.[95] Although human rights law does not absolutely preclude the use of force—and the consequent possibility of killings—during police enforcement operations,[96] it requires very strict conditions to be fulfilled.[97] These strict limitations have now been integrated into the law of the sea and are combined with rules of international law concerning the use of force. It is therefore correct to assert that there is an emerging consensus in the international community concerning minimum safeguards for the interception of vessels at sea and the arrest of people on board, which is filling the gap in the UNCLOS.[98]

In the *Saiga* case, the ITLOS summed up the relevant principles by stating that 'the use of force must be avoided as far as possible and, where force is unavoidable, it must not go beyond what is reasonable and necessary in the circumstances'.[99] The Tribunal went on to consider that firing weapons indiscriminately when on board a vessel and using gunfire to stop the engine did not comply with the conditions qualifying the use of lethal force in police operations. It concluded that the Guinean officers, who had been responsible of the indiscriminate shooting, had 'attached little or no importance to the safety of the ship and the persons on board'.[100]

The Tribunal not only stated the general principles governing enforcement action, but it went further and indicated the specific procedural requirements for the use of force:

The normal practice used to stop a ship at sea is first to give an auditory or visual signal to stop, using internationally recognized signals. Where this does not succeed, a variety of actions may be taken, including the firing of shots across the bows of the ship. It is only after the appropriate actions fail that the pursuing vessel may, as a last resort, use force. Even then, appropriate warning must be issued to the ship and all efforts should be made to ensure that life is not endangered.[101]

Areas on Land and at Sea' (2011) 71 Zeitschrift für ausländisches öffentliches Recht und Völkerrecht 587, 622–23.

[95] *Makaratzis v Greece* App no 50385/99 (Judgment of 20 December 2004) para 49, according to which the right to life 'covers not only intentional killing but also situations where it is permitted to use force which may result, as an unintended outcome, in the deprivation of life'.

[96] Art 2(2)(b) ECHR.

[97] *McCann and Others v United Kingdom* App no 18984/91 (Judgment (GC) of 27 September 1995). Paul Tavernier, 'Le recours à la force par la police' in Christian Tomuschat, Evelyne Lagrange, and Stefan Oeter (eds), *The Right to Life* (Martinus Nijhoff 2010) 44–45. See also 'Basic Principles on the Use of Force and Firearms by Law Enforcement Officials' Eighth United Nations Congress on the Prevention of Crime and the Treatment of Offenders (Havana, 27 August–7 September 1990).

[98] Douglas Guilfoyle, *Shipping Interdiction and the Law of the Sea* (CUP 2009) 266; Robin Geiss and Anna Petrig, *Piracy and Armed Robbery at Sea: The Legal Framework for Counter-Piracy Operations in Somalia and the Gulf of Aden* (OUP 2011) 100.

[99] *Saiga* (n 17) para 155. See also Art 225 UNCLOS; Art 8*bis*(9) SUA Convention; Art 22(1)(f) FSA. On the use of force during maritime police operations see *SS 'I'm Alone' (Canada, United States)* (1949) 3 RIAA 1609, 1617; *Investigation of Certain Incidents Affecting the British Trawler Red Crusader (The United Kingdom, Denmark)* (1962) 29 RIAA 523, 538; *Guyana/Suriname* (n 30) para 445; *Arctic Sunrise* (n 31) para 222.

[100] *Saiga* (n 17) para 158.

[101] ibid para 156. For a detailed discussion of the modalities of the use of force Guilfoyle, *Shipping Interdiction* (n 98) 277–93.

These conditions are further complemented by the positive duties which bind States, in particular the duty to put in place an adequate legislative and administrative framework concerning the use of force during police operations,[102] as well as the duty to investigate and criminally repress any alleged violations of the right to life.[103] In this respect, the ECtHR has accepted that there is some flexibility afforded to States in this respect when 'difficult security considerations' prevail,[104] which may indeed be the case during some police operations at sea, for example in the case of the fight against piracy.[105]

Turning to the second critical moment, the seizure and detention of individuals, it is mostly the ECtHR that has clarified in detail the positive duties of States with respect to the deprivation of liberty at sea.[106] In the first place, the Court has affirmed that whenever a vessel is intercepted, the restrictions imposed upon the crew members may amount to a deprivation of liberty according to Article 5 ECHR, even if there has been no formal arrest. In order to establish whether this is so, it is necessary to assess the precise situation and the 'type, duration, effects and manner of implementation of the measure in question'.[107] Even the mere fact that a ship's course is determined by someone other than the master of the vessel is sufficient to consider that the members of the crew are deprived of their liberty.[108]

According to the ECtHR, any action that restricts the liberty of persons on board a vessel must comply with the conditions under Article 5 ECHR. These are summarized in the following manner:

Article 5 of the Convention is in the first rank of the fundamental rights that protect the physical security of an individual, and that three strands in particular may be identified as running through the Court's case-law: the exhaustive nature of the exceptions, which must be interpreted strictly and which do not allow for the broad range of justifications under other provisions (Articles 8 to 11 of the Convention in particular); the repeated emphasis on the lawfulness of the detention, procedurally and substantively, requiring scrupulous adherence to the rule of law; and the importance of the promptness or speediness of the requisite judicial controls under Article 5 §§ 3 and 4.[109]

In the first place, it is necessary to take into account the fact that the right to personal liberty is the default starting point, and any limitations must be construed narrowly.[110] Furthermore, any deprivation of liberty must be clearly defined by law, and

---

[102] *Makaratzis* (n 95) para 71.   [103] *McCann* (n 97) para 161; *Makaratzis* (n 95) 73–74.

[104] *Al-Skeini and Others v The United Kingdom* App no 55721/07 (Judgment (GC) of 7 July 2011) para 164.

[105] Tullio Treves and Cesare Pitea, 'Piracy, International Law and Human Rights' in Nehal Bhuta (ed), *The Frontiers of Human Rights. Extraterritoriality and Its Challenges* (OUP 2016) 114; Sofia Galani, 'Somali Piracy and the Human Rights of Seafarers' (2016) 34 Netherlands Quarterly of Human Rights 71.

[106] Notably, the provisions of human rights treaties and, consequently, their interpretation by human rights bodies, can be used also by law of the sea tribunals in assessing compliance with the UNCLOS provisions; see *Arctic Sunrise* (n 31) paras 197–98.

[107] *Medvedyev* (n 35) para 73.   [108] ibid para 74.

[109] ibid para 117. On the application of Art 5 ECHR at sea Papastavridis, 'European Convention' (n 45) 133–38.

[110] *Medvedyev* (n 35) para 78.

the law must be foreseeable in its application.[111] The reference to law also includes international law,[112] which needs to be sufficiently precise and foreseeable.[113]

The requirement of precision means that the international instrument relied upon as the basis of the arrest of a person on board a ship must explicitly mention the possibility of arrest or other measure leading to a deprivation of liberty. A generic reference to action against the ship—without any reference to the persons on board—has not been considered as sufficient.[114] Furthermore, a reference to the power to arrest under international law, even if it is contained in a generally accepted norm such as that allowing every State to arrest pirates, may not be sufficient to fulfil the requirement of precision if adequate domestic legislation that defines the conditions for the deprivation of liberty is missing.[115]

The requirement of foreseeability should 'allow the citizen—if need be, with appropriate advice—to foresee, to a degree that is reasonable in the circumstances of the case, the consequences which a given action may entail'.[116] According to the ECtHR, under international law, the requirement of foreseeability may not be met when an arrest is based on an ad hoc exchange of notes between the flag State and the intercepting State, which authorizes a single operation against a vessel and people on board. What the Court seems to require is that there should be in place a permanent framework of cooperation, which may take the form of a bilateral or multilateral treaty. In this regard, the ECtHR refers to a 'permanent' instrument.[117] In the presence of such a framework, for example the United Nations Convention against Illicit Traffic in Narcotic Drugs and Psychotropic Substances, Article 17 of which contains a specific provision for permission to be granted by the flag State, formal requirements can be relaxed and the verbal granting of permission to board is considered acceptable.[118] In the case of piracy, the combination of UNCLOS

---

[111] ibid para 79. For a general discussion of the difficulties in this respect, including in the case of so-called 'consensual boarding', ie boarding which has been authorized by the master of the vessel, see Papastavridis, *The Interception* (n 89) 64–66. On the difficulties encountered to establish the lawfulness of interdiction of vessels transporting weapons of mass destruction or involved in terrorist activities see Papastavridis, *The Interception* (n 93) 158–59.

[112] *Medvedyev* (n 35) para 97.   [113] ibid para 80.

[114] ibid para 99. This point however was strongly contested by a minority of the Grand Chamber, according to which 'it is scarcely possible to dissociate the crew from the ship itself when a ship is boarded and inspected on the high seas'; *Medvedyev and Others v France* App no 3394/03 (Judgment (GC) Joint Partly Dissenting Opinion of Costa, Casadevall, Birsan, Garlicki, Hajiyev, Sikuta, and Nicolaou) para 7.

[115] *Hassan and Others v France* Apps nos 46695/10 and 54588/10 (Judgment of 4 December 2014) para 69.

[116] *Medvedyev* (n 35) para 80.

[117] ibid para 100. This requirement seems however too strict, in light of the long-standing practice by which flag States have routinely authorized interception of their vessels by other States (Douglas Guilfoyle, 'Counter-Piracy Law Enforcement and Human Rights' (2010) 59 ICLQ 141, 160). A solution might be given by an explicit provision in domestic law of the possibility to intercept and arrest a vessel and the people on board when authorized by the flag State. This option was pursued by France following the *Medvedyev* case.

[118] *Rigopoulos v Spain* App no 37388/97 (Decision of 12 January 1999). See Tavernier, 'La Cour' (n 45) 581.

provisions and UN Security Council Resolution 1816 were deemed sufficient to comply with the foreseeability requirement.[119]

The requirement of foreseeability seems also to be reflected in Article 110(1) UNCLOS. The provision, which deals with the 'right of visit' on the high seas, provides that a State other than the flag State may interfere with a vessel on the high seas if 'acts of interference derive from powers conferred by treaty'. The fact that this provision requires the presence of a treaty, and not simply an informal agreement, is not only based on the fact that the generalized practice of States takes the form of treaties, but also because 'the matter is too important to be left to be settled case by case by a telephone conversation'.[120]

A further requirement is that people arrested should be physically brought before a judicial officer promptly,[121] in order to provide effective safeguards against the risk of ill-treatment and against the abuse of powers bestowed on law enforcement officers.[122] In this regard, judicial control must satisfy three requirements. First, it must be prompt, so as to allow the detection of any ill-treatment and to keep to a minimum any unjustified interference with individual liberty.[123] Second, judicial review must be automatic and should not depend on the application of the detained person, since a person subjected to ill-treatment might be unable to submit a complaint.[124] Third, the judge must be a 'judge or other officer authorised by law to exercise judicial power'[125] and must possess certain characteristics and powers. The judge must be independent from the executive and the parties, must hear the arrested individual personally, must review the circumstances in favour or against detention, must decide, by reference to legal criteria, whether there are reasons to justify detention and lastly the judge must have the power to order release if there are no such reasons.[126]

The first requirement, that of promptness, needs however to take into account the specificities of an arrest at sea. In light of the particular conditions of persons arrested at sea, who are often many days' travel from the nearest coast, the ECtHR has adopted the standard of review according to which it must be 'materially impossible to bring the applicant physically before the investigating judge any sooner'.[127] The distance to be covered by the vessel to reach the port where the arrested may be brought before a judge, the conditions of the vessel, and any ensuing incidents on board which may cause delays, are all circumstances that have been taken into account in assessing promptness.[128] Of course, once the

[119] *Hassan* (n 115) para 68.
[120] Louis B Sohn, 'International Law of the Sea and Human Rights Issues' in Thomas A ClinganJr (ed), *The Law of the Sea: What Lies Ahead?* (The Law of the Sea Institute 1988) 51, 59. See also ibid 62.
[121] *Medvedyev* (n 35) para 118.   [122] ibid para 120.   [123] ibid para 121.
[124] ibid para 122.   [125] ibid para 123.   [126] ibid para 124.
[127] *Rigopoulos* (n 118). See also *Medvedyev* (n 35) para 131 and *Hassan* (n 115) para 99. Of course, one thing is to sail immediately after the persons have been arrested towards the State, even if the travel may require some days or even weeks; another is to delay departure, while deciding what to do with the people arrested (Guilfoyle, 'Counter-Piracy' (n 117) 159).
[128] *Rigopoulos* (n 118); in this case, a delay of sixteen days was not deemed incompatible with the ECHR. In *Medvedyev* (n 35) paras 130–31, the delay, which was not considered incompatible with the ECHR, was of thirteen and fourteen days. See also *Hassan* (n 115) para 99 (travels taking nine

ship has reached the port, individuals must be brought before a judge within hours.[129]

Turning now to the moment when the people seized are turned over to someone else, particular guidance is provided in cases of pirates and migrants intercepted at sea. As a preliminary point, upon interception, the State must take steps to identify the individuals, and only then may it decide whether to bring them to its territory or to disembark them in another State.[130]

If the individuals are brought to the intercepting State, they of course enjoy the full array of human rights guarantees, in particular procedural rights during the detention and the trial provided for in international human rights treaties,[131] on the basis of the exercise of territorial jurisdiction over them.[132] This is also recognized in the UNCLOS, which provides that when conducting proceedings, the 'recognized rights of the accused shall be observed'.[133] These rights, arguably, include all human rights duties that bind States.[134] Recalling them would serve not only as a reminder to State authorities, but also as a means for extending the applicability of the compulsory disputes settlement mechanism of UNCLOS to these disputes.[135] As a matter of fact, this provision is contained in Part XII of the UNCLOS and applies only to proceedings in the case of pollution of the marine environment. It would however be absurd to infer, *a contrario*, that in other cases these rights should not be observed, both in light of the absence of any textual element and of the fact that human rights obligations are accepted by States and may be binding on them as a matter of *jus cogens*. This conclusion is confirmed by the ITLOS, which has mentioned the need to take into account 'international standards of due process of law'[136] and 'human rights law, and ... considerations of due process of law' in the treatment of individuals arrested by a State.[137]

If, on the other hand, the intercepting State decides to hand over the people to another State,[138] it will need to take into account the prohibition of *refoulement*,

---

and seven days respectively) and *Ali Samatar and Other v France* Apps nos 17110/10 and 17301/10 (Judgment of 4 December 2014) para 54.

[129] *Medvedyev* (n 35) para 132; *Vassis and Others v France* App no 62736/09 (Judgment of 27 June 2013) para 60: 'the promptness requirement of Article 5 § 3 of the Convention was even stricter than in a situation where the beginning of police custody coincided with the initial deprivation of liberty'. Now confirmed by *Hassan* (n 115) paras 100–04 and *Ali Samatar* (n 128) paras 55–58.

[130] *Hirsi* (n 35) para 185.

[131] Angela Di Stasi, *Il diritto all'equo processo nella CEDU e nella Convenzione americana sui diritti umani* (Giappichelli 2012).

[132] An issue that arose with respect to persons arrested on charges of piracy related to the absence of national legislation on the basis of which they could be tried (Geiss and Petrig (n 98) 137–67; Kenneth Manusama, 'Prosecuting Pirates in the Netherlands: The Case of the *MS Samanyolu*' (2010) 49 Military Law and the Law of War Review 141). In a famous case, the Danish ship *Absalon* eventually set pirates free after unsuccessfully looking for means to prosecute them (Treves and Pitea (n 105) 118).

[133] Art 230(3) UNCLOS.

[134] Oxman (n 91) 426. See also Myron Nordquist, Shabtai Rosenne, Alexander Yankov, and Neil Grandy (eds), *United Nations Convention on the Law of the Sea. A Commentary*, vol IV (Martinus Nijhoff 1991) 370.

[135] Oxman (n 91) 426–27.   [136] *Tomimaru* (n 22) para 76.

[137] *Louisa* (n 23) para 155. Treves and Pitea (n 105).

[138] This became routine in the case of pirates arrested by States patrolling the coasts off Somalia, in particular following the negotiation and adoption of agreements with coastal States of the region

both under refugee law and under human rights law.[139] The legal basis invoked for such a transfer, for example 'extradition' or any other legitimate executive action, does not affect the duty.[140] In particular, the State will have to determine whether, in the light of the personal characteristics of the individuals and the situation in the receiving country, handing over the persons arrested or returning the migrants would put them at a real risk of persecution or of torture or inhuman and degrading treatment.[141] Even if they do not make any claim for asylum or invoke any remedy for the suspension of their transfer, the intercepting State bears the burden of assessing the situation *proprio motu*.[142] If there is any such risk, then the detaining State is prohibited from handing over the people and should keep them, or transfer them to a safe State. In most cases, acquiring diplomatic assurances that there will be no ill-treatment at the hands of the receiving State is not sufficient to legitimize the transfer of an individual vis-à-vis the prohibition of *refoulement*. The conclusion of

for prosecution of pirates by the courts of the latter. On this practice Guilfoyle, 'Counter-Piracy' (n 117) 152; Geiss and Petrig (n 98) 186–207.

[139] Art 33 Convention Relating to the Status of Refugees (adopted 28 July 1951, entered into force 22 April 1954) 189 UNTS 137 (Refugee Convention) and Art 3 Convention against Torture and Other Cruel, Inhuman or Degrading Treatment or Punishment (adopted 10 December 1984, entered into force 26 June 1987) 1465 UNTS 85 (CAT), respectively. See also UN Human Rights Committee, 'General Comment No 20' in 'Compilation of General Comments and General Recommendations Adopted by Human Rights Treaty Bodies' (27 May 2008) UN Doc HRI/GEN/1/Rev.9 (Vol I). *Soering v The United Kingdom* App no 14038/88) (Judgment of 7 July 1989) para 88; *Chahal v The United Kingdom* App no 22414/93 (Judgment (GC) of 15 November 1996) para 74; *Saadi v Italy* App no 37201/06) (Judgment (GC) of 28 February 2008) paras 125–27; *Hirsi* (n 35) para 114. On the distinction between *refoulement* in refugee law and human rights law see Seline Trevisanut, 'The Principle of Non-Refoulement at Sea and the Effectiveness of Asylum Protection' (2008) 12 Max Planck Yearbook of United Nations Law 205. The principle of *non-refoulement* has a primary relevance in the case of interception of irregular migrants. Initial narrow readings of this principle (Richard Barnes, 'The International Law of the Sea and Migration Control' in Bernard Ryan and Valsamis Mitsilegas (eds), *Extraterritorial Immigration Control: Legal Challenges* (Martinus Nijhoff 2010) 103) have now been superseded by the findings of the ECtHR in the *Hirsi* case (Papastavridis, 'European Convention' (n 45) 128–33). For the application of the principle of *non-refoulement* in the context of migration by sea, see, among many others, Guy Goodwin-Gill and Jane McAdam, *The Refugee in International Law* (3rd edn, OUP 2007); Andreas Fischer-Lescano, Tillmann Löhr, and Timo Tohidipur, 'Border Controls at Sea: Requirements under International Human Rights and Refugee Law' (2009) 21 International Journal of Refugee Law 256; Patricia Mallia, *Migrant Smuggling by Sea. Combating a Current Threat to Maritime Security through the Creation of a Cooperative Framework* (Martinus Nijhoff 2010); Guy S Goodwin-Gill, 'The Right to Seek Asylum: Interception at Sea and the Principle of *Non-Refoulement*' (2011) 23 International Journal of Refugee Law 443; Silvia Borelli and Ben Stanford, 'Troubled Waters in the Mare Nostrum: Interception and Push-backs of Migrants in the Mediterranean and the European Convention on Human Rights' (2014) 10 Uluslararası Hukuk ve Politika 29; Francesca De Vittor, 'Il diritto di traversare il Mediterraneo ... o quantomeno di provarci' (2014) 8 Diritti Umani e Diritto Internazionale 63; Natalie Klein, 'A Case for Harmonizing Laws on Maritime Interceptions of Irregular Migrants' (2014) 63 ICLQ 787; Mariagiulia Giuffré, 'Access to Asylum at Sea? Non-refoulement and a Comprehensive Approach to Extraterritorial Human Rights Obligations' in Violeta Moreno-Lax and Efthymios Papastavridis (eds), *'Boat Refugees' and Migrants at Sea. A Comprehensive Approach Integrating Maritime Security with Human Rights*, (Brill Nijhoff 2017) 248. For the application of the principle in the case of pirates see Guilfoyle, 'Counter-Piracy' (n 117) 153; Treves and Pitea (n 105) 122–24; Geiss and Petrig (n 98) 207–20.

[140] Guilfoyle, 'Counter-Piracy' (n 117) 161.

[141] *Hirsi* (n 35) paras 114 and 117. *Non-refoulement* prohibits both direct and indirect return to a place where the person could be tortured; ibid para 146.

[142] ibid para 133.

any agreement with the receiving State, even if it affirms that human rights shall be respected,[143] might equally not be sufficient, as the actual facts on the ground will prevail over any formal commitment.[144]

If the intercepting State decides that there is no risk under Article 3 of the ECHR, it must inform the individuals of their destination and make sure that each of them has access to an effective remedy to challenge the decision, which carries 'suspensive effect', *before* they are transferred.[145] Since it may be impractical, if not impossible, for a State to fulfil all these obligations and to provide for such mechanisms while people are on board State vessels, the persons would have to be brought to a safe place where the State could more easily carry them out. This may be the territory of the intercepting State or that of another State, as long as the prohibition of *refoulement* is respected.

4.2 The protection of human life at sea

Human life is particularly threatened at sea.[146] It is for this reason that a conspicuous body of rules has been developed in order to safeguard human life at sea. These rules belong both to law of the sea instruments and to human rights instruments, and they have been further complemented by the decisions of international judges. In order to reconstruct this normative complex, it is therefore necessary to examine all fields, switching from one to the other.

Beginning with the law of the sea, for centuries there has been a customary duty to render assistance in order to save life at sea.[147] The duty, now codified in Article 98(1) UNCLOS and other treaties,[148] binds States and masters of ships alike, and

---

[143] For example Art 6 Treaty on Friendship, Partnership and Cooperation (Italy and Libya) (adopted 30 August 2008), which relates to the treatment of migrants, and Art 3(5) Agreement between the European Union and the Republic of Mauritius on the Conditions of Transfer of Suspected Pirates and Associated Seized Property from the European Union-Led Naval Force to the Republic of Mauritius and on the Conditions of Suspected Pirates after Transfer (adopted 14 July 2011) [2011] OJ L254/3, relating to the treatment of pirates.

[144] *Hirsi* (n 35) para 129; Guilfoyle, 'Counter-Piracy' (n 117) 163; Treves and Pitea (n 105) 124; Geiss and Petrig (n 98) 219; Josiane Auvret-Finck, 'La conditionnalité des Droits de l'Homme dans les accords de l'UE relatifs à la lutte contre la piraterie maritime' in Constance Chevallier-Govers and Catherine Schneider (eds), *L'Europe et la lutte contre la piraterie maritime* (Pedone 2015) 245.

[145] *Hirsi* (n 35) paras 197–200. For a discussion in the context of piracy Guilfoyle, 'Counter-Piracy' (n 117) 167.

[146] Chapter 1, Section 3.1.

[147] Emer de Vattel, *Le droit des gens ou principes de la loi naturelle appliqués à la conduite et aux affaires des nations et des souverains*, vol 1 (London, 1758) 170.

[148] Regulation 33.1 SOLAS; Art 10(1) International Convention on Salvage. It should be noted that Art 98(1) UNCLOS repeats the content of Art 12(1) Convention on the High Seas (adopted 29 April 1958, entered into force 30 September 1962) 450 UNTS 11 (HSC), which, in turn, was based upon the draft articles prepared by the ILC. The latter proposal drew upon duties found under Art 11 International Convention for the Unification of Certain Rules of Law Relating to Assistance and Salvage at Sea (adopted 23 September 1910) and Art 8 International Convention for the Unification of Certain Rules of Law Related to Collision between Vessels (adopted 23 September 1910) (ILC, 'Second Report on the Regime of the High Seas by Mr. J.P.A. François, Special Rapporteur' (10 April 1951) UN Doc A/CN.4/42, paras 35–38). On the customary nature of this duty see ILC, 'Articles concerning the Law of the Sea with commentaries' *Yearbook of the International Law Commission* Vol II (1956) 281; Barnes (n 139) 49; Goodwin-Gill and McAdam (n 139) 278; Oxman (n 91) 415; Myron Nordquist, Satya

applies to all maritime zones.[149] It applies both in the case of collision between two vessels and also in cases when a vessel receives information that one or more persons are in danger of being lost at sea because their vessel is endangered or has sunk. This duty applies to all persons in distress, without distinction.[150] The nationality of the vessels or of the persons, their legal status, and the activity in which they are engaged are irrelevant.[151]

This traditional duty incumbent on flag States has been supplemented in the twentieth century by the related duty of coastal States to provide search and rescue services. Article 98(2) UNCLOS requires coastal States to promote the establishment, operation, and maintenance of adequate and effective search and rescue services, if necessary collaborating with neighbouring States.[152] While the language of this provision could be considered as hortatory only,[153] its binding character has been clarified in other treaties, such as the SOLAS and SAR Convention.

The UNCLOS does not define these terms, but according to the SAR Convention 'search' is '[a]n operation, normally co-ordinated by a rescue co-ordination centre or rescue sub-centre, using available personnel and facilities to locate persons in distress',[154] while 'rescue' is '[a]n operation to retrieve persons in distress, provide for their initial medical or other needs, and deliver them to a place of safety'.[155] Search and rescue services aim to locate persons in distress at sea and ensure that they are aided, either by State-owned vessels that go to sea for this purpose, such as those of the coastguard, or by other vessels navigating in the area and acting in compliance with Article 98(1) UNCLOS.[156] In this regard, Regulation 2.1.1 SAR Convention provides that '[o]n receiving information that any person is, or appears to be, in

N Nandan, and Shabtai Rosenne (eds), *The United Nations Convention on the Law of the Sea 1982: A Commentary.* vol III (Martinus Nijhoff 1985) 171. It has also been considered a general principle of international law (Tullio Scovazzi, 'Human Rights and Immigration at Sea' in Ruth Rubio-Marín (ed), *Human Rights and Immigration* (OUP 2014) 212, 225).

[149] Art 98 UNCLOS applies to the high seas and, on the basis of the cross-reference in Art 58(2) UNCLOS, to the exclusive economic zone. The applicability of this principle to the territorial sea can be argued in light of the language of Art 18(2) UNCLOS (Scovazzi (n 148) 226; Oxman (n 91) 414; John E Noyes, 'The Territorial Sea and Contiguous Zone' in Donald R Rothwell, Alex G Oude Elferink, Karen N Scott, and Tim Stephens (eds), *The Oxford Handbook of the Law of the Sea* (OUP 2015) 91, 104; Nordquist, Nandan, and Rosenne (n 148) 176–77) and is expressly provided in Chapter 5, Reg 1.1 SOLAS.

[150] Chapter 2.1.10 SAR Convention provides that 'Parties shall ensure that assistance is provided to any person in distress at sea. They shall do so regardless of the nationality or status of such a person or the circumstances in which that person is found'. See also Reg 33.1 SOLAS.

[151] Scovazzi (n 148) 225; Barnes (n 139) 50. This duty applies also to military vessels, both during peacetime and during wartime.

[152] Art 98, para 2 UNCLOS, reflects Art 12 HSC. Interestingly, the draft articles produced by the International Law Commission in 1956 did not contain any reference to the duty of the coastal State to provide search and rescue services. The text of Art 12 HSC was based upon a Danish proposal during the First United Nations Conference on the Law of the Sea (UN Doc A/CONF.13/C.2/L.36). See also Chapter 2.1.1 SAR Convention.

[153] Douglas Guilfoyle, 'Article 98' in Alexander Proelss (ed), *United Nations Convention on the Law of the Sea. A Commentary* (Beck-Hart-Nomos 2017) 726.

[154] Reg 1.3.1 SAR Convention.   [155] Chapter 1.3.2 SAR Convention.
[156] Chapter 5, Reg 7.1 SOLAS.

distress at sea, the responsible authorities of a Party shall take urgent steps to ensure that the necessary assistance is provided'.

While the normative framework concerning search and rescue operations is well developed, there are still gaps in the system. The first gap concerns the identification of the State that must provide assistance,[157] and the second gap relates to the disembarkation of the people rescued. The term 'rescue', in fact, implies that the people assisted should be delivered 'to a place of safety'. While a ship may temporarily be considered as a place of safety,[158] people saved will eventually have to be disembarked on dry land. Disembarkation is rendered more complex by the need to combine the principle of territorial sovereignty with the principle of *non-refoulement*, enshrined in Article 33 Refugee Convention and now extended to any person who might suffer a violation of his or her right to life or freedom from torture.[159] Following the *Tampa* case,[160] the SOLAS and the SAR Convention were amended in an effort to clarify State duties concerning disembarkation.[161] These amendments, however, have not definitively settled the issue and not all States have accepted them.[162]

The duty to rescue people in distress at sea can be considered as the other side of the coin of the right to life, which every individual enjoys under international human rights law.[163] The right to life, also referred to as 'the supreme right',[164] entails both negative and positive duties for States.[165] Positive obligations include both substantial obligations and procedural obligations. From a substantial point of view, the right to life requires the State to take measures to ensure that those at

---

[157] Mallia (n 139).   [158] IMO Guidelines (n 40).

[159] See above, n 139 and accompanying text.   [160] See above, n 40.

[161] Chapter 3.1.9 SAR Convention; similar texts was inserted in the revised Reg 4.1.1 SOLAS. For a discussion see Mallia (n 139) 100–01.

[162] On the issues relating to disembarkation see Jasmine Coppens and Eduard Somers, 'Towards New Rules on Disembarkation of Persons Rescued at Sea?' (2010) 25 IJMCL 377; Violeta Moreno Lax, 'The EU Regime on Interdiction, Search and Rescue, and Disembarkation: The Frontex Guidelines for Intervention at Sea' (2010) 25 IJMCL 621; David Testa, 'Safeguarding Human Life and Ensuring Respect for Fundamental Human Rights: A Consequential Approach to the Disembarkation of Persons Rescued at Sea' (2014) 28 Ocean Yearbook 555.

[163] Art 6 ICCPR; Art 2 ECHR; Art 4 ACHR. For a discussion of different points of view on the relationship between the right to life and the duty to rescue see Efthymios Papastavridis, 'Is there a Right to be Rescued at Sea? A Skeptical View' (2014) *QIL-Questions in International Law* <http://www.qil-qdi.org/is-there-a-right-to-be-rescued-at-sea-a-skeptical-view> accessed 24 August 2017 and Seline Trevisanut, 'Is there a Right to be Rescued at Sea? A Constructive View' (2014) *QIL-Questions in International Law* <http://www.qil-qdi.org/is-there-a-right-to-be-rescued-at-sea-a-constructive-view> accessed 24 August 2017.

[164] UN Human Rights Committee, 'General Comment No 6' in 'Compilation of General Comments and General Recommendations Adopted by Human Rights Treaty Bodies' (27 May 2008) UN Doc HRI/GEN/1/Rev.9 (Vol I). According to the ECtHR it 'forms the supreme value in the hierarchy of human rights'; *Streletz, Kessler and Krenz v Germany* Apps nos 34044/96, 35532/97 and 44801/98 (Judgment (GC) of 22 March 2001) para 94. The IACHR considers that it 'plays a fundamental role in the American Convention, as it is the essential corollary for realizing the other rights'; *Pueblo Bello Massacre v Colombia* (Merits, Reparations and Costs) Inter-American Court of Human Rights Series C No 159 (31 January 2006) para 120.

[165] Positive duties in the context of operations involving migrants are discussed in Stefan Kirchner, Katarzyna Geler-Noch, and Vanessa Frese, 'Coastal State Obligations in the Context of Refugees at Sea under the European Convention on Human Rights' (2015) 20 Ocean and Coastal Law Journal 57, 74–75.

risk of losing their life are assisted, and to take all necessary measures to ensure their safety.[166] It has been convincingly argued that States' duties under Article 2 ECHR would be triggered, for example, in the case where a State knows that a vessel is navigating through waters well-known for piratical attacks.[167] From a procedural point of view, States are required to investigate instances in which an individual has lost his or her life, so as to punish the culprit and avoid similar instances from occurring in the future.[168]

While earlier efforts to bring an action against a State for the violation of Article 2 of the ECHR at sea did not succeed,[169] the right to life recently came under the scrutiny of the ECtHR in a case concerning the death of a crew member of a Lithuanian vessel off the coasts of Brazil. In this case, the ECtHR considered that the positive obligation of the flag State authorities under Article 2 ECHR included taking:

the reasonable steps available to them to secure the evidence concerning the incident, including, *inter alia*, eyewitness testimony, forensic evidence and, where appropriate, an autopsy which provides a complete and accurate record of injury and an objective analysis of clinical findings, including the cause of death ... Any deficiency in the investigation which undermines its ability to establish the cause of death, or identify the person or persons responsible, will risk falling foul of this standard ... Whatever mode is employed, the authorities must act of their own motion once the matter has come to their attention. They cannot leave it to the initiative of the next-of-kin either to lodge a formal complaint or to take responsibility for the conduct of any investigative procedures.[170]

In the circumstances of the case, the duty to investigate entailed the obligation to consider not only the immediate circumstances of the death, but also 'the broader context of [the victim's] working conditions on the [vessel], in order to assess whether there was a link between the allegations of hazardous working conditions and [the victim's] death'.[171]

Turning again to the UNCLOS, it is necessary to refer to 'the other' provision on the protection of life at sea. While this treaty is best known for Article 98 on the protection of the right to life in the case of persons in danger of being lost at sea, it also contains a provision that goes beyond this and has a potentially much broader application. Article 146 of the UNCLOS, in fact, provides that:

---

[166] *Osman* (n 50) paras 115–16.

[167] Stefano Piedimonte Bodini, 'Fighting Maritime Piracy under the European Convention on Human Rights' (2011) 22 EJIL 829, 838; Papastavridis, *The Interception* (n 93) 129–30; Galani (n 105).

[168] *McCann* (n 97) para 161.

[169] In *Xhavara and Others v Italy and Albania* App no 39473/98 (Decision of 11 January 2001), the ECtHR dismissed the application of the victims of the shipwreck of the *Kater I Rades*, a boat which was transporting irregular migrants from Albania towards Italy, mostly because of non exhaustion of domestic remedies. In *Leray and Others v France* App no 44617/98 (Decision of 16 January 2001), the ECtHR considered that the numerous criminal and administrative proceedings enacted in France following the sinking of the cargo vessel *François Vieljeux* complied with France's duties under Art 2 ECHR and that therefore the application was manifestly ill-founded. See Tavernier, 'La Cour' (n 45).

[170] *Bakanova v Lithuania* App no 11167/12 (Judgment of 31 May 2016) para 67.

[171] ibid para 68.

With respect to activities in the Area, necessary measures shall be taken to ensure effective protection of human life. To this end the Authority shall adopt appropriate rules, regulations and procedures to supplement existing international law as embodied in relevant treaties.

The relevance of this provision for the protection of life at sea is paramount, although spatially restricted. First, there is no qualification that diminishes *ab initio* the responsibilities of States and international organizations, in particular the International Seabed Authority. Second, and related to the first point, the protection afforded is particularly broad as it is not limited to situations in which a person is in distress at sea, like the ones envisaged by Article 98 UNCLOS, but can apply to any situation in which life is threatened, for example working and living conditions, the state of repair of the structures used for activities in the Area, as well as the application of enforcement measures.[172] Third, by using the verb 'ensure', the provision points towards a due diligence duty.[173] Fourth, the provision requires that protection be 'effective', thus demanding not only the adoption of legislative measures, but also that of practical measures.

While no case has yet put to the test the scope and content of Article 146, it is suggested that valuable assistance in applying this provision may again come from international human rights law, where it has been recognized that 'the positive obligation to take all appropriate steps to safeguard life for the purposes of Article 2 ... entails above all a primary duty on the State to put in place a legislative and administrative framework designed to provide effective deterrence against threats to the right to life'.[174] This duty applies in particular 'in the case of industrial activities, which by their very nature are dangerous'.[175] In this respect, the ECtHR has clarified the duties of States in the following manner:

In the particular context of dangerous activities special emphasis must be placed on regulations geared to the special features of the activity in question, particularly with regard to the level of the potential risk to human lives. They must govern the licensing, setting up, operation, security and supervision of the activity and must make it compulsory for all those concerned to take practical measures to ensure the effective protection of citizens whose lives might be endangered by the inherent risks. ....

Among these preventive measures particular emphasis should be placed on the public's right to information, as established in the case-law of the Convention institutions. The relevant regulations must also provide for appropriate procedures, taking into account the technical

---

[172] A Soviet proposal to the United Nations Seabed Committee, the work of which was preliminary to the Third United Nations Conference on the Law of the Sea, which eventually led to the adoption of the UNCLOS, suggested the introduction of an article that would ensure that all activities of States on the seabed beyond nations' jurisdiction 'shall be undertaken in compliance with the rules for the protection of human life at sea' (UN doc A/AC.138/43 (22 July 1971). The fact that Art 146 UNCLOS refers to 'human life' generally can be taken to mean that States wanted to ensure not only the safety of people involved in these activities, but also their other rights.

[173] *SDC Opinion* (n 69) para 110. On due diligence duties see Section 3.2.

[174] *Kolyadenko and Others v Russia* Apps nos 17423/05, 20534/05, 20678/05, 23263/05, 24283/05 and 35673/05 (Judgment of 28 February 2012) para 157.

[175] ibid para 158.

aspects of the activity in question, for identifying shortcomings in the processes concerned and any errors committed by those responsible at different levels.[176]

Positive duties under the law of the sea and under international human rights law would in conclusion seem to merge, in an effort to best protect human life at sea. States are required to adopt legislation or take measures imposing on masters of ships flying their flag the duty to proceed to the rescue of those in distress at sea and providing for the creation and management of search and rescue facilities and their coordination among themselves and with those of neighbouring States. They also include operative measures for the implementation of search and rescue facilities and the disembarkation of people rescued. From a procedural point of view, States having jurisdiction are required to investigate allegations that vessels flying their flag or contacted by them have not gone as requested to the rescue of people in distress.

In all cases in which a State has failed to carry out any of the above-mentioned actions, it can be charged with having failed to comply with its obligations under international human rights law. The consequence is that, in those instances in which there are international tribunals competent for determining compliance with a human rights treaty,[177] the State may also be sued before the competent tribunal. This possibility may help to enforce the international duties incumbent upon States, with a further positive repercussion concerning the duties of individuals. Human rights litigation is therefore an option that should be made use of by individuals.

Recourse to human rights mechanisms presents however some difficulties. Apart from procedural issues, including the need to exhaust domestic remedies before submitting a claim to the relevant regional court,[178] two main problems may hinder individuals in getting access to international justice. The first issue is practical and concerns the difficulties in providing evidence. When a vessel in distress is not rescued, the usual regrettable conclusion is that the vessel will sink and the people on board will die, and therefore will obviously not be able to testify as to the lack of assistance from any other vessel.[179] The second issue is legal, and concerns the need

---

[176] ibid paras 158–59. For the application of these principles to a maritime activity see *Vilnes and Others v Norway* Apps nos 52806/09 and 22703/10 (Judgment of 5 December 2013) para 220.

[177] International tribunals with jurisdiction to examine alleged violations of human rights exist only at the regional level in the European, American, and African continents. These are the European Court of Human Rights, established under the ECHR, the Inter-American Court of Human Rights, established under the American Convention on Human Rights (ACHR), 1144 UNTS 144, 22 November 1969 (entered into force 18 July 1978), and the African Court on Human and Peoples' Rights, established under the Protocol to the African Charter on Human and Peoples' Rights on the Establishment of an African Court on Human and Peoples' Rights (Protocol to the ACHPR), Doc OAU/LEG/EXP/AFCHPR/PROT (III), 10 June 1998 (entered into force 25 January 2004). There is no similar tribunal for the Asian continent; furthermore, not all States belonging to America and Africa are parties to the treaties establishing the regional courts.

[178] Art 35(1) ECHR; Art 56(5) African Charter on Human and People's Rights, 1520 UNTS 245, 27 June 1981 (entered into force 21 October 1986).

[179] More generally, investigation of crimes at sea and the collection of evidence is particularly challenging; non-binding guidelines have been adopted by the IMO, see IMO, 'Guidelines on Preservation and Collection of Evidence Following an Allegation of a Serious Crime Having Taken Place on Board a Ship or Following a Report of a Missing Person from a Ship, and Pastoral and Medical Care of Persons Affected' (28 March 2014) IMO Doc A.28/Res.1091. Modern technologies may assist, as they may provide evidence, for example, of the location of the endangered vessel and that of other

to establish a valid jurisdictional link between the persons who risk their life at sea and the State that should act in order to protect that person's right to life. It is however suggested that these difficulties can be overcome thorugh a combined application of human rights law and the law of the sea.

4.3 Options for further integration

While States undoubtedly have negative obligations towards people at sea, it is the positive obligations that assume particular relevance in this field. In light of the dangerous nature of the marine environment, as well as the fact that violations of individuals' rights often occurs at the hands of private actors, positive duties, including duties of due diligence, are paramount in furthering the protection of people at sea.[180] The jurisprudence of both human rights bodies and law of the sea bodies seems to point towards the same direction, requiring the State to act and achieve protection, not only by adopting the necessary laws and regulations, but also by controlling their application and punishing their violation, be it the result of the actions of State organs or that of private persons.

In light of the vagueness of most human rights and UNCLOS provisions concerning positive duties of States towards people at sea, it is necessary to seek guidance elsewhere. There are two main sources of law that provide assistance when seeking to make States' duties more precise, and therefore more operative. The first is the jurisprudence of human rights and law of the sea tribunals and quasi-judiciary bodies. All these bodies concur that States may be under the duty to ensure that non-State actors adhere to certain standards of treatment of individuals. Furthermore, they all concur in some way that positive obligations need to be interpreted and applied in light of the specific elements of the case, so as to ensure that the protection granted by them is effective and tailored to the needs of the person involved, as well as to the specificities of the marine environment. At the same time, they recognize that positive obligations should be realistic and should not create an excessive or disproportionate burden for States. The development of the standard of 'due diligence' goes in this direction.

The second tool that can be used to concretize obligations is the adoption of technical instruments, mostly in the field of maritime law and labour law. These instruments flesh out the duties of States by providing for the specific measures that States must adopt to comply with the broad objectives of safety, security, and respect of labour rights. The detailed nature of these instruments, together with the fact that they are generally developed by highly skilled technical bodies with practical knowledge and a wide representation of the various actors concerned in their implementation, makes them particularly fit for purpose. It is, therefore, hoped that

---

vessels nearby; see Charles Heller, Lorenzo Pezzani, and Situ Studio, 'Report on the "Left-To-Die Boat"' <http://www.forensic-architecture.org/wp-content/uploads/2014/05/FO-report.pdf> accessed 24 August 2017.

[180] Galani (n 105) 80–81 makes the point in the context of piracy and the protection of seafarers' rights.

international human rights bodies may in the future make use of technical instruments as useful tools in examining compliance with positive obligations of States.

At the same time, and in order to enhance this cross-fertilization between legal regimes, it could be useful if more cases concerning non-compliance by States with their human rights obligations at sea were to be brought to the attention of international human rights bodies, and if these cases were argued using the full array of international law norms that are available, which includes, as demonstrated, not only those contained in strictly human rights-oriented instruments, but also those found in other treaties that purport to regulate conduct by States in order to protect humans more generally.

Issues may still remain concerning conduct which, while complying with treaty standards, is deemed not to satisfy the test adopted for positive obligations by human rights bodies. This problem becomes evident in search and rescue operations. In this case, it is open to debate whether it is sufficient for a State to create a SAR zone and to coordinate rescue, or whether the State should also ensure that people are disembarked in a safe country. While human rights tribunals seized with the issue might provide useful guidance, it is eventually to be hoped that clear rules will be incorporated into universally binding instruments.

5. Dividing and Tailoring

Under most international human rights treaties, a State 'undertakes to respect and to ensure to all individuals within its territory and subject to its jurisdiction the rights recognized' in the treaty itself.[181] Does this mean that each State must respect and ensure *all* rights to *all* persons *all* the time? This is, in a nutshell, the issue of severability that has been alluded to already.[182]

The issue is particularly relevant at sea, where the interaction between States and individuals is often occasional and limited in time. This circumstance begs the question whether States that occasionally exercise jurisdiction over people at sea should ensure to those people the full range of rights granted by human rights law. For example, should a State visiting a vessel suspected of being engaged in the slave trade on the high seas take positive measures to ensure the right to education for those on board? Or, in a different context, should the coastal State take steps to ensure freedom of religion for those on board ships exercising the right of innocent passage through its territorial waters?

Severability is inherently connected with jurisdictional limitations. While it is generally accepted that States have to comply with the full array of their obligations with respect to individuals present in their territory, it is debatable whether this obligation extends to areas outside their territory, where they exercise only limited

---

[181] Art 2(1) ICCPR.
[182] Chapter 3, Section 5.1.2.2. Severability is also linked to the admissibility of reservations to human rights instruments. This issue will not be pursued here. In general see UN Human Rights Committee, 'General Comment No 24' (11 November 1994) UN Doc CCPR/C/21/Rev.1/Add.6.

sovereign rights—or no sovereign rights at all. The exercise of temporary and limited power over an area or a person may make it practically impossible to undertake all those positive acts that are often required to fully fulfil human rights obligations. At the same time, exercising jurisdiction or undertaking activities beyond the strict limits allowed under the specific circumstances might infringe upon the rights of another State, for example the territorial integrity and independence of the State in the maritime areas where these acts take place.

In providing an answer to the issue of severability, two opposite and conflicting needs require conciliation. On the one hand, it is argued that the full application of international human rights treaties, albeit in a limited territorial sphere, would consolidate their content and would avoid the possibility of States deciding which rules bind them, picking and choosing those that they consider compatible with other interests.[183] Those who defend severability, on the other hand, take into account the need to ensure that some basic rights of individuals are respected, even under circumstances where it is practically impossible to ensure the enjoyment of all human rights. It would indeed be incompatible with the object and the scope of human rights law to allow States to derogate from their international human rights obligations simply by undertaking action under circumstances that do not allow for a full protection of all human rights.

Following an initial rejection of the severability of human rights,[184] the ECtHR has recently reversed its position and has accepted that:

[w]henever the State through its agents operating outside its territory exercises control and authority over an individual, and thus jurisdiction, the State is under an obligation under Article 1 to secure to that individual the rights and freedoms under Section 1 of the Convention *that are relevant to the situation of that individual.* In this sense, therefore, the Court has now accepted that Convention rights can be 'divided and tailored'.[185]

While this settles the point concerning the severability of human rights, it remains to be considered when human rights can be divided and how they can be tailored.[186] Much will depend on the circumstances of the case, but there are three typical situations at sea: those in which a State enjoys general jurisdiction; those in which it can exercise only functional jurisdiction, albeit on a continual basis; and those, finally, in which a State exercises only limited temporary power.

Beginning with the latter, when States exercise jurisdiction or control over a vessel in the context of the right of visit, interdiction operations, salvage operations, or pollution control, they are under the obligation, in the spirit and words of the ECtHR, to secure to individuals involved the rights and freedoms that are relevant to their

---

[183] *Banković and Others v Belgium and 16 Other Contracting States* App no 52207/99 (Decision (GC) of 12 December 2001) para 75.

[184] ibid para 75.

[185] *Hirsi* (n 35) para 74 (emphasis added). See also *Al-Skeini* (n 104) para 137.

[186] Kirby Abbott, 'A Brief Overview of Legal Interoperability Challenges for NATO Arising from the Interrelationship between IHL and IHRL in Light of the European Convention on Human Rights' (2014) 96 International Review of the Red Cross 107, 126, speaks of 'the degree of control and temporal scope required to trigger a particular right'.

situations. In such instances, human rights that typically come into play are the right
to life, the right not to be tortured or to be subjected to inhuman or degrading treatment with the corollary *non-refoulement* principle, the right to personal freedom,
and the (procedural) right to an effective remedy. If the State arrests the individuals
and brings them onto its territory or holds them under the permanent custody of
its agents, the range of applicable rights will progressively expand until it includes
all human rights.

Other rights may also be relevant, however, if the State aims to preclude individuals enjoying their most fundamental rights. In the *Women on Waves* judgment, the
ECtHR found that the interdiction of the applicants' vessel by the Portuguese Navy
violated their freedom of expression, protected under Article 10 ECHR.[187] In that
case, in fact, a limitation of the freedom of expression was not a by-product of the
State's law enforcement activity, but was the main aim of State action. The potential
applicability of freedom of expression and freedom of assembly at sea was confirmed
by the *Drieman* case, although the ECtHR reached a different conclusion in the
concrete circumstances of the case.[188] All the same, the fact that the Court considered in the merits whether there had been a violation of Articles 10 and 11 ECHR
confirms their applicability at sea.

Turning to situations of the first type, the premise is that the flag State and the
coastal State (in its territorial waters and with respect to installations and platforms
in the exclusive economic zone and the continental shelf) enjoy general jurisdiction
concerning all matters.[189] It logically follows that, since their jurisdiction is permanent and general, they are also under the obligation to respect and ensure all human
rights for all individuals.

As far as the flag State is concerned, the UNCLOS and customary international
law require it to 'exercise its jurisdiction and control in administrative, technical
and social matters' over vessels flying its flag and persons on board.[190] Secondly,
while it has been claimed that it is extremely cumbersome, if not impractical, for
States to control what happens on board vessels navigating on the other side of the
globe,[191] this is not sufficient to exonerate a State from its legal obligations. States
are not obliged to grant their flag to vessels and, if they do choose to do so, they exercise a right rather than a duty. Nationality is granted to vessels at the discretion of
the State, and States know that the exercise of this right entails legal consequences,

---

[187] *Women on Waves and Others v Portugal* App no 31276/05 (Judgment of 3 February 2009).
[188] In *Drieman and Others v Norway* App no 33678/96 (Decision of 4 May 2000), the ECtHR
concluded that the fact that Norway had arrested Greenpeace activists that were taking actions against
whaling vessels in Norway's exclusive economic zone did not violate the activists rights under Arts 10
and 11 ECHR. The reason was that 'in finding that the public interest in taking the contested measures
against the applicants were preponderant, the authorities of the respondent State acted within their margin of appreciation. The Court finds that the interference complained of was supported by relevant and
sufficient reasons, was proportionate for the purposes of Articles 10 § 2 and 11 § 2 of the Convention
and could reasonably be viewed as necessary in a democratic society' (ibid).
[189] cf Art 2(1) UNCLOS; Art 92(1) UNCLOS; Art 60 UNCLOS; and Art 80 UNCLOS.
[190] Art 94(1) UNCLOS.
[191] Marko Milanovic, *Extraterritorial Application of Human Rights Treaties. Law, Principles, and
Policy* (OUP 2011) 170.

which include the obligation to effectively exercise jurisdiction and control. The practical difficulties encountered by States in this respect are well known before any decision is made. If therefore States choose to exercise their right, they cannot evade their obligations by simply referring to practical difficulties, as has been recognized by the ECtHR recently.[192]

More complex issues may arise with respect to the applicability of the coastal State's jurisdiction to individuals in its territorial sea and the identification of the ensuing duties to protect these people. While in this maritime area the coastal State exercises sovereignty, other States enjoy the right of innocent passage for their ships. The right of innocent passage thus limits the sovereignty enjoyed by the coastal State. In an effort to balance these two rights, the UNCLOS promotes a minimalist approach to the exercise of criminal and civil jurisdiction by the coastal State against vessels flying a different flag.[193] Pursuant to this approach, the coastal State should not exercise its jurisdiction over vessels exercising the rights of innocent passage, save in exceptional cases only. While this approach may be in line with the desire not to overburden navigation through the territorial sea, it is not very satisfactory from a human rights perspective. Abstention from the exercise of jurisdiction would in fact mean that the coastal State would not have either the right or the duty to control compliance with human rights on board vessels exercising the right of innocent passage. In respect of gross violations of fundamental human rights in particular, this would however frustrate the aim of these rights. In conclusion, if the qualifications imposed by the law of the sea are transposed to the context of human rights, the result is not one of 'dividing and tailoring' human rights, but rather one of trying to exclude the obligation to ensure human rights.

Even more problematic is the limitation posed by Article 27(5) UNCLOS,[194] which may produce particularly unwelcome effects in the case of gross violations of human rights. Consider, for example, the case of a vessel, the crew of which are systematically subjected to inhuman and degrading treatment that may amount to torture, which proceeds to enter the territorial sea. The coastal State would be precluded from intervening, even if the vessel is in its 'territory' and members of the crew have contacted the local authorities and have asked for help, if the inhuman treatment stops just before entering its territorial waters and then recommences as soon as the vessel has passed through them.[195] It is true that the coastal State may always ask for the authorization of the flag State to intervene, but the outcome will be uncertain as the latter may not only reject the request (evidently breaching its

---

[192] *Bakanova* (n 170) para 74.   [193] Arts 27 and 28 UNCLOS, respectively.

[194] According to this Article, 'Except as provided in Part XII [on protection of the marine environment] or with respect to violations of laws and regulations adopted in accordance with Part V [relating to the exclusive economic zone], the coastal State may not take any steps on board a foreign ship passing through the territorial sea to arrest any person or to conduct any investigation in connection with any crime committed before the ship entered the territorial sea, if the ship, proceeding from a foreign port, is only passing through the territorial sea without entering internal waters'.

[195] One may question whether the coastal State will have any interest to intervene. This may happen not only if there is a link with the perpetrator or the victim, but also in case the State considers that a claim might be brought against it in front of an international tribunal.

human rights obligations) but the State may also simply avoid responding to the request.

One solution may be to refer to the *jus cogens* nature of some duties deriving from human rights, such as the prohibition of torture, the prohibition of slavery, and the duty to protect life, that would make them prevail over the content of Article 27(5) UNCLOS. Following this argument, the duty of the coastal State to intervene and take action against vessels exercising the right of innocent passage in its territorial sea would depend on the type of violation that takes place on board the vessel. Whenever the acts are sufficiently serious to threaten the violation of a *jus cogens* norm, then the coastal State would have the duty to intervene and protect the people concerned.

An additional argument would be to consider that any behaviour violating human rights law, in particular if it included the commission of an international crime according to international criminal law, would breach the peace and good order of the coastal State. This would determine the inapplicability of Article 17 UNCLOS because of the violation of the conditions imposed by Article 19(1) UNCLOS, rendering passage non-innocent. Consequently, the safeguards for the vessel contained in Articles 27 and 28 UNCLOS would be inapplicable,[196] and the duty of the sovereign coastal State to intervene in its territory would revert back to its full extent.

In conclusion, when assessing the extent of the coastal State's human rights duties in its territorial sea, a distinction needs to be drawn between people on board vessels exercising the right of innocent passage and those in any other circumstances. In the latter case, the sovereignty of the coastal State is unrestrained and thus the State is under an obligation to protect the full array of human rights of people in its territorial sea. In the former case, the duties of the coastal State may be restricted due to the right of innocent passage which inherently restricts the sovereignty of that State in its territorial sea. In this respect, it can be argued that the coastal State has at least those duties deriving from human rights norms that have acquired the status of *jus cogens*. Further duties to protect human rights would stem from a qualification of the illegal conduct as a breach of the peace and good order of the territorial State. While this additional argument would help to enlarge the cases in which the coastal State can intervene, it needs to be applied with caution, lest it may be used as an excuse to intervene and unnecessarily limit the right of innocent passage.

The case of installations and platforms in the territorial sea and exclusive economic zone is simpler, since in this case the jurisdiction of the coastal State is exclusive and there is no other State that may exercise jurisdiction.[197] The coastal State is therefore under the obligation not only to respect, but also to ensure the full enjoyment of all human rights for all persons on board these objects. Legislation that purports to exclude the applicability of national rules for the protection of specific

---

[196] It is relevant to note that Arts 27 and 28 UNCLOS apply only to ships exercising the right of innocent passage, as they are contained in a subsection of Part II, Section 3, relating to the right of innocent passage.

[197] Art 60(2) UNCLOS.

human and labour rights has therefore to be assessed in this light, so as to avoid a violation of the applicable human rights.[198]

Finally, the case that leaves a wider margin of uncertainty as to the possibility of dividing and tailoring human rights obligations towards people at sea concerns the second category identified above, that is, cases in which the State exercises only functional jurisdiction, albeit on a continuous basis. This is essentially the case in respect of the jurisdictional rights exercised by the coastal State over vessels in its exclusive economic zone and continental shelf.[199] In this case, it is not possible to determine in advance the extent of the human rights that the State has the duty to safeguard. The State's duties will in fact depend on the specific circumstances of the case and on the specific powers that that State may exercise towards the people and vessels involved.

Taking for example the case of people fishing in the exclusive economic zone, it has already been argued that the coastal State has jurisdiction over them, even if they are working on board vessels that fly a different flag.[200] The jurisdiction of the coastal State extends to all issues relating to fisheries, which also includes the conditions of work on board the vessel. This power is inferred from the rights to regulate enjoyed by the coastal State, in particular the right to adopt laws and regulations concerning, among others, the 'licensing of fishermen, fishing vessels and equipment',[201] 'specifying information required of fishing vessels',[202] 'terms and conditions relating to joint ventures or other cooperative arrangements',[203] and 'requirements for the training of personnel'.[204] It is therefore not excessive to consider that the coastal State has the duty to protect the basic human and labour rights of the people working in its exclusive economic zone, the more so since the coastal State has undoubtedly the right to also enforce its laws and regulations.[205] In addition, it could be further argued that the coastal State also has the duty to protect and ensure those rights, the fulfilment of which depends on its actions. Thus, for example, rights relating to the disembarkation of fishers—such as the right to recreation on land—could also fall under the coastal State's duties.

6. The Special Character of the Sea and its Incidence on the Nature and Content of Legal Obligations

In concluding this overview of the type and content of State duties owed towards people at sea, it is appropriate to address an issue sometimes raised by States: whether the special nature of the marine environment would allow for exceptions in the application of human rights.

---

[198] Case C-347/10 *Salemink v Raad van bestuur van het Uitvoeringsinstituut werknemersverzekeringen* [2012] ECLI:EU:C:2012:17, paras 35–36.

[199] Arts 56 and 77 UNCLOS, respectively.   [200] Chapter 3, Section 5.1.2.2.

[201] Art 62(4)(a) UNCLOS.   [202] Art 62(4)(e) UNCLOS.

[203] Art 62(4)(i) UNCLOS.   [204] Art 62(4)(j) UNCLOS.

[205] Art. 62(4)(k) and 73(1) UNCLOS.

In general terms, this proposition is untenable. A general limitation of the applicability of human rights would be contrary to both the universality of human rights duties and the scope of international human rights treaties. It is however true that factual circumstances and practical issues may require that States take into account the special nature of the marine environment in the application of human rights obligations. This may result in one of two separate, and apparently opposite, consequences. On the one hand, State duties may be broadened to take into account the dangerous nature of the marine environment. On the other hand, the practicalities of being at sea may impact upon the full enjoyment of some human rights.

Turning to the first instance, the special nature of the marine environment may sometimes require additional action by States. Protection of the right to life, one of the most fundamental human rights prevalent in cultures around the world and provided for in all general human rights treaties, clearly illustrates this point.[206] In addition to all other obligations which bind States, the inherently dangerous nature of the marine environment requires particularly pervasive and comprehensive positive action to be taken at times. First, States must require the masters of vessels flying their flag 'to render assistance to any person found at sea in danger of being lost' and 'to proceed with all possible speed to the rescue of persons in distress'.[207] Second, they must 'promote the establishment, operation and maintenance of an adequate and effective search and rescue service regarding safety on and over the sea'.[208] This goes far beyond what is provided in traditional human rights treaties. Third, States must be precautious and adopt all measures necessary to ensure safety at sea.[209] These measures are significantly detailed in relevant international treaties such as the SOLAS, which apply not only to States parties but also, thanks to the framing of Article 94(5) UNCLOS, to all other States. As a result of this complex framework of norms and cross-references, States are required, not only to act to save the lives of people in distress at sea, but also to enact preventive measures concerning the preparation of search and rescue facilities and the safety of navigation, even before any people find themselves in a situation where the right to life is endangered.

In other cases, the peculiarities of the marine environment and the modes of navigation may impose some factual constraints on the full enjoyment of some human rights. It is intuitive that the limited space on board vessels necessarily restricts the movement of crew and passengers and may also reduce private space. This does not mean however that the freedom of movement and the right to private life do not apply at sea, but rather that these freedoms and rights will in fact undergo some restriction. Labour and maritime treaties, including the MLC and SOLAS, take this into account and aim to elaborate a regime that strikes a fair balance between human rights and the practical realities of life at sea.

---

[206] See Section 4.2.
[207] Art 98(1) UNCLOS.
[208] Art 98(2) UNCLOS.
[209] Art 94(3) UNCLOS.

7. Turning Rights into Duties

A question that arises at this point concerns the type of change prompted by the impact of human rights on the law of the sea. For instance, is it just a quantitative change, which has increased the number of single instances in which international law now imposes duties which are owed by States towards people at sea? Or is it also a qualitative one, which has affected the fundamental relationship between States and people at sea and the way in which they interact? My submission is that both effects can be observed. On the one hand, there is undoubtedly an increase in duties owed by States to people at sea. This aspect has been dealt with in Section 3 of this chapter. On the other hand, a qualitative change has happened, which is slowly transforming the rights of States to exercise power at sea into duties to protect persons, whenever a human right is at issue. This section will discuss this shift.

Historically, international law has mostly been concerned with the extent and content of States' *rights* at sea. As discussed in Chapter 2, it is the law of the sea that provides the framework of reference for activities at sea. Initial rules in this field include the freedom of navigation and the sovereignty exercised by the coastal State over the narrow belt of waters adjacent to its coast.[210] As the law developed, more rules attributing powers and rights came into being. The rules on the continental shelf and, later, the exclusive economic zone, aim to attribute the right to exploit resources in waters close to its land territory to the respective coastal State. The principle that the flag State enjoys exclusive jurisdiction over vessels flying its flag on the high seas attributes the power to control activities on board vessels to that State, as well as the right to have its ships sail in waters around the world.

The discourse of rights also prevailed when new or intensifying threats to States emerged and States had to address them. Faced with the menace of piracy, a new law of the sea rule developed, according to which each State has the *right* to seize a pirate vessel and all persons on board.[211] Later on, it was accepted that States had the *right* to visit ships suspected of being engaged in the slave trade.[212] In more recent times, the coastal State was given the *right* to adopt laws and regulations for the prevention, reduction, and control of marine pollution from foreign vessels in its territorial sea,[213] as well as the *right* to inspect and arrest vessels that do not comply with such standards.[214]

The acceptance of rights at the international level was thus viewed as a welcome way of expanding States' powers without imposing burdens they were not prepared to accept. Essentially, rights leave the State free to determine whether it wishes to act or not, whether it is inclined to regulate, or whether it would rather leave matters to

---

[210] Chapter 2, Section 7.1.   [211] Now codified in Art 105 UNCLOS.
[212] Art XLII Slave Trade and Importation into Africa of Firearms, Ammunition, and Spirituous Liquors (General Act of Brussels) (adopted 2 July 1890, entered into force 31 August 1891) (Brussels General Act), later implicitly recalled in Art 46 of the ILC draft articles on the law of the sea (ILC, 'Articles concerning the Law of the Sea with commentaries' in *Yearbook of the International Law Commission*, vol II (1956) 265, 284), in Art 22(1)(b) HSC and Art 110(1)(b) UNCLOS.
[213] Art 21(1)(f) UNCLOS and Art 211(4) UNCLOS.   [214] Art 220(2) UNCLOS.

resolve themselves. The existence of a right does not in any way oblige the State to make use of its right; a State may very well decide not to exercise the right.

Within this paradigm, that partly permeates also the UNCLOS, limitations to a State's rights were to be inferred from the rights of other States, in a bilateral relationship that always involved two States—and no other actor. For example, a State's freedom of manoeuvring was limited by the other States' freedom of manoeuvring; a State's freedom of constructing artificial islands was checked by the correlative freedom of navigation of all other States;[215] a State's right to enact legislation for the protection of the marine environment in its exclusive economic zone was constrained by the freedom of navigation that all other States enjoyed therein;[216] and so on. The 'due regard' duties of coastal States and third States in the exclusive economic zone, introduced by Articles 56(2) and 58(3) UNCLOS, respectively, provide an exemplary illustration of this synallagmatic relationship.

A variation of this pattern occurred only when collective interests started to receive the attention of States. At the end of the nineteenth century, the abolition of the slave trade and the effort to eradicate slavery were the foundations upon which a *duty* of States to take measures at sea was premised. Thus States 'engage[d] to adopt efficient measures to prevent the unlawful use of their flag, and to prevent the transportation of slaves on vessels authorized to fly their colors'.[217] However, it was mainly in the twentieth century that humanitarian (and environmental)[218] considerations prompted a linguistic and semantic change in international law,[219] which slowly seeped into legal instruments relating to the sea.

The settling of the human rights discourse and the attention devoted to the human element has now impacted rules pertaining to the law of the sea. The view that the State is now 'an entity . . . entrusted with protecting the welfare of the human

---

[215] Art 60(7) UNCLOS.

[216] Achieved through the reference to 'generally accepted international rules and standards established through the competent international organization or general diplomatic conference' (Art 211(4) UNCLOS), which are considered to afford an acceptable balance of different interests.

[217] Art XXV Brussels General Act.

[218] This is indeed the field where the greatest impact has taken place. Environmental considerations were among the first to trigger a revolution in the framing of 'structural' law of the sea rules (Catherine Redgwell, 'From Permission to Prohibition: The 1982 Convention on the Law of the Sea and Protection of the Marine Environment' in David Freestone, Richard Barnes, and David Ong (eds), *The Law of the Sea: Progress and Prospects* (OUP 2006) 180, 181). Thus, Art 192 UNCLOS enshrines the obligation for all States to protect and preserve the marine environment. Although it can be easily argued that a clean marine environment and a sustainable use of marine resources would stem benefits for all States, as currently drafted, the duty contained in Art 192 UNCLOS is an absolute duty, unconnected to correspondent rights of other States.

[219] On the role of human rights as providing a paradigm not based on reciprocity ILC, 'Fragmentation of International Law: Difficulties Arising from the Diversification and Expansion of International Law. Report of the Study Group of the International Law Commission Finalized by Martti Koskenniemi' (13 April 2006) UN Doc A/CN.4/L.682 (Koskenniemi Report) para 391; Bruno Simma, 'From Bilateralism to Community Interest in International Law' (1997) 250 Recueil des Cours 217; Sandesh Sivakumaran, 'Impact on the Structure of International Obligations' in Menno T Kamminga and Martin Scheinin (eds), *The Impact of Human Rights Law on General International Law* (OUP 2009) 133. On the effect of community interests on law of the sea instruments see Yoshifumi Tanaka, 'Protection of Community Interests in International Law: the Case of the Law of the Sea' (2011) 15 Max Planck Yearbook of United Nations Law 329.

being for whom responsibility has been assigned to it'[220] is reflected in the elaboration of rules that impose on States the duty to take action and protect people's
rights and interests. In the law of the sea, the significant loss of life due to maritime
casualties generated one of the first law of the sea rules to contain an absolute and
unbound duty for States: the duty to render assistance to persons in distress at sea.
The introduction in the HSC[221] and the UNCLOS[222] of a duty to render assistance
at sea and to save human lives is not tied to a corresponding right of another State,
but stems from the considerations of humanity which had been invoked by the ICJ
in the *Corfu Channel* case.[223]

It should be noted at this point that the introduction of duties took place alongside
the provision of rights, and occasionally without coordination. It is therefore sometimes hard to reconcile the duty with the right. One may cite, by way of example,
the difficulties in coordinating the duty to protect the marine environment under
Article 192 UNCLOS, with the fact that Article 56 of the same treaty provides the
right (jurisdiction) but not the duty to use this right. The super-imposition of rules
on the same matter having a different content—'right' provisions in comparison
to 'duty' provisions—now urges the interpreter to make sense of this accumulation
and to determine whether certain conduct is only discretionary, or whether it is
compulsory.

In some cases, treaty provisions developed in recent decades contain an indication as to whether certain conduct is mandatory or discretionary. The duties
of the flag State provide a well-known illustration. In the past, the exercise of
jurisdiction by a State over a vessel that had its nationality was the object of a
'right' provision. Accordingly, the flag State was of course free to establish rules
concerning living conditions, the treatment of seafarers, and the provision of
adequate training. But it had no obligation under international law to do so.
This lack of duties and the ensuing lack of responsibility led to gross abuses
that eventually became unacceptable as civil, economic, and labour rights were
recognized internationally. As a consequence, abuses were eventually addressed,
first in the 1958 Geneva codification effort[224] and then during the drafting of

---

[220] Tomuschat, *Human Rights* (n 47) 2.   [221] Art 12 HSC.   [222] Art 98 UNCLOS.
[223] *Corfu Channel* (n 12), see Section 2.2.
[224] In 1956, the ILC proposed that a State should be 'required to issue for ships under its jurisdiction
regulations to ensure safety at sea with regard *inter alia* to ... crew which must be adequate to the needs
of the ship and enjoy reasonable labor conditions' (Art 34(1) ILC Draft Articles on the Law of the Sea).
The need to ensure that the flag State exercises effective control over the vessel and the people on board
also in social and labour issues formed the object of discussion and proposals during the First United
Nations Conference on the Law of the Sea. For example, Denmark considered that 'authorization to fly
a flag should entail appropriate obligations in respect of the ship concerned on the part of the country of
registration. Those obligations implied complete jurisdiction and the exercise of effective control, especially with regard to internationally adopted standards of safety and social conditions of the crew. In view
of the progress that had been made over the past fifty years in establishing such standards, states must
have control over ships flying their flag, in order that they might give effect to the international instruments in force.' (United Nations Conference on the Law of the Sea. Official Records, vol IV, UN Doc
A/CONF.13/40, 5). See also the declarations of Italy (ibid 10), the ILO (ibid 26–27), Uruguay (ibid
30), and France (ibid 61) as well as, for a partly different position, those of the United Kingdom (ibid
58) and Israel (ibid 60). The discussion produced two amendments, specifying that the flag States had
to exercise jurisdiction in 'administrative, technical and social matters' (ibid 61), and that they had to

the UNCLOS,[225] by transforming the right of the flag State to exercise jurisdiction into a duty of the flag State to do so. Thus, today Article 94(2)(b) UNCLOS requires the flag State to 'assume jurisdiction ... over each ship flying its flag and its master, officers and crew in respect of ... social matters'. Eventually, the complete abstention from regulation is an option that States can no longer take.

In conclusion, the emergence of human rights has produced changes in the language and substance of law of the sea instruments, mainly by the introduction of duties for States to act to protect people. This has occurred both with the insertion of provisions aiming at the protection of human rights into law of the sea instruments, as in the case of Article 22(1)(f) of the United Nations Agreement for the Implementation of the Provisions of the United Nations Convention on the Law of the Sea of 10 December 1982 relating to the Conservation and Management of Straddling Fish Stocks and Highly Migratory Fish Stocks (FSA), and with the adoption of ad hoc treaties that purport to protect specific rights, such as labour rights in the MLC, but also with provisions which aim to punish conduct that threatens the safety of people at sea, as in the case of acts against the safety of navigation addressed by the SUA Convention.[226]

However, it is also argued that the existence of human rights has produced a further, unexpected, and unprecedented impact on the law of the sea that has received little attention. Before turning to this impact, it is best to address and dispense one possible misconception. Such an impact does not actually relate to the allocation of rights and duties between States at sea, as negotiated during the Third United Nations Conference on the Law of the Sea and as incorporated in the UNCLOS. Indeed, the nature and main purpose of human rights is not to change the relationship of States *inter se*, but rather to detail the rights of individuals that States must protect. The human rights regime is not so much interested in establishing the State that must protect a certain duty, but rather in obliging a State—which is identified on the basis of rules deriving from other regimes—to engage in, or abstain from, certain conduct.[227] Human rights therefore have not affected the *allocation* of competence, in line with the general way that human rights law operates.

---

take measures concerning the 'manning of ships and labour conditions for crews taking into account the applicable international labour instruments'. On the latter wording see the explanation by the United Kingdom (ibid 77).

[225] Nordquist, Nandan, and Rosenne (n 148) 140, and documents cited therein. It is interesting to note that, apart from enlarging on the duties of the flag State provided by Art 10 HSC in what was to become Art 94 UNCLOS, during the negotiations in the Third United Nations Conference on the Law of the Sea, the initial reference to 'applicable international labour instruments', which was copied and pasted from Art 10(1)(b) HSC, was replaced by a reference to 'applicable international instruments' in what was to become Art 94(3)(b) UNCLOS (Nordquist, Nandan, and Rosenne (n 148) 143). This change has visibly broadened the scope of Art 94(3)(b), which now includes not only the ILO instruments, but also the relevant IMO instruments (Nordquist, Nandan, and Rosenne (n 148) 147–48) and arguably human rights instruments, such as the ICESCR and the International Convention on the Protection of the Rights of All Migrant Workers and Members of Their Families.

[226] Further examples are provided in Chapter 1, Section 4.

[227] This approach is however now much softened through the elaboration of an autonomous notion of jurisdiction, proper to human rights law. Chapter 3, Section 2.3.

Rather, human rights are affecting the *existence* of obligations at sea, as well as on land. As already mentioned above, the nature of the rules belonging to the two regimes is different. Law of the sea rules, or at least the basic principles of the discipline, are mostly permissory in nature, granting States the right to exercise specific powers. In contrast, when viewed from the standpoint of States, human rights law is almost entirely composed of obligatory rules, which impose duties upon States which require specific conduct. My submission is that the obligatory nature of human rights law is significantly affecting law of the sea rules, and is one of the driving forces behind the current transformation of many rights into duties. In several cases, duties under human rights law actually oblige States to engage in activities that otherwise would be only discretionary, according to law of the sea provisions.

As a consequence, it is argued at this point, whenever a State has the right to exercise a power under a law of the sea provision, and the exercise of that power is instrumental to the protection of the right of a person, then that State is under the obligation to take such action. This is a consequence of the joint reading of rules on jurisdiction under law of the sea and human rights law. As has been discussed in Chapter 3, law of the sea provisions determine when a State has *de jure* jurisdiction. In turn, *de jure* jurisdiction is the basis for the application of States' duties deriving from human rights law. Accordingly, whenever a State has jurisdiction over an individual (eg on the basis of a law of the sea provision) then that State has the duty to protect the human rights of that individual. This duty derives *from human rights law* and trumps the right or freedom originally provided for by the law of the sea provision, which may have been used as the basis for the determination of jurisdiction.

It is true, as has just been discussed, that in some cases it is the law of the sea itself that accompanies duties to jurisdiction. However, the point made here goes further: the duty to take measures to ensure the protection of human rights applies not only when the duty to act is endorsed in a law of the sea provision, but also when the law of the sea rule envisages only a right, and not a duty. In short, the existence of rights of individuals is now turning States' rights at sea into duties. The interplay between human rights and the law of the sea just described goes beyond the express provision of duties in the UNCLOS and other treaties, such as Article 94 and Article 98 UNCLOS. It produces its consequences also in cases when there is no specific treaty obligation according to which a State must undertake action to protect people at sea—as long as there is an identifiable right that an individual enjoys and a State that has the duty to protect that person. In other words, a systemic reading of the different rights and duties of States brings with it the result that the State must intervene in many more areas than it used to do.

This conclusion, it is further argued, bears consequences for all those situations which have not yet formed the object of a normative update, whereby States' duties are explicitly stated. This is particularly relevant in respect of installations and structures in a State's coastal zones. According to the law of the sea, the coastal State has the *right* to exercise exclusive jurisdiction over artificial islands, installations, and structures in its exclusive economic zone and continental shelf. According to human rights law, the State *must* protect and promote respect for the human rights of all people under its jurisdiction. Therefore, the coastal State is under a duty to protect the rights of people who are on these artificial islands, structures and installations, notwithstanding the fact that no treaty has yet been adopted to provide an obligation similar to that contained in Article 94 UNCLOS. In other words, the coastal State is not only granted the right to exercise its exclusive jurisdiction, as provided in Article 60 UNCLOS, but it may also be considered as having the duty to actually take measures whenever they are necessary to comply with its international human rights obligations.[228]

The same argument could be advanced concerning the coastal State's duty to undertake action to protect the human rights of people fishing in its exclusive economic zone, even if they work on board vessels flying a different flag. This duty derives from its sovereign rights over resources in the exclusive economic zone[229] and from the ensuing jurisdictional powers, which allow the coastal State to adopt measures to regulate different aspects of fishing.[230] As already discussed, according to Article 62 UNCLOS the coastal State has jurisdiction over people on board fishing vessels that fish in its exclusive economic zone.[231] It follows that the coastal State may impose the duty to respect human and labour rights upon these vessels, even if they sail under a different flag. In turn, since the respect for human rights is mandatory under international law, the coastal State will be under an obligation to act so that these rights are protected. Whilst it is true that Article 62 UNCLOS does not *require* the coastal State to regulate the humanitarian and social aspects of fishing in its waters, it does *allow* the State to do so. A lack of regulation in this respect, while compatible with Article 62 UNCLOS if read by itself, would not be consistent with the obligations accepted by the State under the ICCPR, ICESCR, or other global or regional treaties it is a party to.

Any objections to this spreading of duties could be based either on logical or on practical considerations. From a logical point of view, it could be objected that reading a duty in a right-based provision would actually go against the content of the former and would, as such, produce an interpretation inconsistent with the object and scope of the provision.

There is certainly some weight behind such a remark. On the one hand, it is true that rights are often viewed as being the opposite of duties and that the fundamental point in granting a right to a State is to give that State the freedom of choice, that is the power to decide whether to exercise that right or not. In this sense, a duty is the opposite of a right, as it precludes any choice. However, the choice that is inherent in a right could be stretched to also include a renunciation to this faculty through the acceptance of a duty.[232]

---

[228] This was recently recognised by the ECJ in *Salemink* (n 198).

[229] Art 56(1)(a) UNCLOS.

[230] Art 62 UNCLOS. See also Art 73 UNCLOS and Nordquist, Nandan, and Rosenne (n 148) 126, according to which 'the flag state and the coastal state have concurrent jurisdiction on ships (including fishing vessels) in the exclusive economic zone under article 73'.

[231] Chapter 3, Section 5.1.2.2.

[232] It could even be maintained that, in a democratic system, it is only subjects that have rights who might accept duties; otherwise, duties might be imposed on them. This point is however not relevant for the present discussion and will not be pursued further.

Otherwise, and if it is accepted that the State has agreed to two mutually exclusive provisions—one a right, the other a duty—the conclusion does not change. In this latter case, it would be a matter of establishing the relationship between two conflicting norms. At this point, three principles might come into play: *lex posterior*, *lex specialis*, and *jus cogens*. Without entering into a case-by-case examination of the relative dates of adoption of treaty provisions, it is historically true that the powers of the State at sea generally pre-date the duties stemming from human rights. The rights of the coastal State in its territorial sea and those of the flag State vis-à-vis its vessels were well established by the beginning of the twentieth century, when the legal notion of human rights had not yet been born. Even rights on the continental shelf had been incorporated in the Geneva Convention on the Continental Shelf by 1958 and were recognized as part of customary law some time before the adoption of the two international human rights Covenants in 1966.[233] Even when this is not the case, for example in the case of powers over the exclusive economic zone, which became part of customary law with their inclusion in the 1982 UNCLOS, the principle of *lex specialis* would produce a similar conclusion. A duty under a human rights norm can be considered as *lex specialis* in relation to a structural law of the sea norm concerned with the allocation of power at sea. The former, in fact, affects only in part the content of the latter, and leaves a wide margin for its continuing operation. Thus, while the State is obliged to exercise its jurisdiction over artificial islands in its exclusive economic zone in response to the requirement of the human right to bodily integrity or the social right to social security, it is still free to choose not to exercise such jurisdiction when there is no human rights issue at stake. Finally, in relation to those human rights which hold *jus cogens* status—including the prohibition of torture and freedom from slavery—no other rule may supersede them. Thus the State will be obliged to intervene in cases where slave labour exists on a platform on its continental shelf or in its exclusive economic zone and the State cannot waive such duty.[234]

Further objections to the trend that sees the transformation of rights into duties might be based on practical considerations, namely the limited means at the disposal of States to safeguard human rights and the additional difficulties posed by the need to patrol the seas to this end. The vastness of the oceans cannot be ignored, and neither can the scarcity of means at the disposal of most States. Furthermore, the practical difficulties in discovering human rights violations and in collecting the evidence necessary for the prosecution of the perpetrators are also well known. Yet the law cannot be based solely on what is always possible, but it must take into account that there will be cases in which an actor of the legal order will be unable—not to mention unwilling—to comply with its obligations.

Two counter-arguments seem particularly significant when arguing for the acceptance of an increase in duties. The first relates to the need to have objectives—even ideals—in law, that will guide action and that will at least lead to the avoidance

---

[233] But not before the ECHR, although the Convention has been amended successively.
[234] Reference to *jus cogens* alone may not however solve every difficulty, as Andrea Bianchi, 'Human Rights and the Magic of Jus Cogens' (2008) 19 EJIL 491, has argued.

of a wilful disregard for human rights violations, based on the excuse that it is not possible to intervene everywhere. The second takes into account that legal norms are generally not absolute, but are drafted, interpreted, and applied so as to take into account the existing circumstances, including the capacity of States to take concrete measures.

The issue of limited means and the need to strike a balance between collective and individual interests was addressed by the ECtHR, according to which:

In determining the scope of a State's positive obligations, regard must be had to the fair balance that has to be struck between the general interest and the interests of the individual, the diversity of situations obtaining in Contracting States and the choices which must be made in terms of priorities and resources. Nor must these obligations be interpreted in such a way as to impose an impossible or disproportionate burden.[235]

In particular, the recent diffusion of the notion of due diligence, the standard often used in human rights and in the law of the sea, reinforces this argument. With its proactive and dynamic nature, which adapts to the changing landscape of means and methods at the disposal of States, the obligation of due diligence may prompt States to act and minimize the possibility that they may be considered responsible in cases where it is absolutely impossible to prevent human rights violations.[236]

Legal regulation is therefore not oblivious to the particular circumstances of States. It is one thing, however, to say that legal rules must be interpreted and applied in a way which does not impose disproportionate burdens on States, but it is another thing to argue that there should be no legally binding obligations on States whatsoever, just because there may be instances in which it will be impossible for them to adopt action. In conclusion, the current shift from rights to duties does not impose on States impossible or dispoportionate burdens. It should be therefore welcome as it will ensure a better protection of people at sea.

---

[235] *Ilaşcu and Others v Moldova and the Russian Federation* App no 48787/99 (Judgment (GC) (Merits) of 8 July 2004) para 332.
[236] Sections 3.1 and 3.2.

5

From Set of Rules to Legal Regime

1. Scattered Beads or a Strand of Pearls?

The analysis in the previous chapters has shown that international law does not contain a well-established field or sub-regime that alone suffices to adequately regulate the topic of 'people at sea'. At the same time, however, it has revealed that international law does contain many fragments, in the form of treaties, and groups of norms or even single norms, which do provide some guidance as to what duties States owe to people who are at sea. The presentation and discussion of these fragments in this book has been organized around some core questions: Firstly, whether international law contains any norms that explicitly purport to protect people at sea, and what the content of these norms is (Chapter 1); secondly, whether, apart from these norms specifically aiming at protecting people, there exist other norms of international law that may be used towards this end (Chapter 2); thirdly, what the scope of all these norms is (Chapter 3); and finally, and considering both norms identified in Chapter 1 and those identified in Chapter 2, what duties arise for States from these norms (Chapter 4). The scrutiny of international law and people at sea could end here, with an open-ended appeal to scholars to take up the topic and explore the many issues that were necessarily overlooked.[1]

Nonetheless, there is one loose end still to tie up. At the end of Chapter 2, an ontological question was formulated, which still needs to be answered: What is this group of rules? A number of further questions naturally flow from the initial one: Is it just a random group of rules, which includes rules from many different instruments and regimes? Is there some coherence, not to mention unity, in this group? Is it part of an existing regime, and if so, which one? Or could it be construed as a new, autonomous regime? And finally, how does one prove the existence of such a new regime?

Answering these questions is not a mere idle conceptual exercise. Ascertaining what this group of rules is, even if only an idea, would help in at least two ways, one more specific to the topic of people at sea, the other more general. In relation to the topic 'people at sea', an understanding of the nature of the rules identified so far would serve the purpose of better interpreting and applying them in practice. Given

---

[1] There are in fact many issues that still need to be addressed. These include the consequences of the breach of the duties owed by States, including special regimes of responsibility, and the procedural means at the disposal of individuals for achieving compliance by States with their duties.

International Law and the Protection of People at Sea. Irini Papanicolopulu. © Irini Papanicolopulu, 2018. Published 2018 by Oxford University Press.

the relevance of contextual and systemic interpretation, locating the exact sitting of these rules within the international legal system and its regimes would help provide meaning to their commands and address interactions and conflicts.

In a broader light, discussing the nature of this group of norms may help shed light into how international law addresses new issues that emerge at the international level. Starting from the empirical finding that specialized regimes of international law are dynamic—in the sense that they are created, may evolve, and might eventually end—this chapter seeks to examine a regime during the delicate phase of its creation. This examination is instrumental to drawing some general conclusions that might apply beyond the topic of people at sea.

The thesis advanced in this chapter is that we are witnessing the emergence of a new, autonomous, regime on the international protection of people at sea. The starting point for arguing this thesis is that the applicable set of rules is not to be found in one single regime, but derives from the multiple regimes that come into play (general international law, the law of the sea, international human rights law, international labour law, and diplomatic protection, just to mention a few). As a matter of fact, this new regime takes elements from all these regimes and emerges through their interplay.

In order to argue this point, the chapter will first address some underlying conceptual issues, so as to clarify the methodology that will be used to argue the emergence of the new regime. First, the chapter will examine how international law reacts to the normative challenges posed by new issues. It will then turn to the conceptual underpinnings of any discussion of regime creation, sketching a theory for regime emergence. The novelty of the proposed regime on people at sea is that it is a functional, human-centered legal regime. It is functional because the rules that compose it assist in the protection of the core interest—people who are at sea. It is human-centered because rules are selected on the basis of their relevance to individuals, rather than States. Since the quality of 'human-centeredness' is not common language in legal scholarship, it seems necessary to discuss it in some detail. In light of these premises, the chapter will conclude with an assessment of the nature of the legal rules relating to the protection of people at sea.

2. The Interplay between New Challenges and New Regimes, or, How to Deal with a New Issue

The unprecedented blooming of international law during the twentieth century has resulted in an accumulation of treaties and other legal instruments, and in an exponential increase of legal norms. In turn, treaties and other legal instruments have often formed the basis of newly established legal regimes within the system of international law. For example, the Universal Declaration of Human Rights (UDHR) and the (European) Convention for the Protection of Human Rights and Fundamental Freedoms (ECHR)[2] have driven the development of international human rights

---

[2] (European) Convention for the Protection of Human Rights and Fundamental Freedoms (adopted 4 November 1950, entered into force 3 September 1953) 213 UNTS 221, as amended.

law at the global and regional levels. A significant contribution towards this development has come from the various international judicial and quasi-judicial bodies, which have interpreted and applied norms of the regime in a consistent and constructive way, thus furthering the internal coherence of the regimes.

In conjunction with the positive effects, the multiplication of norms has also raised some issues and has created some problems for both decision-makers and judges. On the one hand, decision-makers have to develop new rules taking into account an ever-increasing and interconnected web of instruments, institutions, and rules. The international statute book, to use Jenks' words, is being constantly enriched,[3] and a good knowledge of its content becomes a matter of urgency for lawmakers.[4] On the other hand, international judges are now called upon to ensure not only the internal coherence of the legal regime within which they operate, but also its harmonious integration with and fusion into the system of general international law.[5] These issues were at the core of the discussions on the fragmentation of international law, both within the International Law Commission (ILC) and within the wider scholarly community.[6]

Not all issues deriving from the burgeoning of legal norms and regimes and the ensuing fragmentation have received the same consideration, however. One consequence that has received little, if any, attention concerns the practical and conceptual challenges encountered by anyone seeking to identify the rules applicable to a subject matter that eludes classification under the framework of an 'established' legal regime. Discussion of regimes and their interaction, from a legal perspective, has indeed focused on already established regimes, with their accepted rules and established problems of interpretation and application. Almost no attention has been given to the genesis of regimes, that is, to that particular moment in time—or, rather, period—during which the challenges posed by a new practical issue receive a response by international law in the form of dedicated legal regulation.[7] Yet, it is submitted here, this is an issue also worthy of consideration by legal scholars, in particular in light of the manifold challenges faced by the international community and the ensuing intense normative response triggered by them in these past few decades.

Before entering into the discussion of regimes, a terminological clarification seems useful. A distinction needs to be drawn at this point between legal regimes and framework treaties. While it is true that many regimes are based upon a framework

[3] Wilfred C Jenks, 'The Conflict of Law-Making Treaties' (1953) 30 British Yearbook of International Law 403, 420.

[4] Hence the flourishing of international law courses at all levels.

[5] Yuval Shany, *The Competing Jurisdictions Of International Courts and Tribunals* (OUP 2003). The same author has however pointed out circumstances that may stand in the way of this process in Yuval Shany, 'One Law to Rule Them All: Should International Courts Be Viewed as Guardians of Procedural Order and Legal Uniformity?' in Ole Kristian Fauchald and André Nollkaemper (eds), *The Practice of International and National Courts and the (De-)Fragmentation of International Law* (Hart 2012) 15.

[6] See Chapter 2, Section 2.

[7] For a notable exception, see James Harrison, *Making the Law of the Sea* (CUP 2011). A different discourse has characterized the field of international relations. However, due to its theoretical underpinnings and the focus of scholarly discussion in this field, while international relations scholarship may provide useful insights, it does not solve legal questions and will therefore not be discussed here.

treaty—the ECHR constitutes such a treaty, which has formed the basis for the respective regional human rights law—this is not always the case. Therefore, the lack of a framework treaty would not be as significant as the lack of a dedicated legal regime altogether. Although there is no all-encompassing 'international convention on the protection of the environment', there is no doubt that international environmental law exists and there is a common agreement on its core elements.[8] The lack of a dedicated treaty may therefore be superseded by a widespread recognition in the epistemic community of the individuality of a certain subject matter and the law that relates to it.

Nonetheless, the lack of a recognized field, or regime, constitutes a first stumbling block in the quest to identify the applicable rules. This is the case of people at sea. There is no 'international convention on the law that applies to people at sea' and there is no 'international law of people at sea' section to be found in international law, international human rights, or law of the sea manuals.[9] Given, therefore, the empirical finding that there are people at sea who need protection, anyone who might look for legal rules granting such protection would not face an easy task, not knowing where to begin the search.

In such instances, there are four potential paths that can be taken:

(a) to consider that there is no regulation: 'persons at sea' does not constitute a branch of international law and therefore it is not regulated (although specific instances, such as pirates, seafarers, or fishers may be regulated);

(b) to choose one of the well-established legal regimes potentially related to the topic and try to find rules in it: as the phrase makes clear, 'persons at sea' recalls both international human rights law and the law of the sea—one should therefore choose either one or the other regime and look for rules in it;

(c) to take into account rules appertaining to more than one legal regime: since 'persons at sea' recalls both international human rights law and the law of the sea, it should be regulated by both regimes and it is for the concerned scholar to address conflicts between these two fields;

(d) to develop a dedicated legal regime: the application of international human rights law and the law of the sea alone does not suffice and 'persons at sea' must be subject to a dedicated legal regime.

The first approach rejects any legal analysis and is rare in practice. States may, however, implicitly opt for this solution as the easiest one. The 'catch-and-release' tactics

---

[8] In 1994 Fitzmaurice identified 'certain ways in which special features of the environment as a subject matter of international law have resulted in particular solutions, applications or rules within the general principles of international law which, if not necessarily unique to, are at least particularly characteristic of, environmental law'; MA Fitzmaurice, 'International Environmental Law as a Special Field' (1994) XXV Netherlands Yearbook of International Law 181, 183.

[9] There is however a section entitled 'People at Sea' in the Report of the Secretary General to the General Assembly on Oceans and the law of the sea for recent years; UNGA 'Oceans and the law of the sea. Report of the Secretary-General. Addendum' (1 September 2015) UN Doc A/70/74/Add.1, paras 28–42 and UNGA 'Oceans and the law of the sea. Report of the Secretary-General. Addendum' (6 September 2016) UN Doc A/71/74/Add.1, paras 28–35.

employed by some States involved in anti-piracy operations off the coasts of Somalia may be seen as an application—in practice, though not in principle—of this solution.[10] According to this approach, while it is recognized that piracy is certainly a problem—and that some action is required by States, that is the arrest and prosecution of pirates—it is eventually considered that law cannot be helpful in addressing the issue. Therefore, no legal action is taken and pirates are eventually released.

The second approach, which is germane to the first, draws implicitly and possibly subconsciously on the concept of legal characterization, that is subsuming a topic under a specific law regime.[11] Legal characterization is widely used in private international law to determine the (foreign) law applicable to a specific set of circumstances in a lawsuit.[12] If transposed to international law, however, legal characterization may preclude, *de facto* if not *de jure*, the application of rules and principles deriving from legal regimes other that the one identified as applicable. The end result is usually strongly shaped by ideology and may, in fact, lead to the same conclusion as the first approach: the absence of (adequate) regulation. As a form of 'regime-shopping', the second approach has sometimes been chosen by States when they sought to evade the application of specific rules and the ensuing obligations. This is the case of one of the defences advanced by Italy in the *Hirsi Jamaa* case. Claiming that its push-back operations should be seen as salvage operations, Italy invoked the applicability of the rules on the salvage of life at sea, rather than those on law enforcement operations.[13] The implicit reason was that, allegedly, the first field did not give any indication as to the duties owed towards the persons saved, in particular if they were refugees.

The third approach is more promising and is indeed the one that is currently pursued in many different fields. Early writings concerning the relationship between law of the sea and international human rights law have followed this path, trying to find the commonalities of the two fields and to promote a fruitful interaction and integration between principles, norms, and institutions.[14] This approach is certainly preferable to the two approaches identified above, as it allows for a fertile interaction, which may eventually produce its fruits in the form of a better protection granted to people at sea. In particular, it has the advantage of accepting that norms

---

[10] Chapter 4, Section 4.1.   [11] Adrian Briggs, *The Conflict of Laws* (OUP 2008) 15.

[12] According to Briggs ibid 1, the conflict of laws is 'the rules and principles which tell an English court hearing a case with a foreign element whether to apply English law or a foreign law or a combination of laws to resolve the dispute'.

[13] *Hirsi Jamaa and Others v Italy* App no 27765/09 (Judgment (GC) of 23 February 2012) para 65: the Italian government 'submitted that the vessels carrying the applicants had been intercepted in the context of the rescue on the high seas of persons in distress … and could in no circumstances be described as a maritime police operation'.

[14] Louis B Sohn, 'International Law of the Sea and Human Rights Issues' in Thomas A Clingan Jr (ed), *The Law of the Sea: What Lies Ahead?* (The Law of the Sea Institute 1988) 51; Bernard H Oxman, 'Human Rights and the United Nations Convention on the Law of the Sea' (1998) 36 Columbia Journal of Transnational Law 399; Paul Tavernier, 'La Cour européenne des Droits de l'Homme et la Mer' in *La mer et son droit: mélanges offerts à Laurent Lucchini et Jean-Pierre Quéneudec* (Pedone 2003) 575; Sophie Cacciaguidi-Fahy, 'The Law of the Sea and Human Rights' (2007) 19 Sri Lanka Journal of International Law 85; Tullio Treves, 'Human Rights and the Law of the Sea' (2010) 28 Berkeley Journal of International Law 1.

from different regimes may apply at the same time and may be used by judges of either regime. Furthermore, and as a consequence, it tries to smooth out difficulties arising from norms that are hard to coordinate, or that need to be assessed according to a horizontal or vertical hierarchy.

Nonetheless, this approach still presents two drawbacks. In the first place, this approach, which usually focuses on specific cases, is more suited to address particular instances rather than to produce a coherent group of rules theoretically able to address all situations arising in the subject matter under examination. It is not surprising that early writers have often been well-known judges and practitioners in this area, who have had to face the challenges of arguing and deciding cases which brought to the forefront of legal discussions the—alleged—points of friction between the two regimes. In the second place, while this approach may help to solve cases when there is sufficient and consistent regulation, it may not be as helpful to address situations in which there is no detailed regulation, or the regulation is inconsistent. When regulation is dense enough, substantial rules are already there. It is therefore a matter of interpreting and ordering—hierarchically or otherwise— existing norms. This feat may be achieved through the use of the integration devices provided by general international law and by the specialized regimes themselves.[15] If however substantial regulation is inconsistent or, even worse, lacking, then a discourse of interaction between different regimes lacks its *materia prima*.

The latter danger may be averted through the fourth approach, which purports not only to deliver a solution to a contingent problem but to provide a set of rules, tools, and methods that will limit as much as possible the uncertainties in the application of the law, ensuring consistency and predictability. This in turn will allow the interpreter to fill any apparent gaps in regulation. The fourth approach is achieved by the elaboration of a dedicated legal regime, which may start as a temporary solution to a specific case but often evolves into a more permanent legal regime and may finally be accepted, in due course, among the 'established' categories of international law rules. International human rights law and international environmental law constitute notable examples of how new regimes can be created and established within international law.

In contrast with the first three approaches, which reflect an increasingly flexible engagement with existing clusters of legal rules, the fourth might be considered as qualitatively different in that it requires a discourse *de lege ferenda*. This may often be so but, it is argued here, this need not always be the case. In fact, given the present density of international law, a new legal regime may consist not only of newly created rules and procedures, but it may also result from a different reading of existing ones. In other words, legal regimes may emerge not only from norm-creating exercises, but also as a result of a novel grouping of existing rules, requiring little addition in the way of general frameworks—although possibly a significant amount in terms of detailed regulation.

---

[15] Chapter 2, Section 8.2.

When choosing between a norm-creating approach and a novel-grouping one, it is suggested that the latter approach should be preferred to the former whenever possible. A word of caution is indeed necessary at this stage. We are presently witnessing a proliferation in international law of regimes and sub-regimes. As such, an extremely careful evaluation is demanded before championing the creation of new legal instruments—treaties or international organizations—within a given regime or as a basis for a new regime. This is not to say that it may be unnecessary to adopt new legal instruments or, if this really be the case, advocate the creation of a dedicated institution. It only means that, in the light of the wealth of rules that international law has produced over the last decades, when assessing existing rules, care should be taken to go beyond the existing categorizations and to inquire whether it may be possible to 'create' a new regime simply by aggregating under a new 'regime' rules already existing within separate formal subdivisions of law. The need for 'new' items—that is, rules or instruments—should be carefully assessed and should be advanced only when it becomes apparent, following a thorough and objective assessment, that existing rules do not suffice to effectively regulate conduct so as to achieve the new aims that have emerged within the international community.

3. The Emergence of Regimes in International Law

Before further discussing the nature of the group of rules that purports to protect people at sea, it is necessary to briefly sketch the theoretical conceptions underlying such discussion. A primary issue that comes to the forefront is the different means through which regimes are created. Looking at the practicalities of the genesis of international law, it seems possible to identify two principal modes in which new legal regimes develop in international law: regime creation, based on a conscious effort to create a new legal regime, and regime emergence, which is partly based on conscious efforts and partly reposes on a combination of circumstances that go beyond the will of the parties involved. These two modes of regime development may in turn take the form of three paradigms: treaty-based regimes, institution-based regimes, and function-driven regimes.

The genesis of a legal regime may, in the first place, be traced in a treaty or in another legal instrument that has a comparable normative significance. The legal instrument thus includes a number of provisions which, at best, should provide the basic principles of the regime, the specific rules and, in a number of instances, the institutions tasked with ensuring the application of the regime.[16] This is, for example, the case of the ECHR, which constitutes the basis for the (European)

---

[16] In this sense, ILC, 'Fragmentation of International Law: Difficulties Arising from the Diversification and Expansion of International Law. Report of the Study Group of the International Law Commission Finalized by Martti Koskenniemi' (13 April 2006) UN Doc A/CN.4/L.682 (Koskenniemi Report) para 152, refers to regimes 'set up' by States. See also ibid 157 '[t]he establishment of a special regime in the wider sense ... would also normally take place by treaty or several treaties'.

regime of international human rights law.[17] For present purposes, it is not necessary to dwell upon the reasons for the adoption of the treaty or the actors that have
promoted the adoption of the treaty—more and more often, a coalition of States,
NGOs, and other actors.[18]

From a genetic point of view, a second category of regimes are institution-based
regimes. This expression is used not to signify the regimes that have as their center
an institution,[19] such as the World Trade Organization (WTO) or the regional
seas regimes, but rather those regimes that are created *within* an institution. An
institution-based regime may indeed contain one or more treaties, which include
norms belonging to the regime. If compared with treaty-based regimes, however,
the cohesiveness of institution-based regimes is to be found not in a specific treaty
and the principles that it propounds, but in the principles that permeate the work of
the institution at the basis of the regime. An example of this type of regime is international maritime law, which includes the numerous conventions, codes, circulars,
and other acts developed within the International Maritime Organization (IMO). It
is not possible to point to a specific treaty among the many that have been adopted
that constitutes the basis of the regime. At the same time, all these treaties contribute, through their principles and norms, to the creation of the regime as they are all
inspired by the same principles which guide the action of the IMO.

The third category of regimes includes all those cases in which a group of principles and norms coalesces around a certain purpose, without there being a treaty
or an institution—or a single treaty and institution—which forms the basis of this
phenomenon. An example of a regime having emerged from a multitude of single
acts, instruments, rules, and institutions is international environmental law. There
is, in fact, no general framework treaty in international environmental law, and the
most well-known and widely ratified treaties regulate just parts of the subject matter
of this field of international law.[20] Moreover, there is no single international organization responsible for setting the basic principles of the discipline and furthering
the adoption of detailed regulation. While a significant role is played by the United
Nations (UN), this is certainly not a coherent one, nor is it the only one. It is not coherent, given that environmental matters are addressed by a number of organs, agencies,
and programmes—the UN General Assembly, the United Nations Environmental
Programme (UNEP), the ILC, the United Nations Division on Ocean Affairs and
the Law of the Sea (DOALOS), just to mention a few—the actions of which may be
coordinated to a wider or lesser extent. Furthermore, the United Nations is certainly

---

[17] Another example is the Statute of the International Criminal Court, which represents the conscious effort by States and other actors (primarily NGOs) to set down the ultimate regulation of international criminal law.

[18] Dirk Pulkowski, *The Law and Politics of International Regime Conflict* (OUP 2014) 87.

[19] On the role of international organizations as law-makers see José E Alvarez, *International
Organizations as Law-makers* (OUP 2005).

[20] For example, the Convention on Biological Diversity (adopted 5 June 1992, entered into force
29 December 1993) 1760 UNTS 79; the United Nations Framework Convention on Climate Change
(adopted 9 May 1992, entered into force 21 March 1994) 1771 UNTS 107; and Part XII of the
United Nations Convention on the Law of the Sea (adopted 10 December 1982, entered into force 16
November 1994) 1833 UNTS 397 (UNCLOS) on the protection of the marine environment.

not the only international organization that deals with environmental matters. A significant contribution which has further propelled the development of international environmental law has in fact come from regional organizations, often based on regional treaties, that have promoted new rules and stricter standards, which may then be followed at the global level.

Of course, this enumeration of regime types, catalogued according to their genesis, serves only taxonomic purposes. In reality, regimes are often the product of complex causes and may partake in both regime creation and regime emergence aspects at different times. Thus, while it is true that international human rights law may be traced back to the UDHR, it is also indisputable that judicial and quasi-judicial institutions, and legal scholarship have played a pivotal role in bringing together the different legal instruments later developed at the regional and global level. Conversely, while the law of the sea has been the product of centuries of State practice and scholarly analysis, it is now mostly contained in a single normative instrument, the United Nations Convention on the Law of the Sea (UNCLOS). Even so, a sketch of regime creation models would be useful to the discussion of regime emergence, as it allows us to focus on the peculiarities of function-driven emergence of legal regimes, as opposed to more conscious modes of creation.

In this respect, awareness of the procedure and its aims tends to diminish as one moves from regime creation to regime emergence. In the case of treaty-based regimes and, to some extent, institution-based regimes, the respective regime is deliberately created. There is a conscious effort of States as they congregate around a table and think about the purpose of the regime, its principles, and its rules.[21] On the opposite side of the spectrum, the third type of regimes generally emerge even in the absence of a coherent normative effort of States, as a spontaneous response by the system to new issues and challenges.[22] The regime is recognized as existing *ex post* rather than being created coherently *ex ante*, and emerges 'from the informal activity of lawyers, diplomats, pressure groups, more through shifts in legal culture and in response to practical needs of specialization than as conscious acts of regime-creation'.[23] Regime emergence thus presents the typical problems of an almost wild development of legal regulation, including a lack of well spelt-out principles, parallel engagements, proliferation of normative conflicts,[24] and gaps in regulation. At the same time, however, regime emergence presents one undeniable advantage: it allows subject

---

[21] This of course does not necessarily mean that the regime will be complete and flawless, as political and other circumstances may affect the result of negotiations and may lead to the unclear formulation of legal provisions, exceptions, and gaps in the final text. But even in these cases, the flaws are intentional.

[22] Koskenniemi Report (n 16) para 157: 'it may also occur that a set of treaty provisions develops over time, without conscious decision by States parties, perhaps through the activity of an implementing organ, into a regime with its own rules of regime-administration, modification and termination'.

[23] Koskenniemi Report (n 16) para 158.

[24] While States creating a new regime may negotiate its content taking into account existing obligations so as to avoid conflict, this is not the case for regime emergence, which takes place without consideration of other engagements by States.

matters to receive recognition and to be addressed within the legal framework even in the absence of an active will of States to regulate them.[25]

Regime emergence is partly different from interactional accounts of the emergence of legal rules. According to the latter, legal rules, that is norms, may emerge only in the case of shared understandings accompanied by social legitimacy and legal legitimacy, that is adherence to the criteria of legality.[26] Interactional law theories are therefore focused on the creation of law, rather than the creation of regimes although the two operations, admittedly, have some points of contact. As discussed in the previous section, new regimes may indeed result from the adoption of new rules by States. This is not always the case, however, as they may also emerge from a different polarization of already existing legal norms. The regime emergence theory briefly set out in these pages does not, on the other hand, purport to examine the creation of norms, but rather how novel regimes emerge out of different groupings of norms that have already come into existence.[27]

The secondary position of States in regime emergence has been hinted at above. Indeed, States do participate, but their participation is often cautious and limited, and consists more of practical acts—for example the adoption of a treaty or the amendment of a convention—rather than grand statements of principle. In these circumstances, a crucial role in regime emergence is played by international judges and legal scholars. Indeed, the creation of legal regimes constitutes one of the instances in which judges and scholars may act as subsidiary sources of international law, in the sense advocated by Article 38 of the International Court of Justice (ICJ) Statute. The function of each category is however quite different.

International judges are the best placed, due to the authority of their decisions, to sanction the existence of the regime and apply its principles in their judgments, setting the precedent for those that will follow. The role of the European Court of Human Rights (ECtHR), for example, in establishing the human rights law regime applicable in most of Europe is widely recognized.[28] At the same time, international judges face a particular challenge. It is well known that, absent a generalized judicial function in international law, every judge has to be created by a specific instrument. This instrument sets out the functions of the court or tribunal, thus limiting personally, geographically, and functionally the competence of the judge.[29] With the exception of the ICJ, all other international judges have in fact been created to adjudicate disputes stemming from a particular treaty, be it the treaty that contains

---

[25] According to Hafner, new rules of international law are produced 'only if States feel the urge' to create them; Gerhard Hafner, 'Should One Fear the Proliferation of Mechanisms for the Peaceful Settlement of Disputes?' in Lucius Caflisch (ed), *The Peaceful Settlement of Disputes between States: Universal and European Perspectives* (Kluwer Law International 1998) 25, 33.

[26] Jutta Brunnée and Stephen J Toope, *Legitimacy and Legality in International Law. An Interactional Account* (CUP 2010) in particular 53–54.

[27] Interactional accounts of international law may of course provide appealing insights on how the norms, that will later coalesce around a regime, are formed; see Brunnée and Toope (n 26).

[28] Koskenniemi Report (n 16) para 157.

[29] *The MOX Plant Case (Ireland v United Kingdom)* Order No 3 (Suspension of Proceedings on Jurisdiction and Merits, and Request for Further Provisional Measures) of 24 June 2003, para 19.

the compromissory clause or the *compromis*.[30] Even the ICJ often finds the basis for its jurisdiction in a specific treaty, and is thus limited in its judicial function by the provisions of that treaty.[31] As a consequence, while international judges often do not shy away from the application of principles and rules of new regimes to the matters at hand, they will seldom declare the existence of a new legal regime as such, as this might not only weaken their decisions but could also open to questioning the legal basis for them. A judge must decide according to the law mentioned in its statute or other constitutive instrument, or according to the law indicated by the parties to the dispute. If a judge were to use a regime beyond those identified in such instruments, then the parties might question the validity of the ensuing decision. Nonetheless, a legal regime could also be described as the context within which legal rules are interpreted—also in the sense adopted by Articles 31(1) and 31(3)(c) of the Vienna Convention on the Law of Treaties (VCLT)—and applied. Therefore, creating a new regime means creating a new context within which rules can be interpreted and applied, and it is in this particular light that the role of international judges in the creation of new legal regimes can best be understood.

Scholarly efforts are partly different. On the one hand, they lack the authority that the decisions by international judges enjoy. On the other, scholars do not face the constraints of judges and are therefore more at liberty to conceptualize and reconstruct new groupings of rules, naming them for what they are: new regimes. Additionally, scholars, who are not constrained by the requests of parties and the focus of a judicial decision,[32] are in a better position to elaborate on the new regime, collecting all its elements and exposing them in a rational and well-articulated way.[33] As a consequence, legal scholarship may play a fundamental role in this context, singling out the new regime, naming it, and rationalizing its content. It is thanks to these qualities that scholarly analysis may become reference work, to be consulted not only by State officials who seek a brief synopsis of the regime, but also by national judges called upon to give an answer to highly articulated issues involving international law rules. Eventually, a few scholarly works may become particularly authoritative and may be cited also by international judges.[34]

---

[30] This is the case both for permanent courts and tribunals and for ad hoc arbitral tribunals. ICSID tribunals may be considered slightly different, as the constituent instrument is separated from the basis of claims advanced by one party against the other. Yet the difference is formal rather than substantial, as the ICSID Convention is incorporated into BITs by an ad hoc provision, and can thus be considered as part of the treaty, on the basis of which the claim will be advanced.

[31] *Oil Platforms (Islamic Republic of Iran v United States of America)* (Judgment, Preliminary Objection) [1996] ICJ Rep 803, para 16; *Democratic Republic of the Congo v Rwanda* (Judgment, Jurisdiction, and Admissibility) [2006] ICJ Rep 39, para 88.

[32] Jeffrey L Dunoff, 'A New Approach to Regime Interaction' in Margaret A Young (ed), *Regime Interaction in International Law Facing Fragmentation* (CUP 2012) 136, discusses the limits encountered by international judges and the case-based approach to regime interaction.

[33] According to Neil MacCormick, 'Reconstruction after Deconstruction: A Response to CLS' (1990) 10 Oxford Journal of Legal Studies 539, 556 'the proper task of legal scholarship in the form of doctrine or dogmatics is the "rational reconstruction" of legal materials' (internal citations omitted).

[34] This is however particularly rare. According to Michael Peil, 'Scholarly Writings as a Source of Law: A Survey of the Use of Doctrine by the International Court of Justice' (2012) 1 Cambridge Journal of International and Comparative Law 136, 151 as of 2012 the ICJ had cited legal scholars in only twenty-two of its 139 judgments and advisory opinions.

Recognition by States of the new regime may come at a later moment, in particular with the amendment of existing legal instruments or with the adoption of new ones, which further the aims of the regime. This is the case, for example, with the introduction of Part XII on the protection of the marine environment into the UNCLOS. The relevance that environmental matters had acquired for international law, and the need to have a complete and coherent set of principles in this area, have spurred the participants to the Third United Nations Conference on the Law of the Sea to single out protection of the marine environment as a topic worth consideration—and of its own part within the draft treaty.[35] This understanding was only possible thanks to the groundwork of a great number of actors, including legal scholars, the regional seas programmes, the secretariat of a number of environmental treaties, and NGOs.[36]

4. Conceptualizing Regime Emergence

Having discussed the different modes of regime emergence and the role of the primary actors, it is now time to turn to the practical steps through which regime emergence may be ascertained.

Firstly, it is necessary to establish in good faith the necessity for a regime since, absent such necessity, it would be idle to engage in a regime-finding exercise. Assessing the need for a new regime consists of two steps, one practical and one conceptual. Legal regimes are not created in a vacuum, but they respond to the pressing need to address new and emerging issues in the international community. Therefore the first step—which could be defined as 'factual'—requires us to evaluate whether a new interest has emerged within the international community and whether factual circumstances have made it necessary to regulate a certain type of situation. The second step—which could be defined as 'conceptual' or 'analytical'—requires us to consider and exclude the possibility that a separate legal regime already exists and sufficiently addresses, or has the potential to sufficiently address, these circumstances. In other words, it is necessary to check, one by one, the existing regimes, and ascertain whether they may fruitfully be used in responding to the factual issues. Once it is established that a new issue has emerged at the international level and that there is no specifically dedicated legal field (regime) that satisfactorily addresses it, it is time to turn to the reconstruction of the regime.

Once it has been ascertained that there is an effective need for a regime, it is possible to engage in the reconstruction of the regime, bringing the scattered fragments together and organizing them rationally. This *reconstruction* of a new regime should be distinguished, right from the start, from the *creation* of a new regime. Creation

---

[35] Alexander Yankov, 'The Significance of the 1982 Convention on the Law of the Sea for the Protection of the Marine Environment and the Promotion of Marine Science and Technology: A Paper on Third Committee Issues' in Albert W Koers and Bernard H Oxman (eds), *The 1982 Convention on the Law of the Sea: Proceedings Law of the Sea Institute Seventeenth Annual Conference, July 13–16, 1983, Oslo, Norway* (Law of the Sea Institute 1984) 71.

[36] Harrison (n 7).

entails a norm-creating exercise, and thus the formulation of new rules, which do not exist at the time of writing, but which, it is suggested, should be adopted at the international level to better address a specific issue. Reconstruction, on the other hand, implies a much more modest action. It simply consists in the collection of existing rules, that is, rules that are to be found in legal instruments already adopted by States, and in their interpretation and application given by judges and other international organs.[37] In the end, regime emergence is nothing more than the result of the effort to bring together and group in a reasoned way rules relating to a certain issue, often with a view towards an evaluation of the completeness and satisfactory nature of the existing rules and a thrust towards their completion and refinement, so as to better protect the core interests at play.[38]

From a practical perspective, reconstruction of a regime consists in a number of steps: identifying its purpose, selecting the rules that compose it, and combining these rules. Eventually, the result may be assessed.

In the first place, it is necessary to identify the object of the regime. The object can best be described as a function of the factual circumstances and the aims. The object is key in identifying the principles that will guide the selection of rules and the assessment of their relevance, as well as of gaps that need to be filled in the regime. Furthermore, the object—as expressed by the general principle(s) that will be discussed below—is fundamental in the interpretation and application of the rules of the regime. As the ILC has stated, '[t]he significance of a special regime often lies in the way its norms express a unified object and purpose. Thus, their interpretation and application should, to the extent possible, reflect that object and purpose'.[39]

Secondly, it is necessary to select the elements that compose the emerging regime. Selection entails the preliminary recognition of the factual circumstances, the identification of the legal challenges that they present, and the mapping of useful systems and sub-systems, wherein to look for the relevant rules. Once these systems and sub-systems are mapped, selection is effected through identification of rules and their evaluation in the light of the object of the regime. Thus, those rules that are relevant will be retained whilst other rules will be discharged.[40] This second step consists of dividing legal regimes into the elements that they are composed

---

[37] Thus Douglas Guilfoyle, *Shipping Interdiction and the Law of the Sea* (CUP 2009) 344, after having collected all sorts of rules that apply to the interdiction of vessels at sea, argues that 'there may be a law that is generally applicable to how interdictions are *conducted*' (emphasis in the original). Of course, it can also be considered that a regime does not exist, see, for a contrary argument, Efthymios Papastavridis, *The Interception of Vessels on the High Seas* (Hart 2014) 82.

[38] Natalie Klein, 'A Case for Harmonizing Laws on Maritime Interceptions of Irregular Migrants' (2014) 63 ICLQ 787, 813, after presenting the laws that apply to the interdiction of irregular migrants at sea, argues that '[t]he fragmentation of issues in this area may only be overcome if there is agreement as to the objectives of the *regime*' (emphasis added).

[39] ILC, 'Conclusions of the Work of the Study Group on the Fragmentation of International Law: Difficulties Arising from the Diversification and Expansion of International Law' <http://legal.un.org/docs/?path=../ilc/texts/instruments/english/draft_articles/1_9_2006.pdf&lang=EF> accessed 16 August 2017 (ILC Conclusions) para 13.

[40] Chapter 2, Section 5.1.

of and—provisionally[41]—taking these elements away from their context, so as to evaluate their relevance for the subject matter of the new regime independent of any extra-legal or non-legal considerations that may taint their interpretation or application within the regime of origin. The selection of rules may—or better, should—take place both within specific regimes of international law and within the general system of international law. It requires first to enter the single regimes, so as to single out and evaluate the contribution of each towards addressing the issue at the core of the emerging regime, and then to step into the system of international law, wherein further rules of interest may be found, for example rules on jurisdiction or the composition of normative conflicts between divergent obligations.[42]

Having now identified a number of rules that relate to the subject matter, the third step will consist in combining them, so as to produce a set of rules that not only occasionally address the subject matter, but that compose a new regime through a number of interrelations and interactions. This procedure constitutes the core of the regime reconstruction exercise, since it aims at using the 'bricks' collected during the previous stage to build the new regime.[43] Reconstruction of an emerging regime benefits from the synthesizing quality of systemic thinking discussed in Chapter 2 of this book.[44] The identification of the applicable law, the application of the principle of systemic integration and of the principle of harmonization, the solution of normative conflicts, and the verification of the inclusiveness of the regime are all necessary steps towards regime emergence recognition and reconstruction. The outcome of this process will be the generation of a group of rules that are closely interconnected and—most importantly—that are supported by some basic principles typical of the regime,[45] produced by the fruitful interaction between the single elements collected in the previous stage.

In this respect, combining the selected rules also allows us to identify any general principles that underlie the new group of rules. The general principle or principles may consist of rules of customary international law, they may still be in the form of soft law, or they may constitute normative propositions to the international community. If there is sufficient international practice to prove its existence, then a rule of customary international law may be ascertained. If, however, practice is still uncertain, and there has been no formal recognition yet, the principle may take

---

[41] The context of origin of course cannot be entirely disposed with, since it will intrude—and might even be useful—in determining their scope as well as in interpreting their content.

[42] Chapter 2, Section 6.

[43] MacCormick (n 33) 556: 'In law ... the scholar or researcher is confronted by a vast body of material or of experimental or obserevational data. The materials and/or data may seem confused and disorderly, partly or potentially conflicting, gappy in places ... The task of scholarship or science is then to take these selected items and put them back together, to *reconstruct* them in a way that makes them comprehensible because they are now shown as parts of a well ordered though complex whole.' (emphasis in the original).

[44] Chapter 2, Section 5.

[45] On the use of principles to ensure coherence of a system see Neil MacCormick, 'Coherence in Legal Justification' in Aleksander Peczenik, Lars Lindahl, and Bert Van Roermund (eds), *Theory of Legal Science* (D Reidel Publishing Company 1984) 235, in particular 238. For an account of the significance of coherence for international law see Pulkowski (n 18) 151–54.

the form of soft law.[46] Finally, it is possible that, absent an explicit manifestation of a general principle in a hard or soft law instrument, international practice points towards a common understanding that, although unspoken, underlies normative developments and implicitly guides the acts of States and other international actors. This common understanding, in particular, may result from different rules collected during the regime reconstruction phase. Those who are involved in the reconstruction of the regime may therefore enunciate the principle for the first time, and propose it to the international community for its consideration; a consideration that may eventually lead to the principle acquiring first soft and then hard law status. At this point, regime emergence recognition may intersect regime creation.[47]

Regime emergence recognition may stop here. It is however logical to have one further step which follows the previous three. The fourth and final step will consist in assessing the new regime in order to identify gaps or inconsistencies and to propose means for filling or solving these.[48] It is very rare that a regime that has newly emerged is complete, so that it addresses each and every issue raised under the topic considered. Even regimes consciously created by States are often not characterized by their completeness. They may present gaps due to issues that have proven too hard to be tackled diplomatically or that have simply been overlooked or not previously thought of. In light of the fact that their genesis is not the result of a conscious and coordinated effort, it is even more normal for emerging regimes to be incomplete and to require further elaboration. Assessment of the regime thus opens the door to norm creating exercises, which may be necessary to complete the regime but which need to be kept conceptually separate. At this stage, scholars may only propose new rules, and it is up to those subjects of international law that have a law-making capacity to pick up the challenge and further elaborate the regime.

In conclusion, reconstruction of an emerging regime is rendered possible by three characteristics of international law: the dual nature of legal rules, which allows them to migrate from one regime to another; the possibility given by legal techniques, *in primis* interpretation and harmonization, to construe new contexts, which form the basis for new regimes; and the completeness and autopoietic nature of the international law system, which make it possible for new principles to emerge within the existing legal rules.

---

[46] This is, eg, the case with the precautionary principle in international environmental law. For several decades, this principle was regularly repeated in soft law instruments and was incorporated in multilateral treaties. Yet, it encountered a hard time in being upheld as a positive rule of customary international law, as the waving practice of international judges has shown, until recently when the ITLOS openly stated that there is 'a trend towards making this approach part of customary international law' (*Responsibilities and Obligations of States Sponsoring Persons and Entities with Respect to Activities in the Area* (Seabed Disputes Chamber, Advisory Opinion of 1 February 2011) (*SDC Opinion*) para 135).

[47] The role that principles may play in the creation of international law is explored in Robert Kolb, 'Principles as Sources of International Law (With Special Reference to Good Faith)' (2006) 53 Netherlands International Law Review 1, who argues that general principles are '"transformators" of extra-positive (moral, social, or other) needs into the legal system' (ibid 7).

[48] It is at this stage that other checks, eg that of legitimacy, can be conducted. Legitimacy tests, which involve extra-legal elements, are beyond the scope of this book; on the concept see, among many others, Thomas Franck, 'Legitimacy in the International System' in Joseph Weiler and Alan T Nissel (eds), *International Law* (Routledge 2011) 670; Brunnée and Toope (n 26).

Rules, even when they constitute part of complex instruments, could be considered as having a dual nature, which partly partakes of the instrument in which they are to be found and partly distinguishes them from all the other provisions of the instrument. In other words, legal rules are at the same time a part of a whole (the legal instrument) and independent, self-standing rules that can be taken as isolated commands. For example, Article 98 of the UNCLOS on the duty to save life at sea which has been discussed at length in this book is certainly one part of this overall treaty, and thus it may be read in the context provided by the preamble and the other provisions of the UNCLOS. At the same time, Article 98 is also a standalone provision, which may find application independently from the other UNCLOS rules. This provision shares little, for example, with Article 79 of the UNCLOS concerning the right of third States to lay cables and pipelines on the continental shelf. Therefore, while one may agree with Higgins that international law is a normative system, rather than just rules,[49] it is also true that the system is composed of rules and that these rules also have particular individuality. This is proven by the allowance made in the VCLT for the severability of treaty provisions.[50] This characteristic lends itself to the discourse of regime emergence. It allows the judge, civil servant, or scholar to detach a specific rule from the legal instrument and the regime in which it was originally located and to introduce it into a new regime. Legal rules, in this respect, are like the building blocks of children's games, which can be combined in more than one way to produce new objects—in this case, the regimes.[51]

Looking at the contribution of rules thus collected to the emergence of the regime, it is possible to distinguish between 'positive' and 'negative' contributions. Positive contributions are those that help the regime to achieve its aims or, in more legal terms, that conform to the general principles of the regime. Negative contributions are those that hinder this effort, by positing substantial or procedural restraints upon the actions of the first kind. An honest effort at the reconstruction of a newly

[49] Rosalyn Higgins, 'International Law and the Avoidance, Containment and Resolution of Disputes: General Course on Public International Law' (1991) 230 Recueil des cours de l'Académie de Droit International 9, 23.

[50] Art 44 Vienna Convention on the Law of Treaties (adopted 23 May 1969, entered into force 27 January 1980) 1155 UNTS 331 (VCLT). The limitations encountered by separability of treaty provisions under Art 44 VCLT are not relevant for the present discussion, since, as the ILC had noted in its commentary to draft Art 41 (which was to become Art 44 VCLT), '[t]he question of the separability of treaty provisions for the purposes of interpretation raises quite different issues from the application of the principle of separability to the invalidity or termination of treaties'; *Yearbook of the International Law Commission*, vol II (1966), 238. See also Joost Pauwelyn, *Conflict of Norms in Public International Law: How WTO Law Relates to Other Rules of International Law* (CUP 2003) 65, according to whom 'it is impossible to define a treaty in its entirety as reciprocal or integral in nature. One must look at every provision and every obligation individually'.

[51] This simile is used to highlight one characteristic of legal rules, ie their potential for multiple uses, and should not be taken beyond that. There are of course differences between the building blocks of children's games and legal norms, the principal being that while the former are material objects and their use in one construction precludes their use in another one at the same time, the latter are conceptual products which can be used simultaneously for the construction of more than one notional regime. MacCormick, 'Reconstruction' (n 33) 556 warns that the reconstruction process 'is an intellectual process, involving a new imagining and describing of the found order, not literally a rebuilding of objects in the world'.

emerging regime cannot ignore the second category of rules, but needs to take them into account[52] and may dispose with them only at the evaluation stage of the regime, when subjective choices as to the rules that should be retained and those that should be modified have a place. Thus, in reconstructing the rules on the scope of States' powers at sea, one cannot ignore the jurisdictional limitations of the coastal State provided for by Article 27(5) of the UNCLOS,[53] even though one may wish for this provision to be disposed with in order to ensure a better protection of people on board vessels exercising the right of innocent passage.

This approach may be criticized as being too subjective, since what is positive and what is negative, or—to make it even simpler—what is good and what is bad depends very much upon the person making the evaluation. It is submitted here, however, that this is not the case. The distinction is not based upon the personal belief of the interpreter, but is guided by the object of the regime, which serves as a criterion for distinguishing between those rules that provide a positive contribution from those that have a negative effect. While it is possible to say that all those rules that fall under the first category will have to be included in the legal regime, the opposite is not true. It is not possible, indeed, to exclude all negative contributions from the regime, since the rules embodying the latter may also be significant to protect or advance other relevant interests. The tension between rules giving a positive or negative contribution is evident, since in construing the regime, the former will be used as much as possible to neutralize the effects of the latter.

An objection that could be raised at this point in respect of the capacity for migration, is that legal rules have to be taken in context. Context, as used in this discussion, is not the narrow notion defined in Article 31(2) VCLT, but the wider framework or background within which the norm is to be read.[54] This framework includes the principles that guide the interpretation of the norm, and, more generally, all other norms of international law and its regimes that have a bearing upon the subject matter of the norm under consideration. Context therefore means both the instruments in which rules are embedded, for example a treaty, and the legal context in which they are generated, for example international law or one of its branches or sub-branches, such as general international law, the law of the sea, or international human rights law. These two accounts of context are embodied in Article 31 VCLT, which requires interpretation to take into account contextual and systemic inputs.[55]

---

[52] Thus, according to MacCormick, 'Reconstruction' (n 33) 556, while 'there has to be some discrimination between the parts that belong in the coherent whole and the mistakes or anomalies' it is necessary to take into account the fact that '[e]ven anomalous cases or statutes are real decisions and real laws, whose effect must be taken into account at the same time as they may be put to one side as anomalous, or not reconcilable with the main doctrinal schema reconstructed out of the rest of the material' (ibid 557).

[53] Chapter 3, Section 5.1.2.1.

[54] The relevance of context for the interpretation—and one should add, the application—of legal provisions was underlined by the ITLOS. In a much quoted passage, the tribunal held that identical provisions in different treaties may be interpreted differently having regard, among others, to the context (*MOX Plant case (Ireland v The United Kingdom)* (Provisional Measures, Order of 3 December 2001) ITLOS Reports 2001, para 51).

[55] Respectively, Art 31(1) VCLT and Art 31(3)(c) VCLT.

This objection, however, does not take into account the ability of international law to produce countless regimes. Legal regimes, it is worth reminding, are composed of 'all the rules and principles that regulate a certain problem area that are collected together so as to express a "special regime" '.[56] In this sense, legal regimes equate to the 'legal context', 'framework', or 'law', that is the general background against which rules are to be read.[57] Legal regimes, however, are not a closed category, but they develop continuously. As new problems arise within the international community, new regimes emerge and may replace the old ones. Fortunately, the international regime pertaining to the slave trade no longer exists, as it has been replaced by a group of anti-slavery provisions that may be considered as forming a sub-regime of international human rights law, but also of international criminal law. Legal regimes also evolve, so as to accommodate new needs and changing perceptions. Human rights law, for example, has now been expanded to include, alongside the original negative obligations of States, positive ones. Additionally, we might consider the evolution of the law of the sea, which has developed from a law that purported to guarantee the free use of the sea to all States against claims to exclusivity, to a body of law, the primary purpose of which is to accommodate different uses of the seas, and in which the freedom of the seas is now counterbalanced by significant instances of exclusive rights of coastal States. While international law is unitary in nature, it is also very much alive and changes all the time, producing new regimes, modifying existing ones, and suppressing those that are not necessary any more.

There is therefore nothing new in supporting the idea that legal rules, which were originally incorporated within a particular legal instrument and formed part of a specific legal regime, may also be used beyond that original instrument and regime. Legal rules may migrate from one regime to another, and a rule originally incorporated in a particular regime may form the basis for a new one. At the same time, the fact that rules migrate from one regime to another does not sever the ties with the original regime. Legal rules may 'return' to the original regime whenever necessary or appropriate. Of course, isolating rules under a 'regime' label could potentially mean that rules are developed independently. However, the system is not closed and the perpetual grouping of rules into different sets would be sufficient to minimize, if not to forestall, the danger of an autonomous development.

In conclusion, a new regime provides the context for the interpretation and for the application of legal rules. In the first place, the existence of a new regime, creating a new mental habit for those applying international law,[58] will promote the application of rules originally deriving from different legal regimes to the same facts, once these facts are characterized as falling under the new regime. Secondly, by bringing together rules

---

[56] ILC Conclusions (n 39) para 12.

[57] Thus Guilfoyle, *Shipping Interdiction* (n 37) 339, speaks of a 'law of interdiction'; Klein (n 38) 789, speaks of a 'legal framework for interceptions of irregular migrants at sea'; Margaret A Young, *Trading Fish, Saving Fish. The Interaction between Regimes in International Law* (CUP 2011) 9, refers to 'governance of fisheries'. In a totally different context, Stephan Schill, *The Multilateralization of International Investment Law* (CUP 2009) xiv, considers that 'one can perceive of international investment law as a proper subsystem of international law'.

[58] Chapter 2, Section 2.

belonging to different legal instruments and to separate legal regimes, a new regime will provide a ready-made framework which is useful for a contextual interpretation of the applicable rules.[59] Furthermore, since systemic interpretation logically identifies the rules that are under scrutiny and confers upon them a key central position, the legal regime of reference will constitute the first step in the interpretative exercise.

Of course, any regime or sub-regime is not isolated from the general context and is useful only to the extent that it can be used for better regulation and for a better understanding of the failures of the system. This will explain why functional regimes are useful and why they have a role to play both in the study and conceptual development of the legal discipline and in the context of governance, as they allow the interpreter to better focus on existing rules—so as to avoid unnecessary duplication and toil—and on the existing gaps that need to be filled.

Finally, regime emergence, in particular the emergence of new principles due to a different grouping of legal rules, derives from the autopoietic nature of international law or, in other words, the completeness of the international legal system. This aspect of international law has already been discussed within the general consideration of the system of international law.[60] At this point, it is sufficient to recall that the autopoietic nature is at the heart of the emergence of new principles that stem from a fruitful interaction of legal norms, in particular when they derive from different legal regimes.

5. Conceptualizing a Human-Centered Regime

Legal regimes, including those of international law, may take a number of forms. Traditionally, international law regimes were State-centric. Efforts at regime reconstruction would take the State as the point of reference and would collect rules that would matter for the State: rules that attributed rights and powers to the State, rules that imposed duties on the State, and rules that regulated the consequences of any violation for States—both the State perpetrator and the State victim of the unlawful act.

The emergence of new actors at the international level during the last century has now started to erode this approach. International law today is not used exclusively in an inter-State context, but it is increasingly applied by individuals against States and also against each other, as well as against other entities established under national and international law, such as inter-governmental organizations and corporations.[61] Individuals use international law against the State not only in the human

---

[59] 'Functionally oriented as such regimes are, they also serve to identify and articulate interests that serve to direct the administration of the relevant rules' (Koskenniemi Report (n 16) para 133).

[60] Chapter 2, Section 2.

[61] Although people do not always realize this. For example, Louis B Sohn, 'Making International Law More User-Friendly' in *International Law as a Language for International Relations* (Kluwer Law International 1996) 411, 412, wondered '[h]ow can the general public realize that international law is in fact a part of their daily life, that it is an important and influential friend?'.

rights field, but also in other fields, for example to regulate and protect international investments.

Nonetheless, with the exception of international human rights law, the presentation of international law is still very much focused upon States. Accounts of international law and its regimes address legal rules from the perspective of inter-State relationships, establishing the rights and duties of States towards each other, as well as the possibility for action to be taken before international organizations and international courts and tribunals.

A different approach is however possible.[62] Legal rules are always about people to some degree. They have been created by persons, they are usually addressed at persons (albeit these persons act as organs of the abstract entity 'State'),[63] and they aim to forward the interests of persons, be they the restricted group of individuals that detains the power or the *demos* at large. International law rules are an exception to this general assertion only to the extent that most of these rules are directly addressed at States, and that individuals may benefit from them only indirectly. However, individuals are the end beneficiaries of rules of international law,[64] as evidenced by the text of the most important international instruments. In the preamble to the United Nations (UN) Charter, the peoples of the United Nations pledge 'to reaffirm faith in fundamental human rights, in the dignity and worth of the human person, in the equal rights of men and women' and 'to promote social progress and better standards of life in larger freedom'.[65] The UNCLOS was adopted with a view towards 'promot[ing] the economic and social advancement of all peoples of the world'.[66] Even the WTO was created 'with a view to raising standards of living,

---

[62] See calls to think about the 'users' of international law in Sohn, 'Making International' (n 61) 411 and Emmanuel Roucounas, 'Effectiveness of International Law for the Users of the Sea' in Jorge Cardona Llorens (ed), *Cursos Euromediterráneos Bancaja de Derecho Internacional* (Tirant lo Blanch 2009) 855, 871.

[63] See Georges Scelle, *Précis de Droit des Gens. Principes et Systématique* (Recueil Sirey 1932) 42: 'Une déclaration unilatérale de volonté, un traité, un acte illicite dont on dit qu'ils engagent l'Etat, sont *toujours* des actes émanant d'individus, agents ou gouvernants, investis d'une compétence représentative, et jamais de l'être fictif qu'on appelle l'Etat' (emphasis in the original). Contra Dionisio Anzilotti, *Corso di Diritto Internazionale. Volume Primo: Introduzione—Teorie Generali* (Athenaeum 1928) 112: '[d]estinatari delle norme sono, di regola, gruppi sociali: ciò vuol dire che le norme considerano il gruppo unitariamente, anzichè nei suoi componenti, fanno del gruppo una *unità di riferimento*, in modo che la potestà accordata, il dovere imposto non sono potestà e dovere di singoli individui, ma della collettività'. He adds however that 'anche se, formalmente, sarebbe possibile di scindere la subiettività dell'ente in un complesso di diritti ed obblighi individuali' (ibid).

[64] The International Criminal Tribunal for Former Yugoslavia recalled the roman maxim '*hominum causa ius constitutum est* (all law is created for the benefit of human beings)', *Prosecutor v Tadic* (Decision on the Defence Motion for Interlocutory Appeal on Jurisdiction) ICTY-94-1 (2 October 1995) para 97. Sohn, 'Making International' (n 61) 416, considers that 'All these common activities [of States] result in obtaining consensus on agreements which, though concluded between Governments, have as their purpose to make life easier for individuals'. See also Gerhard Hafner, 'Some Thoughts on the State-Oriented and Individual-Oriented Approaches in International Law' (2009) 14 Austrian Review of International and European Law 27, 28; Antônio Augusto Cançado Trindade, *The Access of Individuals to International Justice* (OUP 2011) 13.

[65] Preamble, para 2 Charter of the United Nations (adopted 26 June 1945, entered into force 24 October 1945) (UN Charter).

[66] Preamble, para 7 UNCLOS.

ensuring full employment and a large and steadily growing volume of real income'.[67] Considering international law norms from the perspective of the individual, therefore, does not constitute such a fundamental departure from their inherent nature, as might appear at first.[68]

In contrast to the State-centered exposition of international law which focuses on the rights and duties that international law sets for States, a human-centered approach compels the interpreter to consider the potential of international law rules to protect individuals and for these rules to be used by them to their advantage. The acceptance of human rights at the international level has been key to this shift of approach, and has greatly helped towards ensuring a better protection of individuals.[69] However, it is worth stressing that an entirely human-oriented approach to international law goes well beyond human rights in two separate ways. Firstly, it also considers other rights granted directly by international law to individuals, which do not fall under the category of 'human rights'.[70] Secondly, it also considers those duties of States that positively affect persons but which, however, do not have a correspondent right of an individual. This is, in fact, the main reason why human rights alone—at least in their present form of development—do not suffice. For their application, human rights require the identification of a specific individual who bears the right and may therefore claim compliance with the correspondent duty. They are thus not apt to provide for situations in which the State has to act in a precautionary manner, so as to avoid a danger that has not materialized yet. While the positive duties of States, as developed under international human rights law,[71] go to a certain extent towards this aim, they still need to be triggered following the identification of a rights-bearer, that is someone who may suffer the potential damage deriving from the State's inaction.

---

[67] Preamble, para 1 Marrakesh Agreement establishing the World Trade Organization (adopted 15 April 1994, entered into force 1 January 1995) 1867 UNTS 3.

[68] The need to put the individual at the center of the legal discourse was advocated by authors with different theoretical understandings of international law; cf Scelle (n 63) 42 with Hans Kelsen, 'Les Rapports de Système entre le Droit Interne et le Droit International Public' (1926) 14 Recueil 227, 281. This view did not go unchallenged, however; see Anzilotti (n 63) 123–25. For an even precedent argument about the centrality of the individual and his human rights see Pasquale Fiore, *Il diritto internazionale codificato e la sua sanzione giuridica* (2nd edn, Unione Tipografico-Editrice 1898). According to Fiore, '[i] diritti internazionale dell'uomo sono quelli che appartengono a ciascuno come uomo, e non come cittadino di un determinato Stato. Questi sono i diritti della personalità umana secondo il Diritto internazionale' (ibid 87–88). For a contextual discussion of Fiore's ideas see Martti Koskenniemi, *The Gentle Civilizer of Nations: The Rise and Fall of International Law, 1870–1960* (CUP 2002) 55. For a discussion of the different positions and their influence in framing international law see Anne Peters, *Beyond Human Rights. The Legal Status of the Individual in International Law* (CUP 2016) in particular 16–21.

[69] According to Theodor Meron, 'International Law in the Age of Human Rights' (2003) 301 Recueil des Cours 9, 22: '[t]he humanization of public international law under the impact of human rights has shifted its focus above all from State-centred to individual-centred.'

[70] *LaGrand (Germany v United States)* [2001] ICJ Rep 466, para 77. 'Based on the text of these provisions, the Court concludes that Article 36, paragraph 1, creates individual rights, which, by virtue of Article 1 of the Optional Protocol, may be invoked in this Court by the national State of the detained person'. For a conceptualization of these 'other' rights see Peters (n 68), in particular 436–49.

[71] See Chapter 4, Section 3.1.

There are many different modes of conceptualizing a human-centered regime. One can look at it from the perspective of the standing of the individual in the international legal order, discussing his or her subjectivity. Different approaches may be identified in this strand of legal research. For a start, it has been maintained that the turn towards the protection of the individual by international law rules has produced a change in international law, whereby interests and value systems ascribed to individuals have gradually appeared alongside the values and interests traditionally originated from and defended by States,[72] although individuals are still mere beneficiaries of international law rules, since treaties create obligations only between States and individuals cannot dispose of the rights that those treaties provide for them.[73] At an intermediate level, it has been argued that individuals possess legal subjectivity in the measure in which they 'derive rights, obligations and capacities directly from international law'.[74] However, this legal subjectivity is still controlled by States,[75] and the rights, duties, and capacities thus conferred upon them are revocable in certain circumstances.[76] Finally, it has been claimed that the individual is granted legal personality by international law norms deriving from all sources of international law as set out in Article 38 of the ICJ Statute. Legal personality would derive not only implicitly from an accumulation of treaty provisions[77] that would have a quasi-irreversible nature,[78] but also a rule of customary law[79] and even a general principle of law.[80] As a consequence, the individual would enjoy internationally protected individual rights, which could fall either under the category of human rights or under that of ordinary rights.[81]

While the issue of the international subjectivity of the individual undoubtedly generates much interest, it does not necessarily need to be settled to argue in favour of a human-centered regime.[82] A more modest approach is also possible. Independently from the position of the individual in international law and its regimes, it is possible to construe a human-oriented regime as a group of rules that relate to the human person and which can be used to protect his or her interests. In this meaning, it is

[72] Gerhard Hafner, 'The Emancipation of the Individual from the State under International Law' (2013) 358 Recueil des Cours 263, 319–20.
[73] ibid 337.
[74] Kate Parlett, *The Individual in the International Legal System: Continuity and Change in International Law* (CUP 2011) 359.
[75] ibid 350: '[b]oth individual rights and individual capacities to enforce rights are dependent on a specific grant of right or capacity by states ... access to the international legal system has remained within the exclusive control of States'.
[76] ibid 353.
[77] Peters (n 68) 416: 'The accumulation of selective individual rights and duties in conjunction with the ripple effect of international human rights and the increasingly strong orientation of current international law towards the individual now permit the presumption that international treaty norms directly affecting the interests of individuals also regularly protect individuals. This means they contain international individual rights and thus implicitly presume the legal personality of the individual.'
[78] Peters (n 68) 417–18.   [79] ibid 419.   [80] ibid 426–27.
[81] ibid 436. See also Christian Dominicé, 'Droits Individuels et Droit de l'Homme: Chevauchements et Différences' in Laurence Boisson de Chazournes and Marcelo Kohen (eds), *International Law and the Quest for its Implementation. Liber Amicorum Vera Gowlland-Debbas* (Brill 2010) 287, 290–91.
[82] According to Giorgio Gaja, 'The Position of Individuals in International Law: An ILC Perspective' (2010) 21 EJIL 11, the ILC itself has not settled the point.

not necessary to establish in what forum—domestic or international—individuals may pursue their interests. Neither is it necessary to restrict the inquiry to rules that attribute rights directly to individuals. Nor is it necessary to elaborate on the standing of individuals in the decision-making process. Rules benefiting the individual may indeed be created by States or by international organizations, within which people are represented only indirectly,[83] and these rules may be actionable before courts and tribunals to which only States have access. While these circumstances make it more difficult for the individual to be able to exploit these rules, they do not impede persons from eventually benefiting from them. Therefore, the nature of their creators and the modes of creation are of no consequence, as long as the rules themselves are useful in protecting people and furthering their interests, and as long as these rules have the necessary normative density.[84]

This hybrid approach to international law, which draws on the *person* as its center of gravity, may be particularly useful in regime emergence recognition. Under this conception, the human person acts as the magnet that draws together, from the scattered fragments of international law, those rules that are of relevance in forming a legal regime of international law, giving them consistency and a self-standing characteristic. Rules are relevant to the extent that they are useful in protecting a person. Their utility may derive from the fact that they attribute a right to the individual, or from the fact that they provide a duty—for States, other individuals, or other entities—to act so as to protect the individual, or from the fact that they create a framework which purports to advance the individual's rights or interests. If the rules so grouped present the characteristics identified in the previous section, their aggregation may lead to the emergence of a new international law regime.

As with regime emergence in general, this operation does not necessarily require that new rules be formulated. Using the individual as the aggregating factor for the identification of the rules that form a new legal regime under international law does not imply that the law be new in its content, since the content may already be there, in the usual international law instruments. It is, rather, a new way of looking at legal rules, grouping them according to the persons' interests and concerns. In turn, this new grouping may help explore the linkages between those rules and may expose the deficiencies in the framework of protection of the individual.

If compared to traditional, State-centered readings of international law, a human-centred recognition and description of international law, or one of its regimes,

---

[83] If at all; see, for some critical comments, Friedrich Kratochwil, 'Human Rights and Democracy: Is There a Place for Actual People(s)' in Ulrich Fastenrath, Rudolf Geiger, Daniel-Erasmus Khan, Andreas Paulus, Sabine von Schorlemer, and Christoph Vedder (eds), *From Bilateralism to Community Interest: Essays in Honour of Bruno Simma* (OUP 2011) 488.

[84] This stance is particularly relevant in the current climate which re-emphasizes the relevance of the State and State sovereignty in international law, as the most appropriate tools to protect and further human rights. According to Peters (n 68) 6, 'State sovereignty is being recognized by positive international law as instrumental for securing the well-being of humans' while for Martti Koskenniemi, 'What Use for Sovereignty Today?' (2011) 1 Asian Journal of International Law 61, 70, 'sovereignty articulates the hope of experiencing the thrill of having one's life in one's own hands'.

presents two significant advantages. On a more practical level, the grouping and rational exposition of all international law rules pertaining to people and their protection results in a ready-to-use tool to be taken advantage of in litigation brought by persons using international law, whether before national courts or international judges. It is often the case that litigation initiated by people tends to focus solely on human rights rules. While these are certainly paramount for the protection of individuals, it is argued here that there are also other rules in international law that may be used to further the protection of human beings.[85] As has been discussed in this book, these rules may help identify the duty-bearer, they may provide more detailed content for the obligations, or they may add to the requirements under human rights law. In the *Salemnik* case decided by the Court of Justice of the European Union (CJEU), for example, the reference to the concept of the continental shelf as it developed under the law of the sea was key in ensuring the applicability of European Union (EU) law to the person who had initiated the domestic proceedings, and, eventually, in ensuring better protection for that person.[86] A human-centered compilation of international law rules will therefore provide a readily available framework of assessment to examine issues that may arise in human rights litigation or other litigation that involves the exercise of power by a State over a person or, conversely, the disregard of a State with respect to a person.

A further advantage may exist on a conceptual level. A human-oriented approach does not only present an intellectual challenge, but it may be instrumental in identifying gaps and inconsistencies in the regulatory and enforcement framework, which may escape detection pursuant to a State-centered overview. The approach means examining existing law through new eyes and finding links and relationships that have been overlooked so far, since attention was focused elsewhere. The examination of these shortcomings may in turn facilitate their emergence as policy issues in international *fora* and their consideration by States and other international actors.

6. Chance Encounter or Regular Interaction?
An Evaluation of the Legal Rules Protecting People at Sea

Having set the conceptual premises for this discussion, it is now time to turn to the final question that needs to be answered before concluding this book: What is the nature of the group of rules collected and analysed in the previous chapters? My thesis is that they create a unique and coherent legal regime that addresses people at sea. Looking at these rules, it is possible to maintain that their points of contact do not merely represent an occasional interaction, but they could be construed in terms of a regular intercourse. Such a regime, it is argued, is logically necessary, legally possible, and factually materializing.

---

[85] Peters (n 68) underlines the relevance of simple international rights of the individual.
[86] Chapter 3, Section 5.2.1.

6.1 A logically necessary and legally possible regime

First, a legal regime is logically necessary due to the obvious plight of people at sea. These people often face a number of serious threats to their life, integrity, health, liberty, and other core human interests. They find themselves in an inherently hostile environment, often far away from the nearest land and from the aid of other humans, and they are at the mercy of the captain of the vessel they sail in or of the vessels they may encounter. The threats faced by people at sea, illustrated in Chapter 1, undoubtedly constitute an issue worthy of consideration. People should not lose protection because they happen to be at sea, out of sight from the lands where laws are developed. On the contrary, it is precisely because of the quantity and nature of the threats that people face that they deserve to be adequately protected. Crucially, protection requires appropriate legal rules to promote, sustain, and develop humanitarian impulses and initiatives.

The necessity of having a dedicated regime appears to be further supported by the paucity of dedicated legal rules. There are few international treaties dedicated to people at sea, and those that do exist only address specific categories of workers.[87] There is no reason, however, why States should be bound to protect seafarers but not people working on offshore platforms. The few additional provisions that have been inserted in international treaties, mostly concerning unlawful activities at sea, do not always provide a similar level of protection, thus creating a disparity that is not supported by any factual circumstance. For instance, it is not clear why the UNCLOS provides that recognized rights of the accused should be observed in the case of individuals charged with pollution of the marine environment,[88] but not in the case of individuals suspected of having violated the coastal State's regulatory framework concerning fishing in the exclusive economic zone,[89] or in the case of pirates.[90] Nor is it clear why human rights have to be observed in the application of the 2005 Convention for the Suppression of Unlawful Acts Against the Safety of Maritime Navigation (SUA Convention),[91] but no such mention is included in the United Nations Convention against Illicit Traffic in Narcotic Drugs and Psychotropic Substances (Convention against Illicit Traffic in Drugs).[92]

Factual and normative considerations therefore demand legal regulation. The factual circumstances of the dangers encountered by people at sea, combined with the legal consideration that dedicated legal rules are few and uneven, lead to the conclusion that there is the need for a set of rules—a legal regime—that will

---

[87] Chapter 1, Section 8.   [88] Art 230(3) UNCLOS.

[89] Art 73 UNCLOS, while providing concerning the penalties that may be imposed, is silent on procedural guarantees.

[90] Art 105 UNCLOS, which establishes the competence of the courts of the seizing State to try pirates, does not contain any procedural safeguard.

[91] Art 2*bis* Convention for the Suppression of Unlawful Acts Against the Safety of Maritime Navigation (adopted 10 March 1988), as amended by the 2005 Protocol (adopted 14 October 2005, entered into force 28 July 2010) 1678 UNTS 222 (SUA Convention).

[92] United Nations Convention against Illicit Traffic in Narcotic Drugs and Psychotropic Substances (adopted 20 December 1988, entered into force 11 November 1990) 1582 UNTS 165 (Convention against Illicit Traffic in Drugs).

work to protect the people who are at sea in a detailed and comprehensive manner. Following the note of caution expressed at the beginning of this chapter, this book has preferred not to merely propose the creation of a new regime from scratch. It has opted, rather, to conduct an examination of existing rules of international law, with a view towards identifying those that may be helpful in protecting people at sea, and assessing whether they provide adequate protection. From this analysis, it has emerged that there are numerous useful instruments and rules in international law and its sub-systems, in particular international human rights law and the law of the sea. While most of these instruments and rules were not developed with people at sea in mind, their scope is broad enough to allow them to be adapted to the protection of people at sea.

It is thus possible to find legal protection in international law norms. However, going further, is it legally possible to construe an international law regime out of the multitude of legal norms that apply, or should apply, or might apply to people at sea? As argued throughout, this is indeed very much the case and in this regard a new regime is currently emerging. To prove this assertion, I will make use of the methodology to ascertain the emergence of a new regime sketched in Section 4 above. The need for a new regime has just been demonstrated. Consequently, I will apply in turn the various steps to determine regime emergence: identifying the object of the regime; selecting the elements that compose the regime; combining these elements, so as to identify any general principle and understand what the main rules of the regime are.

Beginning with the object of the regime, this is identified by the phrase 'people at sea' used throughout this book.[93] This object is relevant and worth pursuing, as argued above and in Chapter 1. Therefore, the recognitory effort will be based on the hypothesis that a legal regime that purports to protect people who are at sea against both natural and manmade threats should indeed exist.

This object is then used as the aggregating device to attract the different rules of international law that may serve it best. In particular, since the focus is on people, a human-centered methodology has been preferred in approaching the selection task, whereby rules are deemed relevant whenever they are instrumental to the protection of the people: either because they attribute these people rights that they can action against the State, or because they impose duties on States to protect people by both negative and positive action.

From a preliminary glance at international law, two regimes have emerged as being particularly promising in furnishing relevant rules: the law of the sea and international human rights law. The law of the sea is obviously relevant because people are at sea and the law of the sea regulates this space.[94] Similarly, human rights are important because they deal with people, who are the focus of this study. Other regimes are however also relevant, including labour law, since many of the people who are at sea are there to work; maritime law, which contains rules addressing the safety of vessels; refugee law, which guarantees the basic principle of *non-refoulement*;

---

[93] On the selection of this focus see Introduction, Section 2.
[94] Establishing the rule of law therein; Oxman (n 14) 402.

and transnational criminal law, which addresses some of the core threats that people face. These regimes have been discussed in Chapter 2, where the contribution of each has been assessed, as well as the limitations that they present.

A significant part of this book has been dedicated to singling out and discussing the norms that are potentially applicable to people at sea. When synthesizing this effort into an embryonic legal taxonomy, it is possible to identify (at least) six categories of instruments and norms that are relevant for the protection of people at sea. The first includes treaties specifically dealing with the protection of a category of persons and in this regard, the Maritime Labour Convention (MLC) and the Work in Fishing Convention have been singled out in particular. The second includes all those provisions which can be found in a diverse range of law of the sea and maritime law treaties, specifically and directly dealing with the protection of people at sea. These include those provisions concerned with the safety of life at sea, such as Article 98 UNCLOS, and provisions concerning the humane treatment of people intercepted at sea, for example Article 2*bis*(1) SUA Convention. The third comprises law of the sea provisions on the distribution of power to States at sea, especially concerning jurisdiction over persons, ships, and platforms, as well as the human rights principle according to which the power exercised by a State over an individual is relevant as *de facto* jurisdiction. The fourth encompasses human rights norms on the protection of fundamental human rights, which give rights to individuals and oblige States not only to abstain from violating these rights, but also to undertake positive action to promote and ensure the enjoyment of these rights vis-à-vis all third parties, be they State organs or private actors. These norms include, among others, the right to life and physical integrity, the right to personal liberty and the guarantees accompanying the deprivation of liberty, the freedom from torture and other inhuman and degrading treatment, the freedom from slavery, and procedural rights. A particularly significant norm in this context is the principle of *non-refoulement*, which is reflected both in refugee law and in international human rights law. The fifth consists of labour law norms concerning the workplace and working conditions. The sixth and final includes maritime law instruments and norms concerned with the safety of shipping and other maritime activities.

Once these norms have been identified and isolated, they need to be combined so as to ascertain their potential for interaction and for the production of an autonomous legal regime. This task may be approached by two different methodologies. The first is to consider one of the two main regimes that apply to people at sea, either the law of the sea or international human rights law, and see how its norms and principles impact on the other. The second methodology takes a different perspective. It tries to find whether there are common principles underpinning all the norms collected and uses these principles to combine the various rules. The difference between the two approaches is considerable. In the first case, there is simply interaction between the regimes, which do however maintain their separate identities. In the second case there is a new regime which is autonomous, at least in part, from the other regimes from which it has emerged.

The first methodology was adopted in early writings on the topic. In probably the first article on the topic, Sohn set out to examine 'how in practice the United States

Government complies with the human rights standards, which it accepts as internationally recognised, in its application of other generally accepted international rules or standards, those of the law of the sea'.[95] According to Oxman, the law of the sea, as codified in the UNCLOS, 'promotes the rule of law at sea by allocating authority to govern and by imposing qualifications on that authority' thus complying with 'an indispensable condition for the protection of human rights'.[96] Treves has pointed out that 'concerns for human beings, which lie at the core of human rights concerns' are present in the 'texture' of the UNCLOS provisions,[97] and has maintained that law of the sea norms must be interpreted in the light of human rights considerations.[98] At a more specific level, a number of community and individual rights have been read into UNCLOS provisions,[99] and it has been highlighted that some of these rights have found their way into decisions rendered by the International Tribunal for the Law of the sea (ITLOS), through the use of Article 293 UNCLOS and Article 31(3)(c) VCLT.[100] Conversely, Tavernier has provided evidence that the ECtHR has applied its traditional principles in the maritime context taking into account the specificities of this context,[101] and in conformity with law of the sea rules.[102]

These findings are particularly relevant because, based on a systemic reading of international law, they highlight the linkages that exist between norms coming from two separate international law regimes, and they suggest methods for accommodating interests permeating one regime in the application of rules deriving from the other. However, arguably the most important contribution is the assertion that there is a common grounding—the rule of law for Oxman, the concern for human beings for Treves, the humanization of international law for Sohn—for all rules, independently from their regime of origin.[103]

This book argues that this common grounding should not constitute the *conclusion* of a discussion of how international law protects people at sea, but should

---

[95] Sohn, 'International Law' (n 14) 52.   [96] Oxman (n 14) 402.
[97] Treves (n 14) 3.   [98] ibid 12.
[99] Oxman (n 14); Treves (n 14) 5, considers that some 'human rights principles or considerations ... are directly stated in the LOS Convention or can be inferred from its provisions'.
[100] Treves (n 14) 6.   [101] Tavernier (n 14) 576.   [102] ibid 589.
[103] In the more restricted context of interception of irregular migrants at sea, Richard Barnes, 'The International Law of the Sea and Migration Control' in Bernard Ryan and Valsamis Mitsilegas (eds), *Extraterritorial Immigration Control: Legal Challenges* (Martinus Nijhoff 2010) 103, 114, noted that 'although the prospects of any formal changes to the UNCLOS are unlikely in the short term, this does not mean that existing UNCLOS rules cannot be applied in a manner more sympathetic to human rights concerns'. A few years later, Klein has pointed out that 'the desire to save human lives' could be the cornerstone for a harmonization of the different regimes that apply: 'Saving human lives is a common theme, and interception operations have been touted by States as a key means for preventing loss of life at sea. This desire to save human lives must be extended to include saving these same lives from persecution or other human rights violations. If this aim is agreed, the regime can hold together.' (Klein (n 38) 813). Similarly, when discussing the applicability of human rights instruments to people on board ships, Urfan Khaliq, 'Jurisdiction, Ships and Human Rights Treaties' in Henrik Ringbom (ed), *Jurisdiction over Ships* (Martinus Nijhoff 2015) 324, 359–60, notes that 'human rights treaties impose obligations upon flag states and upon port states but do so without undermining or even seeking to challenge the fundamental assumptions upon which UNCLOS is based. The two legal regimes thus operate in relative harmony.'

instead be used as the *first stepping stone* to reconstruct a legal regime dedicated to this need. This common grounding, in fact, constitutes the basis of a normative activity that has resulted in the emergence of the general principle requiring States to protect people at sea, discussed in Chapter 4. This general principle belongs neither solely to the law of the sea nor to international human rights law. It is a self-standing general principle of international law, which combines elements from both regimes and which can be fruitfully used as the basis for a new regime. In this role, it will exert its influence in the interpretation and application of all the norms that have been deemed relevant for the protection of people at sea. These norms will have to be considered not only insofar as they belong to international human rights law or the law of the sea or any other regime of origin, but also as they belong to the newly emerging regime of the international protection of people at sea.[104]

It thus becomes apparent how the general principle is in a dual relationship with the group of norms attracted by the object, that is the protection of people at sea. On the one hand, all the instruments and norms already discussed can be considered as manifestations of the practice that has led to the emergence of the principle. It is arguably the case that when States adopt a specific norm or expound a specific treaty, they may not be aware that this act was directed by an underlying principle or that the adoption of this norm or treaty may actually contribute to the consolidation of the principle. However, this argument is valid only if the norms and instruments are considered as separate acts, without any interdependence. As has been argued in Section 4 and in line with what has been considered the task of the legal scholar, all these manifestations of practice are now collected and combined. What emerges is inescapable: a new, separate, principle. This principle can thus be considered as a consequence of the selection and grouping of these rules in a separate set, which puts at the forefront the sparse elements of international practice that, up to then, had not been assessed as a whole, and extrapolates and makes explicit what up to then had been only implied in the *dicta* of judgments and the activity of States. On the other hand, once they have emerged from this set of rules, principles will inform the interpretation and application of the rules themselves and will be crucial to the further development of the regime.

There are two normative consequences stemming from the establishment of the general principle. The first consists in the increment of instances where States—the flag State, the coastal State, or another State—must act to protect people at sea. As argued in Chapter 4, the consolidation of the human rights discourse at the international level is now turning States' rights to act into duties to act. Whenever a State is accorded jurisdiction on the basis of a law of the sea norm, the State will have the duty to protect and ensure the rights of the people subject to its jurisdiction, within the limits that this is mandated by the relevant jurisdictional rules.

---

[104] I have opted for this name in the absence of a better one. Others have spoken of human rights at sea or maritime human rights. These names, however, might lead the reader to consider them as a subbranch of human rights law, thus diminishing the significant contribution that law of the sea brings to the development of this regime.

The second normative consequence of the emergence of a new principle is that States' duties to act must take into account the particularities of the maritime environment. This means that the obligations of States under international human rights law may need to adapt to the practicalities of life at sea, for example by taking into account the time necessary to navigate long distances before a person arrested is brought before a judge. It also means, however, that States may have increased duties, which may require them not only to undertake additional action to protect human rights, such as the right to life, but also to act in a precautionary manner, even before the potential victim of a human rights violation can be identified. Thus, duties concerning the setting up of search and rescue services and the regulation of the construction, equipment, and manning of vessels to ensure their safety are duties that go beyond human rights and derive directly from the particular characteristics of the maritime environment.

The general principle therefore produces consequences at the normative level, and these consequences are in turn informing the main rules of the regime. Stepping away from their initial positioning, the norms that compose the legal regime on the protection of people at sea can be divided into two main sets: norms on jurisdiction and norms on duties. On the one hand, rules concerning the determination of the scope of States' duties are provided by a close reading of law of the sea rules on jurisdiction, together with other rules of international law on the attribution of jurisdiction, in addition to the special notion that this terms assumes under human rights law, that is the notion of *de facto* jurisdiction, as opposed to *de jure* jurisdiction. These rules have been identified and discussed in Chapter 3.

On the other hand, we are able to identify the rules that spell out the duties of States towards people at sea. These duties derive from a variety of regimes and are contained in a multitude of legal instruments. It is often the case that a number of norms, which may derive from separate legal regimes, are based upon the need to protect the same underlying interest. For example, the desire to protect human life is the foundation upon which norms were developed in international human rights law (the rights to life), the law of the sea (the basic duty to rescue), maritime law (the particularly detailed content concerning the duty to rescue, as well as the characteristics that a safe vessel must have), and labour law (eg the adequate training required for a seafarer who rescues people in distress, but also the need for this seafarer to be adequately rested so as to be able to fulfil their functions). All these rules will have to be interpreted and applied jointly, taking into account the principle of systemic integration and the principle of harmonization, and in light of the basic principle of the regime that requires States to effectively protect people at sea, so as to ensure the best possible protection for the persons involved.

The example of the protection of life at sea demonstrates the added value of referring to a separate legal regime of international law that deals with people at sea. If, in fact, the safety of life at sea were to be approached from the angle of one of the already well-established legal regimes, there would be two negative consequences. The first practical consequence would be that, most probably, only the regime rules of reference would be considered, and any other rule might be taken into account only in a subsidiary fashion, and only in the measure in which the interpreter is aware of their existence. In this respect, the reconstruction of a new regime relating to the protection of people at sea allows the scholar to group all relevant norms together and to provide decision-makers, judges, and other international actors with a ready-made set of rules that do not ignore anything of relevance.[105]

The second negative consequence of an examination of the problem under the lens of one of the established regimes would be a technical one. Every regime of international law tends to privilege its own rules and principles,[106] and to consider rules that derive from other regimes only insofar as they are compatible with its own most fundamental principles. This would mean that rules from a different regime would have to undergo a compatibility test, the outcome of which might be uncertain, depending to some extent on the outlook adopted by the interpreter, and might be variable, as different interpreters could reach different results. In contrast, the acceptance of the existence of a regime concerning the protection of people at sea has two implications. First, the acceptance of the general principle already discussed would constitute the parameter against which the admissibility of a certain rule would be evaluated. Second, the compatibility test has been effected once and for all in the selection of the norms of the regime, and therefore all norms that have been deemed relevant *need* to be applied to the specific circumstances, thanks to the application of the principle of harmonization. This does not entirely rule out the possibility to have conflicting rules, but it certainly reduces this possibility and allows any remaining inconsistencies to be smoothed out through recourse to rules of conflict between norms.

The issue of disembarkation of people rescued at sea clearly illustrates the added value of a human-centered assessment of international law in the form of a proposal for a new regime on people at sea. Rules on disembarkation were elaborated having the State, and State interests, in mind. They include the obligation to save life at sea,[107] and the duty to deliver the rescued people to a place of safety.[108] Once the principle that people at danger of being lost at sea must be saved was adopted, State concerns about sovereignty intruded and shaped the applicable rules, which require the consent of the territorial State before these people are disembarked on shore. Looked at from the perspective of States, the group of rules may appear sufficient: people are saved from death at sea, which means that States may claim compliance with their moral duties, and at the same time national boundaries are protected against the unauthorized entry of aliens, upholding sovereignty and the security concerns of States. However, the assessment changes with a shift in perspective. If one looks at the situation from the point of view of the person, it is evident that a gap is present and that existing rules of international law do not guarantee adequate protection. A mismatch clearly exists between the duty to deliver people to a place of safety, and the requirement that disembarkation take place with the consent of the coastal State, a consent which may be withheld at will.[109] Awareness of the

---

[105] Klein (n 38).   [106] See, eg, Art 311(2) UNCLOS.   [107] Art 98(1) UNCLOS.

[108] Chapter 1.3.2 SAR Convention.

[109] Obviously, pointing out gaps and inconsistencies alone does not eliminate them, as further normative action is required by States, but at least brings the focus on issues that otherwise might be neglected and obliges States to justify, in political if not legal terms, their stance.

mismatch led States to adopt the 2004 amendments to the SOLAS and SAR. While these amendments have not settled all issues, they have introduced the concept of 'place of safety' and can be viewed as a first step forward in what is still an ongoing process. Therefore, only if the applicable rules are considered as part of the same regime, can interactions be highlighted and gaps pointed out, which may in turn lead to a clarification of applicable norms and, if need be, the adoption of new rules.

6.2 A factually materializing regime

A new regime on the protection of people at sea, therefore, allows for a better taxonomy of relevant legal rules, facilitates the practical application of these rules, guides normative developments by providing a guiding principle, and facilitates the harmonization of norms. Arguing in favour of the existence of a new regime on the protection of people at sea is not only legally possible—because it is possible to identify the general principle and the specific rules that compose it—but also desirable as it would have an added value if compared to a reading of rules only within the pre-existing regimes. There is, however, more to it than this. If we leave theoretical constructions aside and turn to the actual practice of States and other international actors, we will discover that this regime is not only logically necessary and legally possible, but it is also materializing in the actual practice of international actors.

There are three main elements of international practice that sustain the contention that such a regime is actually emerging at the international level: the practice of States and other international actors, judicial decisions, and scholarly writings. While the practice of the international community, in particular that of States, is paramount, judicial decisions and doctrine can also contribute to the making of international law, as recognized by Article 38(1)(d) ICJ Statute. Each element will therefore be considered in its own right.

The first element is the fact that there are many manifestations which demonstrate the wish of the international community to ensure the better protection of people at sea. While often spurred by disasters,[110] normative activity aiming at the adoption of rules that either directly protect people at sea or that aim at creating the conditions for a safer and more humane environment for them has been going on since the beginning of the twentieth century.[111] This activity has been significantly increasing and its reach has been regularly expanding since the beginning of the twenty-first century. The 2004 amendments to the SOLAS and the International

---

[110] The example of the SOLAS is telling, as the first version of this treaty was negotiated in the aftermath of the *Titanic* disaster.

[111] For example, the provision that examination of a vessel under the right of visit must be carried out 'with all possible consideration' (Art 22(2) Convention on the High Seas (adopted 29 April 1958, entered into force 30 September 1962) 450 UNTS 11 (HSC) and Art 110(2) UNCLOS) was inserted so as to ensure that 'navigation should be interfered to the minimum extent possible and that the rights of the vessel's and cargo's owners and of the captain and the crew have to be respected to the maximum extent possible. While the point of departure ... was to safeguard national sovereignty, the concern about the smooth working of maritime commerce and the rights of individuals involved soon came to the fore' (Sohn, 'International Law' (n 14) 56–57).

Convention on Maritime Search and Rescue (SAR Convention) to better protect human life at sea, the 2005 amendments to the SUA Convention which have notably introduced an express safeguard for the human rights of the persons involved, the adoption of the MLC in 2006 and the Work in Fishing Convention in 2007, are all elements of this practice. Furthermore, the need to protect people at sea and their rights is now routinely included in legal texts relating to maritime activities produced not only by human rights bodies, such as the UNHCR, and maritime bodies, such as the IMO, but also other international actors such as the UN Security Council in its resolutions on piracy and migrant smuggling.[112] The need to protect people at sea and to safeguard their rights, which seemed to be absent in the UNCLOS, has now taken its place among the present concerns of States and international organizations and, it is submitted in this book, is here to stay. According to the UN Secretary General, '[i]mproving the situation of people at sea has been an increasing focus of the international community',[113] and this has been recognized since 2012 by including a section dedicated to 'people at sea' in the Reports to the General Assembly on Oceans and the law of the sea.[114] One might even add to this the fact that civil society is now active in this field, as the creation of new non-governmental organizations dedicated to the protection of people at sea demonstrates.[115]

The second element of international practice that supports the conclusion that there is an emerging regime on the protection of people at sea is the work of international judges. Indeed, international judges have been the principal means through which the basic principle of this regime has consolidated. While lacking an expressly stated cohesive factor, State practice, albeit significant and increasing in measure and reach, could still be considered as a (numerous) series of single isolated instances. In contrast, it is not possible to assume any such conclusion when looking at the decisions rendered by international judges approaching cases involving people at sea. If we first consider human rights judges and their decisions, the oft-repeated statement by the ECtHR that 'the special nature of the maritime environment ... cannot justify an area outside the law where ships' crews are covered by no legal system capable of affording them enjoyment of the rights and guarantees protected' by

[112] For example UNSC Res 1816 (2 June 2008) UN Doc S/RES/1816, para 11 (on piracy) and UNSC Res 2240 (9 October 2015) UN Doc S/RES/2240, paras 10 and 12 (on migration by sea).
[113] UNGA 'Oceans and the law of the sea. Report of the Secretary-General. Addendum' (1 September 2015) UN Doc A/70/74/Add.1, paras 28–42, para 28.
[114] See UNGA 'Oceans and the law of the sea. Report of the Secretary-General. Addendum' (31 August 2012) UN Doc A/67/79/Add.1, paras 26–34; UNGA, 'Oceans and the law of the sea. Report of the Secretary-General. Addendum' (9 September 2013) UN Doc A/68/71/Add.1, paras 25–33; UNGA 'Oceans and the law of the sea. Report of the Secretary-General. Addendum' (1 September 2014) UN Doc A/69/71/Add.1, paras 37–43; UNGA 'Oceans and the law of the sea. Report of the Secretary-General. Addendum' (1 September 2015) UN Doc A/70/74/Add.1, paras 28–42; UNGA 'Oceans and the law of the sea. Report of the Secretary-General. Addendum' (6 September 2016) UN Doc A/71/74/Add.1, paras 28–35.
[115] See eg organizations such as Human Rights at Sea (<https://www.humanrightsatsea.org>), Slave Free Seas (<http://slavefreeseas.org>), and the Oceans Beyond Piracy programme of One Earth Future (<http://oceansbeyondpiracy.org>).

the ECHR[116] clearly supports the argument that there is a law that applies to these persons. Even more importantly, and as has been demonstrated when discussing the principle in Chapter 4, international judges deciding on the basis of the law of the sea have consistently used the concept of 'considerations of humanity' to single out the fact that there are rules that apply to people at sea and that these rules aim at protecting these people by imposing duties on States. Since the notion of 'considerations of humanity' is the groundwork for the principle, and this principle is in turn the backbone of the regime, it is evident that international judges have been key in the emergence of a regime aiming at the protection of people at sea.

An objection that could be raised is that no international judge, be it a law of the sea judge or a human rights judge, has ever openly proclaimed the existence of this regime. There are two possible rebuttals to this objection. The first is that it is rarely the case, if ever, that international judges take it upon themselves to expressly state that a regime exists or has emerged. The most fundamental task of a judge is to adjudicate a case, not to theorize on the regimes of international law. The second rebuttal, which is closely linked to and may explain the first, is that judges are constrained, in the drafting of their decisions, by the terms of the legal instrument that has created them in the first place. As has already been pointed out, a judge must decide according to the law mentioned in the tribunal's statute or other constitutive instrument, or according to the law indicated by the parties to the dispute. At the same time, since the creation of a new regime may take the form of the adoption of a new context within which the rules that the judge must apply will be interpreted and applied, it can be safely said that, by referring to the 'other' legal regime and its rules as well as the general concept of 'considerations of humanity', international judges have *de facto* allowed the emergence of a new regime.

Finally, it is useful to consider the last element of international practice that points towards the emergence of a new regime: scholarly writing. It is a fact that in recent years, at least some of the issues involving people at sea and their protection have received considerable attention by the scholarly community. The upsurge of piracy off the coasts of Somalia has provided the groundwork for an assessment of the rules concerning piracy also from the point of view of their compatibility with international human rights law.[117] In another area, the plight of migrants resorting to sea routes and the restrictive practices adopted by the States more closely concerned have prompted scholars to discuss the compatibility of these practices with the basic requirements under human rights and refugee law.[118] Perhaps less visibly, but still of

---

[116] *Medvedyev and Others v France* App no 3394/03 (Judgment (GC) of 29 March 2010) para 81, recalled in *Hirsi* (n 13) para 178.

[117] Douglas Guilfoyle, 'Counter-Piracy Law Enforcement and Human Rights' (2010) 59 ICLQ 141; Eugene Kontorovich, '"A Guantánamo on the Sea": the Difficulty of Prosecuting Pirates and Terrorists (2010) 98 California Law Review 243; Robin Geiss and Anna Petrig, *Piracy and Armed Robbery at Sea: The Legal Framework for Counter-Piracy Operations in Somalia and the Gulf of Aden* (OUP 2011); Tom Obokata, 'Maritime Piracy as a Violation of Human Rights: A Way Forward for Its Effective Prevention and Suppression?' (2013) 17 The International Journal of Human Rights 18; Tullio Treves and Cesare Pitea, 'Piracy, International Law and Human Rights' in Nehal Bhuta (ed), *The Frontiers of Human Rights. Extraterritoriality and Its Challenges* (OUP 2016).

[118] M Pallis, 'Obligations of States towards Asylum Seekers at Sea: Interactions and Conflicts Between Legal Regimes' (2002) 14 International Journal of Refugee Law 329; Cacciaguidi-Fahy (n 14);

certain importance, texts examining law of the sea issues have now started to add a particular part concerning the protection of the human rights of the persons involved,[119] and even one law of the sea manual is now devoting a section to this topic.[120]

Again, the same objection that has been addressed in the case of international judges might be raised also with respect to the work of scholars. All these writings do not openly advocate the emergence of a new regime of international law. This statement is formally correct. It is however my contention that, although not expressly making such a proposal, all these works contribute to this emerging regime and, to a certain extent, presume the existence of this regime. This is echoed in the suggestions that there is a rule of law that regulates people at sea,[121] that there are considerations of humanity that must be taken into account generally when addressing these people,[122] and that there is a common theme of saving lives at sea that underpins all actions of States.[123] Notably, Sohn seemed to foreshadow the emergence of such a regime when, referring to the Birth of Venus by Botticelli, he hoped that 'out of the marriage of the law of the sea and the law of human rights an equally beautiful creature will be born'.[124]

7. Conclusions

In conclusion, all elements of international practice—the activities of States and international organizations, the decisions of international judges, and the writings of scholars—complement each other in their support for the contention that a new, human-oriented and function-driven regime is emerging, which purports to protect people at sea. This book has discussed the practical and legal circumstances out of which this regime has emerged and it has described its main elements. It is hoped that this analysis has convinced the reader and that it may even trigger the interest of the reader to further investigate the nature and constituent elements of this regime and its application. Of course, the book and the thesis it advances may also raise eyebrows and may meet with diffidence, or even critique.[125] In any case, this is often the fate

Andreas Fischer-Lescano, Tillmann Löhr and Timo Tohidipur, 'Border Controls at Sea: Requirements under International Human Rights and Refugee Law' (2009) 21 International Journal of Refugee Law 256; Barnes (n 103); Klein (n 38).

[119] Guilfoyle, *Shipping Interdiction* (n 37); Papastavridis, *The Interception* (n 37); Geiss and Petrig (n 117). Notably, the latest edition of J Ashley Roach and Robert W Smith, *Excessive Maritime Claims* (3rd edn, Martinus Nijhoff 2012), a classic text on excessive maritime claims, now contains a section dedicated to the 'treatment of seafarers' (ibid 623–30).

[120] Irini Papanicolopulu, 'Human Rights and the Law of the Sea' in David Attard, Malgosia Fitzmaurice, and Norman Martinez (eds), *IMLI Manual on International Maritime Law. The Law of the Sea*, (vol 1) (OUP 2014) 509.

[121] Oxman (n 14) 402.   [122] Treves (n 14) 3–5.

[123] Albeit in the limited context of irregular migrants interception operations; Klein (n 38) 813.

[124] Sohn, 'International Law' (n 14) 63.

[125] There is no doubt that people at sea deserve protection. However, some may feel that the methodology advanced in this book is not appropriate, or effective, or adequate. Clearly, this book has presented some novel conceptions and further research is necessary, which would benefit from constructive critique.

of scholarly works: once they leave their author's laptop, they start a life of their own. Before concluding this book, however, there are two issues that I would like to address.

The first concerns the exact positioning of the regime. Once the existence of the regime is established, one might wonder where exactly the regime would be located. Is it a sub-regime of international human rights law, or is it a sub-regime of the law of the sea? Or, on the contrary, is it an autonomous regime of international law? There is no definitive answer to this question, as the exact positioning of the regime of the international protection of people at sea will very much depend on the perception of the examiner. In light of the research and analysis contained in this book, I would suggest that it should be seen as an independent regime of international law, for two main reasons. On the one hand, it not only contains rules deriving from more than one regime, but it also does not privilege those rules deriving from a certain regime over those deriving from another. Human rights norms certainly are particularly important in this context, but in a number of instances these principles may be superseded by rules deriving from other regimes. As has been seen, while in some cases it is law of the sea rules that will be most significant (eg the establishment of *de jure* jurisdiction), in other cases it is labour law that will play a primary role (eg the determination of the content of the right of the seafarer to rest). On the other hand, the general principle which constitutes the basis of the regime does not belong to either international human rights law or the law of the sea, but it can be seen as an autonomous general principle of international law. Therefore, it would be unnecessarily restrictive to subsume the regime under only one of the two regimes of origin.

There are, however, also arguments in favour of the thesis that the regime of the international protection of people at sea may be positioned within international human rights law and the law of the sea. The main argument in favour of this conclusion is a practical one, but it carries a great weight. Considering it as a sub-regime of the two above-mentioned regimes, would in fact mean that the regime of the international protection of people at sea constitutes part and parcel of these two regimes. This, in turn, would result in the situation that it could—or better, should—be applied by judges deciding issues on the basis of the law of the sea or international human rights law as part of the primary regime under which they operate. There would therefore be no need to justify why recourse is made to the rules of this regime. Neither should judges operate compatibility tests between the rules of the sub-regime and those of the primary regime, be it the international law of human rights or the law of the sea. By qualifying the regime of the international protection of people at sea as a sub-genus of *both* law of the sea and international human rights law, its use in litigation before the judges whose offices were created under the UNCLOS and human rights treaties would be facilitated.

The second issue I would like to touch upon in concluding this work concerns the potential of 'international law and the protection of people at sea' and its limits. Starting from the latter, as highlighted in Chapter 2, regimes are useful tools but they may eventually lead to the development of gnoseological boundaries.[126] This

---

[126] Another issue that would deserve a discussion of its own concerns the threat that the regime might be reduced to a hegemonic struggle for power by the experts of the two main regimes involved;

is something that needs to be kept in mind, as well as the fact that the emergence of this regime has been possible only thanks to the systemic nature of international law. This regime is therefore in a dialectic relationship with both general international law and the specialized regimes which have contributed their norms to its emergence. However, these are issues that affect regimes once they have been well-established. If the international regime for the protection of people at sea were to incur the same issues, this result would vouch for its widespread acceptance and its attested ability to influence concretely the protection of the people concerned.

Turning to the potential of the regime to help overcome the vulnerability of people at sea, this may indeed be significant from a dual conceptual and practical, perspective. At the conceptual level, a web of assumptions, or, in other words, a reference framework, is interwoven in every manifestation of international practice, in particular the making of treaties and other binding instruments and the adoption of judicial decisions. The absence of a conceptualization should not be equated to the absence of principles guiding the actions of international actors. It will only mean that these principles remain hidden, which in turn may render them confused, shifting, or contradictory. Against this picture, conceptualization brings clarity and transparency, which may favour consistency and participation and may in turn pave the way for meaningful normative changes. In fact, only law that is known can be assessed against societal interests, so as to decide whether it should be kept or whether it should be dismissed.

This point leads to the practical potentiality of the regime. The conditions under which many people find themselves at sea are clearly unacceptable. The lack of protection by States, as this book has demonstrated, is not due to the absence of legal rules and principles, but rather to their limited and incorrect application. While this is to a significant extent the result of the inertia of States, it is also due to the absence in this area of the other international actors, who have often led the development of legal and practical measures: international institutions (including international courts and tribunals) and civil society. The activism of some institutions over the last few years has indeed led to the first developments in this area, which have been referred to when the emergence of the regime in practice was discussed. In particular, the role of international judicial bodies, such as the ECtHR and the ITLOS, has been substantial. If the protection of people at sea were to establish itself in the agendas of civil society, international institutions and, eventually, States, then these people would at last benefit from some measure of protection.

Ultimately, this book has attempted to be part of the process and help consolidate an emerging legal regime, making full use of the potential of international law to create new regimes. The regime of the international protection of people at sea is in fact already emerging. Giving this phenomenon a name does not create it. It is simply a recognition of its existence and an open-ended invitation for all to join its epistemic community and further its aims.

---

see Martti Koskenniemi, 'Hegemonic Regimes' in Margaret A Young (ed), *Regime Interaction in International Law. Facing Fragmentation* (CUP 2012) 305, 319–20.

Bibliography

—— 'Fatal Injuries in Offshore Oil and Gas Operations—United States, 2003–2010' (2013) 62 Morbidity and Mortality Weekly Report 301

—— *Out of Sight, Out of Mind. Seafarers, Fishers & Human Rights* (International Transport Workers' Federation 2006)

Abbott K, 'A Brief Overview of Legal Interoperability Challenges for NATO Arising from the Interrelationship between IHL and IHRL in Light of the European Convention on Human Rights' (2014) 96 International Review of the Red Cross 107

Abi-Saab G, 'Cours Général de Droit International Public' (1987) 207 Recueil des Cours 9

—— 'Fragmentation or Unification: Some Concluding Remarks' (1999) 31 New York University Journal of International Law and Politics 919

Ago R, *Scienza giuridica e diritto internazionale* (Giuffre 1950)

Ailincai M, 'Piraterie et droits de l'homme au sein du Conseil de l'Europe' in Constance Chevallier-Govers and Catherine Schneider (eds), *L'Europe et la lutte contre la piraterie maritime* (Pedone 2015) 227

Allison EH, Ratner BD, Åsgård B, Willmann R, Pomeroy R, and Kurien J, 'Rights-based Fisheries Governance: From Fishing Rights to Human Rights' (2012) 13 Fish and Fisheries 14

Allott P, 'Power Sharing in the Law of the Sea' (1983) 77 AJIL 1

Alvarez JE, *International Organizations as Law-Makers* (OUP 2005)

Andenas M and Bjorge E (eds), *A Farewell to Fragmentation: Reassertion and Convergence in International Law* (CUP 2015)

Anderson D, 'Freedoms of the High Seas in the Modern Law of the Sea' in David Freestone, Richard Barnes, and David Ong (eds), *The Law of the Sea: Progress and Prospects* (OUP 2006) 327

Antonucci A, Papanicolopulu I, and Scovazzi T (eds), *L'immigrazione Irregolare via Mare nella Giurisprudenza Italiana e nell'Esperienza Europea* (Giappichelli 2016)

Anzilotti D, *Corso di Diritto Internazionale. Volume Primo: Introduzione—Teorie Generali* (Athenaeum 1928)

Auburn FM, 'International Law and Sea-Ice Jurisdiction in the Arctic Ocean' (1973) 22 ICLQ 552

Auvret-Finck J, 'La conditionnalité des Droits de l'Homme dans les accords de l'UE relatifs à la lutte contre la piraterie maritime' in Constance Chevallier-Govers and Catherine Schneider (eds), *L'Europe et la lutte contre la piraterie maritime* (Pedone 2015) 245

Baillet C, 'The Tampa Case and Its Impact on Burden Sharing at Sea' (2003) 25 Human Rights Quarterly 741

Balloun OS, 'The True Obstacle to the Autonomy of Seasteads: American Law Enforcement Jurisdiction over Homesteads on the High Seas' (2012) 24 University of San Francisco Maritime Law Journal 409

Barnes R, 'The International Law of the Sea and Migration Control' in Bernard Ryan and Valsamis Mitsilegas (eds), *Extraterritorial Immigration Control: Legal Challenges* (Martinus Nijhoff 2010) 103

Barrett J and Barnes R (eds), *Law of the Sea. UNCLOS as a Living Treaty* (BIICL 2016)

Baslar K, *The Concept of the Common Heritage of Mankind in International Law* (Martinus Nijhoff 1998)

Berkes F, 'Fishermen and "The Tragedy of the Commons"' (1985) 12 Environmental Conservation 199

Besson S, 'The Extraterritoriality of the European Convention on Human Rights: Why Human Rights Depend on Jurisdiction and What Jurisdiction Amounts to' (2012) 25 Leiden Journal of International Law 857

Bianchi A, 'Human Rights and the Magic of *Jus Cogens*' (2008) 19 EJIL 491

Bonafe BI and Palchetti P, 'Relying on General Principles in International Law' in Catherine Brölmann and Yannick Radi (eds), *Research Handbook on the Theory and Practice of International Law-Making* (Edward Elgar 2016) 160

Borelli S, 'Positive Obligations of States and the Protection of Human Rights' (2006) 15 Interights Bulletin 101

Borelli S and Stanford B, 'Troubled Waters in the Mare Nostrum: Interception and Push-backs of Migrants in the Mediterranean and the European Convention on Human Rights' (2014) 10 Uluslararası Hukuk ve Politika 29

Boyle A, 'Further Development of the 1982 Convention on the Law of the Sea: Mechanisms for Change' in David Freestone, Richard Barnes, and David Ong (eds), *The Law of the Sea: Progress and Prospects* (OUP 2006) 40

Breda G and Perini JP, 'Legal Issues Surrounding Maritime Counterdrug Operations and the Related Question of Detention as Highlighted in the *Medvedyev and Others v. France* Decision of the European Court of Human Rights' (2008) 47 Military Law and the Law of War Review 167

Briggs A, *The Conflict of Laws* (OUP 2008)

Brown N, 'Jurisdictional Problems Relating to Non-Flag State Boarding of Suspect Ships in International Waters: A Practitioner's Observations' in Clive R Symmons (ed), Selected Contemporary Issues in the Law of the Sea (Martinus Nijhoff 2011) 69

Brownlie I, *Principles of Public International Law* (7th edn, OUP 2008)

Brunnée J and Toope SJ, *Legitimacy and Legality in International Law. An Interactional Account* (CUP 2010)

Cacciaguidi-Fahy S, 'The Law of the Sea and Human Rights' (2007) 19 Sri Lanka Journal of International Law 85

Caflisch LC and Cançado Trindade AA, 'Les Conventions Américaine et Européenne des Droit de l'Homme et le Droit International Général' (2003) 108 Revue Générale de Droit International Public 5

Cançado Trindade AA, *The Access of Individuals to International Justice* (OUP 2011)

Cannizzaro E, *Corso di Diritto Internazionale* (Giuffre Editore 2011)

Carballo Piñeiro L, 'Port State Jurisdiction over Labour Conditions: a Private International Law Perspective on Extra-territoriality' (2016) 31 IJMCL 531

Carbone SM, *Conflits de Lois en Droit Maritime* (Martinus Nijhoff 2010)

Cassese A, *Diritto Internazionale. Problemi della Comunità Internazionale* (Il Mulino 2004)

——*Diritto Internazionale* (10th edn, Editoriale Scientifica 2014)

Cellamare G, 'Brevi note sulla sentenza della Corte europea dei diritti dell'uomo nell'affare *Hirsi Jamaa e altri c. Italia*' (2012) 7 Studi sull'Integrazione Europea 491

Charlesworth H, Chinkin C, and Wright S, 'Femminist Approaches to International Law' (1991) 85 AJIL 613

Charney JI, 'The Implications of Expanding International Dispute Settlement Systems: The 1982 Convention on the Law of the Sea' (1996) 90 AJIL 69

Chevallier-Govers C and Schneider C (eds), *L'Europe et la lutte contre la piraterie maritime* (Pedone 2015)

Churchill RR, 'Port State Jurisdiction Relating to the Safety of Shipping and Pollution from Ships—What Degree of Extra-territoriality' (2016) 31 IJMCL 442

Churchill RR and Lowe AV, *The Law of the Sea* (3rd edn, Manchester University Press 1999)

Clapham A, *Brierly's Law of Nations: An Introduction to the Role of International Law in International Relations* (OUP 2012)

Cohen JL, *Globalization and Sovereignty* (CUP 2012)

Combacau J and Sur S, *Droit International Public* (11th edn, LGDJ 2014)

Conforti B, 'Reflections on State Responsibility for the Breach of Positive Obligations: The Case-Law of the European Court of Human Rights' (2003) 13 The Italian Yearbook of International Law 3

Conroy M, 'Sealand: the Next Haven?' (2003) 27 Suffolk Transnational Law Review 127

Coomans F and Kamminga MT (eds), *Extraterritorial Application of Human Rights Treaties* (Intersentia 2004)

Coppens J and Somers E, 'Towards New Rules on Disembarkation of Persons Rescued at Sea?' (2010) 25 IJMCL 377

Crawford J, *Brownlie's Principles of Public International Law* (8th edn, OUP 2012)

——*State Responsibility. The General Part* (CUP 2013)

den Heijer M, 'Reflections on "Refoulement" and Collective Expulsion in the "Hirsi" Case' (2013) 25 International Journal of Refugee Law 265

De Sena P, *La nozione di giurisdizione statale nei trattati sui diritti dell'uomo* (Giappichelli 2002)

De Vattel E, *Le droit des gens ou principes de la loi naturelle appliqués à la conduite et aux affaires des nations et des souverains*, vol 1 (London, 1758)

De Vittor F, 'Il diritto di traversare il Mediterraneo … o quantomeno di provarci' (2014) 8 Diritti Umani e Diritto Internazionale 63

De Wet E and Vidmar J, *Hierarchy in International Law. The Place of Human Rights* (OUP 2012)

Di Pascale A, 'La sentenza *Hirsi e altri c. Italia*: una condanna senza appello della politica dei respingimenti' (2012) Diritto, Immigrazione e Cittadinanza 85

Di Stasi, *Il diritto all'equo processo nella CEDU e nella Convenzione americana sui diritti umani* (Giappichelli 2012)

DOALOS, *The Law of the Sea: Obligations of States Parties Under the United Nations Convention on the Law of the Sea and Complementary Instruments* (United Nations 2004)

Dominicé C, 'Droits Individuels et Droit de l'Homme: Chevauchements et Différences' in Laurence Boisson de Chazournes and Marcelo Kohen (eds), *International Law and the Quest for its Implementation. Liber Amicorum Vera Gowlland-Debbas* (Brill 2010) 287

Doyle C, 'Extraterritorial Application of American Criminal Law' (CRS Report 15 February 2012)

Dupuy PM, 'L'unité de l'Ordre Juridique International: Cours Général de Droit International Public' (2000) 297 Recueil des Cours 9

Dworkin R, 'A New Philosophy for International Law' (2013) 41 Philosophy & Public Affairs 2

EJF, *All at Sea—The Abuse of Human Rights aboard Illegal Fishing Vessels* (Environmental Justice Foundation 2010)

Faiss RD and Cabot AN, 'Gaming on the High Seas' (1986) 8 New York Law School Journal of International and Comparative Law 105

Fauchald OK and Nollkaemper A (eds), *The Practice of International and National Courts and the (De-)Fragmentation of International Law* (Hart 2012)

Fischer-Lescano A and Teubner G, 'Regime-Collisions: The Vain Search for Legal Unity in the Fragmentation of Global Law' (2004) 25 Michigan Journal of International Law 999

Fischer-Lescano A, Löhr T, and Tohidipur T, 'Border Controls at Sea: Requirements under International Human Rights and Refugee Law' (2009) 21 International Journal of Refugee Law 256

Fitzmaurice MA, 'International Environmental Law as a Special Field' (1994) XXV Netherlands Yearbook of International Law 181

Fitzpatrick D and Anderson M (eds), *Seafarers' Rights* (OUP 2005)

Focarelli C, *Trattato di Diritto Internazionale* (UTET 2015)

Fornari M, 'Soccorso di Profughi in Mare e Diritto d'Asilo: Questioni di Diritto Internazionale Sollevate dalla Vicenda della Nave Tampa' (2002) 57 Comunità Internazionale 61

Forowicz M, *The Reception of International Law in the European Court of Human Rights* (OUP 2010)

Force R, Yiannopoulos AN, and Davies M, *Admiralty and Maritime Law*, vol 2 (Beard Books 2008)

Franck T, 'Legitimacy in the International System' in Joseph Weiler and Alan T Nissel (eds), *International Law* (Routledge 2011) 670

Fredman S, *Human Rights Transformed: Positive Rights and Positive Duties* (OUP 2008)

Freestone D (ed), *The 1982 Law of the Sea Convention at 30: Successes, Challenges and New Agendas* (Martinus Nijhoff 2013)

Gaja G, 'Does the European Court of Human Rights Use Its Stated Methods of Interpretation?' in *Divenire sociale e adeguamento del diritto: Studi in onore di Francesco Capotorti*, vol 1 (Giuffré 1999) 213

—— 'The Position of Individuals in International Law: An ILC Perspective' (2010) 21 EJIL 11

Galani S, 'Somali Piracy and the Human Rights of Seafarers' (2016) 34 Netherlands Quarterly of Human Rights 71

Gammeltoft-Hansen T, *Access to Asylum. International Refugee Law and the Globalisation of Migration Control* (CUP 2011)

Garfinkle MS, Catz CL, and Saratchandra J, *The Psychological Impact of Piracy on Seafarers* (The Seamen's Church Institute 2012)

Gavouneli M, *Functional Jurisdiction in the Law of the Sea* (Martinus Nijhoff 2007)

Geiss R and Petrig A, *Piracy and Armed Robbery at Sea: The Legal Framework for Counter-Piracy Operations in Somalia and the Gulf of Aden* (OUP 2011)

Giuffré M, 'Watered-Down Rights on the High Seas: *Hirsi Jamaa and Others v Italy* (2012)' (2012) 61 ICLQ 728

—— 'Access to Asylum at Sea? Non-refoulement and a Comprehensive Approach to Extraterritorial Human Rights Obligations' in Violeta Moreno-Lax and Efthymios Papastavridis (eds), *'Boat Refugees' and Migrants at Sea. A Comprehensive Approach Integrating Maritime Security with Human Rights* (Brill Nijhoff 2017) 248

Gonsaeles G, 'Of Mice and Men: Some Observations on the EU Approach towards Seafarers' Liability for Marine Pollution' in Kris Bernauw, Ralph De Wit, Wouter Den Haerynck, Benoît Goemans, Frank Stevens, and Erik Van Hooydonk (eds), *Free on Board. Liber Amicorum Marc A. Huybrechts* (Intersentia 2011) 317

Goodwin-Gill GS, 'The Extra-territorial Reach of Human Rights Obligations: A Brief Perspective on the Link to Jurisdiction' in Laurence Boisson de Chazournes and Marcelo

Kohen (eds), *International Law and the Quest for its Implementation: Liber Amicorum Vera Gowlland-Debbas* (Brill 2010) 293

Goodwin-Gill GS and McAdam J, *The Refugee in International Law* (3rd edn, OUP 2007)

Goy R, 'Le Pêcheur Devant le Juge Pénal en Droit International' in Giuseppe Cataldi (ed), *La Méditerranée et le Droit de la Mer à l'Aube du 21e Siècle* (Bruylant 2002) 113

Gradoni L, Regime Failure *nel Diritto Internazionale* (CEDAM 2009)

Guilfoyle D, *Shipping Interdiction and the Law of the Sea* (CUP 2009)

—— 'Counter-Piracy Law Enforcement and Human Rights' (2010) 59 ICLQ 141

——*Modern Piracy* (Edward Elgar 2013)

Hafner G, 'Should One Fear the Proliferation of Mechanisms for the Peaceful Settlement of Disputes?' in Lucius Caflisch (ed), *The Peaceful Settlement of Disputes between States: Universal and European Perspectives* (Kluwer Law International 1998) 25

—— 'Some Thoughts on the State-Oriented and Individual-Oriented Approaches in International Law' (2013) 14 Austrian Review of International and European Law 27

—— 'The Emancipation of the Individual from the State under International Law' (2013) 358 Recueil des Cours 263

Harrison J, *Making the Law of the Sea* (CUP 2011)

Hart HLA, *The Concept of Law* (2nd edn, OUP 1997)

Heller-Roazen D, *The Enemy of All. Piracy and the Law of Nations* (Zone Books 2009)

Higgins R, 'International Law and the Avoidance, Containment and Resolution of Disputes: General Course on Public International Law' (1991) 230 Recueil des Cours 9

——*Problems and Process: International Law and How We Use It* (Clarendon Press 1994)

—— 'A Babel of Judicial Voices? Ruminations from the Bench' (2006) 55 ICLQ 791

Hosch G, Ferraro G, and Failler P, 'The 1995 FAO Code of Conduct for Responsible Fisheries: Adopting, Implementing or Scoring Results?' (2011) 35 Marine Policy 189

Hunnings NM, 'Pirate Broadcasting in European Waters' (1965) 14 ICLQ 410

ICC and Oceans Beyond Piracy, 'The Human Cost of Somali Piracy 2011'

ILO, *Safety and Health in the Construction of Fixed Offshore Installations in the Petroleum Industry* (International Labour Office 1981)

——*Conditions of Work in the Fishing Sector. A Comprehensive Standard (A Convention Supplemented by A Recommendation) on Work in the Fishing Sector* (International Labour Office 2003)

Iovane M, 'L'influence de la multiplication des juridictions internationales sur l'application du droit international' (2017) 383 Recueil des Cours 233

Jakubowski A and Wierczyńska K (eds), *Fragmentation vs the Constitutionalisation of International Law. A Practical Enquiry* (Routledge 2016)

Jenks WC, 'The Conflict of Law-Making Treaties' (1953) 30 British Yearbook of International Law 403

Joseph S and McBeth A, *Research Handbook on International Human Rights Law* (Edward Elgar 2010)

Kalin W and Kunzli J, *The Law of International Human Rights Protection* (OUP 2009)

Kelsen H, 'Les Rapports de Système entre le Droit Interne et le Droit International Public' (1926) 14 Recueil des Cours 227

Khaliq U, 'Jurisdiction, Ships and Human Rights Treaties' in Henrik Ringbom (ed), *Jurisdiction over Ships* (Martinus Nijhoff 2015) 324

Kirchner S, Geler-Noch K, and Frese V, 'Coastal State Obligations in the Context of Refugees at Sea under the European Convention on Human Rights' (2015) 20 Ocean and Coastal Law Journal 57

Klabbers J, 'Setting the Scene' in Jan Klabbers, Anne Peters, and Geir Ulfstein (eds), *The Constitutionalization of International Law* (OUP 2009) 1

Klein N, *Maritime Security and the Law of the Sea* (OUP 2011)

—— 'A Case for Harmonizing Laws on Maritime Interceptions of Irregular Migrants' (2014) 63 ICLQ 787

Kontorovich E, ' "A Guantánamo on the Sea": the Difficulty of Prosecuting Pirates and Terrorists' (2010) 98 California Law Review 243

Koskenniemi M, *The Gentle Civilizer of Nations: The Rise and Fall of International Law, 1870-1960* (CUP 2002)

—— 'What Use for Sovereignty Today?' (2011) 1 Asian Journal of International Law 61

—— 'Hegemonic Regimes' in Margaret A Young (ed), *Regime Interaction in International Law. Facing Fragmentation* (CUP 2012) 305

Koskenniemi M and Leino P, 'Fragmentation of International Law? Postmodern Anxieties' (2002) 15 Leiden Journal of International Law 553

Koutrakos P and Skordas A (eds), *The Law and Practice of Piracy at Sea: European and International Perspectives* (Hart Publishing 2014)

Krasner S, 'Structural Causes and Regime Consequences: Regimes as Intervening Variables' in Stephen Krasner (ed), *International Regimes* (Cornell University Press 1983) 2

Kratochwil F, 'Human Rights and Democracy: Is There a Place for Actual People(s)' in Ulrich Fastenrath, Rudolf Geiger, Daniel-Erasmus Khan, Andreas Paulus, Sabine von Schorlemer, and Christoph Vedder (eds), *From Bilateralism to Community Interest: Essays in Honour of Bruno Simma* (OUP 2011) 488

Krueger RB, Nordquist MH, and Wessely RP, 'New Technology and International Law: The Case of Deepwater Ports' (1977) 17 Virginia Journal of International Law 597

Kulesza J, *Due Diligence in International Law* (Brill | Nijhoff 2016)

Lagoni R, 'Commentary' in Alex G Oude Elferink (ed), *Stability and Change in the Law of the Sea: The Role of the LOS Convention* (Martinus Nijhoff 2005) 49

Laly-Chevalier C, 'Lutte contre la piraterie maritime et droits de l'homme' (2009) 42 Revue Belge de Droit International 5

Lauterpacht H, *The Function of Law in the International Community* (OUP 2011)

Lavelle J (ed), *Maritime Labour Law Convention 2006. International Labour Law Redefined* (Informa Law 2014)

Lawson R, 'Life After Bankovic: On the Extraterritorial Application of the European Convention on Human Rights' in Fons Coomans and Menno T Kamminga (eds), *Extraterritorial Application of Human Rights Treaties* (Intersentia 2004) 83

Legg A, *The Margin of Appreciation in International Human Rights Law: Deference and Proportionality* (OUP 2012)

Lenzerini F, 'Il principo del "non-refoulement" dopo la sentenza "Hirsi" della Corte europea dei diritti dell'uomo' (2012) 95 Rivista di diritto internazionale 721

Li KX and Ng JM, 'International Maritime Conventions: Seafarers' Safety and Human Rights' (2002) 33 Journal of Maritime Law & Commerce 381

Liguori A, 'La Corte europea dei diritti dell'uomo condanna l'Italia per i respingimenti verso la Libia del 2009: il caso Hirsi' (2012) 95 Rivista di diritto internazionale 415

Lowe AV, 'The Right of Entry into Maritime Ports in International Law' (1977) 14 San Diego Law Review 597

—— 'The Politics of Law-Making: Are the Method and Character of Norm Creation Changing?' in Michael Byers (ed), *The Role of Law in International Politics: Essays in International Relations and International Law* (OUP 2001) 207

——*International Law* (OUP 2007)

—— 'Ships' in Tullio Scovazzi, Nerina Boschiero, Cesare Pitea, and Chiara Ragni (eds), *International Courts and the Development of International Law: Essays in Honour of Tullio Treves* (Asser Press 2013) 291

Lowe AV and Staker C, 'Jurisdiction' in Malcolm D Evans (ed), *International Law* (OUP 2010) 313

Lowe AV and Talmon S, *The Legal Order of the Oceans: Basic Documents on the Law of the Sea* (Hart 2009)

Lukas W, 'Leadership: Short-term, Intercultural and Performance-Oriented' in Alexis Papathanassis (ed), *Cruise Sector Growth Managing Emerging Markets, Human Resources, Processes and Systems* (Gabler 2009) 65

MacCormick N, 'Coherence in Legal Justification' in Aleksander Peczenik, Lars Lindahl, and Bert Van Roermund (eds), *Theory of Legal Science* (D Reidel Publishing Company 1984) 235

—— 'Reconstruction after Deconstruction: A Response to CLS' (1990) 10 Oxford Journal of Legal Studies 539

Mallia P, *Migrant Smuggling by Sea. Combating a Current Threat to Maritime Security through the Creation of a Cooperative Framework* (Martinus Nijhoff 2010)

Mann FA, 'The Doctrine of International Jurisdiction Revisited after Twenty Years' (1984) 186 Recueil des Cours 9

Mann I, *Humanity at Sea. Maritime Migration and the Foundations of International Law* (CUP 2016)

Manusama K, 'Prosecuting Pirates in the Netherlands: The Case of the *MS Samanyolu*' (2010) 49 Military Law and the Law of War Review 141

Marsden RG, *Documents Relating to Law and Custom of the Sea*, vol I (Navy Records Society 1915)

Martineau A-C, *Le debat sur la fragmentation du droit international: une analyse critique* (Bruylant 2016)

Mathew P, 'Australian Refugee Protection in the Wake of the Tampa' (2002) 96 AJIL 661

McLachlan C, 'The Principle of Systemic Integration and Article 31(3)(c) of the Vienna Convention' (2005) 54 ICLQ 279

Mendelson MH, 'Fragmentation of the Law of the Sea' (1988) 12 Marine Policy 192

Meron T, 'International Law in the Age of Human Rights' (2003) 301 Recueil des Cours 9

Michaels R and Pauwelyn J, 'Conflict of Norms or Conflict of Laws?: Different Techniques in the Fragmentation of Public International Law' (2012) 22 Duke Journal of Comparative & International Law 349

Milano E and Papanicolopulu I, 'State Responsibility in Disputed Areas on Land and at Sea' (2011) 71 Zeitschrift für ausländisches öffentliches Recht und Völkerrecht 587

Milanovic M, *Extraterritorial Application of Human Rights Treaties. Law, Principles, and Policy* (OUP 2011)

Miller S, 'Revisiting Extraterritorial Jurisdiction: A Territorial Justification for Extraterritorial Jurisdiction under the European Convention' (2010) 20 EJIL 1223

Molenaar EJ, 'Port State Jurisdiction: Toward Comprehensive, Mandatory and Global Coverage' (2007) 38 ODIL 225

Moreno Lax V, 'The EU Regime on Interdiction, Search and Rescue, and Disembarkation: The Frontex Guidelines for Intervention at Sea' (2010) 25 IJMCL 621

—— 'Hirsi Jamaa and Others v Italy or the Strasbourg Court versus Extraterritorial Migration Control?' (2012) 12 Human Rights Law Review 574

Moreno Lax V and Papastavridis E (eds), *'Boat Refugees' and Migrants at Sea: A Comprehensive Approach. Iintegrating Maritime Security with Human Rights* (Martinus Nijhoff 2017)

Mowbray A, *The Development of Positive Obligations under the European Convention on Human Rights by the European Court of Human Rights* (Hart 2004)

Nelson D, 'Maritime Jurisdiction' in Rüdiger Wolfrum (ed), *Max Planck Encyclopedia of Public International Law* (OUP 2012)

Nga Essomba S, 'La protection de la personne physique, victime d'actes de piraterie maritime' (2015) 20 Annuaire du Droit de la Mer 209

Nordquist MH, Nandan SN, and Rosenne S (eds), *The United Nations Convention on the Law of the Sea 1982: A Commentary. Volume III* (Martinus Nijhoff 1985)

Nordquist MH, Rosenne S, and Sohn LB (eds), *United Nations Convention on the Law of the Sea, 1982: A Commentary. Volume V* (Martinus Nijhoff 1989)

Nordquist MH, Rosenne S, Yankov A, and Grandy N (eds), *United Nations Convention on the Law of the Sea. A Commentary, Volume IV* (Martinus Nijhoff 1991)

Noyes JE, 'The Territorial Sea and Contiguous Zone' in Donald R Rothwell, Alex G Oude Elferink, Karen N Scott, and Tim Stephens (eds), *The Oxford Handbook of the Law of the Sea* (OUP 2015) 91

Obokata T, 'Maritime Piracy as a Violation of Human Rights: A Way Forward for Its Effective Prevention and Suppression?' (2013) 17 The International Journal of Human Rights 18

O'Connell DP, *The International Law of the Sea*, vol II (Clarendon Press 1984)

Oude Elferink A (ed), *Stability and Change in the Law of the Sea: The Role of the LOS Convention* (Martinus Nijhoff 2005)

—— 'The "Arctic Sunrise" Incident: A Multi-faceted Law of the Sea Case with a Human Rights Dimension' (2014) 29 IJMCL 244

Oxman BH, 'Human Rights and the United Nations Convention on the Law of the Sea' in Jonathan I Charney and Donald K Anton (eds), *Politics, Values and Functions: International Law in the 21st Century. Essays in Honor of Professor Louis Henkin* (Martinus Nijhoff 1997) 377

—— 'Human Rights and the United Nations Convention on the Law of the Sea' (1998) 36 Columbia Journal of Transnational Law 399

Paine L, *The Sea and Civilization. A Maritime History of the World* (Atlantic Books 2013)

Pallis M, 'Obligations of States towards Asylum Seekers at Sea: Interactions and Conflicts Between Legal Regimes' (2002) 14 International Journal of Refugee Law 329

Papanicolopulu I, 'La Nozione di Giurisdizione ai Sensi dell'Art. 1 della Convenzione Europea dei Diritti Umani nella Recente Giurisprudenza della Corte Europea dei Diritti Umani' in Tullio Scovazzi, Irini Papanicolopulu and Sabrina Urbinati (eds), *I diritti Umani di Fronte al Giudice Internazionale. Atti della Giornata di Studio in Memoria di Carlo Russo* (Giuffre 2009) 83

—— 'The Law of the Sea Convention: No Place for Persons?' (2012) 27 IJMCL 867

—— 'Hirsi Jamaa v. Italy' (2013) 107 AJIL 417

—— 'International Judges and the Protection of Human Rights at Sea' in Nerina Boschiero and others (eds), *International Courts and the Development of International Law* (Asser Press 2013) 535

—— 'Considerations of Humanity in the Enrica Lexie Case' (2015) QIL - Questions of International Law <http://www.qil-qdi.org/considerations-of-humanity-in-the-enrica-lexie-case>

—— 'Seafarers as an Agent of Change of the Jurisdictional Balance' in Henrik Ringbom (ed), *Jurisdiction over Ships. Post-UNCLOS Developments in the Law of the Sea* (Martinus Nijhoff 2015) 301

Papastavridis E, 'Enforcement Jurisdiction in the Mediterranean Sea: Illicit Activities and the Rule of Law on the High Seas' (2010) 25 IJMCL 569

—— 'European Court of Human Rights *Medvedyev et al v France* (Grand Chamber, Application No 3394/03) Judgment of 29 March 2010' (2010) 59 ICLQ 867

—— 'European Convention on Human Rights and the Law of the Sea: the Strasbourg Court in Unchartered Waters?' in Malgosia Fitzmaurice and Panos Merkouris (eds), *The Interpretation and Application of the European Convention of Human Rights: Legal and Practical Implications* (Martinus Nijhoff 2013) 117

—— 'Is There a Right to be Rescued at Sea? A Skeptical View' (2014) *QIL-Questions in International Law* http://www.qil-qdi.org/is-there-a-right-to-be-rescued-at-sea-a-skeptical-view

——*The Interception of Vessels on the High Seas* (Hart 2014)

Parlett K, *The Individual in the International Legal System: Continuity and Change in International Law* (CUP 2011)

Pauwelyn J, *Conflict of Norms in Public International Law: How WTO Law Relates to Other Rules of International Law* (CUP 2003)

Payre F, 'Les passagers clandestins' (1996) 14 Annuaire de Droit Maritime et Oceanique 265

Peil M, 'Scholarly Writings as a Source of Law: A Survey of the Use of Doctrine by the International Court of Justice' (2012) 1 Cambridge Journal of International and Comparative Law 136

Peters A, 'Membership in the Global Constitutional Community' in Jan Klabbers, Anne Peters, and Geir Ulfstein (eds), *The Constitutionalization of International Law* (OUP 2009) 153

——*Beyond Human Rights. The Legal Status of the Individual in International Law* (CUP 2016)

Petrig A, *Human Rights and Law Enforcement at Sea. Arrest, Detention and Transfer of Piracy Suspects* (Brill Nijhoff 2014)

Pisillo Mazzeschi R, 'Responsabilité de l'Etat pour Violation des Obligations Positives Relatives aux Droits de l'Homme' (2008) 333 Recueil des Cours 175

Pitea C, 'Interpreting the ECHR in the Light of "Other" International Instruments: Systemic Integration or Fragmentation of Rules on Treaty Interpretation?' in Nerina Boschiero, Tullio Scovazzi, Cesare Pitea, and Chiara Ragni (eds), *International Courts and the Development of International Law. Essays in Honour of Tullio Treves* (Asser Press 2013) 545

—— 'Azioni di Contrasto alla Pirateria e Convenzione Europea del Diritti Umani: Questioni di Attribuzione e di Applicazione Extraterritoriale' (2015) 9 Diritti Umani e Diritto Internazionale 489

Proelss A (ed), *United Nations Convention on the Law of the Sea. A Commentary* (Beck-Hart-Nomos 2017)

Prost M, Unitas Multiplex: *Unité et Fragmentation en Droit International* (Bruylant 2013)

Pulkowski D, *The Law and Politics of International Regime Conflict* (OUP 2014)

Raz J, *Ethics in the Public Domain: Essays in the Morality of Law and Politics* (Clarendon Press 1995)

Redgwell C, 'From Permission to Prohibition: The 1982 Convention on the Law of the Sea and Protection of the Marine Environment' in David Freestone, Richard Barnes, and David Ong (eds), *The Law of the Sea: Progress and Prospects* (OUP 2006) 180

—— 'Mind the Gap in the GAIRS: the Role of Other Instruments in LOSC Regime Implementation in the Offshore Energy Sector' (2014) 29 IJMCL 600

Roach JA and Smith RW, *Excessive Maritime Claims* (3rd edn, Martinus Nijhoff 2012)

Robertson H, 'The Suppression of Pirate Radio Broadcasting: A Test Case of the International System for Control of Activities Outside National Territory' (1982) 45 Law and Contemporary Problems 71

Rodière R and Rèmond-Gouilloud M, *La mer: droits des hommes ou proie desétats?* (Pedone 1980)

Rothwell DR, 'The Law of the Sea and the MV Tampa Incident: Reconciling Maritime Principles with Coastal State Sovereignty' (2002) 13 Public Law Review 118

Rothwell DR and Stephens T, *The International Law of the Sea* (Hart 2010)

Roucounas E, 'Effectiveness of International Law for the Users of the Sea' in Jorge Cardona Llorens (ed), *Cursos Euromediterráneos Bancaja de Derecho Internacional* (Tirant lo Blanch 2009) 855

—— 'Facteurs Privés et Droit International Public' (2002) 299 Recueil des Cours 9

Rousseau C, 'De la Compatibilité des Normes Juridiques Contradictoires dans l'Ordre International' (1932) 6 Revue General de Droit International Public 133

Ryngaert C, *Jurisdiction in International Law* (OUP 2008)

Salerno F, *Diritto Internazionale. Principi e Norme* (CEDAM 2008)

Scelle G, *Précis de Droit des Gens. Principes et Systématique* (Recueil Sirey 1932)

Schill S, *The Multilateralization of International Investment Law* (CUP 2009)

Sciso E, *Gli Accordi Internazionali Confliggenti* (Cacucci 1986)

Scott SV, 'The LOS Convention as a Constitutional Regime for the Oceans' in Alex G Oude Elferink (ed), *Stability and Change in the Law of the Sea: The Role of the LOS Convention* (Martinus Nijhoff 2005) 9

Scovazzi T, 'The Evolution of International Law of the Sea: New Issues, New Challenges' (2000) 286 Recueil des Cours 39

—— 'La tutela della vita umana in mare, con particolare riferimento agli immigrati clandestini diretti verso l'Italia' (2005) 88 Rivista di Diritto Internazionale 106

—— 'Human Rights and Immigration at Sea' in Ruth Rubio-Marín (ed), *Human Rights and Immigration* (OUP 2014) 212

Shany Y, *The Competing Jurisdictions of International Courts and Tribunals* (OUP 2003)

——'One Law to Rule Them All: Should International Courts Be Viewed as Guardians of Procedural Order and Legal Uniformity?' in Ole Kristian Fauchald and André Nollkaemper (eds), *The Practice of International and National Courts and the (De-)Fragmentation of International Law* (Hart 2012)

Shaw M, *International Law* (CUP 2008)

Shearer IA, 'Problems of Jurisdiction and Law Enforcement Against Delinquent Vessels' (1986) 35 ICLQ 320

Shelton D and Gould A, 'Positive and Negative Obligations' in Dinah Shelton (ed), *The Oxford Handbook of International Human Rights Law* (OUP 2013) 563

Simma B, 'Self-Contained Regimes' (1985) 16 Netherlands Yearbook of International Law 112

—— 'From Bilateralism to Community Interest in International Law' (1997) 250 Recueil des Cours 217

Simma B and Pulkowski D, 'Of Planets and the Universe: Self-contained Regimes in International Law' (2006) 17 EJIL 483

Simmons G and Stringer C, 'New Zealand's Fisheries Management System: Froced Labour an Ignored or Overlooked Dimension?' (2014) 50 Marine Policy 74

Sivakumaran S, 'Impact on the Structure of International Obligations' in Menno T Kamminga and Martin Scheinin (eds), *The Impact of Human Rights Law on General International Law* (OUP 2009) 133

Sohn LB, 'International Law of the Sea and Human Rights Issues' in Thomas A Clingan Jr (ed), *The Law of the Sea: What Lies Ahead?* (The Law of the Sea Institute 1988) 51

—— 'Making International Law More User-Friendly' in *International Law as a Language for International Relations* (Kluwer Law International 1996) 411

Steglich E, 'Hiding in the Hulls: Attacking the Practice of High Seas Murder of Stowaways through Expanded Criminal Jurisdiction' (2000) 78 Texas Law Review 1323

Steiner HJ, Alston P, and Goodman R, *International Human Rights in Context* (3rd edn, OUP 2007)

Stone J, *Legal System and Lawyers' Reasonings* (Stanford University Press 1968)

Stringer C, Simmons G, and Coulston D, 'Not in New Zealand's Waters Surely? Labour and Human Rights Abuses Aboard Foreign Fishing Vessels' (2011) New Zealand Asia Institute Working Paper Series 11-01 <http://docs.business.auckland.ac.nz/Doc/11-01-Not-in-New-Zealand-waters-surely-NZAI-Working-Paper-Sept-2011.pdf>

Suman D, 'Regulation of Ocean Dumping by the European Economic Community' (1991) 18 Ecology Law Quarterly 559

Swan J, 'Port State Measures—from Residual Port State Jurisdiction to Global Standards' (2016) 31 IJMCL 395

Swanson S, 'Google Sets Sail: Ocean-Based Server Farms and International Law' (2011) 43 Connecticut Law Review 709

Symmons CR, 'Use of the Law of Piracy to Deal with Violent Inter-Vessel Incidents at Sea beyond the 12-Mile Limit: The Irish Experience' in Clive R Symmons (ed), *Selected Contemporary Issues in the Law of the Sea* (Martinus Nijhoff 2011) 169

Tanaka Y, 'Protection of Community Interests in International Law: the Case of the Law of the Sea' (2011) 15 Max Planck Yearbook of United Nations Law 329

——*The International Law of the Sea* (2nd edn, CUP 2015)

Tanzi AM, *Introduzione al Diritto Internazionale Contemporaneo* (3rd edn, CEDAM 2010)

Tavernier P, 'La Cour Européenne des Droits de l'Homme et la Mer' in *La Mer et son Droit: Mélanges Offerts à Laurent Lucchini et Jean-Pierre Quéneudec* (Pedone 2003) 575

Testa D, 'Safeguarding Human Life and Ensuring Respect for Fundamental Human Rights: A Consequential Approach to the Disembarkation of Persons Rescued at Sea' (2014) 28 Ocean Yearbook 555

Teubner G, *Constitutional Fragments. Societal Constitutionalism and Globalization* (OUP 2012)

—— 'Introduction to Autopoietic Law' in Gunther Teubner (ed), *Autopoietic Law: A New Approach to Law and Society* (De Gruyter 1988) 1

Thomson JE, *Mercenaries, Pirates, and Sovereigns: State-Building and Extraterritorial Violence in Early Modern Europe* (Princeton University Press 1996)

Thirlway H, 'The Sources of International Law' in Malcolm D Evans (ed), *International Law* (OUP 2010)

Tomuschat C, 'Human Rights: Tensions between Negative and Positive Duties of States' (2009) 14 Austrian Review of International and European Law 19

—— 'International Law as a Coherent System: Unity or Fragmentation?' in Mahnoush Arsanjani (ed), *Looking to the Future: Essays on International Law in Honor of W. Michael Reisman* (Martinus Nijhoff 2011) 323

——*Human Rights. Between Idealism and Realism* (3rd edn, OUP 2014)

Tomuschat C, Lagrange E, and Oeter S (eds), *The Right to Life* (Martinus Nijhoff 2010)

Tondini M, 'The Legality of Intercepting Boat People under Search and Rescue and Border Control Operations: With Reference to Recent Italian Interventions in the Mediterranean Sea and the ECtHR Decision in the Hirsi Case' (2012) 18 The Journal of International Maritime Law 59

Treves T, *La Giurisdizione nel Diritto Penale Internazionale* (CEDAM 1973)

—— 'Military Installations, Structures and Devices on the Seabed' (1980) 74 AJIL 808

—— 'Codification du Droit International et Pratique des Etats dans le Droit de la Mer' (1990) 223 Recueil des Cours 9

—— 'Fragmentation of International Law: The Judicial Perspective' (2007) 23 Comunicazioni e Studi 821

—— 'Piracy, Law of the Sea, and Use of Force: Developments off the Coast of Somalia' (2009) 20 EJIL 399

—— 'Human Rights and the Law of the Sea' (2010) 28 Berkeley Journal of International Law 1

Treves T and Pitea C, 'Piracy, International Law and Human Rights' in Nehal Bhuta (ed), *The Frontiers of Human Rights. Extraterritoriality and Its Challenges* (OUP 2016)

Trevisanut S, 'The Principle of Non-Refoulement at Sea and the Effectiveness of Asylum Protection' (2008) 12 Max Planck Yearbook of United Nations Law 205

—— 'Search and Rescue Operations in the Mediterranean: Factor of Cooperation or Conflict?' (2010) 25 IJMCL 523

—— 'Is There a Right to be Rescued at Sea? A Constructive View' (2014) *QIL-Questions in International Law* <http://www.qil-qdi.org/is-there-a-right-to-be-rescued-at-sea-a-constructive-view>

UNODC, *The Globalization of Crime. A Transnational Organized Crime Threat Assessment* (UNODC 2010)

—— *Transnational Organized Crime in the Fishing Industry* (United Nations 2011)

—— *Combating Transnational Organized Crime Committed at Sea* (United Nations 2013)

van Ginkel B and van der Putten FP (eds), *The International Response to Somali Piracy* (Martinus Nijhoff 2010)

Viñuales JE, *Foreign Investment and the Environment in International Law* (CUP 2012)

Vukas B, 'Droit de la Mer et Droits de l'Homme' in Giuseppe Cataldi (ed), *La Méditerranée et le droit de la mer à l'aube du 21e siècle* (Bruylant 2002) 85

Walker C, 'Jurisdictional Problems Created by Artificial Islands' (1973) 10 San Diego Law Review 638

Webb P, *International Judicial Integration and Fragmentation* (OUP 2013)

Wegelein FHT, *Marine Scientific Research* (Martinus Nijhoff 2005)

Weil P, 'Towards Relative Normativity in International Law?' (1983) 77 AJIL 413

Weis P, 'The Hague Agreement Relating to Refugee Seamen' (1958) 7 ICLQ 334

Wilde R, 'Compliance with Human Rights Norms Extraterritoriality: Human Rights Imperialism?' in Laurence Boisson de Chazournes and Marcelo Kohen (eds), *International Law and the Quest for its Implementation: Liber Amicorum Vera Gowlland-Debbas* (Brill 2010) 319

Wilson B, 'Human Rights and Maritime Law Enforcement' (2016) 52 Stanford Journal of International Law 243

Woodliffe JC, 'Some Legal Aspects of Pirate Broadcasting in the North Sea' (1965) 12 Netherlands International Law Review 365

Yankov A, 'The Significance of the 1982 Convention on the Law of the Sea for the Protection of the Marine Environment and the Promotion of Marine Science and Technology: A Paper on Third Committee Issues' in Albert W Koers and Bernard H Oxman (eds), *The 1982 Convention on the Law of the Sea: Proceedings Law of the Sea Institute Seventeenth Annual Conference, July 13–16, 1983, Oslo, Norway* (Law of the Sea Institute 1984) 71

Young MA, *Trading Fish, Saving Fish. The Interaction between Regimes in International Law* (CUP 2011)

——*Regime Interaction in International Law. Facing Fragmentation* (CUP 2012)

Zanobetti Pagnetti A, *Il Rapporto Internazionale di Lavoro Marittimo* (Bononia University Press 2008)

Index

slavery 16, 30, 86, 132, 147, 149,
    174, 194, 201–202, 226,
  freedom from 70, 89–90, 140,
    168, 198, 207, 235
  slave-like practices 30
  see also forced labour, human
    trafficking
smuggling
  arms 18, 23
  drugs 58, 134, 137
  migrants 11, 55, 57
  people 45, 87–88, 105, 109, 112, 115,
    125, 135, 137, 146–147, 151, 241
social security, right to 35, 36, 41,
    90, 93, 145, 150, 207
soft law 89, 94, 104, 159, 169, 222, 223
Sohn, Luis 235–236, 243
Somalia 1, 81, 109, 169, 185, 213, 242
sovereignty 16, 76, 81–82, 84, 94,
    101–102, 115–117, 131, 138–139,
    142, 152, 156, 161, 166, 169, 189,
    197–198, 201, 231, 239–240
Spain 116, 121, 145, 151
standards, generally accepted 55,
    106–108, 176–179, 202
stateless persons 40, 41
stowaways 21–23, 27, 57, 123, 150, 257
  repatriation 23
structures 4, 17, 24, 27, 29, 31, 33,
    40–41, 48, 50–51, 54, 57, 130, 154,
    170, 196, 198, 205–206, 233
  continental shelf 145–146, 156, 198, 205–207
  exclusive economic zone 145, 156, 205
  high seas 146–148
  jurisdiction 113, 128, 130–131,
    143–148, 150–152, 156, 160, 235
  International Seabed Area 191
  offshore 19, 20, 41, 51, 144
  registration 147
  safety 48, 50–51, 146, 191
  safety zones 146
  used for fishing 20, 146
submarine cables and pipelines 118, 129, 224
systemic integration, principle of 73, 75,
    76, 78, 97, 99, 104, 122, 222, 238
systemic thinking 60, 71–76, 78–79, 96, 98, 222

Tavernier, Paul 236
territorial waters 18, 23, 31, 47, 81, 126,
    133, 140, 143, 151, 162, 194, 196, 197

terrorism 23, 31, 46, 115, 117, 169, 183
Thailand 4
Titanic 2, 26, 48, 83, 240
torture 28, 140, 186, 197
  prohibition of 70, 89–90, 95,
    140, 168, 171–174, 180,
    189, 196, 198, 207, 235
traffickers 3–4, 18, 23–24, 33
training 16, 28–29, 54, 203, 238
transnational criminal group 24
transnational criminal law 235
transnational organized crime 30
transport of slaves *see* slavery
Treves, Tullio 236
Tunisia 22

United Kingdom 203–204
United Nations 1, 46, 106,
    110, 167, 169, 216
  Division on Ocean Affairs and the Law
    of the Sea (DOALOS) 1, 106, 216
  General Assembly 169, 216
  Secretary General reports on Oceans
    and the law of the sea 241
  Security Council 169, 190, 241
United Nations Environment
    Programme 216
United Nations High Commissioner
    for Refugee 6, 167, 241
United States 16, 25–26, 92, 235
Universal Declaration of Human
    Rights 4, 57, 89, 104, 210
use of force 1, 16, 31–32, 44, 45, 63, 76, 136,
    151, 155, 163, 165–166, 180–182

vessel
  definition 144
  endangered 26, 27, 49, 54, 86, 192
  military 111, 188, 121
  State-owned 188
  working place 3, 17, 18, 19, 20, 27, 35
  see also arrest of vessels, fishing
    vessel, jurisdiction, safety

whaling 132, 142, 196
work, right to 90, 177
working conditions
  decent 35–36, 38, 166, 178
  inhuman and degrading 3,
    16, 27–29, 93, 147